GETTING TO SCALE

GETTING TO SCALE

How to Bring Development Solutions
to Millions of Poor People

LAURENCE CHANDY
AKIO HOSONO
HOMI KHARAS
JOHANNES LINN

Editors

BROOKINGS INSTITUTION PRESS
Washington, D.C.

Library of Congress Cataloging-in-Publication data

Getting to scale : how to bring development solutions to millions of poor people /
Laurence Chandy, Akio Hosono, Homi Kharas, and Johannes Linn, editors.
    pages cm
Includes bibliographical references and index.
ISBN: 978-0-8157-2419-3
1. Economic development projects—Developing countries. 2. Economic assistance—
Developing countries. 3. Poverty—Developing countries. 4. Economic development—
Developing countries. I. Chandy, Laurence. II. Hosono, Akio. III. Kharas, Homi J.,
1954– IV. Linn, Johannes F.
HC59.72.E44G48 2013
338.9109172'4—dc23   2013004915

9 8 7 6 5 4 3 2 1

Printed on acid-free paper

Typeset in Adobe Garamond

Composition by Cynthia Stock
Silver Spring, Maryland

Printed by R. R. Donnelley
Harrisonburg, Virginia

Contents

Preface

I n 2004 the World Bank and Chinese government co-hosted a major conference in Shanghai to identify lessons on delivering global development solutions at scale. In the ensuing decade, a small group of development thinkers and practitioners has sought to explore this topic further. Among them are Brookings Institution scholars who have built a dedicated work program on scaling up to support new research, advise implementing organizations, and bring interested parties together from across the global development community.

This volume captures some of the diversity of views and experiences within that community. Chapter authors include academics and practitioners, and among the latter, representatives of the public and private sectors. Some chapters contain personal accounts of success and failure; others offer rigorous analysis of what those in the field have been able to accomplish.

While there is a wealth of ideas and experience packed into this volume, reflecting a decade of learning, our understanding of how to bring successful development interventions to scale remains limited. The editors hope that this work will spur further research, analysis, and experimentation to answer this question, which is pivotal to understanding how development cooperation, in all its forms, can have an impact commensurate with the scale of the challenges to be addressed.

The volume is the outcome of an eighteen-month collaborative project between the Brookings Institution and the Japan International Cooperation Agency (JICA). Earlier drafts of the volume's chapters were discussed at a two-day workshop held in Washington, D.C., in January 2012. The editors are grateful to the following individuals who attended the workshop and provided feedback on those drafts: Raj Desai, Alan Gelb, Nick Lovegrove, Paul Isenman, Jane Nelson, Dennis Whittle, Rohit Wanchoo, Mwangi Kimenyi, Molly Kinder, Noam Unger, Ernesto Araújo, Han Fraeters, Niloy Banerjee, Heather Baser, Navtej Dhillon, Rajul Pandya-Lorch, Tom Kelly, Keiichiro Nakazawa, Richard Ponzio, and Go Shimada.

The editors would also like to thank Kathy Sierra for reviewing the entire volume; Natasha Ledlie, Veronika Penciakova, Steven Rocker, and Cory Smith for proofreading; and Janet Walker, Diane Hammond, and Susan Woollen from Brookings Institution Press.

The chapters reflect the views of their authors and not the official position of any specific organization.

This project would not have been possible without the financial and intellectual support of JICA—an agency that is acknowledged as a pioneer in promoting and institutionalizing a scaling-up agenda.

1

Overview: The Challenge of Reaching Scale

LAURENCE CHANDY, AKIO HOSONO, HOMI KHARAS,
AND JOHANNES LINN

The challenges of global development can be counted in millions, if not billions: 2 million preventable infant deaths a year from pneumonia and diarrhea, 61 million children out of school, 850 million malnourished people, a billion people living in city slums, 1.3 billion people without access to electricity, 1.5 billion people living in conflict-affected states, 2.5 billion people without access to formal financial services. Meeting these challenges hinges on finding sustainable solutions that can have a transformational impact on the lives of millions of the world's poorest people.

Developed countries have, by definition, solved these problems.[1] These countries are identifiable by both their superior level of income and the institutions through which their societies and politics are organized, which enable their living standards to be sustained. Over the last half century, a handful of countries have succeeded in making the transition from developing to developed, and the hope is that many more will do so in the next.

However, such transitions are extremely hard to pull off. Using past performance as a guide, it would take nearly 6,000 years for the poorest countries to reach the level of income currently enjoyed by the United States of America.[2]

1. This is not to imply that developed countries are entirely harmonious societies; no country is without its unique socioeconomic problems and political failings. The point, rather, is that the challenges of development represent a unique kind of problem.
2. Pritchett, Woolcock, and Andrews (2010).

Similarly, improvement in the capacity of poor countries to deliver basic public services to their citizens is proceeding at a glacial pace. Extremely optimistic estimates, using the performance of the fastest-improving countries as a yardstick for what is possible, suggest that the waiting time to eradicate extreme poverty and deprivation should still be measured in generations. For instance, were Haiti to somehow adopt the rate of progress in government quality of the twenty fastest-improving countries in the world, it would be another twenty-six years before it reached the current standard of Malawi.

To speed up this process for today's poor countries would require a recipe for development—something that after years of looking has not yet been found, and maybe never will be. Countless studies have been undertaken examining what countries such as Japan and Korea did to advance so quickly. But it is quite another thing to translate these studies into a meaningful plan for today's poor countries. This explains much of the skepticism around foreign aid. If the role of aid is to encourage countries to grow faster and to accelerate up the development ladder, then it is easy to conclude that the mission has been a failure and is probably futile.

There is an alternative and more hopeful view. It submits that there is much that can be done to address global development challenges without altogether altering the trajectories of poor countries. A number of targeted solutions have been found that can solve specific challenges: vaccines and water treatment to prevent child death; conditional cash transfers to nudge parents to encourage school attendance; micronutrient supplements and the promotion of breastfeeding to vanquish malnourishment. These solutions can permit poor countries today to overcome many of the deprivations associated with their low levels of income and to improve the lives of their people.

To succeed, however, these solutions need to be scaled up to reach poor people everywhere. Herein lies the problem.

Reaching Scale

There are certainly examples of scale being reached in a developing country context. Mexico rolled out its Oportunidades program, a conditional cash transfer scheme, to all of its regions, reaching around one-quarter of the entire population with cash incentives designed to improve health and educational attainment among poor families.[3] Brazil dramatically reduced poverty with its Bolsa Família program, which today reaches 12 million families.[4] Indonesia's Kecamatan Development Program provides grants to half of all villages in the country for small infrastructure projects chosen by the community. Oral rehydration

3. Levy (2006).
4. Duffy (2010).

therapy, introduced by UNICEF, has almost halved deaths from diarrhea, cholera, and related diseases. Long-lasting insecticide-treated bed nets have dramatically reduced malaria. China has initiated vast poverty reduction programs, including those affecting millions of poor farmers of the Loess Plateau.

Yet these examples are the exception as opposed to the rule. Many development solutions create more of a whimper than a wave. This is surprising when one considers that scaling up is at the core of the development model that donor agencies purport to follow. They regularly develop pilot projects with the supposed intention of replicating or expanding successes, or handing them over to developing country governments to do the same. But only a small share makes it beyond a pilot phase. This is why donors are more likely to report one-time, localized success stories than examples of transformative wide-reaching progress.

Even when a dedicated effort is made to transition from pilot to program, scale is rarely achieved. The use of fuel-efficient cooking stoves in India, for example, has proceeded very slowly. Ten years after their introduction through the National Improved Stoves Program, improved stoves accounted for less than 7 percent of all stoves in use.[5]

We believe this deserves a full inquiry. Remarkably little is understood about how to design scalable projects, the impediments to reaching scale, and the most appropriate pathways for getting there. Despite its centrality to development, scaling up is rarely studied in its own right and has undergone little scrutiny.[6] Scaling up has been treated as something that occurs spontaneously and organically when successful development interventions are identified rather than as a challenge in and of itself.

This book is about increasing the number of people who are assisted through development programs so they can be counted in the hundreds of millions and in a time frame that is measured in decades rather than centuries. It asks what could be done to improve living conditions in poor countries in a way that is financially affordable and technically feasible. It is the contention of this book that scaling up is mission critical if extreme poverty is to be vanquished in our lifetime.[7]

Already, the idea of accelerating poverty reduction is taking root among development practitioners. This is evidenced by the Millennium Development Goals (MDGs), which are expressed in terms of the pursuit of results at scale, reflecting the desire to transform lives and to bring about far-reaching, sustainable change. In 2011 the international development community congregated in Busan, Korea, at the High Level Forum on Aid Effectiveness, to discuss

5. World Bank (2011).

6. One exception is the study by Hartmann and Linn (2008).

7. The phrase *mission critical* is borrowed from the International Fund for Agricultural Development, which provides a rare example of an aid agency that has made scaling up an integral and explicit part of its modus operandi.

how approaches to development need to change if accelerated results are to be achieved. The outcome document for the meeting concludes, "We recognize that progress has been uneven and neither fast nor far-reaching enough. . . . We reaffirm our commitment to scale up development cooperation . . . scaling up our support of development results . . . scaling up the use of triangular approaches to development cooperation . . . and scaling up of efforts in support of development goals."[8] Easier said than done.

But perhaps such pledges are not so unrealistic. What if scaling up was being held back by some well-defined obstacles, which could be overcome through a dedicated effort? This claim has become associated with two schools of thought.

The first can be caricatured as a West Coast "Silicon Valley" perspective. It puts its emphasis on finding innovative technological solutions to development challenges through scientific advances and visionary entrepreneurship. From this perspective, the reason that scaling up rarely occurs in developing countries is the dearth of scalable opportunities. If scientists, engineers, and innovators focused on the problems of poor people, as opposed to those of the rich, new opportunities could be discovered. New vaccines and off-grid lighting solutions are examples of what can be achieved when innovators turn their attention to development problems.

The second camp is associated with what we call the East Coast "Kendall Square" perspective, named for the location of MIT's Abdul Latif Jameel Poverty Action Lab. Researchers there have organized a massive effort to compile compelling statistical evidence of what development interventions work best, based on randomized trials. Their aim is to equip policymakers with sufficient information to determine how resources can be efficiently allocated: in other words, what interventions should be taken to scale and what interventions should be discarded. A good example of the former is the Kenya National School-Based Deworming Program, which has treated millions of school children at modest cost, thereby substantially improving attendance rates and learning outcomes throughout the country. Public backing for the program followed the publication of an impact evaluation that demonstrated the intervention's unequivocal success when attempted on a small scale.[9]

This book argues that the challenges to scaling up are more complex and more numerous than either a lack of appropriate technology or a lack of evidence of what works. Without understating the importance of both technological innovation and rigorous evaluation for development and scaling up, we believe that neither can be viewed as the binding constraint for the failure of many existing successful interventions to reach scale.

8. Busan Partnership for Effective Development Cooperation (2011, p. 2ff).
9. Miguel and Kremer (2004).

Instead, the challenge of scaling up development impact cannot be reduced to a single constraint but is better approached as a process challenge. The business model—the specific combination and design of product, distribution, supply chain, financing, pricing, payment, and sales—is often far more important in determining success than a specific technology or piece of evidence. It is attention to the details of implementation at a large scale that makes the difference between successful and unsuccessful scaling up.

This poses a challenge for the development community. Donors have traditionally resolved implementation problems by breaking up projects into small and "doable" efforts, which they can supervise from abroad. Many governments of poor countries, meanwhile, have limited capacity for scaling interventions competently. The private sector has enjoyed more success when interventions have been proven to have a commercial return—witness the explosion of microfinance through the private sector—but is rarely involved in development activities affecting poor people.

Given this reality, it is useful to try and learn systematically how to scale up development impact by analyzing examples of success and failure. Each of the essays in this book documents one or more contemporary case studies or syntheses of cases, which together provide a body of evidence on the challenges, opportunities, risks, and rewards of pursuing a scaling agenda. Cases of scaling up by the private sector and by the public sector are included. They reveal some hard truths. Scaling up is difficult to plan because it involves transformational change. Tools like cost-benefit analysis, the workhorse for analyzing development projects, are not helpful because scaling up often involves changing cost curves, altering beneficiary behavior, and an endogenous policy environment. Business models to implement scaled solutions cannot be taken off the shelf or easily replicated from one context to another—what is called external validity—but need to be designed and fine-tuned for scale over many years.

There are high risks to trying to reach scale, with more failures than successes. That is typical of most innovations, as entrepreneurs can attest. According to one estimate, it takes an average of fifty-eight new product ideas to deliver one that is viable.[10] This is enough to scare off bureaucrats, whether in donor agencies or governments, whose expected rates of success are set impossibly high. (For instance, the World Bank aims for a project success rate of 85 percent.) Their strategy has been to seek modest impacts across many small interventions, rather than attempting to scale their best investments. By contrast, corporations are usually willing to take on risks, as huge returns from a few successes can compensate for the financial losses of failures, so long as the latter are truncated efficiently. But the same calculus doesn't apply when corporations operate in

10. Mullins and Komisar (2009).

the development sphere. There, the returns to a successful scaled-up intervention may be large in terms of development impact but are typically small in terms of profits. The financial returns, therefore, do not compensate for the costs incurred in failed pilots.

In each of the cases in this book, we show that the scaling-up challenge can be divided into two. There is the challenge of financing scaled-up interventions, because poor people cannot afford to pay full cost for many services. These costs can be especially high when new markets or products, like solar power, are being introduced. The second challenge is managing delivery to large numbers of beneficiaries. The logistics, training, recruitment, and systems needed to deliver goods and services efficiently to poor people spread out throughout a country are incredibly complex and depend on a strong customer-oriented design. Very few actors—whether governments, donors, nonprofits, charities, or corporations—have the management ability to operate efficiently at scale. Large corporations are most adept at handling this challenge, but development activities are not at the top of their priorities. In every case, scaling up requires sustained commitment from top leadership, something that can be hard to achieve in most environments.

Scaling Definitions

In this book, we are particularly interested in the range of interventions that can transform the lives of poor people. Transformation may entail providing them with goods and services to which they otherwise have no access, such as education, health, finance, and energy, or involving them directly in the design or implementation of development projects, making them partners and providers as well as potential beneficiaries. For example, when poor farmers are linked into commercial agricultural value chains, they can achieve unprecedented improvements in income. Or when children are enrolled in schools that teach them literacy and numeracy skills to a minimum standard, their lifetime earnings opportunities are expanded hugely. When lives are saved through medical attention at birth, and illnesses avoided by reducing indoor air pollution or improving nutrition, the development benefits are startling.

In other words, we define scaling-up development impact in terms of not just reaching large numbers of poor people but doing so with interventions that transform their lives. These interventions often lead to behavioral changes in poor households that trigger further innovations and development: poor families invest more in their children when they are more likely to survive; they save more when they see opportunities for further income advancement; they work more when they are not sick; their children go on to higher education when they excel at the basics.

What constitutes scale can differ according to circumstances. Scale may be defined in terms of the level at which objectives are set: for instance, a mayor's pledge to a city, a government's national development strategy, or the global MDGs. We do not limit ourselves to a rigid definition of scale here, but the case studies are principally oriented to experiences where the goal is transformational impact at the country level. With this definition, we exclude the activities of many small social enterprises and nonprofit organizations, which can have enormous transformational impact on the lives of those they reach but do not have the resources or capacity to implement national programs. However, we do include so-called franchise models, where many of these entities replicate a similar business model and thereby achieve scale in aggregate. In other words, we do not restrict ourselves to scaling up through a single program or organization. Sometimes, a successful business model leads to imitation and replication, and that becomes the process for reaching scale. That has been true for the microfinance and the mobile phone industries, for example.

Although our interest is in understanding how to transform the lives of poor people, we do not focus only on scaling up interventions that reach the poorest of the poor. For the most part, poor people are not a well-defined, static group. Poor families may have good years, when they would be classified as near poor, and bad years, when they fall back into poverty. But if they benefit from a scaled-up intervention when they are just above the poverty threshold, they are far less likely to fall back into poverty at a later stage. Hence the impact on poverty reduction over time can be just as large by including the near poor in the target group compared to interventions that target only extremely poor populations. While the precise target group varies from organization to organization, most of the examples presented here are aimed at those individuals spending less than 4 dollars a day.

Scaling Up Today

Scaling up is an inherently complex process involving the management and organization of vast numbers of dollars and people: dollars, to cover the cost of establishing and running large-scale operations; and people, to manage those operations, serve as intermediaries in the delivery of interventions, and to interface with low-income beneficiaries. In other words, any attempt at getting to scale hinges on establishing a business model—the nexus of finance and delivery—that can support a scaled-up operation.

Figure 1-1 provides a stylized schematic of how this works in practice today. Development interventions are arranged according to whether they require subsidies or can be made profitable. Typically, when subsidies are needed,

Figure 1-1. *Scaling-Up Models: The Status Quo*

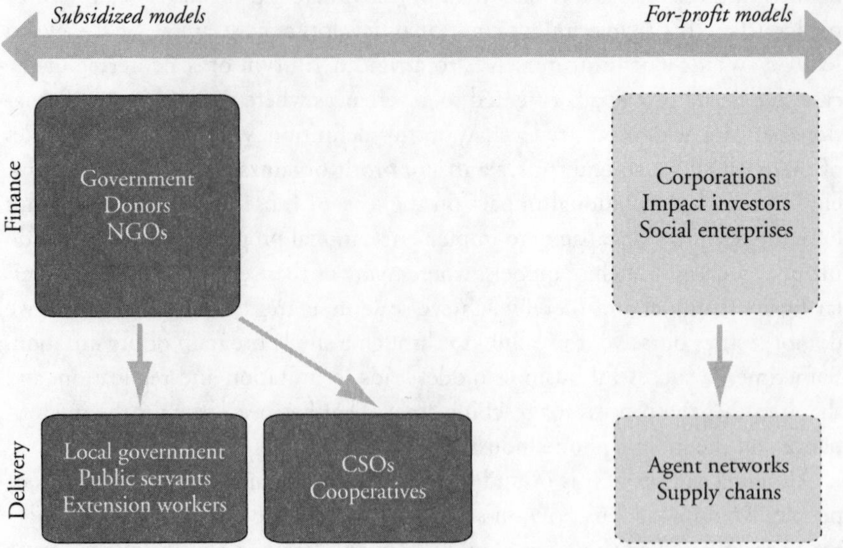

government, aid donors, or large international NGOs take the lead. Examples range from vaccine programs to national employment guarantee schemes. When profits are feasible, it is the private business sector that undertakes scaling up. In the last decade, small sachet shampoos, community water, and biomass stoves have demonstrated market potential when poor households are viewed as a specific customer segment, while contract farming models show the commercial viability of viewing poor communities as low-cost producers.[11] Whether scaling up is financed through subsidies or on a commercial basis determines whether interventions are ultimately delivered through the public or private sector.

Subsidy Models

The financial challenge of scaling up subsidized interventions is straightforward enough: subsidies cost money. Even with the benefit of scale economies, total costs typically increase with the number of beneficiaries, so the availability of resources can determine the degree of scale that is ultimately achieved. Sustaining subsidized interventions at scale requires a long-term commitment, far beyond the duration of the domestic political cycle or a donor's strategy for a country. While governments, international NGOs (INGOs), and donors command large budgets, the number of interventions they can feasibly scale remains finite.

11. Prahalad (2004).

Take, for instance, the treatment of people living with HIV/AIDS in the developing world, which is considered to be one of the most comprehensive and successful examples of a subsidized model of scaling up in the development field. In 2011, 8 million individuals received antiretroviral therapy, at a cost of $16.8 billion: $8.6 billion collectively spent by developing country governments and $8.2 billion spent by the donor community.[12] The latter represents a sizable share of all foreign aid (6 percent). The goal of universal provision for all 34 million people living with HIV/AIDS—a number that is rising by 2.5 million a year—demands additional resources, despite a steep reduction in per person costs. Recent cost estimates for meeting global demand by 2015 indicate the need for an additional $7 billion of annual spending.[13] Critics question whether such large expenditure on HIV/AIDS crowds out spending on other diseases that can save lives at a lower cost.[14]

To be viable, a business model that relies on subsidies has to be narrowly focused on a specific issue. If the range of activities is too broad, resources must be thinly spread, and scale becomes unachievable. That forces a trade-off: scaling up can require taking a narrow approach, potentially limiting development impact, while the alternative of broadening the range of activities to encompass the multisectoral interventions that are often required for sustained development impact can make scaling up unaffordable. The United Nations' Millennium Villages project has been criticized for exactly these reasons. Its critics argue that it is too broad and expensive to be scalable.[15] On the other hand, when global education resources were channeled in a focused way for building new schools to meet the enrollment targets of the MDGs, school quality and learning outcomes fell in some countries, causing a backlash against such programs.[16] These examples show how difficult it can be to find the right balance between scaling up to reach more people—a public good imperative—and providing the range of services that truly achieves a transformational impact in beneficiaries' lives.

Subsidized models also have difficulty organizing efficient delivery. As an intervention's scale increases, so do logistical demands. Systems need to be developed to monitor effective implementation and to manage personnel. Even in the most easily mechanized activities, distribution models require the identification of reliable individuals and the development of their skills to perform different roles. With large numbers of people involved in a scaled-up operation, there is a premium on effective recruitment, training, and managing churn. The

12. Figures represent total HIV/AIDS spending, not just expenditure on antiretroviral therapy.
13. UNAIDS (2012).
14. For instance, see World Bank (2012).
15. Quote by Bunker Roy in Bishop and Green (2010).
16. Lewin (2008); Kenny (2010).

relationships between individuals along the distribution channel must be managed so as to provide the right incentives and to promote accountability and productivity.

Subsidized models rely on implementing organizations to provide these systems and manage personnel. Governments tend to work through ministries, subnational government, state-owned enterprises, and extension networks, whereas INGOs typically partner with local civil society organizations (CSOs) or cooperatives. These implementing organizations provide the networks for reaching poor populations, extending down to the level of individual villages and communities.

The difficulties of achieving scale with these delivery systems are well known. Government ministries and local authorities often lack the capability for effective administration, including financial management, procurement, and service delivery, and despite their public service mandate, struggle to foster a customer-service orientation and adopt a customer-driven design.

Few countries have meritocratic-based civil services that reward employees for the efficiency and effectiveness of their performance. Hiring is as likely to be based on patronage as on merit. In developing countries, government information and payroll systems, structured learning, willingness to innovate and experiment to fine-tune delivery, and training programs for employees are notoriously poor. Corruption, absenteeism, and theft can be widespread. In India and Uganda, for example, teacher absenteeism in public schools still reaches over 25 percent.[17]

When programs are administered by local CSOs, results tend to be better, but few of these organizations have national reach. Indeed, in some cases their effectiveness is a consequence of their small size, and their organizational systems are not capable of expansion. A franchise model, involving multiple CSOs, may provide a path to scale but can imply higher transaction costs and greater variability in quality.

Donor agencies are acutely aware of these weaknesses and have oscillated between establishing their own delivery systems and working through government or CSO delivery channels. Over the last decade, donors have made commitments to working through government in recognition that long-term sustainable development depends on countries being in control and having viable institutions of their own, consistent with the principle of ownership. Despite this rhetoric, donors have made less progress in practice. Less than half of all aid is channeled through government systems, and less than half employs programmatic approaches, which pool government and donor efforts around government-led plans.

17. Devarajan (2010).

Box 1-1. *Lessons from BRAC*

Over the course of forty years, BRAC has evolved from an organization dedicated to relief and rehabilitation in the wake of Bangladesh's independence to the world's largest development NGO. Its presence in Asia, Africa, and the Caribbean benefits an estimated 126 million people. BRAC's growth reflects a strong focus on bringing successful interventions to scale, which it has achieved in a variety of areas, including income generation, health, education, agriculture, food security, water, and sanitation.

BRAC's visionary founder, Fazle Hasan Abed, identifies a number of factors to which the organization's success in scaling up can be attributed.[a] First, BRAC has the goal of achieving scale engendered in all its activities from the outset. This vision informs its choice and pursuit of business models. Second, BRAC adopts a well-trodden pathway in getting to scale: demonstrating the *effectiveness* of a given intervention, then achieving *efficiency* by lowering cost, and finally *expanding* to reach large numbers of beneficiaries. This sequence is crucial in giving BRAC the confidence to invest in the right interventions. Third, BRAC puts an emphasis on strong internal systems to support operations at scale. These include a focus on human resources, management, monitoring, performance metrics, financial accounting, and delivery.

a. Abed (2012).

Large donor investments have focused on boosting governments' capacity to deliver and on improving government systems, from public financial management to procurement to sector policy, planning, and evaluation. But achieving progress in these areas has proven to be much harder than expected. Civil service reform and public capacity building are among the least well performing and most challenging of all development cooperation efforts.[18]

Taken together, the obstacles to financing sustained large-scale subsidies and building efficient and effective delivery systems are daunting. Developing country governments have no choice but to muddle through and to provide interventions at scale to the extent and to a standard that fiscal and capacity constraints allow. Scale, in a literal sense, is often achieved, but poor quality of delivery and an inappropriate level of focus constrains impact. Few NGOs have the resources and interest in sustaining large-scale subsidized interventions, although there are some notable exceptions (box 1-1).

What about donors? Their best chance for achieving scale is to play a catalytic role, with a focus typically on supporting government or NGO efforts. In practice, however, donors have often favored more modest interventions,

18. UK DFID (2008).

diversifying their investments widely and avoiding working through others where this weakens their ability to account for money spent. Interventions are favored that can generate immediate results, with little consideration given to the fact that development impact rarely unfolds in a linear and monotonic fashion.[19] This is reflected in the characteristics commonly associated with today's aid investments, characteristics that emerge from the peculiar set of factors that shape donor choices (box 1-2). Incentives such as short termism and an extreme aversion to institutional risk inform aid allocations and modalities and permeate agency culture.

For-Profit Models

It used to be thought that subsidized models presented the most, and possibly only, viable way of delivering development solutions at scale to poor people. But this idea was challenged with the 2004 publication of C. K. Prahalad's *The Fortune at the Bottom of the Pyramid*. Prahalad argues that there exist significant, untapped profitable opportunities in low-income—or base of the pyramid (BoP)—markets, which can be seized if businesses adjust for the circumstances, preferences, and behavior of low-income customers.

This concept offers a radical, alternative route to scaling up development impact. Whereas subsidized models depend on government planning to spur the transition to scale, for-profit models harness market forces and the universal motivation to make profits. (In fact, Prahalad argues that being profitable in low-income markets relies more on turnover than margins, providing a further spur to the achievement of scale.) Private corporations replace governments, donors, and INGOs as the investors behind these ventures. Corporations are joined by a growing cadre of social enterprises committed to using market-based solutions to address development goals. Meanwhile, private networks of agents and supply chains provide a delivery route to beneficiaries.

For-profit models of scaling up face an immediate problem: achieving a financially attractive rate of return. Margins at the base of the pyramid are very low—some 3 to 10 percent, compared to an opportunity cost of capital for most multinationals of 20 percent or more.[20] Further, the upfront costs of penetrating or sometimes creating those markets are high. In the first instance, funding is needed to finance research and development, to design and refine consumer products, to test consumer interest among low-income households, and to identify ways to lower unit costs. If this stage is successful, additional investments can be required to lay the groundwork for expansion. This may include building a business infrastructure, institutions, or skills, where the enabling environment

---

19. Woolcock, Szreter, and Rao (2011).
20. Kubzansky (2010).

Box 1-2. *Aid Characteristics*

An analysis of aid interventions reveals three salient characteristics.

First, they are typically very *small.* In 2010, $133.5 billion was spent on foreign aid by the OECD Development Assistance Committee (DAC) countries and multilateral agencies on 19,186 projects.[a] This was broken up further into 139,832 activities, giving a mean activity size of approximately $1 million. Half of these activities had a value of under $50,000. Given that there can be no rigorous definition of a *project* or an *activity*—essentially, there are no limits on the degree to which interventions are bundled together—these figures can give only a rough indication of the degree of atomization within the official aid system. Nevertheless, official data point to a steady fall in the average size of activities over time. It seems fair to assume that the typical aid intervention is dwarfed in size by the development challenge (or challenges) it is intended to address.

Second, interventions tend to have a *short* duration. Those same 19,186 projects had a mean length of 613 days from start to expected completion, with half occurring within a single year. Given such a fast rate of turnover, less than one in ten of the 19,186 projects in 2010 will still be running in 2014.[b] Again, this seems at odds with the type of problems facing the world's poor, problems that are often deeply rooted and persistent. While it is possible that a series of short interventions may succeed at overturning persistent challenges, it is hard to marry this approach to the challenge of achieving structural improvements in developing economies, such as institution building and developing skills.

Third, interventions are largely *discrete,* in the sense that they are disconnected from each other both within and across time. This is partly a result of fragmentation; with hundreds of actors delivering hundreds of brief, small-scale interventions, coordination is hard to pull off. However, the problem runs deeper than this. Interventions are supposed to serve a common, focused agenda as defined by national development strategies. But in reality, strategy documents perform the opposite role: defining objectives in the broadest possible terms and providing justification for interventions regardless of how tenuous and superficial their link is to others.

Interventions that are mostly small, short, and discrete can still have a positive impact on the world's poor, albeit one that is below the aid system's potential.[c]

a. There is no standardized way of measuring a project size. We adopt the methodology used by Birdsall and Kharas (2010) in which activities reported to DAC's creditor reporting system database are collapsed into a single project if they have the same donor name, agency name, recipient name, project title, and expected start date. Small projects (those with less than $250,000 in funding) are excluded, as they often represent line-item adjustments to existing projects rather than new projects. For a detailed account of this methodology, see www.cgdev.org/userfiles/quoda/QuODA%20Second%20Edition%20Report.pdf.

b. Calculations based on those projects of known duration.

c. Linn (2011).

is otherwise deficient, and generating demand for products through marketing and educational campaigns.

A key feature of for-profit models is that they take considerable time to reach scale, and firms must be willing to absorb losses over this trial period. For some products, low-income consumers are already active purchasers even when these markets are informal, expensive, and unregulated. For these market-entry and "pull" products, the time to reach a scaled-up sales volume for better or cheaper products is two to five years. But it can be considerably longer when poor people are being introduced to new market-creation and "push" products, even if buying these has a major social benefit. In these cases, time is required to build beneficiaries' trust of a new product or to induce behavioral change. BoP markets like microfinance and contract farming are still maturing after thirty and fifty years, respectively.

The time and money spent on nurturing the market for push products are a public good. They benefit not only the first mover, who incurs the expense, but also all other potential suppliers. For that reason, individual companies are often unwilling to take on the burden themselves, preferring to wait until another firm covers the initial costs.

For-profit actors are well suited to building efficient delivery systems at scale. Private companies have a strong pedigree in product-testing and customer-oriented design. They are free to hire and fire and to experiment with different delivery models. Building networks of agents or supply chains to reach poor beneficiaries is still a challenge, but these can often piggyback onto existing structures. For example, MicroEnsure, a company that seeks to provide a safety net to reduce economic setbacks for those living on less than 4 dollars a day, uses the customer network of existing microfinance enterprises for selling its products.

Of all private sector actors, large, multinational (or at least national-scale) companies are best placed to build the systems required for scale. They have experience with logistics, personnel, information technology, and other back-office functions. But they also have alternative priorities. For now, the BoP space is dominated by social enterprises with hybrid profit and development motives. These enterprises are small and thus have a hard time developing the institutional wherewithal for large-scale delivery.

Thus for all the enthusiasm that for-profit models have generated, there have been disappointingly few examples of their interventions reaching scale. In some cases, market fragmentation or poor market linkages have inhibited growth by forcing prices too high for large numbers of low-income customers to afford. More often, ventures have never even gotten off the ground, as the fixed costs incurred in early discovery and pilot phases, or in creating a new market, cannot be met. Potential financiers are put off by the anticipation of high-risk, low-return, and long-term investments. Patient capital for development does not exist as an asset class. Social enterprises have shown glimmers of promise but remain too small in number and size to make a difference. Some view the failure of for-profit models as a saving grace, protecting poor consumers from exploitation at the hands of powerful corporations, which they cannot hope to hold to account.

Revolutions in Finance, Delivery, and Partnerships

Until now, the number of scaling-up success stories is relatively small, reflecting the limitations of existing business models.

First, financial resources for development are not being effectively utilized. Public and NGO resources are thinly spread across the many challenges that confront poor people and lack a sufficient degree of focus. Donor resources, in particular, have struggled to perform a catalytic role. Significant additional resources for scaling up could be unleashed through private finance, but this has been constrained by the large up-front costs and low rates of return incurred in identifying and developing scalable commercial opportunities.

Second, systems for managing delivery at scale in developing countries have been found wanting. While succeeding at turning delivery at a small scale into an art, donors and NGOs have struggled to master the complexities of developing large-scale delivery operations that are sustainable, cost effective, and customer oriented. Government implementation capabilities are often especially weak and are undermined by inadequate information and communication technology and by poor internal incentive and accountability mechanisms. Private sector know-how in this area has yet to be successfully harnessed to serve the world's poor people. More fundamentally, many poor people remain hard to reach, and the high transaction costs incurred in connecting to them drive up the price of sub-sidy models and reduce the scope for identifying commercially feasible for-profit models. However, these structural factors are starting to shift, creating a sense of excitement about the possibilities for scaling up in the near future.

Among the drivers of change are the evolving roles of actors in the development community. A wave of successful entrepreneurs is entering the world of philanthropy, seeking to apply to social problems the calculated risk taking, discipline, and drive for scalable solutions that served them well in their for-profit ventures.[21] In addition, there has been a dramatic expansion in the number and range of social enterprises in advanced and developing countries, blurring the lines between traditional categories of profit and nonprofit actors. The official donor community has also expanded to include members from emerging

---

21. Worthington and Pipa (2011); Bishop and Green (2010).

economies who exhibit different ways of working. Traditional donors, meanwhile, are looking to leverage increasingly scarce aid dollars into greater value for money. Finally, developing country governments wish to translate greater domestic resources into stronger leadership and more effective service delivery.

Another driver is technological progress. A cluster of new technologies—identification, communication, payment, digitalization, and data processing—are being combined in ways that could alter how global efforts to tackle poverty are forged. For instance, mobile money promises to strengthen consumers' participation in markets and thus expand the scope for market-based service delivery. Improved targeting technology and real-time data collection and analysis can improve management capacity and strengthen systems for large-scale interventions. And the dramatic expansion of mass media has introduced transparency to all development efforts, which has given fresh confidence that partners with different agendas but shared goals can come together and be accountable to civil society at large.

As the case studies in this volume attest, these dynamics are generating innovative approaches to scaling up. They are still too few to yield a complete science of execution, but they offer tantalizing examples of how scaled-up development impact may soon become the norm rather than the exception.

We have organized the case studies into three groups, indicating the ways in which business models for scaling up are changing: finance, delivery, and partnerships.

Finance for Scale

The flows of official development assistance from OECD countries fell in 2011 for the first time since 1997, and projections of future aid levels up to 2015 indicate continued risks to the downside, resulting from the poor economic outlook in most donor countries. This prompted Oxfam to warn of "hundreds of thousands of poor people [going] without life-saving medicines and many more children [missing] out on school."[22] Given this backdrop, now seems a strange time to make the argument that the prospects for resources for scaling up are strong.

However, to focus exclusively on the value of official flows is to miss the forest for the trees. Aid flows have never been sufficient to meet all development challenges. In fact, they equate to only 30 cents a day, per poor person, after excluding aid devoted to extraneous issues beyond development programs and projects.

Instead, aid flows have to be looked at in the context of all resources available for development, both domestic and international. The significance of these additional resources has increased in recent years. Despite rising aid volumes over the past decade, average aid dependence in low-income countries has

22. Oxfam (2012).

fallen sharply, with the number of governments relying on aid for at least 30 percent of their public expenditure falling from forty-two to thirty.[23] This is the result both of faster economic growth in the developing world and a dramatic expansion in government capacity to collect taxes. As a share of total international capital flows to developing countries, aid has fallen from 70 percent in the 1960s to 13 percent today, due to the takeoff in trade, remittances, equity, and foreign direct investment.

Of course, numbers alone cannot tell the whole story. Understanding the prospects of finance for scale requires an assessment not only of the size of resources but also of how resources are being applied: whether sufficient attention is given to the objective of scale, whether investments have an appropriate degree of focus, and whether specific resources succeed at crowding in others to support scalable programs.

One of the largest potential new sources of finance for development comes from the private corporate sector. This is distinct from the corporate social responsibility of charitable contributions, which large firms have long been making. Rather, it concerns the direct engagement of major corporations in development through their core business strategies. As economic growth in the advanced countries has slowed, multinational corporations are looking to developing countries for the bulk of their own growth. That has shifted the priority of development from an afterthought to a central priority of major business leaders.

Private financing offers the potential for significant expansion in capital flows to poor countries. The OECD's Development Assistance Committee reports $330 billion in such flows destined for low- and middle-income countries. This is mostly direct foreign investment and bank loans that are not directly related to development, although in many cases, such as infrastructure investments in telecommunications, toll roads, and power plants, the profit motive of the private sector is well aligned with the development motive of creating the enabling environment for growth and poverty reduction.

There are, however, the new phenomena of inclusive business and impact investing that promise to align incentives between private capital and the achievement of social impact more closely and in many more fields. Inclusive business is defined as a profitable core business activity that tangibly expands opportunities for the poor and disadvantaged as producers, employees, or consumers in formal markets and commercial value chains. Impact investments are investments made in companies, organizations, and funds with the intention of generating measurable social and environmental impact alongside financial return. While it is difficult to estimate the amount of money flowing into such efforts, the Global Impact Investing Network (GIIN) estimates that $50 billion

23. ActionAid (2011).

has already been mobilized for impact investing (although largely in advanced countries) and that $9 billion in new commitments are expected in 2013 by respondents to their survey.[24] A recent J. P. Morgan report suggests that impact investing could emerge as an asset class with committed funds of $400 billion to $1 trillion within ten years, just counting five sectors: housing, rural water delivery, maternal health, primary education, and financial services.[25]

Can these new funds and business models make a material difference in developing countries? Mike Kubzansky explores the potential for private capital to contribute to scaling up development impact (chapter 2). He challenges the assumption that a single entity offers the best route to scale in all circumstances, whether through a multinational corporation or a social enterprise. He posits two alternative routes to scale using the for-profit model. One route is to replicate a proven business model through hundreds of small and medium enterprises, as has happened with microfinance and contract farming. The key to exploiting this route is the demonstration of effectiveness in transforming poor people's lives. The second route is to leverage existing informal providers, who are legion in developing countries, by organizing them, providing them with technical assistance, and improving and upgrading their services. This latter route is similar to a franchise model, and while examples are few, they indicate the potential for success. The Greenstar network in Pakistan, for example, a franchise of small clinics, has been shown to provide better quality health services, to poorer clients, at lower unit cost than either government health clinics or private for-profit clinics.

Kubzansky highlights the dearth of funding for early-stage investments to get good ideas off the ground and to test new business models before they can be taken to a growth and expansion phase. But he also points to constraints on the amount of grants for technical assistance, training, and the establishment of networks that franchising requires. If these gaps can be filled, Kubzansky believes that for-profit scaling up could take off. His suggestion: donors and philanthropists interested in scaling up should try to identify and fill key financing gaps in conjunction with for-profit businesses and social enterprises in new hybrid arrangements.

This leads to the question of whether donors can alter the way they work to achieve scaled-up development impact. Laurence Chandy (chapter 3) reviews the past decade of rising aid flows to explore how agencies made use of additional resources. He argues that growing aid budgets generate competing pressures within donor governments. In combination, these pressures produce an ambiguous effect in terms of whether donors strive for scale.

24. Stabile (2010); Saltuk and others (2013).
25. J. P. Morgan (2010).

Chandy shows that to understand the success of subsidized models requires much more than a simple assessment of the volume of resources committed. He submits that few donors have an approach to aid management that is conducive for scaling up as it is classically conceived, whereby good ideas emerge from the field, are rigorously evaluated, and are ultimately propagated with support from donor headquarters. For other donors, the best opportunity for achieving scale is to choose development problems that lend themselves to more mechanized solutions, where the challenge consists mainly in overcoming logistic and resource constraints rather than institutional strengthening and sustainability challenges, and the drive for scale can come from the top. This suggests that donors could be much more effective in achieving scale if they were matched to particular development challenges based on their expertise. A division of labor, based on the operational models of different donors, offers the chance of greater impact without any growth in global aid budgets.

To be viable, a business model that relies on subsidies has to be narrowly focused on a specific issue. David Gartner and Homi Kharas (chapter 4) look at the efforts to scale up resources and impact through vertical funds: specialized aid agencies that adopt a strong focus by providing a critical mass of expertise, identifying results in measurable ways, and mobilizing highly targeted financial support. These organizations have been controversial among development practitioners because, while they scale up impact and results in one area, they may inadvertently dilute resources going into other areas.[26] If vertical funds are truly efficient, however, then the net impact on development by operating through vertical funds could potentially be larger.

Gartner and Kharas find that there is considerable variation in the practices of vertical funds. Some are highly successful, with considerable impact, while others have made less of a difference. They attribute this to the governance arrangements of the funds. Those with more independence, greater beneficiary involvement, and clear performance-based metrics do better in terms of impact, resource mobilization, and learning. These, they submit, are all attributes necessary for scaling up. The authors conclude that a vertical fund approach can lead to scaled-up impact, but only if management, governance, and implementation practices are properly designed.

Together, these three chapters demonstrate that resources for scale could be dramatically enhanced over the near future, by both unlocking pools of private finance for development and altering the way in which donor resources are utilized to derive greater impact.

26. Isenman and Shakow (2010).

Delivery at Scale

Earlier in this chapter we define delivery as being a problem about managing people. Delivery is what makes getting to scale not merely difficult but complex. Securing finance for scale may be extremely hard to achieve, but there is normally a clear vision from the outset as to what the end goal should look like. By contrast, successful delivery at scale is more an art than a science. This is especially apparent when operating at the base of the pyramid, where the last mile of delivery involves not merely a transaction but also obtaining beneficiaries' trust and understanding and often changing their behavior. A strong customer-oriented design can be of critical importance in shaping products, prices, distribution, marketing, and sales, which together create a viable business model.

The chapters in this section touch on many aspects of delivery: strategic, institutional, and administrative. It is no surprise that they put forward no silver bullet solutions. However, recent experimentation and learning from implementers justify optimism and indicate opportunities for progress in many areas.

Johannes Linn (chapter 5) examines incentives and accountability within and between governments and aid agencies as they grapple with scaling up. He frames the transition to scale as a classic principal-agent problem, where success hinges on the alignment of stakeholders' interests. In theory, he argues, all parties should share the goal of expanding the reach of successful public goods and services. Yet a collection of government and market failures results in a wedge being driven between parties. Moreover, the longer the chain of accountability between development planners and ultimate beneficiaries, the greater the likelihood that interests will diverge and that scaling up will not be pursued, or will fail.

Linn identifies a variety of instruments that can be deployed to better align incentives around the objectives of scaling up. These include ways to amplify the voice of beneficiaries, to unite donors and recipient governments behind shared strategies and approaches, and to introduce market mechanisms that induce competition around the achievement of specified goals. He views experimentation as a valuable path to innovation and improvement. However, Linn's greatest interest is in opening the black box of government and donor agencies to shed light on internal institutional incentives. He argues that too often "internal management practices do not provide for effective incentives and accountability between top management and the front-line staff." Fixing these—to pinpoint aspects that discourage scaling up—requires top-to-bottom reviews of institutions to assess their corporate missions, strategies, operational policies, processes, and instrumentalities, and human resource and budget management. Linn makes the case that this more systematic approach to scaling up can identify small reforms that result in significantly improved institutional performance.

Chris West (chapter 6) is enthusiastic about the application of private sector know-how for delivering development solutions at scale. He calls this "business DNA," which he defines as an understanding of how "to develop and execute viable models to deliver products or services to customers in ways that they value." West's enthusiasm is informed by a decade of experience with the Shell Foundation, an angel investor committed to catalyzing scalable development solutions through supporting social enterprises. When the foundation focused narrowly on providing short-term grants, 80 percent of those enterprises failed to achieve any evidence of scalability. However, when grants were incorporated into long-term partnerships and coupled with hands-on business skills support and the identification of market linkages, the foundation's results turned around dramatically.

Through a collection of case studies, West highlights the wide variety of business skills required for scaling up social enterprises. The foundation supports its clients in project management competencies, such as developing operating systems and setting milestones, as well as in more specialized areas, such as product marketing and market analysis. In addition, by using its own network of partners, the foundation has been able to pair its clients with investors, sources of business, route-to-market partners, and others with close links to local communities. This testifies to the complexity of mastering delivery at scale, but it also highlights that typical efforts to support social enterprises are not sufficiently focused on building these critical skill sets. Greater attention to these weaknesses could help unleash the potential of social enterprises, which have traditionally been written off as unscalable.

The story of M-PESA, the mobile money service in Kenya, presents one of the most celebrated cases of scaled-up development impact and is quite possibly the quickest the world has seen. M-PESA offers a commercially viable business model for serving poor customers where traditional banking falls short. M-PESA overcomes the constraint of access by substituting mobile phone ownership and networks of agents for physical banks; and it allows small-value transfers and minimal fees by encouraging a shift away from cash to electronic money in which simple movements of money incur virtually no transaction costs. The adoption of mobile money by 73 percent of adults in Kenya—where 67 percent of the population lives below 2 dollars a day—suggests that it should be possible to conceive of a world where virtually all poor people are "banked."

Pauline Vaughan, Wolfgang Fengler, and Michael Joseph (chapter 7) provide a unique insiders' view on how M-PESA triumphed. They identify many contributing factors concerning the company's approach to management, design, and delivery. Robust internal processes, the setting of targets, and visionary leadership are all identified as important components of success, in which the objective of reaching scale was fully reflected. However, arguably the most ingenious aspect of the business model is the approach to reaching customers through the formation, training, and retention of a cadre of M-PESA agents.

M-PESA recognized from the outset that its success would critically depend on its agents. Agents would be the most visible element of the company and would have to earn the trust of potential customers to bring about the behavioral change required in the adoption of a new product. Rather than creating agents from scratch, M-PESA identified existing networks of competent operatives in the Kenyan economy, which they could readily employ. These included their own airtime dealers (sellers of prepaid mobile phone credit), the fuel retailer Caltex, Group 4 Securicor courier services, supermarket chains and other retailers, dry cleaners, and the Pesa Point ATM network. By the end of 2011 the number of agent outlets exceeded 35,000, or 1 for every 700 adult Kenyans. Regular interactions between M-PESA and its agents provided an opportunity for training (to ensure a high quality of service), information gathering (to identify possible improvements to the service), and instilling loyalty (to retain agents and avoid rehiring costs). From a scaling-up perspective, the virtue of this approach was to ensure that delivery could expand swiftly while transaction costs are kept low.

Inspirational though the story of M-PESA is, its consequences for scaling up go much further. The possibility of introducing poor people the world over into the banking system provides a route for engaging them in other and new BoP markets. In Kenya today, over 500 organizations use M-PESA to pay bills and conduct transactions, including utilities, medical saving plans, crop insurance for smallholder farmers, and teacher payment programs (as an alternative to standard school fees). Of course, so long as poor people remain poor, their purchasing power in these markets will be limited. However, mobile banking services provide a means for governments, donors, and charities to give money directly to poor populations and allow them to buy the goods and services they seek, rather than attempting to supply these themselves. When poor people have access to funds, markets for goods and services spring up spontaneously. That has been the experience with schools in slums, rural water supply, health clinics, and a range of other products. Scaling up is most likely to take off by increasing the purchasing power of poor people rather than by organizing the delivery of specific goods and services.

Mobile money is one of a number of new technologies that can expand the scope for scaling up (box 1-3). The internet provides another fast track for reaching vast numbers of customers at low cost. This is demonstrated in one of two highly successful case studies examined by Hiroshi Kato and Akio Hosono (chapter 8) in which the private sector plays a leading role. The authors describe how the Micro Finance International Corporation (MFIC), a social enterprise,

Box 1-3. *Technological Innovations for Delivery*

The creative application of modern technologies can push out the possibility frontier of future development efforts by enabling better targeting, real-time data collection and analysis, and responsiveness to beneficiary feedback.

Around half a billion people in the developing world have had their biometric identification recorded in a government database using fingerprinting, or iris or facial recognition, a number that is currently rising at an astounding 25 percent a year. As biometric identification expands, so does the possibility of more accurate programs to assist poor and vulnerable communities. Spatial identification and mapping can also enhance the targeting of programs. These technologies are increasingly being deployed to ensure equitable distribution across geographical areas and in supporting coordination across donors and NGOs. Most recently, they have proven valuable in responding to crises such as the monitoring of violence in Nairobi and the search for missing earthquake victims in Haiti, both organized by the NGO Ushahidi.

Modern technologies allow data to be collected and analyzed in real time (or with drastically reduced lags), with greater reliability, at less cost, and in larger quantities. Cell phone surveys allow data collection to be conducted remotely in conflict-affected environments and to bypass weak institutions, which are often the underlying cause of low-quality data. Electronic platforms that manage finances create an auditable trail, typically running from the issuing agency all the way to ultimate beneficiaries. This trail can then be analyzed, helping to evaluate interventions and make them more effective.

Over the past decade, there has been growing interest in social accountability mechanisms, which strengthen citizens' ability to monitor and demand accountability from service providers and funders. Technologies can be employed to facilitate ex ante consultation of beneficiaries and support ex post consultation, to strengthen the feedback loop from beneficiaries to service providers and aid agencies.

New media are transforming the way that citizens can hold governments and other development actors accountable for their efforts. Advocacy efforts can now be organized at speed and at low cost. Pressure for greater transparency has encouraged governments to simplify processes: Kenya's Revenue Authority has placed customs, excises, and value-added taxes on an electronic portal, and Tanzania's mobile payments system permits taxes to be filed without citizens having to visit a government office. The accountability promoted by media access and scrutiny in developing countries extends to all development resources, not just aid, and to all development actors, not just governments. Donors, NGOs, and private corporations are subject to the same standards to promote development or at least avoid harm.

established a low-cost online facility to enable rapid and low-cost remittance transfers for "unbanked" migrant workers. The facility is supported by a new payment platform called Arias, which employs COBIS (core banking system) technology. This technology is associated with fast-speed intrabank transactions, as opposed to the more cumbersome traditional SWIFT technology. Recipients receive remittances via local microfinance branches that partner with MFIC. In 2010, MFIC and KDDI, one of the largest telecommunication companies in Japan, announced a new partnership to jointly promote a global remittance and payment platform for telecommunications carriers. This will allow users to make remittance payments using prepaid international telephone cards and prepaid mobile phones.

In their second case study, Kato and Hosono tell the story of the development and propagation of the Olyset net, a long-lasting insecticidal net created by the company Sumitomo Chemical to support the fight against malaria. Over the past decade, the Olyset net has been rapidly disseminated in sub-Saharan Africa, as a result of a unique approach to production and delivery supported by a diverse group of partners. The manufacture of the Olyset net has been transferred to A to Z Textile Mills in Tanzania under a joint venture with Sumitomo Chemical, resulting in the elimination of shipping costs. Delivery is handled by a combination of local government, NGOs, and commercial retailers, depending on the terms of sale.

Partnerships for Scale

The Global Partnership for Effective Development Cooperation, which emerged from the Fourth High Level Forum on Aid Effectiveness, acknowledges the critical role of partnerships in supporting development and seeks to forge closer cooperation between the traditional development community, emerging economy donors, civil society, and corporations. Partnerships can expand the scope for achieving scale in two related ways: first, by pooling the resources and expertise of different parties to enable larger and more ambitious programs and goals; and second, by recognizing the strengths and weaknesses of different parties and effecting an appropriate division of labor.

It is this latter rationale that provides the motivation for the partnerships explored in this section of the book. The case studies promote alternative allocations of roles for tackling the twin challenges of finance and delivery from the organizational arrangements assumed by standard subsidized and for-profit models.

For all their promise, the case studies show that partnerships are much easier to conceive than to agree on, operate, and sustain. Working in partnership can involve large transactions costs, and when these exceed the benefits to individual parties of working with others, they will choose to go it alone. Another problem is overcoming the cultural differences associated with different institutions.

Goals, time horizons, decisionmaking, risk tolerances, and commitments vary enormously from one party to another and can feed mistrust. This is especially apparent in public-private partnerships (PPPs), which have been experimented with for over fifty years. In spite of their long history, until recently only a few examples have delivered impact at scale. These constraints are important to keep in mind when assessing the feasibility of various partnership approaches.

One partnership structure that received significant acknowledgment at the Fourth High Level Forum on Aid Effectiveness was South-South cooperation, in which developing countries share know-how on solving common challenges. While this practice is growing fast, it typically involves only small, one-off projects, so the scope for scaled-up impact is limited. Akio Hosono (chapter 9) suggests that a slight modification of this type of partnership can radically alter the prospects for achieving scale. He advocates for what is called triangular cooperation, in which a traditional donor facilitates a South-South exchange. The role of the traditional donor is twofold: to complement knowledge exchange with assistance for capacity and institutional development; and to propagate South-South cooperation across countries by organizing, institutionalizing, and programming the replication of effective interventions.

Hosono's argument is backed by a number of case studies drawn from the Japan International Cooperation Agency's (JICA's) long-standing focus on capacity development and its creation of centers of excellence in developing countries. He draws an analogy between establishing these centers and the concept of training the trainers, in which a center provides a vehicle for reaching beneficiaries far beyond the number that JICA could feasibly reach directly. JICA views itself as a catalyst in enabling Southern partners to become donors and providing them with the institutions to assist others. Hosono uses the Brazilian Agricultural Research Corporation (Embrapa) as an example of an organization that reached global standards of excellence, thanks in part to collaboration with Japanese researchers, and that is now transferring this know-how to transform tropical agriculture in Mozambique. Japan complements these efforts with related investments in Mozambique to support the development of its agricultural export markets.

An honest assessment of the role of partnerships in getting to scale requires an understanding of the responsibilities and scope of different parties. Tessa Bold, Mwangi Kimenyi, Germano Mwabu, Alice Ng'ang'a, and Justin Sandefur (chapter 10) describe a fascinating experiment in Kenya to test the government's ability to implement and scale up an NGO intervention of proven effectiveness: a contract teacher program. The government was unable to replicate the success achieved by World Vision when it took responsibility for selecting, paying, and monitoring contract teachers. Since the government is the dominant actor in Kenya's education sector and the only party capable of scaling up education policies, this collaboration between the NGO and government failed to produce a truly scalable model.

The authors draw sharp conclusions from their work. While it is tempting to devise and study pilots as a way of understanding what might work at scale, the act of scaling up can pose political economy obstacles that a small pilot does not encounter. During the implementation of the contract teacher program, the government faced resistance from the teachers' union and committed to hiring all contract teachers into the regular civil service at the end of their contracts—a factor the authors cite as a possible cause of the intervention's failure. This case study is a reminder that scalable models are not just large, replicated pilots but often have their own unique characteristics. However, the experiment is one of the first to show how controlled trials can be used to inform a scaling-up operation, using similar techniques to those used to evaluate pilot interventions.

Shunichiro Honda and Hiroshi Kato (chapter 11) provide an account of the scaling up of another popular education reform, this time in Niger. Encouraged by experiences elsewhere, the Niger government mandated each primary school to establish a school management committee composed of the principal, a teacher, and representatives from parent-teacher and school mother associations. These committees were given extensive autonomy to manage community funds, monitor the performance of teachers, and procure supplies and basic infrastructure in a way that responded to local needs.

At the core of this program was a partnership between a weak government, donors, and civil society. Niger is one of the poorest countries in the world, and the government's strong focus on poverty reduction over the past decade could not make up for its very limited capacity. Sharing responsibility for school oversight with civil society, twinned with low-cost interventions to raise capacity, offered a way of leveraging community strength to improve education across the country quickly and to sustain improvements. Honda and Kato demonstrate that the program also displayed a high degree of cooperation among official and nongovernment donors as part of a sectorwide approach. This included joint evaluations of alternative models of school management, joint selection of the preferred model, and joint support for implementation.

Jane Nelson (chapter 12) documents the evolution of PPPs into new sectors and structures and asks what potential these have for driving scaled-up impact where traditional models fall short. She identifies four sectors where PPPs are demonstrating particular promise: health, nutrition, sustainable agriculture, and mining and energy. In these sectors, PPPs take on many forms, from project-based partnerships to country-based alliances and global multistakeholder platforms. She argues that effective scaling up often involves close linkages among these PPPs, providing a bridge between global resources, policymakers and decisionmakers, and local beneficiaries and knowledge.

Nelson offers some powerful recommendations for enabling PPPs to better support the scaling-up agenda. Among these is the establishment of large-scale replication funds that employ competitive bids (like today's challenge funds) and combine financial resources with technical advice, brokerage, and government policy dialogue. She also advocates the creation of joint investment networks for science and technology to identify breakthrough technologies and mobilize financing, research, development, and delivery through multistakeholder platforms.

A New Framework for Scaling Up

The emergence of new approaches for tackling development problems calls into question traditional ways of conceptualizing the scaling-up challenge. The dichotomy of public-led and private-led efforts to reach scale makes less sense in an ecosystem containing hybrid actors and hybrid partnerships. We suggested earlier that development interventions are normally arranged according to whether they require subsidies or can be made profitable, but what happens if both are true at once? Almost all cases of successful scaling up, including those where the private sector led the charge, have involved some soft money.

We submit that a large number of scalable development solutions occupy the middle ground on the spectrum between subsidized and for-profit models. Delivering these solutions requires the promotion of new hybrid models.

Hybrid models would combine the development efforts of a government, donor, foundation, or INGO with the efforts of a private corporation under a joint venture, drawing on the financial strengths of the nonprofit sector and its accountability to citizens and on the management and delivery strengths of the private sector. These ventures offer most promise in those instances where the fixed costs associated with creating a new product or product market prohibit a commercial intervention from moving forward but where variable costs could feasibly be recovered through market-based delivery once scale economies are achieved.

Finance from the nonprofit actor would provide a temporary subsidy to support the intervention during the early stages of scaling up, to cover costs such as research and development, market testing, piloting and evaluations, and marketing and education campaigns. These costs may not be recoverable in a commercial sense but would have the potential to generate large social returns and serve the development objectives pursued by government, donors, or INGOs.

Another aspect of hybrid models is a clearer division of labor between those responsible for the finance aspects of scaling up and those responsible for the delivery aspects. Subsidized and for-profit models have usually paired up financing institutions and implementing organizations along traditional lines:

Figure 1-2. *A New Framework for Scaling Up*

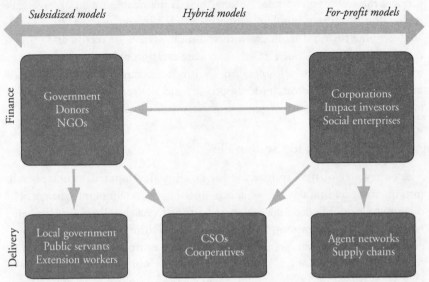

government with government, NGOs with NGOs, corporations with other private actors. Under hybrid models, partnerships would be determined by best fit for the particular challenge. Witness, for instance, the growing interest of pharmaceutical and agribusiness companies in partnering with and training health-care professionals and agricultural extension officers. This would drastically expand the possibilities for scaling up and lead to significant efficiency gains (figure 1-2).

M-PESA is an example of a hybrid model designed to solve a social problem: a technology developed with financial support from both the multinational corporation, Vodafone, and a challenge fund operated by the UK's Department for International Development; piloting conducted in collaboration with a microfinance institution, Faulu, to deepen understanding of the customer; exemplary customer-driven design, management, and execution, including the formation of a network of trusted agents by M-PESA; new public regulations to ensure no abuse of monopoly power despite a network covering most poor communities; and a further round of innovations by NGOs and social enterprises in response to the changed circumstances of "banked" poor people.

The role of the Kenyan government in this case is especially notable. Not only did it look to safeguard the rights and interests of users through consumer protection and market oversight, it also provided a supportive public policy and regulatory environment in which M-PESA could emerge and ultimately flourish. It should be noted that, at the time M-PESA was piloted, no regulations existed for e-money initiatives or for the involvement of mobile phone opera-tors in any kind of financial transactions. The willingness of the government to allow regulation to follow innovation is an integral part of M-PESA's suc-cess story. This reinforces our belief that scaling up is fundamentally a process challenge. That process can entail not only identifying the right business model but policy reform and policy innovation. In a case such as M-PESA, it was the interaction between the new business model (notably its approach to financing, delivery, and partnerships) and the progressive and enabling policy environment that facilitated scaling up; both were necessary and neither was sufficient with-out the other.

The propagation of hybrid models starts with nonprofit actors and their investment choices. Altering these choices requires a fundamental change of cul-ture for some organizations: one that accepts a higher frequency of failure, is comfortable with providing subsidies to profitable entities, and is sufficiently flexible to allow partners to operate freely rather than being excessively bound by the stipulations of an operational manual. A number of donor agencies are making efforts to move in this direction.

This emergence of hybrid models does not spell the end of traditional sub-sidized and for-profit models. The case studies suggest a number of ways in which these too can advance. Moreover, the typology of subsidized, for-profit, and hybrid models for scaling up is not mutually exclusive. An intervention that starts with a subsidy model, for instance, may metamorphose into a for-profit or hybrid model over time.

For subsidized models, new technologies offer great promise for overcom-ing long-standing weaknesses in delivery. However, these will be of little help unless organizations—donors especially—can tackle the perverse incentives that drive many away from the goal of achieving scale and lead instead to small, fragmented efforts. A stricter division of labor among nonprofit actors could advance scaling up but has proven hard to implement over the past decade. New approaches, such as triangular cooperation and vertical funds, offer prom-ise but only if they are designed for scale; today, many are not.

The scope for growth in for-profit models could receive a major boost through the expansion of financial services to poor populations. Nevertheless, it remains unclear whether multinational corporations can be drawn into BoP markets. Social enterprises cannot be expected to completely fill their shoes, but they are capable of delivering at scale if they are supported with technical assistance and incorporated into market networks. Steps to leverage existing, informal providers into upgraded franchises offer an alternate route to scaling up impact. Ultimately, more information is needed on the unit costs of ser-vice provision in order to determine which sectors offer the most promise for BoP markets.

Any attempt to scale up encounters both opportunities and hurdles. The successful examples from our case studies took the commitment of leaders over long periods of time. These leaders were willing to take risks even when the business model remained unproven, because they understood the transformational impact of a scaled-up effort for the BoP market and the intangible value that could be generated in terms of a brand or an expanded network. They also demonstrated skill and empathy in understanding the perspective of their customers and earning their trust. In many cases, such trust is a prerequisite to the behavioral change required for new product markets to succeed.

Furthermore, effective partnerships are at the core of all successful scaling-up initiatives. Rarely can any one organization—public or private—tackle a major development challenge on its own. But partnerships do not happen without deliberate efforts on all sides to establish clear and transparent mechanisms of cooperation and a division of labor. Partnerships require a common vision, shared goals, and agreements over execution details, including resources, responsibilities, and risks. Sustained implementation of partnership agreements in turn requires institutional leadership, mutual trust, and staying power among the partners.

Are we at a tipping point in terms of the takeoff of scalable solutions for development? Some caution here may be prudent. Theory tells us that identifying a viable business model and reaching scale can take years but that, once a model is proven, it should be possible to replicate it quickly. Yet the case of mobile money doesn't seem to fit this model. M-PESA reached large scale in Kenya in only two to three years but replication in many other countries has proven harder and slower.

It is unclear what can account for this. One explanation is that business models that appear replicable, like M-PESA's, may not be universally applicable after all. Safaricom saw M-PESA as a loyalty driver to protect and expand its market share in its core profitable mobile business; it did not need to turn a profit from mobile money. Furthermore, the main appeal of M-PESA to consumers was the ability to send money home, a practice that is less common in other countries. This is a reminder that external validity applies only weakly in scaling up.

Another explanation is that the demonstration effect can have a more insidious side. Kenyan regulators and policymakers may have played a less supportive role in the emergence of mobile money if they had known what a tremendous success it would turn out to be and the subsequent opportunities created for rent seeking. Officials in other countries are better prepared to seize such opportunities when mobile money offerings are launched, with potentially negative consequences for whether these offerings succeed. In some circumstances, then, scaling up could become its own worst enemy.

At the same time, M-PESA has developed a virtuous circle of scaling up. Other services that piggyback on M-PESA's infrastructure in Kenya are experiencing their own rapid transitions to scale. The propagation of hybrid models could trigger a similar effect. If corporations and other private sector actors (social enterprises, impact investors) can be drawn into BoP markets with the assistance of, and in partnership with, governments, donors, and INGOs, agent networks will expand, driving down unit costs and further increasing the number of market-based opportunities. This will broaden the scope of for-profit models in delivering development solutions, creating yet more momentum. The provision of cash transfers directly to poor populations by governments and donors, channeled through mobile money services, can enhance the participation of poor people in BoP markets, providing a further channel of reinforcement.

These opportunities for scaling up will not solve all development problems, but offer the best chance for improving the lives of millions of poor people. We hope through this book to encourage more development actors to think systematically about getting to scale.

References

Abed, Fazle Hasan. 2012. Remarks. Asia Foundation, Washington, September 19.

ActionAid. 2011. "Real Aid 3."

Birdsall, Nancy, and Homi Kharas. 2010. "Quality of Official Development Assistance Assessment." Center for Global Development (www.cgdev.org/section/topics/aid_effectiveness/quoda).

Bishop, Matthew, and Michael Green. 2010. *Philanthrocapitalism: How Giving Can Save the World*. London: A and C Black.

Busan Partnership for Effective Development Cooperation. 2011. "Outcome Document, Fourth High-Level Forum on Aid Effectiveness" (www.aideffectiveness.org/busanhlf4/images/stories/hlf4/OUTCOME_DOCUMENT_-_FINAL_EN.pdf).

Cohen, Jessica, and Pascaline Dupas. 2008. "Free Distribution or Cost-Sharing? Evidence from a Malaria Prevention Experiment." Working Paper 14406. National Bureau of Economic Research (www.nber.org/papers/w14406).

Duffy, Gary. 2010. "Family Friendly: Brazil's Scheme to Tackle Poverty." *BBC News*, May 25 (www.bbc.co.uk/news/10122754).

Hartmann, Arntraud, and Johannes Linn. 2008. "Scaling Up: A Framework and Lessons for Development Effectiveness from Literature and Practice." Working Paper 4. Wolfensohn Center, Brookings.

Isenman, Paul, and Alexander Shakow. 2010. "Donor Schizophrenia and Aid Effectiveness: The Role of Global Funds." Practice Paper 5. Institute of Development Studies (www.ids.ac.uk/files/dmfile/Pp5.pdf).

J. P. Morgan. 2010. "Impact Investments: An Emerging Asset Class" (www.rockefellerfoundation.org/uploads/files/2b053b2b-8feb-46ea-adbd-f89068d59785-impact.pdf).

Kenny, Charles. 2010. "Learning about Schools in Development." Working Paper 236. Center for Global Development (www.cgdev.org/files/1424678_file_Learning_About_Schools_in_Development_FINAL.pdf).

Kubzansky, Michael. 2010. "Inclusive Markets Report 2010." Monitor Group.

Levy, Santiago. 2006. *Progress against Poverty: Sustaining Mexico's Progresa-Oportunidades Program*. Brookings.

Lewin, Keith M. 2008. "Why Some Education for All and Millennium Development Goals Will Not Be Met: Difficulties with Goals and Targets." *Southern African Review of Education* 13, no. 2: 41–60.

Linn, Johannes F. 2011. "Scaling Up with Aid: The Institutional Dimension." In *Catalyzing Development: A New Vision for Aid,* edited by H. Kharas, K. Makino, and W. Jung. Brookings.

Miguel, Edward, and Michael Kremer. 2004. "Worms: Identifying Impacts on Education and Health in the Presence of Treatment Externalities." *Econometrica* 72, no. 1: 159–217.

Mullins, John, and Randy Komisar. 2009. *Getting to Plan B: Breaking through to a Better Business Model.* Harvard Business Press.

Oxfam. 2012. "First Global Aid Cut in 14 Years Will Cost Lives and Must Be Reversed" (www.oxfam.org/en/pressroom/pressrelease/2012-04-04/first-global-aid-cut-14-years-will-cost-lives-and-must-be-reversed).

Prahalad, C. K. 2004. *The Fortune at the Bottom of the Pyramid: Eradicating Poverty through Profits*. Wharton School Publishing.

Pritchett, Lant, Michael Woolcock, and Matt Andrews. 2010. "Capability Traps? The Mechanisms of Persistent Implementation Failure." Working Paper 234. Center for Global Development (www.cgdev.org/content/publications/detail/1424651).

Saltuk, Yasemin, Amit Bouri, Abhilash Mudaliar. and Min Pease. 2013. "Perspectives on Progress." January (www.thegiin.org/cgi-bin/iowa/download?row=489&field=gated_download_1;).

Stabile, Tom. 2010. "Architects of a 'Social Investment Data Engine.'" *Financial Times*, April 11 (www.ft.com/intl/cms/s/0/e297b7de-440b-11df-9235-00144feab49a.html#axzz27Oglc9xY).

UK DFID. 2008. "Capacity Building in Research." In Department for International Development, "Research Strategy 2008–2013 Working Paper Series" (www.dfid.gov.uk/r4d/PDF/Outputs/Consultation/ResearchStrategyWorkingPaperfinal_capacity_P1.pdf).

UNAIDS. 2012. "Factsheet: Getting to Zero" (www.unaids.org/en/media/unaids/contentassets/documents/epidemiology/2012/201207_FactSheet_Global_en.pdf).

Woolcock, Michael, Simon Szreter, and Vijayendra Rao, 2011. "How and Why Does History Matter for Development Policy?" *Journal of Development Studies* 47, no. 1: 70–96.

World Bank. 2011. "Household Cookstoves, Environment, Health and Climate Change. A New Look at an Old Problem." *World Bank Report.*

———. 2012. Nineteenth International AIDS Conference Debate (http://live.worldbank.org/debate-global-health-funding-hiv-aids-liveblog-webcast).

Worthington, Samuel A., and Tony Pipa. 2011. "Private Development Assistance: The Importance of International NGOs and Foundations in a New Aid Architecture." In *Catalyzing Development: A New Vision for Aid,* edited by Homi Kharas, Woojin Jung, and Koji Makino. Brookings.

2

Why Business Models Matter

MICHAEL KUBZANSKY

I n the last decade, several events have conspired to substantially raise the level of effort and attention to private-sector-led approaches to addressing development needs. C. K. Prahalad's *Fortune at the Bottom of the Pyramid* provided an important analytic underpinning, but probably more influential has been the rise of commercially viable microfinance and, more recently, mobile money solutions like M-PESA, which have demonstrated that it is feasible to serve very large numbers of very low-income households in a commercially viable manner and achieve some social impact.[1] Microfinance serves almost 100 million borrowers (table 2-1) and almost 67 million savers.

More quietly and less celebrated, examples from contract farming demonstrate that it is equally feasible to engage large numbers of small, poor farmers in commercially viable supply chains. Some examples, like the Kenya Tea

---

1. Prahalad (2004). The social impact of microfinance is a highly charged topic, with evidence ranging from studies indicating it has little impact on incomes and livelihoods ("Microcredit therefore may not be the 'miracle' that is sometimes claimed on its behalf, but it does allow households to borrow, invest, and create and expand businesses" [Banerjee and others, 2009]) to those that suggest other important impacts, including income smoothing ("There is evidence from a number of studies . . . suggesting that microfinance is good for microbusinesses" [Grameen Foundation, 2010]). It is beyond the scope of this chapter to take on the question of the impact of microfinance; moreover, its impact has arguably been the less important driver of the rush to replicate microfinance's success. Inspiration is driven largely by the ability to cover costs in many models and reach hundreds of millions of people.

Table 2-1. *Microfinance: A Business Model at Scale*

	Assets (billions of $)	Borrowers (millions)	Depositors (millions)
Africa	6.7	4.5	16.6
East Asia/Pacific	8.4	15.8	5.8
Europe/Central Asia	11.9	2.8	2.8
Latin America	29.2	15.0	15.5
Middle East/North Africa	1.6	2.2	0.1
South Asia	11.3	58.0	26.0
Total	69.1	98.3	66.8

Source: MixMarket, 2010 data (www.mixmarket.org).

Development Authority (KTDA) in Kenya, KRBL in India, and AICO in Zimbabwe, do business with 70,000 or more smallholder farmers at a time (figure 2-1) and contribute to substantial increases in incomes.[2]

As a result, many development actors now believe that one of the primary ways to achieve large-scale social impact is via commercially sustainable solutions—or what has been termed *inclusive business*. Private firms, social entrepreneurs, impact investors, and donors have invested substantial time and effort in supporting new initiatives at the intersection of the private sector and development in the last decade.[3] While it is difficult to estimate the amount of donor money flowing into such efforts, or to quantify funding from multinational corporations (MNCs) or other large commercial enterprises, the Global Impact Investing Network estimates that impact investing has already capitalized $50 billion, and J. P. Morgan suggests that impact investing will be a $1 trillion asset class in the future.[4] The newest J. P. Morgan/GIIN survey of

2. As a comparator, Standard Bank, typically cited as one of Africa's largest employers in Forbes surveys, employs about 30,000 people (https://members.weforum.org/pdf/Initiatives/GHI_HIV_CaseStudy_StandardBank.pdf). Safaricom in Kenya boasts 2,400 permanent employees (Safaricom, 2010). A Monitor Group analysis of Pradhan's contract farming operations in poultry in India, for instance, suggests that it resulted in a 125 percent income increase for women who participated (Monitor Group, 2009).

3. The amount of donor spending on private sector or market-based solutions to poverty is not tracked, but IADB invested $150 million in its region between 2007 and 2011 (http://browndigital.bpc.com/publication/?i=92819), and the International Finance Corporation (IFC), which takes an expansive view, suggests that "in 2010 IFC's outstanding portfolio included approximately $6 billion in investment and advisory services to more than 200 firms with inclusive business models" (www1.ifc.org/wps/wcm/connect/AS_EXT_Content/What%20We%20Do/Advisory%20Services/Inclusive%20Business).

4. *New York Times*, April 24, 2010 (www.nytimes.com/2010/04/24/your-money/24wealth.html?_r=2&pagewanted=all&); J. P. Morgan (2010).

Figure 2-1. *Scale of Selected Outgrower and Other Smallholder Farmer Engagement Schemes in Africa*

Number of farmers engaged (thousands)

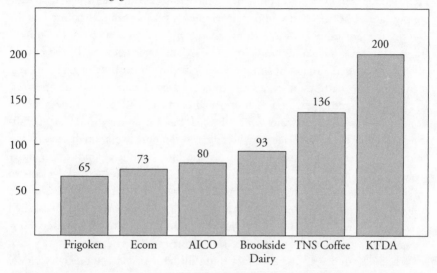

Source: Monitor Group primary research in India and Africa study countries, including Frigoken (export horticulture, Kenya), Ecom (coffee, East Africa), AICO (cotton, Zimbabwe), Brookside (dairy, Kenya), TNS/Technoserve (coffee, East Africa), KTDA (tea, Kenya).

impact investors, released in January 2013, suggests that such investors expect to place about $9 billion in capital in 2013 alone, up from $8 billion in 2012.[5] At $9 billion of committed funds, if impact investors were a country, they would rank sixth globally in terms of official development assistance, behind only the United States, Germany, the United Kingdom, France, and Japan; put differently, they would be the equivalent in size to all aid from Canada and Switzerland combined.[6] All of this new activity is premised on the assumption that scale, at least at the level achieved by microfinance, is achievable by such private-sector-led approaches.

It's about the Business Model First

Such scale is, indeed, possible, as microfinance and other sectors have already demonstrated. But to get there, the focus must be on finding business models

5. See Saltuk and others (2013).
6. Data from OECD DAC (http://webnet.oecd.org/oda2011).

that can scale. Getting the business model right is the single biggest factor in enabling such private-led approaches to reach meaningful scale.

In over five years of work and research in this area, the Monitor Group's inclusive markets team has confirmed Prahalad's central assertion—that scale simply cannot be achieved without developing a business model tailored to the exacting circumstances of low-income markets. The real scale stories of micro-finance and mobile money hinge upon first (and over decades, in the case of microfinance) perfecting a business model that can successfully engage this segment in terms of affordability, access, and commercial viability for the operator. In the well-documented case of microfinance, this involves a business model fundamentally different from typical branch banking: peer groups as guarantors, less-educated mobile agents who come to the borrowers, small amounts of credit, and often no bricks and mortar. It also involves liberal amounts of early-stage grant capital—more than $20 billion by some estimates—to allow time to tinker with the delivery model.[7] In mobile money, the central business model innovation (building on billing platforms that mobile operators had established to track very small prepaid transactions) was building out a trusted money transfer agent network on top of the lower-skilled airtime seller network.

While it sounds easy, it is in fact quite difficult to get the business model right, even in the same product and market. Take, for instance, funeral insurance in South Africa, where several sophisticated major commercial insurers entered the market in recent years—both out of commercial objectives and regulatory nudges—to serve low-income South Africans (table 2-2).[8] Sanlam had been building its business for years, and it chose a route that relied on informal channels; it worked with and through the ZCC Church, which partnered and handled all of the agent-level transactions. It reached over half a million customers, profitably. Hollard chose to partner with PEP stores, a formal retail chain that serves the base of the pyramid (BoP) segment, and it also reached hundreds of thousands of customers. But both MetLife and Old Mutual tried other approaches, including Old Mutual's "pay when you can" product, which in theory should have been appealing due to its flexibility to match consumer cash flows. However, it did not achieve any meaningful scale, due to a range of factors, primarily its choice to deliver via mainstream supermarkets.

This story is not unique to the insurance sector or even to the financial services sector. It is equally applicable in selling productivity-enhancing

---

7. Hudon (2005).

8. Funeral coverage in Africa is an essential product, which can save a household from years of vulnerability and indebtedness, especially in cases of death early in life, as from HIV/AIDS. In South Africa, on average, households spend on funerals the equivalent of a year's total expenditure on food and groceries (Case and others, 2008). For a more colorful account of Ghana's elaborate coffin industry, see Murray (2011). For more details, see http://makinganexit.net/.

Table 2-2. *Funeral Insurance in South Africa: Three Business Models, Three Results*

Old Mutual: Pay When You Can	Hollard/PEP Stores	Sanlam Sky/ZCC Church
• 5,000 policies • Sold through retail supermarket channel, starter pack includes cover • No monthly premium, but cover can be flexibly "topped up" as desired at any point during the life of the policy	• 360,000 policies • Sold through retail mass market store (PEP) channel, starter pack includes cover • Premiums paid monthly with SMS reminders • Claims and servicing via mobiles	• 500,000 policies • Sold through ZCC Church to its low-income members • ZCC owns 49% of scheme, administers it and collects cash premiums. Committees offer assistance with organizing funerals • Discretionary fund to top up a policy if payment is missed • Premiums paid through booklets with bar codes

Source: Monitor Group primary research. Data as of 2010.

agricultural inputs, health services, and clean drinking water; each of these sectors offers examples of enterprises that have achieved scale and enterprises that have flopped, with the differentiator being the business model chosen.

Getting a Business Model Right Takes Time

The good news is that one can achieve large-scale impact if one gets the business model right. Some models can scale quickly, but many require years, or decades, to perfect before moving to scale. Many participants in an inclusive business tend to have overly optimistic expectations about how quickly a given model can reach large numbers of customers or suppliers. There is still too much of a one-size-fits-all expectation around business models and expectations framed more by Silicon Valley venture capital than by the harsh realities of engaging the poor with socially beneficial goods and services.

Monitor's India report notes that most commercial and social enterprises that succeed need at least a decade to achieve a reasonable measure of scale for the Indian market.[9] That conclusion is borne out by the more recent Africa study, where 40 percent of the enterprises encountered that had achieved significant

9. Monitor Group (2009).

Figure 2-2. *Years to Reach Scale or Sales Volume, Eight Examples*

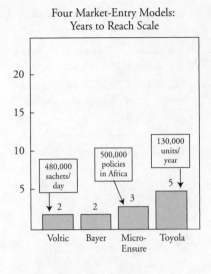

Four Market-Entry Models:
Years to Reach Scale

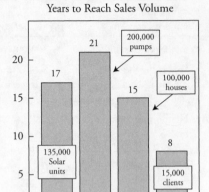

Four Market-Creation Models:
Years to Reach Sales Volume

Source: Monitor primary research.

Note: The different industries for the companies listed above include Voltic, drinking water in Ghana; Bayer, chemical crop protection in Kenya; MicroEnsure, bundled credit life coverage via microfinance institutions; Toyola, clean cookstoves in Ghana; Selco, solar home systems in India; Kickstart, irrigation pumps in East Africa; Mwanza, rural housing Tanzania; and Selfina, microleasing in Tanzania.

reach did so in the first five years, and 36 percent required over eleven years to get to significant size.[10]

The ability of a given business model to scale depends on four factors: first, whether it is promoting a pull product (such as mobile phones or credit) or a push product (such as contraception or solar lanterns); second, the degree of maturity of the business model (in other words, its ability to provide socially beneficial goods or services and recover its costs at large scale); third, how much of the surrounding ecosystem the business model has to also manage and organize; and fourth, whether the task at hand requires market entry or market creation. The time to scale will depend on a combination of all four of these (figure 2-2).

Market entry business models typically—though not always—take much less time to perfect and to scale. These efforts target markets where the low-income consumer is already accustomed to paying for a good or service—albeit informally, expensively, and sometimes for life-endangering quality. Examples include credit, where microfinance substitutes for informal money lenders; money transfer, where

10. Kubzansky and others (2011).

M-PESA substitutes for expensive and insecure bus transfers of cash; cookstoves, where many consumers often already pay for both cookstoves and, in many cases, fuel; or budget private schools, where parents are often already paying government school fees. In these entry cases, the presence of underlying demand can make it faster to achieve large-scale operations, since the demand-creation task (and associated cost) is much less, giving more leeway to the business model to adjust. Most of the 40 percent of the fast-scaling models seen in Monitor's Africa study fell into this category—for instance, Hollard funeral insurance (South Africa), Flash mobile cash (South Africa), and Gyapa cookstoves (Ghana).

Market creation business models, conversely, often require much longer times to scale—typically a decade or more.[11] They are often attempting to create markets among the BoP for socially beneficial goods and services that are not usually paid for by low-income households, require a significant amount of trust, and often entail behavior change. These tasks include most clean drinking water schemes or water filtration devices, which ask the poor to pay for something (such as water) they can typically get free, certain preventive health services and products, agricultural index insurance, solar lanterns, and even some agricultural inputs where the alternative can be recycling seeds or relying on rain for irrigation.

In most cases there is a strong payoff to the low-income consumer from purchasing the market-creation good, but that benefit is often difficult and expensive to convey. As a result, the business models can take a long time to develop and can be costly, both in the experimentation and in the accompanying persuasion campaigns usually required to create a market. It is not surprising, then, that returns on investment for businesses that typically target market creation activities are low. Monitor's analysis of several successful businesses selling water to BoP consumers suggests that margins are, at best, in the 3 percent to 5 percent range, usually not including what it costs to activate demand. Other analysis—for instance of slum health clinic/pharmacies targeting the BoP in India—suggests that such enterprises take twenty-four months to break even, rather than the nine months projected for equivalent services targeting middle-market consumers.

Many of these market-creation enterprises and models are further complicated by the fact that they tend to target rural households. In rural areas in emerging economies, distribution channels tend to be poor, layered, and thin. As such, the enterprise often needs to develop not just a business model but an end-to-end solution, incorporating more than the product or service being sold. As figure 2-2 indicates, many social enterprises take substantial time to figure out their business model and, even with that time, still struggle to reach scale.

11. See Monitor Group (2009), which examines hundreds of market-based approaches in India and their required time to scale.

Box 2-1. *Water Model Comparison: Rural Kiosks versus Individual Purifying Powder Sachets*

The water sector has been a hotbed of experimentation to serve the poor with affordable, high-quality, potable water. In India more than 2,200 water kiosks, serving mainly small rural villages, are managed by six different operators. These kiosks offer daily purchase of purified water in a fifteen-to-twenty-liter jerry can for about 4 cents (21.5 paise) a liter. The kiosks are remarkably successful—they cost between $8,000 and $20,000 to capitalize and can be operated easily with local village staff. Many break even financially, encouraging large water companies like Eureka Forbes to enter the market. Assuming an average village population of about 4,000 and conservative utilization rates of 25 percent, these facilities reach about 2.3 million people.

In 2002 Procter and Gamble (P&G) began testing its PUR sachet. The sachets retailed for about 10 cents and yielded treated water at a cost of about 1 cent a liter. But the product requires stirring, repouring, and waiting thirty minutes for the water to purify, limiting its popularity. In 2007, despite the marketing savvy and reach of a global FMCG giant like P&G, there were only an estimated 216,000 users.[a] This comparison is a clear indication that the business model in water treatment matters greatly and can require significant effort, investment, and time to get it right.

a. See www1.ifc.iorg/wps/wcm/connect/ca723600489124d3b110f78dd77ebd3/IFC_Water Report.pdf?Mod+AJPERES.

There is not always a hard and fast line between market entry and market creation tasks and models. Fifteen years ago there was no market in rural Africa or India for mobile phones—let alone for mobile money services—yet telephone companies succeeded in creating one in relatively short order. In some water markets—for instance, sachet water in West Africa—consumers were already paying about 3.4 cents for 500 milliliters of sachet water from informal providers (box 2-1). So Voltic's entry in Ghana resulted in a very short time to scale.

Mature business models often take time to develop. This is hardly true only in the social enterprise space; it applies equally to any commercial business, and especially one operating in frontier customer segments in emerging markets. Research for the Templeton Foundation notes, for instance, that "McDonald's opened its first franchised restaurant in 1955, 15 years after the company's founding. Subway waited nine years before opening its first franchise outlet, and Holiday Inn waited five. It takes a good deal of time to test the profitability and sustainability of a business model and to prepare the processes, products, and procedures for reliable replication."[12]

12. Beck, with Deelder and Miller (2010).

Microfinance took over three decades to get the model right, and it still receives a substantial subsidy. As recently as 2011, according to MixMarket and CGAP, over 52 percent of funding commitments to microfinance in Africa came in the form of grant capital. Grameen Bank (the pioneer in South Asia) took seventeen years to break even. However, this paved the way for subsequent Grameen replicators—in India SKS took only six years to break even, and Equitas just one.[13] Contract farming is a model that has existed in the United States and Europe since the early twentieth century and has been actively employed in emerging markets for almost seventy years.[14] So it is hardly surprising that some of the largest examples of a business model at scale are found in such outgrower schemes. Time to prove out a model, in other words, matters; investment from either commercial or public sources allows the time for experimentation, failure, and recalibration.

There is broad diversity across business models, and each varies in its maturity and ability to cover costs and serve the poor. This has broad implications for investors, enterprises, policymakers, and sources of grant funding. Analysis of business models encountered by the Monitor Group across more than 600 enterprises in India and Africa from 2007 to 2011 suggests that a number of business models are already mature, as defined by ability to cover costs, multiple enterprises deploying the model, and large numbers of buyers or suppliers engaged.[15] Figure 2-3 notionally charts the maturity of the business models encountered, with a key break at the ability to cover costs.

However, a number of business models can operate profitably and cover operating costs but cannot sustain the fixed costs if they must charge the full capital investment to their low-income customers. Models that fall into this category include, not surprisingly, a range of infrastructure solutions like village energy microgrids, urban water kiosks, some rural water kiosks, direct procurement from small farmers, and direct sales and distribution models for health products. In the first three examples the key driver is the fixed capital cost of equipment.

Microgrid energy in Africa is a good example, where Monitor examined models in Kenya, Senegal, Tanzania, and Uganda for villages of less than 5,000 people. Capital expenditure costs per installation are relatively low; none cost more than $2,000 per kilowatt hour of capacity, irrespective of generating technology. In most cases the actual capital required is less than $100,000, depending on generating capacity. Revenues typically cover operating costs, even in environments where operators were unable to raise prices for almost a decade.

13. Koh, Karamchandani, and Katz (2012).

14. Kirsten and Sartorius (2002) offer a history of contract farming, noting that "contract farming has . . . spread rapidly in Asia, Latin America and Africa owing to the higher returns earned by high-value export crops and the impact of new technologies."

15. Karamchandani, Kubzansky, and Frandano (2009); Kubzansky, Cooper, and Barbary (2011), esp. chap. 4.

Figure 2-3. *Maturity of Fifteen Entrepreneur-Led Business Models*[a]

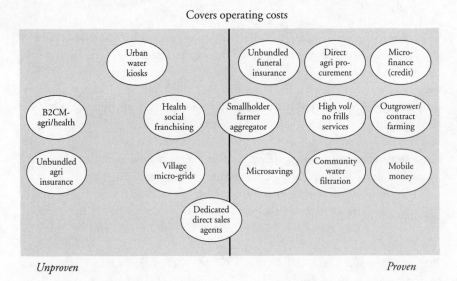

Covers operating costs

Urban water kiosks

Unbundled funeral insurance

Direct agri procurement

Micro-finance (credit)

B2CM-agri/health

Health social franchising

Smallholder farmer aggregator

High vol/ no frills services

Outgrower/ contract farming

Unbundled agri insurance

Village micro-grids

Microsavings

Community water filtration

Mobile money

Dedicated direct sales agents

Unproven   *Proven*

Source: Kubzansky (2012).
a. Maturity based on ability to cover costs and number of players engaged.

But partly because of the price ceiling due to serving low-income rural households, and limited numbers of available connections, no operator covers its fully capitalized costs. And this does not even take into account the obstacle of upfront one-time fees for household connections, which, as figure 2-4 suggests, are very expensive for individual households, ranging from 6 percent to 36 percent of average annual household income in the village.

In the direct procurement example, the main cost driver is the cost of training thousands of small farmers to meet the quality and other requirements of large buyers, such as Olam in rice in Nigeria, Suguna in poultry in India, and Coca-Cola in fruit juice in Uganda.[16] In the health agent example, the primary fixed cost is in the recruitment and training of sales agents, especially in environments of high churn among sales agents. In 2010 the training of agents accounted for 49 percent of the operating costs of running a network like Living Goods.[17] If the social enterprise did not have to account for this cost, it could break even. And in other models, especially market-creation models, there is

16. Some agriculture models can afford this training cost, depending on their market and the relative competitiveness of smallholder farmers versus larger commercial farms. But in many cases, the cost of engaging and training large numbers of small farmers is more expensive than sourcing from a few large commercial estates.
17. For more on direct sales agent models in health, see Kubzansky and Cooper (2013).

Figure 2-4. *Connection Fees for Village Microgrids and Household Income, Three Countries*[a]

U.S. dollars

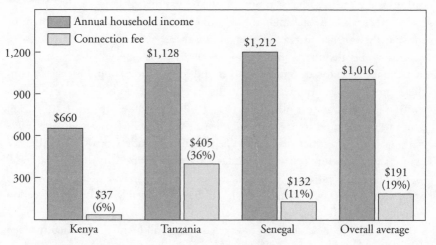

Source: Monitor Group, customer interviews (*n* = 46), May 2010.
a. Tanzania connection fees vary; figure shows those from Lugarawa.

frequently a substantial fixed cost that must be incurred in stimulating demand. Kickstart in Africa and IDE in India report very large fixed costs in promoting the adoption of low-cost irrigation pumps. Demand activation is costly, and the first entrants are often building demand not just for their own products but also for any followers or new entrants. Thus with no early adopters and easily copied products, there are few private returns to demand stimulation for the first entrant.[18] Even for pull products like mobile phone service, mobile phone carriers in emerging markets typically spend 10–15 percent of revenues on demand stimulation through above- and below-the-line advertising.

The Expectation That a Single Entity Will Scale

The conventional wisdom of how to scale a private-sector-led solution is often implicitly grounded in a Silicon Valley or large MNC paradigm of continued investment in, and growth of, a single entrepreneurial entity or firm addressing a key market or challenge, inspired by, for instance, Google, Carrefour, Coca-Cola,

18. On the basis of this argument, the Gates Foundation granted $16 million to IDE in India to generate demand for its drip irrigation product. For more details, see Koh, Karamchandani, and Katz (2012).

or Nokia. While these expectations are most apparent among impact investors, they are also present among donors, as the design of USAID's new Grand Challenges facility confirms. This model does indeed constitute one tried and true path to scale, and it is the first, but not the only, route to scale.

In certain cases, reaching scale due to the efforts of a single large firm or entity is the optimal answer. These are the firms, after all, with the resources, systems, and scale to serve millions of people. This is especially so in challenges that entail complicated route-to-market and distribution issues for socially beneficial products like oral rehydration salts and fortified foods.[19] Monitor's Africa study notes that almost all of the successful approaches on route-to-market issues were executed by large national firms or MNCs. Large-scale, commercially viable efforts that reach into the millions include Coca-Cola SABCO's manual distribution centers, Standard Bank's community banking model (8,300 outlets), Safaricom's M-PESA service (45,000 agents), Voltic-SABMiller's water sachets (480,000 sachets a day), and Bayer's Green World crop protection program (200,000 customers a month).

Conversely, social enterprises have encountered all manner of difficulty when developing their business models to address critical route-to-market issues. Living Goods in Uganda and Health Keepers in Ghana have set up direct sales forces to distribute a basket of health products to the rural poor, products ranging from contraception and bed nets to antiseptics and soap. In India and other countries, VisionSpring set up a similar direct sales force to distribute low-cost reading glasses. But all have struggled to cover costs with this grant-funded, direct sales model. In its 2008 Growth Capital offering, VisionSpring candidly disclosed that it lost $641,000 on $150,000 of sales in 2007.[20] It sold 100,000 pairs of glasses in its first seven years. As a result, it changed its distribution model and has achieved better sales volume and cost recovery.[21] But many social and commercial enterprises still routinely struggle with the task of direct distribution into fragmented, informal, and less dense rural markets.

This would seem to argue in favor of MNCs and large-scale organizations taking on the task of scaling such solutions, at least from a public-good perspective. However, as figure 2-5 indicates, these firms are concerned about the high cost of reinventing a business model, typically have higher return activities

19. *Route to market* is defined here as the set of decisions about, and configuration of, physical distribution, sales channel activation, incentives in the channel, and sales and marketing activities. For socially beneficial products and services, route to market often encompasses demand stimulation and persuasion activities.

20. Beck, Deelder, and Miller (2010), p. 160.

21. New distribution models include, in El Salvador, hub-and-spoke models centered on a village store; and in India, a fleet of mobile vans that doubled sales from 2010 to 2011. For details, see Koh, Karamchandani, and Katz (2012, p. 55).

Figure 2-5. *Five Most-Cited Obstacles to Growing BoP Business by Large Companies*

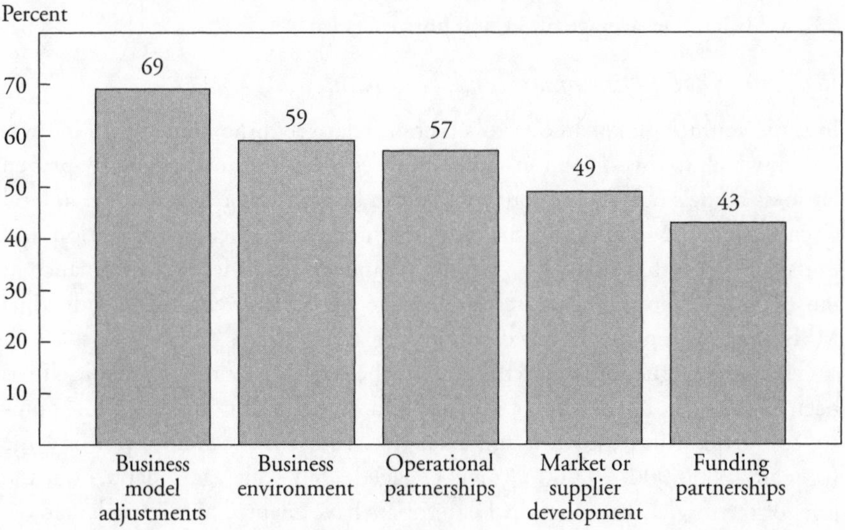

Percent

Source: Kubzansky, Cooper, and Barbary (2011, p. 175).

to take on with their investment capital, and are wary of striking operating or funding partnerships with donors or NGOs to achieve these inclusive business solutions. Not surprisingly, and most important, many do not wish to target the poorest customers in the hardest to reach areas.

This suggests that it is perhaps inappropriate to hope that scale will be achieved primarily by either large MNCs providing social benefit or entrepreneurial firms taking the decade or longer required to create a market. This certainly needs to be one piece of the solution but should not be the only solution. It is but one route to scale.

Two Additional Routes to Scale

In many cases, and particularly in frontier markets, there are two other routes to scale that investors, entrepreneurs, and donors must consider and support. These other routes to scale are based on examples witnessed in the field in Africa and India and also on two observations: that no single enterprise is able to address millions in poverty on its own, and that the spread of microfinance demonstrates that scale can be reached by an aggregate, as much as a solo, effort. As an example, in South Asia in 2011, the 486 microfinance institutions (MFIs) that report data to MixMarket serve 50.2 million customers in aggregate, or about 103,000 customers per institution, despite the presence of giant MFIs like BRAC, SKS, and Grameen Bank. In Latin America the figures are lower: 532 MFIs have an average of 34,400 borrowers each.[22]

Replicate, Adapt, Disseminate, and Transplant

In some countries and some sectors there is relatively little homegrown innovation in which to invest. And in some instances there is a stock of already proven business models outside the country that can be relatively easily adapted to local circumstances. Microfinance in most countries is a story of adaptation and transplanting rather than of homegrown innovation. Indeed, microfinance in most countries, in aggregate, serves customers at scale, even though individual MFIs often serve relatively few customers.

The same is true for contract farming. The contract farming model itself has been replicated across many countries and many commodities—from poultry to horticulture to cotton and even rice. Individual schemes can be large (as many as 60,000–70,000 farmers engaged), but scale again happens at the level of the model that individual enterprises have adapted and transplanted. In 2010 Kenya was home to outgrower schemes in horticulture that have adopted a model involving numbers of farmers ranging from 2,000 (AAA Growers) to 65,000 (Frigoken).

Mobile banking has inspired similar imitation now that M-PESA, G-Cash (Philippines), and others have proven the concept. GSMA's estimate of December 2011 suggests a 76 percent annual rate of increase in "live" mobile money deployments between 2009 and 2011. And in India there is evidence that the same is now happening with village water kiosks: at least seven operators have opened broadly similar networks of kiosks that in aggregate serve several million people in a way that covers costs.[23] The spread of microfinance and mobile banking illustrates how a successful enterprise model (Grameen, M-PESA) can be replicated elsewhere. This is perhaps best illustrated by the low-cost, more fuel-efficient, bucket cookstove.

In the 1970s, low-technology bucket stoves, which used less charcoal and wood than other stoves and which could be manufactured locally, were successfully introduced into Thailand. Following this, Keith Openshaw and Max Kinyanjui introduced the stove to Kenya (as the Jika stove). The stove quickly achieved success in the Kenyan market as well, with penetration rates of over 50 percent in urban homes and 15 percent in rural ones. In the absence of homegrown solutions, the stove was also introduced and well received in Rwanda, Tanzania, and Ethiopia.[24]

22. Data from MixMarket (www.mixmarket.org/mfi/region/South%20Asia).
23. Monitor Group (2009).
24. USAID (2007, pp. 34–39).

In 2003 USAID and the Shell Foundation funded Enterprise Works to bring the proven technology to Ghana (branded as the Gyapa stove). By 2010, following the seeding of over eighty local manufacturers and an effective public awareness campaign, over 150,000 units had been sold.

We identify three primary methods of replicating and spreading successful enterprises: geographic expansion of the originating firm, imitation, and transplanting by a different entity. Pursuing scale through replication rests on collaboration among key players. Knowledge of what works (and, crucially, what does not) needs to be shared. By providing a license to copy, successful enterprises extend their impact beyond their local markets. But this raises issues about returns to investment for the originator of an idea and about providing some incentive other than the purely public good for pioneering an idea that can be replicated by others.

Leverage and Improving Existing Entities

Low-income segments in emerging markets participate mainly in informal and quasi-formal economies. Often, the main task of most inclusive businesses is to supply formal-sector quality products and services at informal-sector prices and flexibility—to improve the lives and livelihoods of the poor. Many of these efforts look to replace or bypass small, fragmented, often informal providers, outlets, and channels. Increasingly, however, rather than bypass these fragmented structures, businesses work with them, upgrading and improving them. This shift stems from a recognition of the facts on the ground:

—In India, 93 percent of all retailers are still informal, Walmart's impending entry notwithstanding. Modern retail, even in Latin America, accounts for only 40 percent of trade.[25]

—In Nigeria, where 67 percent of health care costs are paid out of pocket, the private sector has 11,473 physicians and 56,400 nurses and midwives.[26] By our estimates, these providers serve about 15 million to 20 million patients monthly.

—In the poor urban and periurban areas of Lagos State, Nigeria, 75 percent of schoolchildren were in small private schools in 2006. The corresponding figure for the periurban district of Ga, Ghana, was 64 percent, and for the low-income areas of Hyderabad, India, it was 65 percent.[27]

—Recent estimates suggest that 37 percent of sub-Saharan Africa's economy and over 25 percent of South Asia's is informal.[28]

25. According to *The Economist*, "At the moment 'organised retail' accounts for a mere 7% of the country's $470 billion retailing business—a far lower share than in other countries" (www.economist.com/blogs/schumpeter/2011/12/indias-retail-reform). For Latin America data, see Treewater and Price (2007).

26. USAID (2009, p. 4).

27. See Tooley (2006).

28. Schneider, Buehn, and Montenegro (2010).

Over time, as emerging economies get wealthier, the proportion of small, fragmented, and informal trade will diminish (one study estimates the informal economy to be only about 15 percent of GDP in OECD countries).[29] But these small outlets represent a base that already trades extensively with the BoP. A faster route to scale, therefore, may well be in leveraging and upgrading this existing infrastructure, but such an approach is vastly different from growing a single firm or government agency to address the issue and reach large numbers of people. Not surprisingly, this route to scale has been least developed.

Yet the formalization trend and the practice of leveraging informal assets can and do coexist. Most of the route-to-market MNC success stories described required a formal company to work through existing informal outlets, whether in selling mobile airtime, financial transactions, fortified foods, agricultural inputs, or other fast-moving consumer goods. The Bayer Green World program is particularly instructive on the combination of training, upgrading, product packaging, and marketing and demand stimulation required to implement this approach among small, fragmented agrodealers.[30] This has been, and will continue to be, a source of experimentation and activity as large firms aim to distribute their goods through these channels.

However, the most novel work in building on and upgrading fragmented, informal assets has been done on the services side, in efforts to upgrade and improve the services extended by small individual providers, so that quality, affordable services can be provided by a cluster of independent players rather than a single firm. The most common example is in the world of social franchising for health, where donors like USAID support programs like Pakistan's Greenstar Network and Bangladesh's Bluestar Network. These programs "roll up" and train independent clinicians, midwives, and other operators to provide health services, usually those related to reproductive health and family planning (table 2-3).

Few if any of these social franchise networks fully cover their costs.[31] But many have reached substantial scale, so they signal an opportunity to take on such a task with a more commercial business model. They deliver results comparable to or better than what government services provide; one study concludes that Greenstar "provided higher quality services . . . than other private facilities surveyed" and that it "also served a higher proportion of poor clients than government facilities" and served them "more efficiently . . . than government facilities."[32]

29. Schneider, Buehn, and Montenegro (2010).

30. See Monitor Group (2011).

31. In most cases the operations are profitable for the individual provider but not for the umbrella organization.

32. Bishai and others (2008).

Table 2-3. *Social Franchising for Health, Six Countries*

Country	Network	Clinic	Sponsor (year started)
Pakistan	Greenstar	8,000	PSI (1995)
South Africa	ARV Care	4,500	BroadReach (2002)
Bangladesh	Bluestar	3,600	Social Marketing (1998)
Nepal	Sangini	2,928	Nepal CRS (1994)
Peru	Red Plan Salud	1,660	INPPARES (2002)
India	Dimpa Network	1,150	PSP-One (1998)

Source: Montagu and others (2009).

The scale and results of this work in the health sector also signal the possibility of undertaking similar roll-up efforts. For this route to scale, the intervention is quite different from a pure grant or a commercial investment: it is instead a combination of a small amount of financing, technical assistance, sometimes certification, and some standardized materials in terms of protocols, curricula, or medicines, depending on the type of entity targeted. The capital required tends to be small: the average entity typically requires between $10,000 and $50,000 of reasonably priced debt. Also in health, Banyan Global–SHOPS secured USAID credit guarantees for commercial banks or for MFIs (such as Diamond Bank and Acción in Nigeria) to lend to individual medical providers; USAID accompanied its financing with technical assistance. Medical Credit Facility undertakes a similar set of tasks in Africa, including credit to small providers, technical assistance, and certification.

The key add-on is technical assistance. For instance, Indian Schools Finance Company provides credit, bookkeeping assistance, and some standardized curriculum to improve the performance of the local, budget private school. Tedcor in South Africa secures master municipal solid waste management contracts in low-income areas and provides the overall contract as a surety to allow individual truck-owning entrepreneurs to finance garbage trucks to fulfill the contract. Tedcor subcontracts to these owner-operators and provides training and technical assistance. There are currently 700 subcontractors, serving 400,000 customers.

Other solutions have been led by government. For example, Tanzania's ADDO (accredited drug-dispensing outlets) program provides government certification to small retailers (box 2-2). In addition, AGRA supports the training of agrodealers in Tanzania and other countries via training and certification carried out by CNFA. The agrodealer training enables the retailers to distribute fertilizer vouchers. In this way governments and donors create networks of trained retailers, independent of any specific product or service.

In other words, increased reach, or growth in scale, in these circumstances can require quite different actions in this third route to scale compared to those

Box 2-2. *The Initiative for Accredited Drug-Dispensing Outlets (ADDOs) in Tanzania*

The ADDO initiative in Tanzania trains and provides licenses to small, privately owned retail outlets in rural and poor areas to sell certain essential medicines, including selected prescription drugs. This initiative has formalized private retail outlets into an official sales channel and, by increasing the number of medicine outlets in rural and poor areas, has increased the availability of medicines in these areas. There are currently 900 ADDOs, serving four regions.

undertaken to scale a single enterprise. Given the substantial installed base of small, fragmented service providers in many emerging market countries, this is an area with a potentially vast scale for impact and activity.

Policy and Partnership Implications

Governments and donors have a strong interest in promoting private-sector-led solutions. The motivation can range from outcome and efficiency considerations—as noted in the Greenstar case—to a desire to "crowd in" private investment and activity to provide social benefit, to working with the system to improve what it can deliver affordably. Private-sector-led solutions offer the promise to also help fiscally strapped governments—whether in emerging markets or in donor countries—to target their funds to the poorest segments or the most difficult situations. Focusing on partnerships with private, nonstate actors can also expand service delivery—for instance, in infrastructure, where if the capital cost can be covered, then the service can be delivered sustainably and at little or no cost to the public sector.

However, such approaches have their risks. Most donor agencies are not accustomed to the long horizons required to prove out a business model or to the risks entailed in investing in companies rather than in government or even NGO programs. Many agencies are uncomfortable with the notion that their public funds will be contributing to the profits of private enterprises, especially MNCs.[33] They are even more squeamish about the notion that those profits

33. It is worth noting that many donors explicitly and actively subsidize small and medium enterprises that are (or aim to be) profit making. This support may be in the form of technical assistance, loan guarantees, or outright grants. Many fewer programs offer support to MNCs or large national firms in emerging markets, even though their scale and success on key issues (such as distribution) are arguably far greater. This could be a reflection of many factors, but one of them is surely a discomfort in being seen as subsidizing companies that could, in theory, pay for such programs themselves.

may come at the expense of the poor. Moreover, to succeed in this area often requires governments and donors to be able to evaluate winning and losing business models, a competence that many donors do not possess. And many donors—in a commendable effort to validate that their funds have actually paid for social returns—require substantial evidence of impact, but working with private firms to produce rigorous or randomized control group data can often be much trickier than working with governments or NGOs.[34]

For donors and governments to invest in this approach, a business model lens becomes an important means for looking at how, where, and when to invest, but few donors have adopted such a lens to date. There are at least two scaling strategies distinguished by the stage of the business model:[35]

—Supporting early or unproven business models: support in early stages, especially to prove out the model, is warranted and, in many cases, essential, as there is little risk capital willing to fund a private business to target the customers or suppliers with the least income and skills.[36]

—Defraying fixed costs for proven business models: here, support should be provided to make a proven business model viable by underwriting the fixed costs that a private operator cannot recoup through operations or given pricing-affordability ceilings, whether in terms of capital expenditure, supplier training costs, or the costs of stimulating customer demand (such as persuasion campaigns on the use of latrines).

There are two additional scaling strategies distinguished by route to scale. Either of the above strategies can be used with a single firm or entity or with a cluster of firms or entities, using the same business model:

—Replicating or transplanting business models that work: this should be targeted at bringing models that work elsewhere into new regions, jurisdictions, and settings and at defraying the risk or providing expansion capital to do so.

—Rolling up a fragmented set of (predominantly informal) enterprises that are already at scale as a group and are already serving low-income segments: this

34. For instance, GAFSP (a new multidonor program with $1.3 billion in donor pledges to support agriculture that trades with smallholder farmers and to improve food security) has stated that "up to 30% of GAFSP investment projects will undergo in-depth impact evaluations using experimental or quasi-experimental methods" (www.gafspfund.org/gafsp/content/monitoring-and-evaluation).

35. This chapter deals primarily with donor strategies to scale promising or fragmented enterprises and their impact through time-limited support. There are other important strategies that donors can and do undertake to use subsidies with commercial enterprises, but often these strategies tend to address the issue of improving affordability and reach (which improves scale), which typically entails continuous rather than time-bound support. For instance, governments and donors often provide ongoing subsidies to water utilities (as in Zambia's Kafubu water utility), to enable them to extend their reach and affordability to the poor. This is a significant tool, but it is more concerned with extending the reach of a given service to the poor than with scaling it. For more on Zambian water utilities and slum kiosk tariff subsidies, see Monitor Group (2011).

36. This has been described extensively in Koh, Karamchandani, and Katz (2012).

support would enable them to improve their quality, reach, and affordability and enable more successful ones to grow larger.

Mapped against Monitor's framework for scaling up private market-based solutions to poverty, the four suggested approaches cover the spectrum of potential interventions (table 2-4). Monitor's broader four-stage framework for enterprise philanthropy applies equally to bilateral or multilateral financing (figure 2-6).[37]

Each stage has an end milestone, to allow a donor and an enterprise to recognize when it is time to move from one stage to another. The first three stages are the most important for subsidized donor or government capital, with an expectation that, by the time a business reaches stage four, it should be able to attract commercial or impact capital. These three stages are the ones most in need of fixed-cost support, whether in developing a blueprint, validating a model, or preparing the market (or supply chain).

Many of these approaches can lead policymakers and funders into tricky and sometimes uncomfortable territory, as they can entail supporting private firms and making decisions about whether supporting them fulfills a sufficiently charitable purpose or public-good outcome. This is a tension that policymakers and funders will need to wrestle with and trade off against the outcomes desired. This chapter argues that such investments, if structured well, can have enormous social-good payoffs and are worth the risks and trade-offs.

Supporting the Development of an Early-Stage Business Model

Early-stage support is most relevant to the paradigm of scaling an individual enterprise or firm, although it could just as easily support multiple entities trying the same business model as a deliberate research-and-development strategy. This approach is also the closest fit to the increasing availability of impact-investing capital. Most capital is structured to support later-stage enterprises serving the poor, enterprises that have track records and developed models (figure 2-7). There is relatively little capital available for very early stage idea development. In particular, there is a dearth of angel-stage capital available to allow enterprises to pilot an idea before attracting commercial finance.

Even impact investors, who are explicitly looking for positive impact and the engagement of poor customers or suppliers, find this stage of investing too speculative and risky. This is so despite the fact that many of them are backed by donor funds from bilaterals or multilaterals. The early stage of testing an idea and proving out the business model is inherently risky; in purely commercial investing in OECD countries, venture capital firms and angels can recoup this

---

37. The four phases of the enterprise philanthropy process form the heart of Koh, Karamchandani, and Katz (2012), and ideas in this chapter are adapted from that report.

Table 2-4. *Four Stages of Enterprise Philanthropy Support*

Stage	Blueprint	Validate	Prepare	Scale
Definition	Develop blueprint for the future business	Validate by testing and refining the business model	Prepare by enhancing the conditions required for scaling	Scale up by rolling out the model to reach larger numbers
Key activities	—Understand customer needs —Develop initial customer proposition —Develop business plan —Develop core technologies or product prototypes	—Conduct market trials —Test business model assumptions —Refine business model, technologies, or product	—Stimulate customer awareness and demand —Develop supply chains, upstream and downstream —Build organizational capability to scale (systems, talent, plant)	—Move into new geographies and segments —Invest in assets and talent —Enhance systems and processes —Exploit scale efficiencies —Respond to competitors
Key needs	—Innovation capability —Strategy development and business planning —Talent networks —Seeding funding	—Operationalizing the model —Focusing on cost, value, and pricing —Learning orientation and flexibility —Innovation capability —Funds to facilitate market trials and refinement	—Marketing strategy and execution —Supply chain design and implementation —Systems and processes —Talent and networks —Funds for marketing, supply chain, fixed assets, inventory	—Competitive strategy —Realizing scale efficiencies —Risk management —Formalizing impact standards and expectations —Stakeholder management —Funds to support expansion
End milestones	—Compelling initial business plan —Demonstrated core technologies or product prototype	—Refined business model, technologies, product —Validation of viability and scalability —Indication of customer demand	—Strong customer awareness and demand —Effective supply chains —Organizational systems, talent, assets in place to support scaling	—Sustainably reaching all BoP customers or suppliers

Source: Koh, Karamchandani, and Katz (2012, p. 13).

Figure 2-6. *Four Approaches for Donors in Scaling Inclusive Business Models*

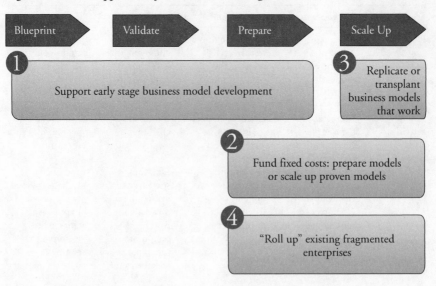

risk because markets are well developed, and a few will pay off spectacularly to cover the costs of the rest failing.

In inclusive business, this equation is far less likely to succeed. The customers targeted are the segment of emerging markets with the lowest purchasing power, with the least skill in operating commercial farms, and with the most variable cash flows. A recent Monitor analysis estimates that net operating margins of about fifty of these inclusive business enterprises in Africa and India were, at best, 10–15 percent.[38] Acumen Fund, the pioneer impact investment fund that invests in health, water, and agriculture, reports an even more sobering number: an average after-tax profit of –20 percent. The fund's eight most profitable portfolio firms earned an after-tax profit of only 6 percent.[39] The good news is that the margins suggest that none of these firms trading with the poor are doing so on exploitative terms. But the bad news is that these margins offer insufficient returns to entice commercial funds to take on the risk of developing a new business model to serve these important segments. Not surprisingly, relatively little

38. Monitor Group (2011).
39. Koh, Karamchandani, and Katz (2012, p. 9). Acumen may also be an extreme case: few impact investors target health and water to the degree that Acumen does, and these two sectors often require more market creation and demand stimulation than sectors like financial services. Until more impact investors publish their returns, it will be difficult to calibrate. A recent World Bank study of CDC's investment in commercial stakeholder and estate agriculture and agriprocessing from 1948 to 2000 across thirty-two countries suggested that "when equity investment was involved, one in six received compound equity rates of return of over 12 percent" (Tyler and Dixie, 2012, p. 7).

Figure 2-7. *Impact Investment by Investment Stage, India, Africa, and Global, Mid-2011*[a]

Percent

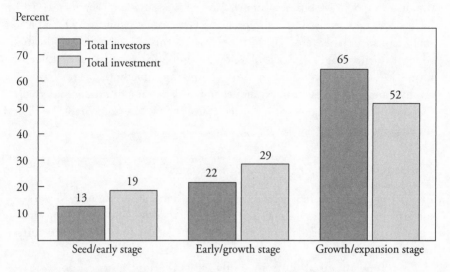

Source: Kubzansky (2012).
a. Survey of 90 funds.

of the new wave of impact investing capital is invested in such enterprises in the early stages of developing their business models.

Donors and governments can fill this market gap by funding early-stage efforts to develop and prove business models that aim to serve the poor in new ways, either directly or, more commonly, through intermediaries. Challenge funds, like the DFID-originated Africa Enterprise Challenge Fund, which has $150 million to invest, are potential vehicles for doing this.[40] But there are other potential structures, including direct placement of funds with early-stage facilities like the Acción Venture Lab. This kind of risk capital—to experiment with different business models—should also have different time horizons, depending on whether the task addressed is market entry or market creation and whether the enterprise is targeting the 2-dollar-a day segment or the 6-dollar-a day segment. Capital often needs to be accompanied by some form of technical assistance to help enterprises figure out key aspects of their business model. These business models are often attempts to invent a new way of serving and reaching their low-income customers or suppliers. Given the margins the models have to operate with, government and donor support is critical.

40. DFID's Financial Deepening Challenge Fund in the mid-2000s provided matching grant support to Safaricom's efforts to develop M-PESA.

Given that larger MNCs or national corporates (such as Hollard in South Africa and ITC in India) typically do not express that they need external capital to pursue an inclusive business model, most of this early-stage support tends to focus on smaller, earlier-stage entrepreneurial enterprises, which may be NGOs, small firms, social enterprises, or other legal forms. As figure 2-7 indicates, support to encourage MNCs to develop a new business model takes different forms. MNCs also have different, and competing, time horizons for payback on investment in a new business model and are often under pressure internally to generate payback quickly—or at least in a time frame comparable to their middle- and upper-market businesses.

Covering Fixed Costs for Proven Business Models

Another method of scaling is by focusing on business models known to work— for instance, village water kiosks and village microgrids—and developing facilities that can support expansion on a much larger scale. This approach requires two components:

First, fund the fixed up-front capital costs that operators cannot recover at affordable price points (for instance, water kiosks, microgrid generation, microgrid household connections). In this approach, governments and donors must be careful to not oversubsidize models that can fully cover their own costs nor to use the funding of such models as a reason to decrease funding of other public supply and distribution projects, such as public utilities in urban areas. However, the right formula can vary: in some cases a build-operate-transfer model could work, or a model in which the government builds the asset and provides a long-term lease to a private operator, or a model in which the government commits to buying the asset at the end of a defined period.

These frameworks are already being deployed in utility PPPs. The challenge is to apply them on smaller projects, and in larger quantity on a multisite basis to realize economies of scale. Figure 2-8 illustrates the difference that a 50 percent subsidy made in achieving coverage and long-term sustainability of a village solar-diesel microgrid project in Senegal. The underwriting of about $43,000 of the up-front capital costs could ensure the financial viability of the asset over time, while still preserving incentives for the operator to manage the facility effectively.

Second, fund the fixed cost of demand stimulation or supplier and agent training—that is, noncapital costs that prevent solutions from operating in a commercially sustainable way. Too often the cost of farmer training or behavior change communication, especially in market-creation contexts, can make the difference between a model being self-sustaining and a model that generates negative returns. In some cases (for instance, Ecom's work in the coffee

Figure 2-8. *Project ERSEN Solar-Diesel Microgrid, Casamance, Senegal*

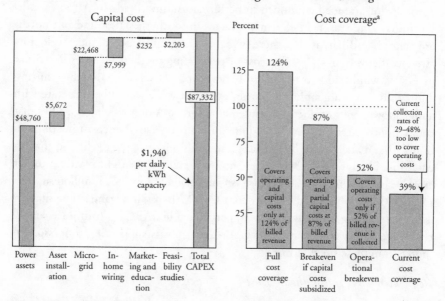

Source: Monitor interviews with Project ERSEN management, May 2010.
a. Percentage of billed revenues required to collect in order to cover costs.

sector in East Africa) the firm will pay the cost of organizing and training farmers as a part of securing needed supply. But in many cases these one-time costs can make a business uneconomic. This is especially so in contexts where the establishment of basic demand (say, for latrines, or drip irrigation, or doctor-attended childbirth) is a public good, and benefits will accrue not just to the first enterprise to provide such services or goods but also to any imitators or competitors who, it is hoped, will come in behind the first mover.

To support such financing, donors and policymakers have multiple options, but they need not invest directly in firms that are undertaking such training. Nor do the options for scaling take the form of conventional NGO grants or aid. They can be in the form, for instance, of category campaigns that apply to all manufacturers of a given product, like clean cookstoves, where a campaign is coordinated with a program to introduce the product or service. This is the approach that USAID and Shell Foundation took with Gyapa cookstoves in Ghana. Other approaches could include a centrally capitalized grant facility to which enterprises could apply for competitively awarded funds to stimulate demand alongside a new product or service. This kind of facility would be better where multiple providers do not operate and where there may only be one or two enterprises aiming to serve the BoP.

A good example is LifeSpring Hospital, which offers low-cost ($40 to $50), doctor-attended childbirth in periurban Andhra Pradesh (AP), in southern India. One reason LifeSpring operates in southern states (and not northern states like Bihar) is that there is higher community acceptance of doctor-attended delivery in AP.[41] The cost of persuading mothers in states like Bihar or Orissa would add to the cost of the hospital's services, thereby limiting affordability. Yet arguably LifeSpring's greatest value would be in a state with a much lower level of doctor-attended childbirths. A donor-funded facility that could absorb these one-time and quite long-term persuasion costs, in conjunction with a market entry by the hospital, could increase the likelihood that an enterprise like LifeSpring will scale—and will scale in the right places. Another example of one-time cost absorption is Gates Foundation's $7.5 million support to Coca-Cola and its local bottler, Coca-Cola SABCO, in Uganda. The support is for the training of small farmers to participate in SABCO's fruit juice supply chain, making it cost neutral for Coca-Cola and its supporting processors to source from these small farmers.[42]

Replicating or Transplanting Business Models That Work

This type of support becomes relevant once enterprises have passed the "prepare" stage and business models have been validated. Support for scaling up in this realm appears at first to be straightforward: find business models that work and fund them to expand their scope and adapt to local conditions, as in the Jika cookstove example. But to do this, policymakers and donors will need to develop the following three tools:

—Identify which business models are successful and articulate some metrics to define success. This could include number of people reached, income levels of those served, development effectiveness or financial viability. The definition could also be a measure of readiness to transplant. USAID's Development Innovation Ventures program attempts to do this with its three-stage process, which

41. One indicator of this is data from the government of India, which suggest that attended birth rates in Andhra Pradesh in 1999 stood at 28 percent, compared to 20 percent in Bihar. For the underlying data, see www.cehat.org/infocentre/r51tables1.pdf#page=11.

42. Jenkins and others (2010). The authors note that "in early 2009, the Bill & Melinda Gates Foundation approached the Coca-Cola Company with market assessments showing a clear business case for developing local supplies of mango and passionfruit in Kenya and Uganda, where the company had been struggling with a shortage of quality fruit for its growing juice business. After 10 months of negotiation—a 'relatively quick' process—Gates, Coca-Cola, its East African bottler Coca-Cola Sabco, and TechnoServe entered a four-year partnership to develop the market. Gates is funding TechnoServe, which organizes farmers, provides them with agricultural extension services, and facilitates access to financing. Coca-Cola is contributing 50% of the total project cost, a market for some of the fruit produced, and an 'anchor' effect that—combined with Gates' convening power—helps attract additional companies. There are now 15 companies involved, including Jain Irrigation. Over the next five years, the project aims to double the incomes of 54,000 farmers."

requires evidence (usually based on randomized control trials) to justify investment in scaling up.

—Develop a licensing regime that will provide fair returns and recognition to entities that have done the hard work of developing and proving a business model that delivers social benefit, a model that is bound to be copied and implemented in another region by another player. This is particularly important for ideas developed by, for instance, local NGOs, which may be more focused on serving their own communities than on expanding to others. There may well be trapped value in some NGO ideas and models.

—Find successful business builders who can take proven ideas and implement them elsewhere. In some cases, like microfinance in Afghanistan and Uganda, turning to the NGO BRAC (Bangladesh Rural Advancement Committee) was an easy decision. In other cases, it is far less obvious who can or should take on the task of introducing a business model that seems to work elsewhere, especially in low-capacity frontier markets.

The task therefore requires some degree of matchmaking in the service of market making (box 2-3). Typically the process of transplanting will require some experimentation to see how well the business model works in a new setting or new operating conditions. Thus the scaling process will require a more networked approach from donors and policymakers than they are accustomed to.

Rolling Up Fragmented Enterprises

Rolling up fragmented enterprises differs from conventional approaches and does not require social entrepreneurs or corporate models. The underlying premise is that there is a large-scale, installed base already serving this segment and that the task at hand requires upgrading that base en masse. While efforts are beginning to unfold focusing on health and education, it is still surprising how little has been attempted within agriculture and especially aggregating small, informal agrodealers.[43] These rural retailers form an essential part of the smallholder agriculture economy in most countries and are the distribution channel most critical to improving Africa's dismal level of productivity inputs for small farmers. The NGO IFDC (International Fertilizer Development Center) has identified at least 3,000 agrodealers in Ghana, all operating largely independently.[44]

Donors, policymakers, and governments have a range of options, many of which are geared to create the necessary conditions for either improving a

43. A notable exception already mentioned is AGRA in Africa, which has been working through its PASS program and other interventions to build networks of certified agrodealers in a number of countries, including Kenya, Tanzania, Ghana, and Malawi.
44. See www.modernghana.com/news/294308/1/ifdc-and-agra-to-enhance-food-security-situation-i.html.

Box 2-3. *Market Making*

There is an emerging awareness not only of multiple routes to scale but also of the need to "make" a market (or even a whole sector) rather than just investing in a given firm. The leading exponent of this view is the Omidyar Network.[a] Matt Bannick and Paula Goldman's argument is that, just as microfinance grew as a series of individual microfinance institutions, there was a parallel investment in policy change, in fieldwide institutions to share data and research (like CGAP and MIX), and even in new entities, like M-CRIL in India, to provide micro-finance-specific rating services to help these institutions address currency risk issues. Similar investments in policy, supporting infrastructure, intermediaries, and other elements are required in order to make a market.

Bannick and Goldman argue that "an excessive focus on the individual firm . . . also has caused many impact investors to underestimate the importance of policy and political sensitivity, particularly when serving the disadvantaged." Moreover, this focus on the firm as the central actor can lead to poor system-level outcomes. "Everyone loves to invest in the occasional impact-investing 'home run' that promises strong financial and social returns—and these home runs have an important demonstration effect for the viability of the industry as a whole. Unfortunately, relatively few appear willing to step up to the hard and uncertain work of sparking and nurturing the innovations that ultimately generate a robust flow of investable, high-return impact investments. It is as if impact investors are lined up around the proverbial water pump waiting for the flood of deals, while no one is actually priming the pump!"

These observations are consistent with Monitor's experience in making the market for affordable housing in urban India, where all of these challenges persist. Beyond these challenges, there is one other important element to consider: even if one agrees that market making is critical, who actually can and should take on the task? Little is known about this set of tools, but new research is now under way to begin to develop a more nuanced and rigorous understanding of what it takes to succeed.

a. Bannick and Goldman (2012).

cluster of small players who are already at scale in aggregate; or creating the shared infrastructure that will allow other players to operate and serve the BoP at scale, especially in fragmented, rural, distribution tasks. A partial list of possible interventions follows:

—Provide certification, as with ADDO in Tanzania and Licensed Chemical Sellers in Ghana. However, for the certification to be effective, it must offer more than one-time training, so this represents an ongoing expense and effort.

—Aggregate and create membership organizations (plus training), as AGRA has funded the IFDC in Ghana, as the Indian government has formed federations

Figure 2-9. *Funds Needed to Upgrade Four Types of Medical Provider, Nigeria*[a]

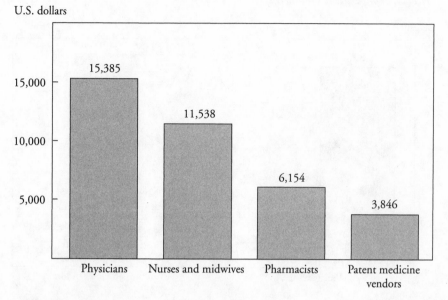

U.S. dollars

Source: McKeon (2009).
a. Sample of 156 physicians; 201 nurses and midwives; 176 pharmacists and 349 patent medicine vendors.

of credit-linked self-help groups, and as spaza shops have formed the Shop-Net program in South Africa. As with certification, this step does not increase scale, but it does create the infrastructure that can support increased scale.

—Capitalize roll-up funds, which can act as the catalyst to upgrade large numbers of facilities, invest in training, increase bankability, and standardize services and products. Figures 2-9 and 2-10 illustrate the relatively small amount of capital required for small-scale medical providers, from physicians through patent medical vendors, and the improvement in medicine availability that could be triggered. Given the low levels of capacity, these funds are as much a vehicle for delivering technical assistance and upgrading capability as they are for financing. This implies that donors, governments, or other sources of funding need to finance not just capital but also advisory services. Commercial banks are typically reluctant to invest in the delivery of technical assistance, so it usually falls upon donors to cover these costs.

—Support variants on social franchising, which can operate on more commercially viable terms than most of the current health examples. This option for delivering scale is the least well understood and can potentially deliver on a large scale quickly, if roll-up funds can be successfully established (figure 2-11). The

Figure 2-10. *Likelihood of Drug Purchase if Provided Financing,*
Two Types of Medical Provider, Nigeria

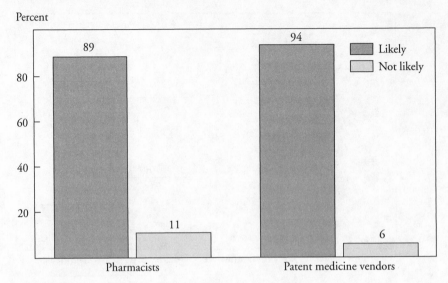

Percent

Source: McKeon (2009).

benefit, unlike for options that rely on a single firm, is a distribution infrastructure that multiple parties can work with and that is not proprietary to individual firms or their specific products.

Implications for Donors and Governments

It is worth pausing to consider whether the activities described above are even feasible for donor and government agencies, given that they differ from private sector actors in almost every respect: cultures, incentives, time horizons, procurement requirements, and risk tolerances. Furthermore, several of the interventions described above could be interpreted as picking winners, in terms of both entrepreneurs and business models. Is it a mistake to even contemplate a role for donors in this area?

The preliminary answer is a qualified no: some donors have already succeeded in accomplishing some of the tasks described above. The Gates Foundation, for instance, manages a range of large grants that address the fixed costs (that is, the "prepare" stage) of training farmers to participate in various agriculture supply chains in Africa. These programs often support firms at the precompetitive stage, to raise the capability of a group of suppliers so that the

Figure 2-11. *Example of Financing-Led Roll-Up Models*

ISFC	Gray Ghost created the Indian School Finance Company (ISFC) to provide expansion capital and technical assistance to low-cost private schools serving the poor in India
Banyan Global	Banyan Global and USAID/SHOPS partnered with Diamond Bank in Nigeria and USAID to provide loans ($3,000–$5,000 for small providers; $40,000–$100,000 for large providers) and TA for health care providers
Medical Credit Fund Africa	PharmAccess created the Medical Credit Fund (MCF) to provide financing to small private health care providers in Africa, typically $7,000–$45,000
IFC	IFC developed joint ventures with local partner banks to increase lending to budget private schools in Ghana and Kenya via Equity Bank and Trust Bank

Source: Impact Investor Interviews, IFC, Gray Ghost, ISFC, PharmAccess, SHOPS, Banyan, Monitor Analysis.

intervention supports a number of private firms, rather than just building one proprietary supply chain. However, this approach is unusual for organizations that are primarily in the business of providing grants.

A number of donor agencies have attempted to address this cultural mismatch by moving the function out of the donor agency altogether to an arm's-length fund manager, recognizing that the donors are culturally ill suited to run such a process directly. Most such programs are geared to identifying and supporting smaller, growing enterprises that have real potential for development impact and commercial viability and are less focused on large MNCs.[45] The best examples of this approach can be found in the challenge funds referenced above, where donors typically engage (through a competitive-bid process) a professional fund manager to find businesses in which to invest capital. Challenge

45. Donors like GIZ, USAID, and the Dutch government have programs for supporting activities with MNCs in particular. There are also many donor-supported forums established for peer learning and activity among large MNCs, like the World Business Council on Sustainable Development, Frontier 100, Business Action for Africa, and the International Business Leaders Forum. Recently, the African Union, WEF, and USAID have supported the Grow Africa process to encourage large private sector investment in African agriculture that engages smallholder farmers (Monitor Group, 2011).

funds are hardly new ideas, but they are increasingly being used to channel donor funds into businesses with social purposes—and do so at arm's length in ways that improve speed to market and coverage.

However, these donors also wrestle with the issues of whether these facilities are sufficiently integrated into their mainstream operations to influence how staff think about solving problems or whether they can link to larger pools of onward funding from donors. And in recent years, some donors have capitalized pools of grant funding to assist with some of these costs; for instance, the Gates Foundation and the International Finance Corporation capitalized a technical assistance fund alongside the $105 million of for-return capital to be invested by Aureos' Health in Africa Fund.[46] The technical assistance fund can cover some of the business model development costs by assisting investees, but it provides a relatively low proportion of the overall funding.

Donors have funded related programs in, for instance, agriculture in the Beira Corridor in Mozambique, where AgDevCo manages a $20 million facility capitalized by a consortium of donors to make both at-risk and grant investments in business model development and fixed farmer-training costs.[47] Indeed, the creation of AgDevCo itself is a response to the need for deploying donor funds on market-based, arm's-length terms: to take a catalytic, early-stage risk in jump-starting small, smallholder, farmer-based businesses and to replicate or build successful business models. AgDevCo is capitalized as a separate not-for-profit company and has more operating leeway than a typical donor agency.

Other donors have kept this function in house through, for instance, Grand Challenges, or through direct funding that they operate themselves, such as USAID's Development Innovation Ventures program (DIV). Indeed, DIV has introduced a new level of sophistication, with different windows for public programs and private enterprises and different funding amounts and criteria by stage of maturity of the innovation. Helpfully, DIV has also introduced a requirement for rigorous evaluation of impact and, even more helpfully, a willingness to pay for that evaluation. More and more donors are beginning to support impact enterprises, either as a direct goal or as a component of a broader program. A recent Monitor Group analysis for Rockefeller Foundation indicates that almost thirty (nonmicrofinance) donor programs provide above $5 million a year in nonreturnable capital to such businesses, with new programs announced by at least seven donor agencies (box 2-4).[48]

46. Aureos is now owned by Abraaj Capital and has announced six investments. For more on Aureos fund investing in African health businesses that serve BoP patients and consumers, see www.aureos.com/region/africa/aureos_health_fund.

47. For more details, see http://seedinvestors.blogspot.com/2012/04/catalytic-capital-realising-africas.html. Also see AgDevCo's own site (www.agdevco.com).

48. Rockefeller Foundation and Monitor Group (forthcoming).

Box 2-4. *Donor Support for Impact Enterprises*

Monitor Group's 2012 analysis for Rockefeller Foundation of over 500 donor programs (excluding microfinance) finds 110 that could potentially support such enterprises, although most donors lack even a common definition of "inclusive business" or "impact enterprise."[a]

From this long list, thirteen programs explicitly focus on supporting inclusive businesses directly with grants, technical analysis, or other noninvestment capital. Another sixteen programs employ such support as part of a broader agenda to promote a given sector (such as cookstoves and smallholder agriculture). The thirteen narrowly focused programs (such as JICA's BoP Business Promotion Preparatory Survey Support) account for about $55 million in annual funding, with an average of $5 million a year. The sixteen more broadly focused programs offer an additional $458 million of funding for impact enterprises as part of wider-ranging programs, where inclusive business is but one component (for instance, Gates Foundation's work in sanitation).[b]

These programs, however, are still quite small in comparison to the intended for-return investment of fifty-two GIIN members in impact enterprises, an investment estimated to be about $2 billion.[c] However, the analysis also identifies another eight new programs in the planning and development stage. These are from SIDA, DFID, JICA, GIZ, ADB, and others. Many of these programs are expected to be operational by the time this volume is published.

a. Rockefeller Foundation and Monitor Group (forthcoming).
b. Over half the funds in this second category of programs are Gates Foundation funds.
c. Saltuk and others (2013).

Nonetheless, despite the uptick in donor activity, when these agencies or governments are in the direct business of investing in or supporting firms, there is a real likelihood of a mismatch between what donors are capable of and what firms need, especially as donor concerns for reputational risk, procurement, contracting, use of funds for charitable purpose, and other considerations come into play and restrict the freedom of donor agencies to engage with enterprises.[49] Systems for efficiently picking businesses to support, and then engaging with them, are nearly diametrically opposed to most other systems that large donors have in place. Moreover, the typical skill set for evaluating a business and its feasibility as an investment is not usually found in donor job descriptions, and donor pay scales are unlikely to compete with pay scales of analysts who have the experience to evaluate a business on both commercial and social terms.

49. Other considerations include the concern that donors should not be seen as subsidizing a large firm's profits.

Consequently, this is a function typically best done at arm's length and out-side the donor or the government agency itself.[50] Most interventions thus far have been in the form of new intermediaries, like challenge funds (for example, AECF, noted above), or in the form of specialized entities, like Root Capital, Oikocredit, AgDevCo, Medical Credit Facility, and DFID's Business Innovation Facility, rather than vehicles capitalized within existing for-profit invest-ing entities. But over time more research will be required to determine which approach is more scalable, successful, and sustainable.[51] It is worth noting that, inasmuch as these new intermediaries may be offering debt in addition to grants or equity, there will be a longer-term issue with the balance sheets of these inter-mediaries and their ability to make loans at scale. This is one reason that pro-grams like the International Finance Corporation and the Development Credit Authority of USAID tend to work with commercial banks that have adequate balance sheets and, in most cases, knowledge of how to select businesses in which to invest.[52] In all events, however, some form of larger scale intermediar-ies will undoubtedly be required to enable donors to participate in supporting businesses and business models in a meaningful way.

Beyond funding such enterprises, if donors are to take on the idea of sup-porting impact enterprises using a business model lens, they will also need to undertake a variety of other tasks, including the following:

—Fund research and activities that solve issues that block business models from a range of sectors from being successful—for example, distribution, pay-ment, aggregation, customer education, and supplier training. These solutions can and should be cross-cutting, and donors should help make these elements cost neutral for any firm undertaking an impact-oriented business serving the poor.

—Develop data, a staging framework, a point of view, and rigorous stan-dards on when a business model is mature and ready for the next stage—or when it is ready to be cut off from grant subsidy funds (either through commer-cial viability or failure to achieve stated goals).

---

50. A strong exception to this observation are facilities or entities, like the IFC and IADB's Multilateral Investment Fund, that are already predominantly in the business of investing in private firms. In these cases, the task at hand is to incentivize and frame new approaches that prioritize inclusive business and impact as much as generating deal flow for conventional private investments.

51. There has been relatively little research, at least in the public domain, to evaluate the effec-tiveness and scalability of such intermediaries. Such analysis is needed to guide future efforts.

52. Commercial bank financing for inclusive businesses (or the lack thereof) is an oft-lamented topic. In many cases banks have expensive capital, high levels of risk aversion, lack of interest in lending early in the enterprise's development, and low levels of understanding of these businesses. Moreover, such businesses' focus on selling to poor consumers or on engaging small, fragmented suppliers makes them appear to be high-risk investments, unlike businesses that serve the emerging middle classes, which have more purchasing power.

—Generate data on additional business models to learn from. (This chapter notes only a fraction of the potential business models that could successfully engage BoP populations.)

—Issue grand challenges around not just particular problems (like maternal and child health) but specific business models or elements of them that need solving—for example, correspondent banking, social franchising, and direct sales agent models.

—Pursue sectorwide or market-making approaches that address not just individual firms but the broader infrastructure, ecosystem, and policy environment in which inclusive businesses with promising business models operate.

Investing in inclusive businesses and patiently nurturing business models that engage the poor require an approach that will usually take policymakers and funders into unaccustomed territory. Nonetheless, few other actors can mobilize the required capital and absorb the risk necessary to develop and try new models and to help successful ones reach the maximum number of people. There is, in other words, much to be done to organize the significant resources of the donor community if its members are to take enterprise solutions to poverty—and the business models that they employ—seriously. The task may be difficult, but it is important—and almost certainly worth the effort.

References

Banerjee, Abhijit, and others. 2009. "The Miracle of Microfinance? Evidence from a Randomized Evaluation" (www.povertyactionlab.org/publication/miracle-microfinance-evidence-randomized-evaluation).

Bannick, Matt, and Paula Goldman. 2012. "Sectors, Not Just Firms." *Stanford Social Innovation Review* (www.ssireview.org/blog/entry/sectors_not_just_firms).

Beck, Steve, with Wouter Deelder and Robin Miller. 2010. "Franchising in Frontier Markets: What's Working, What's Not, and Why." *Innovations: Technology, Governance, Globalization* 5, no. 1: 153–62.

Bishai, David, and others. 2008. "Social Franchising to Improve Quality and Access in Private Health Care in Developing Countries." *Harvard Health Policy Review* 9, no. 1.

Case, Anne, and others. 2008. "Paying the Piper: The High Cost of Funerals in South Africa." Working Paper 14456. National Bureau of Economic Research.

Grameen Foundation. 2010. "Creating a World without Poverty" (http://grameen foundation.wordpress.com/2010/06/10/measuring-the-impact-of-microfinance-taking-another-look-2).

Hudon, Marek. 2005. "On the Efficiency Effects of Subsidies in Microfinance: An Empirical Enquiry." Working Paper. CGAP, Mapping of Funding Flows.

Jenkins, Beth, and others. 2010. "Inclusive Business: Expanding Opportunity and Access at the Base of the Pyramid." International Finance Corporation.

J. P. Morgan. 2010. "Impact Investments: An Emerging Asset Class" (www.jpmorgan.com/pages/jpmorgan/investbk/research/impactinvestments).

Karamchandani, Ashish, Michael Kubzansky, and Paul Frandano. 2009. "Emerging Markets, Emerging Models. Monitor Group (www.mim.monitor.com/downloads/emerging markets_full.pdf).

Kirsten, Johann, and Kurt Sartorius. 2002. "Linking Agribusiness and Small-Scale Farmers in Developing Countries: Is There a New Role for Contract Farming?" *Development Southern Africa* 19, no. 4.

Koh, Harvey, Ashish Karamchandani, and Robert Katz. 2012. "From Blueprint to Scale: The Case for Philanthropy in Impact Investing." Monitor Group (www.mim.monitor.com/blueprinttoscale.html).

Kubzansky, Michael. 2012. "The Importance of Business Models." Policy brief for the Brookings Blum Roundtable. Brookings.

Kubzansky, Michael, and Ansulie Cooper. 2013. Direct Sales Agent Models in Health. Bethesda, MD: SHOPS Project, Abt Associates.

Kubzansky, Michael, Ansulie Cooper, and Victoria Barbary. 2011. *Promise and Progress: Market-Based Solutions to Poverty in Africa.* Monitor Group.

McKeon, Kimberley. 2009. "Financing and Business Development Needs of Private Health Care Providers in Nigeria." Market research report, September. Abt Associates.

Monitor Group. 2009. *Emerging Markets, Emerging Model.*

Montagu, D., and others. 2009. *Clinical Social Franchising: An Annual Compendium of Programs.* Global Health Group, University of California, San Francisco.

Murray, Sarah. 2011. *Making an Exit.* Coptic Publishing.

Prahalad, C. K. 2004. *Fortune at the Bottom of the Pyramid: Eradicating Poverty through Profits.* Dorling Kindersley.

Rockefeller Foundation and Monitor Group. Forthcoming. *Impact Enterprises: Mapping the Landscape of Donor Support.*

Safaricom. 2010. *Annual Report.*

Saltuk, Bouri, and others. 2013. "Perspectives on Progress." January (www.thegiin.org/cgi-bin/iowa/resources/research/489.html).

Schneider, Friedrich, Andreas Buehn, and Claudio E. Montenegro. 2010. "New Estimates for the Shadow Economies All over the World." *International Economic Journal* 24, no. 4: 443–61.

Tooley, James. 2006. "Educating Amaretch: Private Schools for the Poor and the New Frontier for Investors." *Financial Times,* September 17.

Treewater, Evette, and John Price. 2007. "Navigating Latin American Distribution Channels." *Logistics Today* 48, no. 9.

Tyler, Geoff, and Gramahe Dixie. 2012. Investments in Agribusiness: A Retrospective View of Development Bank's Investments in Agribusiness in Africa and East Asia, World Bank.

USAID. 2007. "Implementation Plan for Increasing the Adoption and Use of Efficient Charcoal Cookstoves in Urban and Peri-Urban Kigali," Market Research Report.

———. 2009. "Financing and Business Development Needs of Private Health Care Providers in Nigeria." Market research report.

3

From Scaled-Up Budgets to Scaled-Up Impact: A Decade of Rising Foreign Aid in Review

LAURENCE CHANDY

I very much welcome—as should we all—the recent decisions by
President Bush and the European Union to boost aid spending. . . .
But we must not stop there. This is not just about resources. It is
about scaling up—moving from individual projects to programs,
building on and then replicating, for example, microcredit for
women or community-driven development, where the poor are at
the center of the solution[,] not the end of a handout.

—James Wolfensohn
at the Monterey International Conference
for Development, March 2002

The first decade of the twenty-first century saw a rapid increase in official
aid flows (figure 3-1). From 2000 to 2010 net annual official development assistance (ODA) from countries of the Development Assistance Committee of the Organization for Economic Cooperation and Development (OECD
DAC) and multilateral agencies increased over 60 percent, from $78.7 billion
to a new record of $128.5 billion (2010 prices). Measured as a share of member
countries' economic size, aid in 2010 reached its equal highest level since 1992,
at 0.32 percent of OECD DAC gross national income. This resulted in an extra
$278 billion of aid for developing countries, over and above 2000 levels. This is

Figure 3-1. *Official Development Assistance, OECD DAC Countries and Multilateral Agencies, 2000–10*

Billions of constant 2010 U.S. dollars

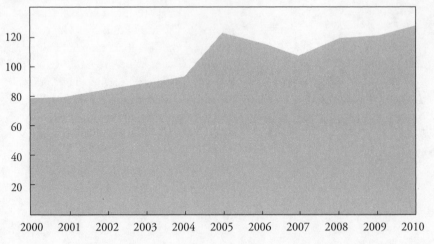

Source: OECD (2012a).

consistent with the lower range of costing estimates for the achievement of the Millennium Development Goals.[1] It almost certainly underestimates the growth of global ODA, since aid from non-OECD DAC donor countries is believed to have risen at a faster pace than OECD DAC aid.[2]

While there were various motivations for this increase in aid, among them was a desire to spur faster development and poverty reduction by, inter alia, systematically expanding the delivery of basic services to poor populations and financing the replication of other interventions that had achieved demonstrable success at a limited scale. In other words, scaled-up aid volumes would finance the scaling up of development impact.

With the expectation that the period of rising aid flows is now likely over following a drop of OECD DAC aid flows in 2011, now is a good time to take stock of the preceding period.[3] This chapter attempts to bridge the two notions of scaling up by examining to what extent increased aid volumes were used to support the scaling up of development impact. In doing so, it seeks to shed light on the relationship between these two related, but separate, agendas.

1. For a range of estimates, see Atisophon and others (2011).
2. Park (2011).
3. For details of the drop in aid flows, see DAC (2012).

To definitively answer this question would require a level of analysis far beyond the scope of this research: tracing the evolution of individual projects and programs from their inception, observing the mechanisms of the project cycle, and scrutinizing other operational and institutional aspects (staff guidelines, incentive systems, culture) of aid agencies and recipient governments.[4]

This essay is considerably more modest. I begin by examining the common motivations, planning, and challenges associated with increasing aid volumes. I then identify some readily observable characteristics of aid programs that appear supportive of scaling up development impact and test whether their incidence can be explained by the growth in aid programs over the past decade. Finally, I look at a sample of donor-country case studies and review their experiences in managing increasing levels of aid and their attempts to translate these into greater development impact (or otherwise).

To avoid confusion, the term *scaling up* is used hereafter to refer only to the scaling up of development impact.

Motivations for More Aid

Aid budgets are the responsibility of individual donor governments and are therefore shaped by country-specific factors. Nevertheless, one can identify three factors that have played an important role in driving increased aid volumes over the previous decade and that are common across many donor countries.

First, the September 11 terrorist attacks sparked new concerns over the threats posed by fragile states, prompting several governments to adopt a more activist foreign policy in which aid has played an important role. Aid has been used to complement military interventions and other security-driven measures: financing postwar reconstruction, supporting new or strategically important governments, and seeking to win the hearts and minds of affected populations. Aid programs have been at the vanguard of Western efforts to tackle fragility, focusing on fighting poverty, strengthening institutions, and tackling corruption in weak and unstable states.

Second, a number of countries started or expanded their aid programs to mark their growing economic stature. Most prominent among these are emerging economy donors that remain outside of the OECD DAC club; they have challenged the old order and blurred the distinction between donor and recipient classifications. In addition, some of the newer members of the OECD DAC, including Spain, Ireland, and Korea, have quickly established themselves as major players in the international development sphere, while the expansion of

4. For a good example of an institutional agency review, see two Brookings studies of IFAD (Linn and others, 2010; Hartmann and others, 2013).

the EU has encouraged countries in eastern Europe to begin supporting global development efforts.

Third, there has been growing international sympathy and support for the moral cause of eradicating poverty, as encapsulated—and in some part, likely driven—by the UN Millennium Development Goals (MDGs). Increased aid volumes were initially seen as a small piece of the jigsaw in achieving the MDGs; the Millennium Declaration explicitly mentions only debt relief, and a "fairer aid deal" for Africa and the "Least Developed Countries." Over time, however, aid generosity has become increasingly prominent in assessments of MDG commitment and progress.[5] Support for the MDGs has been assisted by well-organized and harmonized civil society campaigns in many donor countries.

These three factors inspired a series of international pledges to increase aid flows. In 2002 the UN Financing for Development Conference at Monterrey elicited commitments from the United States to raise its annual aid budget by 50 percent and from the European Union to reach an aid to gross national income (GNI) share of 0.39 percent by 2006. In May 2005 the European Council built on its previous commitment by setting a new collective ODA/GNI percent target of 0.56 for 2010 and 0.7 for 2015. Two months later, G-8 members at Gleneagles pledged a series of individual aid increases that, together with those from other donor nations, would raise annual aid levels by approximately $50 billion (2004 dollars) by 2010, of which half would go to Africa.

Progress in meeting these targets has been mixed. While the Monterrey outcome document (the Monterrey Consensus) is best remembered for urging developed countries "to make concrete efforts" toward the ODA/GNI target of 0.7 percent, a level that today still seems far out of reach for most OECD DAC countries, the specific pledges made by the United States and the EU at the conference were both fulfilled. The EU fell short of its subsequent 2010 target, however, leaving its 2015 target very unlikely to be met. Finally, only $30 billion of the G-8's envisaged $50 billion aid increase was delivered, while the fulfillment of its pledge to Africa fell well short, with only an $11 billion increase.

Nevertheless, these targets have almost certainly played their own part in motivating increased aid levels. Those countries that set themselves more ambitious targets have tended to be the ones to achieve significant increases in their aid budgets, even if increases ultimately fall short of their promised level.[6] While the manner in which targets have been structured is occasionally quite complex, pledges have been made publicly, enabling civil society organizations to play a supportive role in holding governments to account. Governments that ignored their own

5. See MDG Gap Taskforce Reports (UN, 2010, 2011) and the online platform for monitoring commitments made to the MDGs (UN, 2012).

6. Kharas (2010).

commitments risked reputational damage.[7] Indeed, Italy's woeful failure to deliver on its Gleneagles pledge was cited as among the factors that allegedly caused other G-8 members to call for the country to be expelled from the group in 2009.[8]

In addition to the above factors, the increase in aid over the decade was, in hindsight, made possible by a conducive economic environment, in which the global economy purred along at a healthy rate of growth before the global financial crisis began in 2008. It is inconceivable that the same record would have been possible had today's sovereign debt crisis in the West occurred a decade earlier.

The MDGs

The MDGs provide the most direct link between the increase in aid volumes and the agenda for scaling up development impact. As already mentioned, MDG advocacy has become synonymous with calls for increased global aid volumes. Indeed, additional aid is regularly described as a necessary condition for the achievement of the goals.[9] While this claim has the ring of hyperbole, it is consistent with a particular interpretation of the development process regularly espoused within the donor community. According to this view, the condition of poverty typically results from countries being locked in a low saving-investment trap, in which investments in human capital, knowledge, and infrastructure, all of which are vital for sustained economic growth, are constrained by the limited availability of capital. Aid can help poor countries break free from such a trap by temporarily financing these investments, until domestic finance or other sources of capital become available.[10]

The link between the MDGs and the scaling up of development impact is self-evident. The MDGs set forth an ambitious vision of transforming the lives of hundreds of millions of poor people throughout the world. This vision is distilled into a collection of high-level targets and indicators, which are defined principally in terms of access to basic services and so respond to specific

7. UK Prime Minister David Cameron said the following at the GAVI replenishment conference, July 13, 2011: "When you make a promise to the poorest people in the world you should keep it. I remember where I was during the Gleneagles Summit and the Live 8 concert of 2005 and I remember thinking at the time how right it was that those world leaders should make such pledges so publicly. For me it's a question of values. . . . It was the right thing to promise; it was the right thing for Britain to do, and it is the right thing for this government to honor that commitment."

8. Borger (2009).

9. See, for instance, the 2002 Monterrey Consensus: "We recognize that a substantial increase in ODA and other resources will be required if developing countries are to achieve the internationally agreed development goals and objectives" (UN, 2002).

10. This description of the role of aid in escaping poverty traps is an amalgamation of two alternative ways of looking at the same problem: filling the financing gap with the amount required to support a certain growth rate; and financing basic service delivery for underserved populations. Costing exercises for the MDGs typically employ one or the other approach.

interventions. The MDGs stress the need for replication and expansion of interventions based on the simple intuition that to achieve high-level targets requires interventions that are commensurate in scope to that challenge.[11]

Whether support for the MDGs has served to advance a scaling-up agenda, as well as increased levels of aid, is another matter. Indeed, the promotion of the MDGs, in at least three respects, has been associated with an oversimplified account of the development process, which in turn may have led to a distorted understanding of how scaling up occurs.

First, some MDG advocates argue that the specific interventions needed to achieve the MDGs are already known. The veracity of this claim is the subject of one of the liveliest debates in development economics but is tacitly supported by many donors.[12] This reduces the challenge of scaling up to successful program implementation and expansion, with only a modest role for discovery, experimentation, and learning.

Second, the MDGs are often construed as an adequate expression of what is meant by development.[13] According to this perspective, the literal targeting of the goals through dedicated programs represents an efficient (and sufficient) approach to ending poverty. To the extent that systems, institutions, norms, and capacity matter, they too can be built and strengthened through programs at scale. This programmatic vision of how development occurs both misrepresents the objective of development and underplays the distinction between merely replicating interventions successfully and bringing into being highly functional, prosperous, and resilient states.

Third, MDG costing studies based on unit cost estimates have been interpreted as accurate calculations of what is required to achieve the targets. These studies typically derive unit costs from the prevailing level of expenditure for service delivery related to the MDGs—primary schooling, pre- and postnatal care, family planning, vaccines and treatment against infectious and other

---

11. This is consistent with a criticism often leveled at the global aid system that, by focusing on small-scale interventions, it generates "islands of excellence" rather than country-wide results (Uvin, Jain, and Brown, 2000).

12. See Sachs (2005); Easterly (2006); Banerjee and Duflo (2011). The veracity of the claim is passionately defended by, among others, the UN Millennium Project, whose 2005 report states, "The world has the practical knowledge, tools, and means to reach the Millennium Development Goals. Development can be achieved through specific actions on the ground. We know how to prevent mothers from dying in labor. We know how to encourage girls to complete sixth grade so that they have more choices than their mothers. We know how to vastly increase maize yields to feed villages. We know how to make sure that hospitals have uninterrupted electricity. We know how to plan cities to avoid the misery of slums and how to connect remote villages to markets and schools. We know how to combat violence against women and girls. We know what it takes to make sure all citizens have the equal right and opportunity to make choices. Even if we don't know everything about such challenges, we know enough to achieve the Goals" (UN, 2005).

13. Pritchett (2010).

preventable diseases, HIV/AIDS services, water, and sanitation—and estimates of the number of people who are being served. The cost of meeting the MDGs is then determined by multiplying unit costs by the size of underserved populations. There is undoubtedly value to carrying out these exercises, but when taken at face value, they again oversell the role of scaling up in meeting goals and oversimplify how scaling up occurs. For a start, these studies reduce the challenge of achieving the MDGs to a simple supply constraint, when there is evidence that demand for services and the quality of services can be of equal, if not greater, importance.[14] In addition, they ignore the role of policies and institutions in managing and utilizing aid investments.[15]

These issues should not take away from the core, correct inference that scaling up is rightly seen as a vital strategy for achieving the MDGs. However, they serve as a reminder of the complexity of successfully getting to scale, even when goals have been clearly defined, enjoy strong support, and are backed by substantial resources.

Global Planning for Increasing Aid

Given the number of international commitments to increase aid levels, it is perhaps surprising how few plans were made at an international level to guide how anticipated additional aid dollars could be effectively managed.[16]

14. For instance, in a study of primary education in rural areas in twenty-one low-income countries, each with considerable numbers of children not attending school, it was estimated that if the distance between children and their nearest school was eliminated, enrollment rates would rise by more than 4 percentage points in only three of the countries (Filmer, 2004). See also discussion in Clemens, Kenny, and Moss (2004).

15. The 2004 World Development Report found that there is no significant relationship between public spending per child on education and the primary school completion rate, or between public spending per child on health and the under-five mortality rate, once countries' income levels are controlled for.

16. The UN Millennium Project—an independent advisory body commissioned by the UN secretary general to identify the best strategies for meeting the Millennium Development Goals—advocated for a systematic approach to planning as part of its broader recommendations for how the global community could achieve the MDGs. Its ideas never took hold, but it is nevertheless interesting to examine its proposals as they powerfully incorporate scaling up as a strategy for supporting the employment of new aid. In keeping with the recommendations of others, the UN Millennium Project agreed that country development strategies represented a key instrument for directing the allocation of new aid flows. However, its vision of these strategies was more clearly defined. All strategies were to be organized around seven common clusters, each representing an area for public investment and policy reform. Public investments would "be based on known interventions that can be rapidly scaled up" (UN, 2005, pp. 64–65), though adapted to the local setting. In addition, three global initiatives were proposed that could make effective use of greater aid volumes, each embodying a scaling-up strategy: identifying a group of "fast-track counties" that were ready to absorb a rapid increase in aid due to strong governance; establishing a global human resource training scheme, in recognition that skills are required to meet all the goals and need to be built up simultaneously with other investments; and delivering seventeen "quick-win" interventions, which could be scaled up the world over within no more than three years, to jump-start MDG progress.

There are a number of possible reasons why this occurred. The sovereignty of individual donor countries over their aid budgeting and allocations may have served as a constraint on a more cooperative approach. Another limitation may have been uncertainty as to which global governance institution was responsible for managing the increase in aid flows: the UN as organizer of the Monterrey Conference and architect of the MDGs; the OECD DAC as the principal forum for coordinating development assistance and a source of aid norms and standards; or the Development Committee of the World Bank and the IMF, which facilitates intergovernmental consensus building on development issues with a focus on resource flows.

The most compelling explanation, however, may be that the rise in aid levels coincided with the ascendancy of the country-based model in donor-recipient relations. This model, embodied in the development of Poverty Reduction Strategy Papers in 1999 and the Paris Declaration on Aid Effectiveness six years later, stressed the sovereignty of the recipient country in determining its own development plans and the need for donors to align behind that vision. Any supranational efforts to direct new aid to particular ends could therefore be construed as crowding out recipient country voices.

The country-based model is typically contrasted with vertical funds, whose rapid emergence in the last decade represented a significant innovation for the aid industry. Vertical funds were not created to absorb additional aid flows, but in the case of the Global Fund to Fight AIDS, Tuberculosis, and Malaria (and to a lesser extent, others), they represented a deliberate attempt to advance action toward the MDGs. While a number of vertical funds had significant success in raising finance, the claim that the country-based model remained ascendant is well founded; vertical funds together can account for only $50 billion of global aid disbursements over the decade, which is less than a fifth of marginal global ODA flows above 2000 levels.

The promotion of the country-based model was evident when the Development Committee briefly took up the issue of planning for greater aid volumes following the G-8 summit in Gleneagles.[17] Three objectives were identified by the committee: designing national development strategies that were country-owned and results-focused, which would provide clear guidance for donors on how to align and harmonize; improving macroeconomic conditions so that increased aid flows could be absorbed without creating destabilizing effects, such as Dutch disease and volatility; and improving institutional capacity for service delivery, including through improving public financial management,

---

17. These discussions were informed by a series of joint World Bank–OECD DAC technical meetings. See Development Committee (2006, 2007).

monitoring and evaluation, results management, statistical systems, and subnational governance.[18]

The Development Committee recognized the need for deeper dialogue and coordination between recipient governments and donors if aid resources were to be effectively utilized. Operational-level meetings were encouraged that would enable medium-term expenditure planning and improved performance management. These activities have been implemented to a varying degree in many aid recipient countries.[19] It is important to note, however, that many of the same steps were already being advocated or undertaken independent of the expected rise in aid flows.

In addition, the Development Committee recommended improving forecasts of future aid spending through new DAC surveys and improving the effectiveness of aid through the implementation of the Paris Declaration. It is notable that the Paris Declaration had little to say on the issues of aid architecture and fragmentation—two aspects of effectiveness that present direct challenges to the successful utilization of additional aid flows. No explicit mention was made by the Development Committee of using scaling up as a basis for employing increased aid. The use of scaling up as a strategy to guide the allocation of new aid flows would depend on recipient countries adopting such an approach in their individual development strategies.

Donor-Country Planning for Increasing Aid

Within donor countries, decisions regarding the size of aid budgets are overtly political.[20] The planning for increasing aid levels tends to reflect this reality; increasing aid flows is perceived first as a political problem and only second as a technical one. A consequence of this is that the programming challenges in effectively employing additional aid have tended to be underplayed or are contemplated after, rather than before, budgets have been agreed. It is rare for donor countries to develop specific strategies for managing increasing aid levels. More common is for an increase in aid levels to prompt a revamp of a country's overall aid policy, providing confidence that additional spending will be informed by a sound policy framework. Irrespective of the degree of planning, the consequence of rising aid volumes is to focus attention on four overarching priorities or pressures.

First, donors need to find a way to channel their increased ambition. As the aid budgets increase, donors have typically pursued more lofty goals, more

18. Note overlap with the seven constraints identified by Barder (2006).

19. Berg and others (2012).

20. This section focuses on donor countries, but many of the ideas apply equally to multilateral agencies facing a growing aid budget.

influence, and more leverage. At a global level, this may mean seeking to inform the evolving global development agenda or to reform the international aid system. A common target for such efforts is the multilateral system, where targeted increases in capital contributions for a single agency can usually be converted into significantly expanded governance shares.[21] At a recipient-country level, donors often expect to engage in more detailed policy dialogue in return for larger bilateral flows.

Second, donors need to find reliable ways of spending more money. To make the case for an increased aid budget to parliaments, donor agencies must usually demonstrate their ability to spend their existing budgets within the allotted fiscal year—a rigid time frame, which is blind to the many obstacles that aid spending can regularly encounter. In expectation of rising aid budgets, donors often look to identify either those elements of their existing aid program that have the potential to absorb more funding or new financing opportunities that offer such potential. These may include particular projects, aid modalities, or partners.

Third, donors need to strengthen or alter their capacity to manage a larger aid program. Reforms may focus on adapting internal systems for human resources, management, procurement, financial management, budgeting, performance measurement, and reporting. On occasion, entirely new institutions are developed to manage new aid programs. Critically, the skills required of donor staff must also be able to respond to an evolving aid program.

Fourth, donors need to prepare for greater scrutiny from parliaments, the media, and civil society. In recognition that with increased resources comes increased responsibility, donors often seek to strengthen oversight and introduce new measures to avoid corruption, improve their results management, and constrain growth in their administrative costs to demonstrate efficiency.

Scaling-up strategies rarely feature explicitly in donor preparations for rising aid budgets.[22] However, the pressures identified above can have important effects on the extent to which donors pursue a scaling-up agenda. Whether those effects are positive or negative depends on how donors respond to these pressures. Does ambition spur a dispersion or a concentration of effort? Are highly absorptive expenditure choices also those that generate a high development impact? Do donors have the necessary policy and evaluation capacity and a sufficiently coherent approach to knowledge management to function as a learning institution? How do donors weigh development and institutional risk when encountering higher levels of scrutiny? The following sections reveal how donors responded to these questions over the past decade.

21. This is made possible by the messy aid architecture, in which there exist a large number of multilateral agencies of varying sizes.
22. An obvious exception here are vertical funds. Also, see later description of DFID's 2011 bilateral aid review.

Analysis of Global Aid Trends

This section begins by identifying a number of aid program characteristics that appear supportive of a scaling-up agenda. Changes in these characteristics are then observed to determine whether the international aid system has become, over the past decade, more or less conducive to scaling up.

Identifying such characteristics is far from easy. There is no consensus within the development community on how donors should organize their aid programs to best support a scaling-up agenda, and the outward features of an aid program can reveal only so much about the aid activities it contains. Some donors have developed discrete initiatives that explicitly support scaling up, but these are largely disconnected from their core approach to programming, which is our concern here.[23] Moreover, the choice of aid program characteristics is limited to those for which there exist internationally and temporally comparable data.[24] Among the characteristics chosen, some are almost certainly more relevant to scaling up than others.

Analyzing characteristics that are at best indicative of scaling up cannot, by definition, lead to very emphatic conclusions. Nevertheless, they provide a useful starting point for this study. The subsequent section on country case studies provides a basis for reviewing the validity of the choice of characteristics in light of donor practice.

As in the previous section, we focus on the characteristics of donor countries as opposed to donor agencies. A weakness of this approach is that multilateral aid is analyzed only in terms of the multilateral policies bilateral donors pursue, rather than considering multilateral institutions as important actors in their own right, actors that must also navigate the challenges of growing aid programs and that play an important role in supporting scaling-up endeavors globally.

Altogether, eight characteristics of a scaling-up-conducive aid program are postulated. These are arranged into two groups: four characteristics concerning resource allocation choices, followed by four characteristics concerning aid modalities.

—High country-programmable share. Country programmable aid is a narrow definition of aid that strips away aid that is unpredictable by nature (humanitarian aid and debt relief), entails no cross-border flows (administrative costs, scholarships), is not subject to donor cooperation agreements (food aid

---

23. Examples are USAID's Development Innovation Ventures or the World Bank's Development Marketplace.

24. A number of the characteristics identified in this section are consistent with those promoted by the Paris Declaration. An obvious reason for this is that the Paris Monitoring Survey represents one of the few available sources of comparable aid data across donors and time. It is notable, therefore, that the declaration had nothing to say on the issue of scale.

and aid from subnational government), and is not programmable by the donor (core NGO funding). A necessary condition of aid being used to support scaling up is that it is country programmable.

—High country selectivity. Donors that concentrate their aid among a few recipients are more likely to succeed in scaling up, as they can acquire greater knowledge of the local environment and commit a greater share of resources. This indicator captures the number of bilateral relationships between donors and recipients.

—High sector selectivity. Similar to the previous characteristic, donors that invest in particular sectors are more likely to succeed in scaling-up efforts, as they can draw on relevant sector expertise and learning. This indicator looks at the share of a donor's aid program spent in sectors in which it has a revealed comparative advantage: that is, its investment in the sector relative to other donors is at least comparable with its overall weight in the global aid system.

—Large project size. The size of a project gives some indication of its scope. Large projects are more likely to achieve impact at scale than small projects. Aid programs with a large median project size are therefore interpreted as being more supportive of a scaling-up agenda.

—Support for multilateral giving. For many successful aid projects, reaching optimal scale is far beyond the scope of any individual donor. Multilateral agencies are designed to pool donor resources and efforts, which enables projects to be scaled up to a higher level. Some multilateral agencies specialize in a particular region or sector, in which they can draw on deep experience and knowledge. Aid programs that provide a large share of their aid in support of multilateral agencies are therefore expected to be more supportive of scaling up.[25]

—Highly cooperative approach. Donors that act more collaboratively are more likely to support the type of joined-up efforts often required to bring activities to scale. This indicator looks at the extent to which donors cooperate on two simple operational activities: analysis and missions.

—Highly programmatic approach. Programmatic aid is a class of aid modality whereby donors' efforts are coordinated around a government-owned-sector policy, government and donor resources are entered into a single budget framework, and a formal process is followed for donor-recipient coordination. Examples include general and sector budget support, sectorwide approaches (SWAps), and pooled or basket funds. Programmatic aid is likely to support scaling up for a number of reasons: first, it pools the efforts of various donors and the recipient government; second, it supports government plans that target performance at

25. Note that this indicator measures only core funding for multilateral aid and not noncore (earmarked) funding that also uses the multilateral system.

Table 3-1. *Characteristics of OECD DAC Members' Aid, 2000 and 2010*

Characteristic	2000 or nearest year	2010
Country programmable aid share (%)	74.4	72.4
Number of bilateral relationships	2,346	2,534
Specialization by sector (%)	70.5	71.3
Median project size ($)	86,600	108,300
Multilateral share (%)	30.9	27.1
Shared missions and analyses (%)	37.6	47.7
Use of programmatic aid (%)	34.1	42.2
Use of recipient country systems (%)	39.6	53.6

Source: Author's calculations, based on OECD (2012a).

the national level; and third, it is purposefully designed to increase the sustainability of results and to support opportunities for learning.

—Reliance on country systems. Similar to programmatic aid, aid channeled through recipient country procurement and public financial systems is likely to support government country-level plans and to achieve results that, by virtue of being aligned to the recipient country, have a greater chance of being sustained.

Table 3-1 summarizes the performance of OECD DAC aid, taken as a whole, on the eight characteristics in 2000 and 2010, or the nearest available year. It shows some improvement on five of the indicators, with deteriorating performance on the others. From this, one can draw some very limited inferences regarding the degree to which the international aid system has become more or less supportive of a scaling-up agenda over time.[26]

However, this chapter is not concerned merely with trends in scaling up in the aid industry but rather with how these trends relate to the increase in aid flows recorded over the previous decade by donor countries. To explore this question, changes in the eight aid characteristics are regressed on changes in aid volumes for each donor.[27] Initial levels of both aid characteristics and aid volumes are controlled for, in recognition of the range of circumstances facing donors at the start of the decade.

---

26. The eight indicators are chosen to capture characteristics of donor aid programs as opposed to characteristics of the aid system itself. Furthermore, many actors within that system are missing from this analysis, including multilateral agencies, non–OECD DAC donors, and private sector donors.

27. Regressions are not weighted to account for donor size. While weighting would provide a more accurate estimate of the relationship between aid volumes and aid characteristics for a given dollar of aid, this study is focused on donor aid programs as the principal unit of analysis, as it is at this level that aid budgets and plans for using aid are generally determined.

Despite some technical limitations, this analysis generates some interesting findings (see appendix).[28] As one would expect, the explanatory power of the change in aid volumes for any of the eight characteristics is at best partial; there are a number of other factors at work that can explain changes in the different indicators. Nevertheless, significant results were obtained in three cases: country selectivity, multilateral giving, and donor cooperation.

—Country selectivity. The increase in donor aid volumes has spurred donors to disperse their resources more widely among a larger number of recipient countries. This phenomenon is consistent with the hypothesis that greater resources raise donors' ambitions; establishing new bilateral relationships allows donors to spread their influence and to boost their international prestige. It may also be viewed as a straightforward means of spending more money, quickly. Neither the administrative cost nor the human resource demands of establishing new bilateral partnerships are sufficient to constrain this tendency.[29]

—Multilateral giving. There is evidence that the growth in donor aid programs has driven down the share of aid devoted to multilateral agencies. While increasing core contributions to multilateral agencies represents a relatively easy way to spend money (incurring very little administrative cost, minimal capacity to administer, and no absorptive constraints), two factors may draw donors in the opposite direction when overseeing a growing aid program. First, donors may feel unable to adequately account for how multilateral aid is used and the results it achieves, which prevents them from using this aid modality at a time when they face growing levels of scrutiny. Second, by eating into the discretionary power that a growing budget confers, the transferral of aid management may be inconsistent with a donor's ambition for greater influence and agency. It is possible that donors make more use of noncore funding to multilaterals at a time when their aid budgets are increasing, since this would appear to give donors the benefits of both options. However, a lack of data prevents this hypothesis from being tested.

—Donor cooperation. The growth in aid programs can account for some of the improvement in the extent to which donors act cooperatively. Cooperating on the conduct of analysis and country missions may be viewed by donors as a simple means of keeping administrative costs down at a time when their aid programs are growing. More speculatively, cooperative approaches may also facilitate donors' entry into new sectors and countries.

28. The small number of observations is among the most obvious limitations.
29. To explore this finding further, similar regressions were run swapping the dependent variable for two other characteristics: the share of each donor's aid program spent in a country in which it has a revealed comparative advantage; and then the concentration of each donor's aid program, using the Herfindahl index. In neither case was a significant result obtained. The results of these regressions appear in the appendix.

Of these three results, the first and second indicate that the growth in aid programs has decreased the potential for scaling up, while the third suggests the reverse. The net impact is clearly ambiguous. Adding weight to this conclusion are the insignificant results obtained for each of the remaining aid characteristics. Among these, perhaps the most surprising is the absence of evidence that the growth in aid programs has driven a shift toward larger average aid projects. This is a reminder that the translation of growing aid programs into scaled-up impact is far from inevitable.

Country Case Studies

Country case studies provide a complementary and more detailed means of assessing the relationship between increasing aid flows and support of scaling up. The case studies build on the analysis of the preceding section in two ways. First, they allow a reexamination of the eight aid program characteristics that are the focus of the previous section—but this time accounting for differences among donors. This is important, as the regression analysis demonstrates that the impact of changing aid volumes on aid program characteristics is not uniform. Second, they broaden the focus to additional aid program characteristics, including those that cannot easily be quantified.

The case studies are developed from a review of public documents, with a particular reliance on the OECD DAC peer reviews, which provide a rich and broadranging account of donor experience.[30] Figure 3-2 illustrates the changing size of OECD DAC donor aid programs over the previous decade relative to their 2000 volumes, which are normalized to 100. Of the twenty-three countries, only two ended the decade with a smaller program than at the start. We focus our analysis on four of the seven countries whose aid programs more than doubled in size over the period: the United Kingdom, Spain, the United States, and Ireland.[31]

United Kingdom

A distinguishing feature of the UK's experience is that it made plans to grow its aid program long before its aid budget started to rise. The Labour government

---

30. DAC (2001, 2002a, 2002b, 2003, 2006a, 2006b, 2007a, 2007b, 2007c, 2009, 2010, 2011a, 2011b, 2012).

31. The decision to focus on countries that record the largest growth rates is consistent with the proposition that donor aid programs represent the most relevant unit of analysis for examining aid management decisions (see note 27). An alternative approach would be to select case study countries that record the largest absolute increase in aid volumes, which would provide the most accurate account of how growing global aid volumes have been deployed. The choice of four countries was determined by the ease with which the author was able to obtain public information on each aid program. The three other donors that more than doubled their aid budget but are not studied here are Korea, Finland, and Belgium.

Figure 3-2. *Normalized Net Official Development Assistance,*
OECD DAC Countries, 2000–10

2000 value = 100

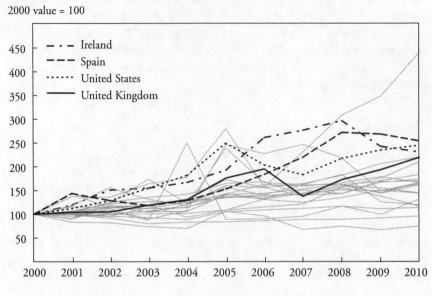

Source: OECD (2012a).

made clear its intention to increase the size and profile of its foreign assistance in its 1997 election manifesto, yet a commitment to medium-term fiscal consolidation prevented it from meaningfully acting on this for five years hence.

This allowed time for the government to develop a strong institutional foundation underpinning its development cooperation. During this period, the Department for International Development (DFID) was created, headed by a cabinet minister; its mandate and objectives were defined and enshrined in law in the International Development Act 2002, identifying poverty reduction as its singular goal; and the first two of four white papers were published setting forth the government's development policy agenda.

Institutional reforms were accompanied by bureaucratic strengthening. DFID expanded its workforce, with a premium placed on technical expertise as much as on project management, providing it with the in-house capacity to conduct quality research and policy development, engage in policy dialogue in partner countries, and undertake rigorous evaluations. This process was helped by DFID's rising profile, making it the most popular choice among entry-level applicants to the UK civil service and enabling the agency to recruit from the very best candidates. Meanwhile, middle and top management were strengthened by attracting leaders from the UK's vibrant NGO community.

A condition of DFID's elevation to a stand-alone government department was a demand that it meet the professional standards expected of equivalent parts of government. DFID rose to this challenge and in 2005 was ranked first among government departments for its financial procedures and systems.[32] Internal systems consequently underwent periodic reforms, guided by capability reviews led by the Cabinet Office. Public service agreements were reached that defined targets against which the department's performance would be judged. These targets helped to align efforts around the agency's core goals, mapping the International Development Act and key MDG indicators in the UK's largest partner countries with the department's organizational structure and country offices. The targets also provided incentives to value evidence and results.

The sequence of "capacity strengthening first, budget increase second" has obvious benefits in increasing the chances that marginal aid dollars are effectively spent and achieve impact. For many donors, attempts to improve capacity struggle to keep pace with budget increases. This tension is exacerbated by pressure to reduce administrative costs to avoid the perception of waste and profligacy. The UK's ability to implement successive rounds of efficiency reforms over the decade without any noticeable deterioration in its aid program management suggests that this problem was largely avoided.[33]

Given that the increase in the UK's aid budget came with prior warning and occurred over several years, it is noteworthy that no dedicated plan was made for deploying increased aid flows during this time. Instead, the anticipation of budget increases appears to have been an implicit motivation behind the operational model it employed and its pursuit of greater aid effectiveness.

Four features of this model are particularly notable from the perspective of a scaling-up agenda: first, respect for country ownership and significant devolved authority to country offices to ensure that programming decisions were attuned to country needs and program performance; second, a preference for programmatic aid modalities, ideally in the form of general budget support, twinned with policy dialogue as a strategy for improving partner-country governance, especially of public finances and service delivery; third, a long time horizon, reflected in multiyear planning and partnership agreements; and fourth, an effort to leverage the resources and efforts of partner governments and other donors through cooperative programming.

Certain aspects of this model are borne out in the indicators identified in the previous section. The UK scored consistently strongly in its use of programmatic aid and country systems over the period studied, reinforcing the claim

32. DAC (2006a).
33. A 2005–08 efficiency plan included a 10 percent reduction in DFID staff numbers and support-service costs. Additional commitments in 2009–11 included a 5 percent annual cut in administrative costs.

that the UK began the decade with a robust operational model, which it was then able to sustain throughout the phase of budgetary growth. Indeed, its adoption of these approaches preceded their inclusion in the Paris Declaration and is evidence of the UK's influence in shaping the global aid effectiveness agenda. General budget support was promoted by DFID as the ultimate manifestation of country ownership and alignment, but it also had the advantage of providing an efficient means of expending rising aid volumes. This was noted by the parliamentary International Development Committee, which raised concerns in 2008 that general budget support might be seen as an "easy option for spending a rising aid budget."[34]

This same concern has more recently been raised in response to the UK's use of multilateral aid.[35] However, the UK's share of aid devoted to core multilateral contributions remained virtually unchanged between 2000 and 2010. What did change is the allocation of multilateral giving toward agencies with a proven record of effectiveness. This resulted, most prominently, in a stronger commitment for the World Bank's low-income concessionary window, IDA. During its fourteenth and fifteenth replenishments, the UK increased its contribution to IDA by 43 percent and 49 percent, respectively, overtaking the United States to become its largest donor in 2007.[36]

The UK government made the case for increasing contributions to IDA not only by pointing to IDA's strong performance but by highlighting the potential for the UK to exert greater influence on the agency and to motivate necessary reforms. This reflected a broader effort by the UK to enhance the effectiveness of the aid industry through agenda setting, consensus building, and promoting good ideas and practice.[37] One such area that has gained considerable traction is the UK's work over the past decade on social protection and social safety nets, where it has actively sought to collect evidence, build interest in key partner countries, and collaborate with other donors.[38] These efforts were complemented at the political level by the actions of successive prime ministers, Tony Blair and Gordon Brown, each of whom demonstrated a strong personal

34. UK (2008).

35. UK (2011).

36. The United States moved marginally ahead following the IDA16 replenishment in 2010. The share of UK net ODA devoted to IDA rose from an average 6.1 percent from 2000 to 2005, and to 10.5 percent from 2006 to 2010, the latter period reflecting IDA14 and IDA15.

37. This strategy of increasing impact by influencing others reflected the recognition, made repeatedly in DFID White Papers, that the UK could make only a modest difference to global development by operating on its own.

38. UK (2009). Another recent example, taken from just after the period being studied, is the much-cited meta-evaluation on the impact of microfinance commissioned by DFID. See Duvendack and others (2011).

commitment to international development and who used his position to raise the profile of aid volumes and effectiveness on the international agenda.

One significant change in resource allocation not picked up by the preceding analysis is the choice of partner countries. In 2002, DFID pledged to devote 90 percent of its bilateral aid to low-income countries, driven by the goal of having a greater impact on poverty. This meant a shift away from its middle-income country partners, a move that was hurriedly brought forward the following year, when half of the residual 10 percent share was consumed by a new country program in Iraq following the onset of the Second Gulf War.

A further shift in partner choice occurred in the second half of the decade, as DFID's attention honed in on fragile states. This reflects an evolution in the agency's conception of efficient poverty targeting toward long-term threats to development and the underlying causes of poverty. Fragile states account for all five countries that featured in the UK's ten largest bilateral aid programs in 2010 but were not present in 2000: Ethiopia, Pakistan, Nigeria, Democratic Republic of Congo, and Afghanistan. The turn toward fragile states during a period of rising aid volumes was a courageous move. First, the difficulty of using general budget support in these environments challenges DFID's standard operation model and reduces the scope for expeditiously expending budgets. Second, cynicism as to the utility of aiding fragile states invites further scrutiny of the aid program.[39] Third, there was an implicit acknowledgment that achieving transformational impact in these environments would incur a greater cost, requiring a more nuanced explanation of the UK's claims of efficiency, value for money, and management for results.While this essay is focused on the decade ending in 2010, the growth in the UK's aid budget is ongoing, with a commitment to reach the UN's ODA/GNI target of 0.7 percent by 2013. Furthermore, the UK's approach to managing this increase has undergone some significant changes under the new coalition government elected in 2010. Most significant are the two major reviews undertaken in 2010 and 2011 to guide the allocation of bilateral and multilateral aid. These reviews were designed to maximize value for money in the aid program by basing allocations on the estimated costs of achieving results, costs that are informed, in the case of bilateral aid, by an internal bidding process. Notably, these assessments took account of whether the results proposed were scalable and enabled a continued focus on fragile states by making allowances for the cost premium in achieving results in these environments. Other changes ushered in by the new government were the abolition of public service agreements and a significant shift away from

39. See, for instance, Easterly and Freschi (2009) and, more recently, BBC (2011) and Bunting (2011).

general budget support. These changes are attributed to concerns over account-ability and corruption.

Spain

Spain's increase in aid was concentrated between 2004 and 2008. It began with the election of the Social Party government, which campaigned on a pledge to adopt a more cosmopolitan, multilateral, and compassionate foreign policy, drawing on public anger against the previous government's support of the Iraq War. It ended with the onset of the global financial crisis and the European debt crisis.

In contrast to the UK, in Spain the absence of any lead time between the plan and the execution of Spain's aid budget increase, plus the short period over which that increase took place, increased the challenge of using additional aid dollars effectively. Exacerbating this effect was Spain's relative inexperience as a donor. Spain was still a recipient of aid as recently as 1977 and only joined the OECD DAC in 1991. The modest capacity of Spain's aid management was evident in several aspects: its policies, which were incomplete; its evaluation function, which was contracted out; and its choice of aid modalities (specifically, its reliance on technical cooperation and loans, which were deemed more straight-forward to administer than traditional projects and programs).[40] Indeed, the secretary of state for international cooperation described the Spanish development cooperation system in this period as "lagging behind in all areas."[41]

Despite a clear commitment to and motivation for increasing aid levels, a coherent strategy for how aid should be deployed took several years to develop. Arguably, such a strategy only truly emerged with Spain's third four-year master plan, which began in 2009, when aid levels were already in decline. Until then, Spain's operational model retained many of its old features, which led to ad hoc programming decisions. For instance, country strategies were defined in terms of their modalities, rather than their goals, and were void of allocation plans; and multilateral allocations were driven by funding opportunities rather than strategic considerations.

Given the above constraints, it is to Spain's credit that it was able to put in place some major reforms to its operation model over a small space of time. For instance, Spain's use of partner-country systems ramped up quickly from 16 percent to 60 percent over the second half of the decade, despite its limited prior experience in policy dialogue and public finance oversight, outside of middle-income countries. However, other reforms have taken longer to bring

40. In 2003, projects and programs represented only 7 percent of gross ODA, which was half the size of technical cooperation (14 percent) and a third of the size of concessional loans (20 percent).
41. DAC (2007c).

about. For instance, Spain's use of programmatic approaches remains very low (12 percent in 2010), and its efforts to improve its evaluation capability and results management are ongoing. Tight controls of administrative costs during Spain's budget increase may, in hindsight, have hampered additional progress, given the shortage of skilled staff at both headquarters and in country offices.

Arguably the biggest constraint Spain faced in translating more aid into more impact is the diffusion of effort caused by the fragmentation of its aid program. Fragmentation has long been a feature of Spanish aid, both in terms of its institutional organization and its aid allocations. In 2009, Spanish ODA was programmed through fourteen government ministries, seventeen autonomous regions, and approximately 8,000 local authorities. Spain's official aid agency, AECI—itself something of an artifact, having been formed of several institutions whose traditions have persisted—accounted for only 19 percent of Spanish aid. An equivalent share was the responsibility of subnational institutions, which channel half their aid via NGOs—themselves highly independent actors. The degree of institutional autonomy is so extreme that it is common for Spain's aid program to be represented by multiple independent offices in partner countries, each a satellite of a distinct domestic institution.

Over the decade the number of countries receiving aid from Spain increased from an already high 98 to 127. Successive master plans sought to make sense of this multitude of relationships by designating priority status to individual partner countries, but to no obvious effect. For instance, the third master plan identifies 50 priority partner countries, a list that simultaneously excludes 26 countries in which Spain had a significant presence—according to the OECD DAC definition—and includes 24 countries in which it didn't.[42]

A similar pattern is apparent in the distribution of Spanish aid across sectors. The share of Spanish aid spent in sectors in which it has a revealed comparative advantage declined over the decade, from 63 percent to 58 percent—the second lowest among OECD DAC members.[43] The third master plan offered a similarly half-baked account for this spread, putting forward an exhaustive menu of areas in which Spanish aid should focus, composed of twelve sectors, four areas for special attention, and five cross-cutting issues.

This level of fragmentation presents obvious constraints to the achievement of development impact. Interventions tend to be small and unconnected; opportunities for learning across the aid program are limited; and the various institutions that make up Spain's aid architecture do not feel bound to the same vision,

42. The OECD DAC measure of fragmentation captures the importance of a donor from a recipient's perspective. A relationship is deemed significant when a donor is among the fewest possible number of donors that can cumulatively account for at least 90 percent of a recipient's aid. See DAC (2009).

43. Belgium's is the lowest.

despite the efforts of the federal government to define a common agenda. This argument can equally be turned around: the absence of a better strategy for how to achieve impact may have contributed to a growing level of fragmentation over the past decade. Spain's growing ambition for influence found its clearest expression in the broadening of its aid program's reach, rather than in leadership of particular development issues or deepened ties with select partner countries.

Arguably the most propitious element of Spain's aid increase has been its use of the multilateral system. The share of Spain's aid program devoted to core multilateral funding remained relatively constant over the decade, but the share routed through multilateral organizations as earmarked funds rose to the highest within the OECD DAC.[44] This resulted in Spain having the second highest share of its aid going through the multilateral system, coupled with the more dubious honor of the largest ratio of non-core to core funding, at 183 percent.

Spain's extensive use of the multilateral system reflects both an ideological preference for working with others in the international arena and a pragmatic approach to seeking greater development impact. Delivering aid via multilateral institutions was perceived as a means "to enhance the quality of aid through large-scale actions with longer time frames."[45] But Spain's bilateral aid program could not achieve this, given its widely acknowledged weaknesses.

The most ambitious and strategic element of Spain's multilateral aid was the creation of the Spain-UNDP MDG Achievement Fund in 2006. Endowed initially with $700 million from the Spanish aid program, the fund was intended to accelerate progress toward the MDGs by supporting "innovative actions with the potential for wide replication and high impact in select countries and sectors."[46] Furthermore, all programs would be delivered jointly by multiple (on average, six) UN agencies, to advance progress on interagency harmonization in accordance with what would become the "delivering as one" initiative. Despite these noble intentions, midterm evaluations and a recent peer review describe unsatisfactory progress.[47] These are attributed to both the numerous flaws in the design of the fund and the capacity constraints of the UNDP, which have affected the fund's oversight and the monitoring of activities on the ground.

United States

At the 2002 Monterrey conference, President George W. Bush set out a radical vision for an increase in U.S. foreign assistance. All new funds would be

---

44. Historical data on the use of earmarked funding are incomplete. But high levels of earmarking are seen as a new phenomenon, so it is fair to assume that Spain's use of earmarking has increased.

45. DAC (2007c, p. 39).

46. UNDP (2006, p. 1).

47. DAC (2011a).

channeled through a new Millennium Challenge Account, administered by the soon to be established Millennium Challenge Corporation (MCC).

This was significant in two related respects. First, the MCC model was deliberately designed to bring about transformative impact in developing countries and presented a persuasive case for how this might be achieved. The agency would invest large sums of money in poor but well-governed countries on select projects that had undergone rigorous cost-benefit analysis, that were backed up by strong evidence and research, and whose beneficiaries would be counted in the hundreds of thousands, if not millions. Furthermore, projects would be multiyear efforts and country owned and implemented.

Second, the MCC model would serve as an alternative to the U.S.'s traditional approach to aid giving. The design of the MCC was in many respects a reaction to that model, whose weaknesses have been well documented. Those weaknesses include the balancing of multiple objectives epitomized by the antediluvian U.S. Foreign Assistance Act, the aid program's legal foundation, which lists 140 priorities and 400 special directives for their implementation; a system of earmarks and an approach to budgeting that distorts allocations, is deaf to country needs, and fuels unpredictability; a myopic approach to accountability and results management, which stresses project performance over impact; and a weak and understaffed lead agency in USAID. The creation of the MCC as a separate entity, with its own separate legal foundation, agency, and processes immediately relieved it of these various constraints.[48] By 2005 it was envisaged that the MCC would be responsible for administering $5 billion of aid a year, or roughly a third of U.S. foreign assistance, putting the differences between the two approaches in sharp relief.

However, this vision was never fully realized. Despite a rapid increase in the volume of U.S. assistance, outstripping the commitments made by the government, the MCC today is only a fraction of what it was envisaged to be. Ten years after Monterrey, only $3.2 billion has been dispersed by the agency, and annual appropriations have settled below $1 billion a year, representing around 3 percent—as opposed to 33 percent—of U.S. foreign assistance. Even this more modest amount has recorded some impressive results and at a reasonable scale: 188,846 farmers trained and 3,074 enterprises assisted in agriculture and irrigation; 1,162.9 kilometers of roads rehabilitated or constructed; 353,293 rural hectares formalized through land reforms; 300 water points constructed; and 2,603 instructors trained or certified and 155,513 students benefited

---

48. The MCC's creation exacerbated one additional weakness of the U.S. model: the fragmentation of the U.S. aid program across multiple departments and agencies and the weak coordination across these bodies.

Figure 3-3. *Normalized Net Official Development Assistance,*
OECD DAC Countries, 2000–10[a]

Millions of constant 2010 U.S. dollars

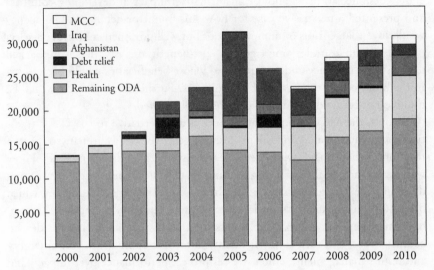

Source: DAC (2012); USAID (2005, 2008, 2012).
a. All official development assistance reflects disbursements (other than for health, where only commitment data are available).

through education investment.[49] However, the scale of impact is undoubtedly limited by the volume of resources appropriated to the agency.

While the MCC cannot account for a significant share of the increase in U.S. assistance, neither, it turns out, can the much-maligned traditional model. Between 2000 and 2007, the bulk of the growth in the aid budget can be attributed to four ends—Afghanistan, Iraq, debt relief, and health sector spending—each representing a departure from the standard aid program (figure 3-3).

An analysis of U.S. aid to Afghanistan and Iraq is not attempted here. It is certainly possible to distinguish elements of these country programs that were brought to scale, but the blurring of development and security objectives in these cases calls into question the applicability of the scaling lens used elsewhere in this essay.[50] One effect of the two country programs was to pass responsibility for aid management and delivery toward the Department of Defense, an

49. MCC (2011).
50. Two of the most celebrated development programs in Afghanistan are the National Solidarity Program and the Basic Package of Health Services. Both explicitly incorporated and executed a scaling-up strategy and were partially financed by U.S. foreign assistance.

agency with little experience in delivering aid that scores poorly on at least one international assessment of aid agency effectiveness.[51] Its share of U.S. foreign assistance peaked at 19 percent in 2005.

Of the four ends, spending on health demonstrated the clearest application of a scaling approach. Over the course of the decade, aid to the health sector rose eightfold from under $800 million to over $6 billion a year. Most of this increase was devoted to two presidential initiatives: the President's Emergency Plan for AIDS Relief (PEPFAR) and the President's Malaria Initiative (PMI).

PEPFAR is the largest international health initiative to fight a single disease in history. It was launched in 2003 with the explicit aim of combating HIV/AIDS by scaling up treatment, prevention, and care interventions in partner countries. By the end of the decade, it had exceeded its scale-based targets. In 2010 alone it was responsible for providing 3.2 million patients with antiretroviral treatment (ART) and a further 1.5 million through U.S. contributions to the Global Fund; for providing 600,000 women with drugs to prevent mother-to-child transmission of HIV, resulting in an estimated 114,000 babies born free of the disease; and for providing care to over 11 million people, including approximately 3.8 million orphans and vulnerable children. PEPFAR's large size relative to collective global efforts—approximately two-thirds of patients in developing countries on ART can be accounted for by U.S. assistance—means that the initiative can claim significant responsibility for progress in fighting the disease, including a steady decline in the number of HIV/AIDS–related deaths.

Sustaining the reach of PEPFAR depends on ongoing financing, which remains relatively secure thanks to bipartisan support. Extending treatment to all individuals living with HIV/AIDS and achieving the U.S. goal of an AIDS-free generation will incur a far greater cost, one that will likely have to draw more heavily on partner countries than on existing cost shares.[52] Sustaining impact also depends on building integrated health programs and a strong workforce in partner countries—two objectives that have belatedly been integrated into PEPFAR's strategy.

The PMI was launched in 2005 with a similar objective of fighting malaria in Africa by scaling up (four) proven interventions for treatment and prevention. Cumulative results to 2010 include the distribution of 30.3 million bed nets, 16.1 million rapid diagnostic tests, and 67.5 million treatments. In addition, in 2010, PMI was responsible for the spraying of 6.7 million houses with insecticides, protecting over 27 million people. Significant progress has also been made in scaling up training and the capacity of health systems. In contrast to PEPFAR, the PMI represents a smaller share of global efforts, making

51. Birdsall, Kharas, and Perakis (2011).
52. UNAIDS (2012).

the attribution of results less straightforward. Nevertheless, there is growing evidence of the success of global efforts as a whole: malaria deaths are significantly down and reported cases of the disease are also declining. Moreover, recent data reveal a substantial reduction in infant mortality in a number of African countries, for which malaria interventions likely account for a large share.[53]

Both of these initiatives were able to avoid some of the weaknesses of the traditional U.S. aid model, partly by virtue of the presidential support they enjoyed. In each case objectives were clearly defined, efforts were focused on a small set of partner countries, and new mechanisms for coordination were established among U.S. agencies. In other respects, weaknesses of the traditional model persisted: the use of earmarks, the establishment of project-implementation units, a preference against using country systems and program-based approaches, and a tendency to go it alone rather than working with other donors. These are borne out in the indicators of overall U.S. assistance, many of which went from bad to worse over the decade: use of programmatic approaches fell from 27 percent to 18 percent, while the use of country systems fell from 11 percent to a paltry 4 percent; the U.S. multilateral funding share halved, from 24 percent to 12 percent; and cooperative activities fell from 34 percent to 23 percent.

It is notable that U.S. success in scaling up in the health sector, especially with HIV/AIDS, has been in an area that lends itself to top-down planning, where interventions are largely homogeneous and the challenge to achieving scale lies particularly in raising sufficient financial resources and overcoming logistical constraints. This undoubtedly plays to U.S. strengths as a donor. Equally significant is that the United States was responsible for much of the pioneering work in tackling HIV/AIDS in the developing world. For instance, the United States has been a long-term provider of assistance to two of the largest indigenous NGOs working on HIV/AIDS in Uganda, which have served as models for the rest of Africa.[54] Nevertheless, questions concerning the sustainability of PEPFAR's impact rightfully linger, as they should for any donor-led program of such a grand scale.

One effect of the growth in aid volumes occurring outside of the traditional aid model was to marginalize and further weaken USAID. USAID began the decade after undergoing a dramatic reduction in staffing in the 1990s. This evisceration continued as governance arrangements for new programs subordinated USAID to other parts of government, undermining the agency's claim to

53. UNICEF (2012).
54. USAID was the first international donor to support the AIDS Information Center (AIC), the first and largest organization in Africa to provide voluntary counseling and training. USAID has also been a major funder of The AIDS Support Organization (TASO), the first indigenous HIV/AIDS organization in Africa, which has provided care and support to affected families since the late 1980s.

development leadership and denying it a mandate that would justify its empowerment. Agency restaffing began belatedly in 2008, but a series of reforms have, in some respects, reinforced the agency's reduced status.[55]

Ireland

The increase in Ireland's aid budget between 2000 and 2008 represents a continuation of a trend that began in the early 1990s, coinciding with the country's rapid economic expansion. By the start of the new millennium, the aid program had already established a well-defined mandate and operational model, despite its modest size. Its salient features included a strong poverty orientation and a focus on the social sectors, which aligned neatly with the emerging MDG agenda. Aid was strongly concentrated on half a dozen least-developed countries in sub-Saharan Africa, in which Ireland had developed experience and expertise.[56] In addition, the program worked in close cooperation with Ireland's large and respected international NGO community, providing it with the means to operate effectively at subnational and community levels in partner countries.

In 2000 the government set a timetable for the attainment of the UN ODA/GNI 0.7 percent target. In the following year it appointed a committee to conduct a review of the aid program and to advise on how the anticipated growth of the aid budget could most effectively be managed. The committee's report reaffirmed the virtues of the existing program, thereby ensuring that its main features would be retained.[57] Its recommendations included a small number of steps to institutionalize these features and to leverage the growth in the aid program to achieve greater effectiveness. These proved influential in shaping how the aid program evolved over subsequent years.

Among the recommendations were changes in the nature of Ireland's relationships with both NGOs and multilateral agencies. In practical terms, this meant narrowing down to fewer partners, increasing the level of engagement and funding to these partners, and putting in place multiyear arrangements to negotiate more ambitious objectives, underpinned by mutual accountability. These relationships increasingly came to resemble those agreed upon with partner countries, and they employed similar criteria to judge effectiveness. Up to a quarter of Irish ODA was channeled through NGOs, a higher share than any other OECD DAC donor.[58] More than half of these funds were accounted for by five major NGO partners. The shift in Ireland's relationship with

55. Interaction (2008); U.S. Department of State (2010).
56. Ethiopia, Lesotho, Mozambique, Tanzania, Uganda, and Zambia.
57. Government of Ireland (2002).
58. DAC (2009).

multilateral agencies was evidenced in its support of UN agencies: partnership agreements were signed with five priority agencies, and symbolic contributions to many others were eliminated.[59]

Ireland also refined its operational model so that it could confidently employ best-practice aid modalities, despite the challenges of working predominantly in low-capacity and often poorly governed environments and despite its own staffing constraints. The default use of programmatic aid and country systems was made possible by a more rigorous approach to monitoring and evaluation and an explicit consideration of risk management. Equally important was ongoing discipline in its degree of country focus, so that high-quality country teams could be relied upon to conduct checks and balances. The recruitment of national auditors within each Irish embassy is also seen as a factor in reinforcing oversight.[60]

Both these sets of reforms laid the groundwork for expending increasing volumes of aid in the same broad pattern as had been pursued before the review but with continued confidence that spending could remain effective and withstand scrutiny. The majority of bilateral aid continued to be devoted to priority countries, but now three additional countries have been promoted to priority status.[61] Ireland's use of programmatic aid rose from 64 percent to 73 percent, while its recorded use of country systems reduced only marginally, from 93 percent to 88 percent. On both of these indicators, Ireland's shares topped the ranks of OECD DAC donors.

After more than a decade of growth in its aid budget, Ireland remains a relatively small donor, responsible for a little over $1 billion in ODA at its peak in 2007 and 2008. Even with well-managed growth, the potential for achieving wide-reaching impact over the previous decade was necessarily limited by the size of its ODA. Nevertheless, Ireland was able to raise its potential for impact by working strategically. Two strategies stand out.

First, Ireland has been a leading proponent of cooperative programming arrangements, enabling its resources to be combined with those of other donors for greater effect. It has been a supporter of multidonor trust funds in several postconflict countries and has engaged in silent partnerships and delegating authority arrangements as part of the Nordic Plus group of like-minded donors. Given Ireland's relatively small size, this strategy may have offered a more satisfying means of leveraging impact than working through the multilateral system.

Second, Ireland has used programmatic aid modalities creatively to exert influence on partner countries' decisionmaking. Programmatic aid—particularly budget support—has traditionally been viewed by donors as, inter alia, a

---

59. Note, however, that the 2009 peer review points to "marginal" contributions to many vertical funds.
60. DAC (2009).
61. Malawi, East Timor, and Vietnam.

means for influencing and ultimately crowding in partner-country resources by securing a seat at the table of budget and sector meetings. However, this relies on donors providing sufficient amounts of money relative to both partner countries and other donors. Ireland has instead used a combination of programmatic modalities to exert influence another way. Within its priority partner countries, Ireland has simultaneously employed budget support, SWAps, and area-based programs (multisector partnerships with local governments). Through this approach, Ireland has been able to feed its local-level experience into national-level policy dialogue, monitor the impact of national policies at subnational levels, and support capacity building to help sustain successful interventions.

Conclusion

In the first decade of this century there was widespread consensus that more aid dollars were needed to meet international development goals, and more aid dollars were forthcoming. Fast forward to today, when discussions on what might replace the MDGs in the post-2015 era have begun, and the difference could not be greater: the consensus now is that official aid volumes are unlikely to grow in the foreseeable future, but this has not caused significant alarm, as perceptions of the role of aid have evolved. Official aid is increasingly seen as only one of a number of flows that support development and as a catalyst, rather than a driver, of the development process. Moreover, expectations as to what additional aid can deliver have been tempered. Aid volumes are one of a number of factors that determine whether development efforts can have transformative impact.

This chapter reinforces this conclusion. The donors that recorded large increases in aid volumes over the previous decade each tell a unique story. While the pressures faced when undergoing budget increases are similar across donors, these pressures prompted a variety of responses: some enhancing, but some mitigating, aid's development impact and its focus on achieving results at scale. While certain trends were found to be commonly associated with increasing aid budgets—less multilateral giving, less country selectivity, and more cooperation on missions and analysis—other factors may help to explain the differences among donors. These include each donor's level of preparedness for budget increases and its degree of risk aversion.

The empirical analysis in this chapter began by speculating what characteristics might connote an aid program that is supportive of a scaling-up agenda. It advocated something akin to a "Paris approach," whereby aid employs modalities that promote country ownership, alignment and harmonization, and a results focus. Less easy to quantify but equally important to this approach is an emphasis on evaluation, on decentralized authority to country-based staff, and on a long time horizon. In theory, this approach facilitates scaling up through a bottom-up process in which successful programming experiences readily emerge from the field, are studied and adapted and then expanded, replicated, and sustained through an organic process of endogenous learning supported by donor headquarters and by partner-country governments.

However, many donors simply don't fit this mold. Furthermore, evidence from the case studies suggests that these donors may have an alternative route for achieving scaled-up impact that is applicable in certain areas. For interventions that are easily standardized, and where the challenge of scaling up lies chiefly in raising finance and the logistics of delivery, a project-based, donor-driven approach may be feasible.[62] The scaling up of antiretroviral treatment through PEPFAR is a case in point and demonstrates how quickly such efforts can be mobilized, notwithstanding important questions regarding the sustainability of impact. This suggests that a stronger division of labor, which matches donor type and problem type, could improve the scope for achieving scaled-up impact without an increase in the overall volume of aid.

While official aid dollars from OECD DAC donors are no longer growing, resources from other actors are. The Busan Partnership, which emerged from the Fourth High Level Forum on Aid Effectiveness, acknowledges both the growing number of players involved in supporting development and the diversity of their approaches. With aid claiming a smaller share in overall resources available to developing countries, its catalytic role could become especially critical, not least in relation to private finance, where the potential to support scaling-up impact is evident.

62. This distinction between types of intervention echoes the contrast made between technical and adaptive problems characterized by Woolcock (2009).

Table 3A-1. *Impact of Change in Aid Volume on Change in Aid Characteristics*[a]

Variables	(1) Specialization by sector	(2) Median project size	(3) Share of aid to multi-laterals	(4) Number of recipients	(5) Specialization by recipient country	(6) Concentration across recipients	(7) Coordination of missions and analysis	(8) Use of programmatic aid	(9) Use of country systems	(10) Country programmable aid share
Change in ODA	-0.040	0.392	-0.371**	0.172**	-0.004	-0.250	1.331**	0.258	-0.507*	-0.084
	(0.078)	(0.502)	(0.161)	(0.078)	(0.056)	(0.342)	(0.480)	(0.261)	(0.281)	(0.096)
	-0.511	0.781	-2.299	2.198	-0.079	-0.730	2.771	0.991	-1.804	-0.874
Initial ODA	0.000	-0.000	-0.000	0.000***	-0.000	-0.000	-0.000***	0.000	0.000	-0.000
	(0.000)	(0.000)	(0.000)	(0.000)	(0.000)	(0.000)	(0.000)	(0.000)	(0.000)	(0.000)
	0.543	-0.712	-1.658	2.996	-1.235	-0.579	-2.497	0.557	0.077	-0.113
Initial quality	-0.160**	-0.107	-0.037	-0.001***	-0.084***	-0.300**	-0.869***	-0.406*	-0.400**	-0.051*
	(0.063)	(0.186)	(0.057)	(0.000)	(0.027)	(0.130)	(0.143)	(0.200)	(0.156)	(0.029)
	-2.546	-0.577	-0.638	-6.499	-3.165	-2.302	-6.058	-2.027	-2.568	-1.751
Constant	0.114**	0.044	0.033	0.082***	0.069***	0.053	0.459***	0.184**	0.334***	0.041*
	(0.049)	(0.054)	(0.024)	(0.011)	(0.023)	(0.031)	(0.064)	(0.084)	(0.081)	(0.022)
	2.324	0.817	1.369	7.562	2.956	1.738	7.123	2.187	4.099	1.851
Observations	21	21	23	23	23	23	21	22	22	23
R-squared	0.395	0.180	0.275	0.723	0.348	0.220	0.738	0.312	0.353	0.211

Source: Author's calculations based on OECD (2012b).

*** $p < 0.01$, ** $p < 0.05$, * $p < 0.1$.

a. Standard errors in parentheses. Changes are calculated using compound annual growth rate.

References

Atisophon, Vararat, and others. 2011. "Revisiting MDG Cost Estimates from a Domestic Resource Mobilisation Perspective." Working Paper 306. OECD Development Center (www.oecd.org/social/povertyreductionandsocialdevelopment/49301301.pdf).

Banerjee, Abhijit V., and Esther Duflo. 2011. *Poor Economics: A Radical Rethinking of the Way to Fight Global Poverty*. New York: PublicAffairs.

Barder, Owen. 2006. "Are the Planned Increases in Aid Too Much of a Good Thing?" Working Paper 90. Center for Global Development (www.cgdev.org/files/8633_file_WP90edited.pdf).

BBC. 2011. "Ethiopia Using Aid as Weapon of Oppression." *Newsnight.*

Berg, Andrew, and others. 2012. *Enhancing Development Assistance to Africa: Lessons from Scaling-Up Scenarios*. International Monetary Fund.

Birdsall, Nancy, Homi Kharas, and Rita Perakis. 2011. "Measuring the Quality of Aid." Center for Global Development, Brookings.

Borger, Julian. 2009. "Calls Grow within G8 to Expel Italy as Summit Plans Descend into Chaos." *Guardian,* July 6.

Bunting, Madeleine. 2011. "Value for Money Is Not Compatible with Increasing Aid to 'Fragile States.'" Poverty Matters blog. *Guardian,* April 11.

Clemens, Michael A., Charles J. Kenny, and Todd J. Moss. 2004. "The Trouble with the MDGs: Confronting Expectations of Aid and Development Success." Working Paper 40. Center for Global Development.

DAC (Development Assistance Committee). 2001. "United Kingdom (2001) Peer Review." OECD.

———. 2002a. "Spain (2002) DAC Peer Review." OECD.

———. 2002b. "United States (2002) Peer Review." OECD.

———. 2003. "Ireland (2003) Peer Review." OECD.

———. 2006a. "United States (2006) Peer Review." OECD.

———. 2006b. Statement made by Richard Manning, Seventy-Third Meeting.

———. 2007a. "Country-Based Scaling Up: Assessment of Progress and Agenda for Action." OECD.

———. 2007b. "Joint Ministerial Committee of the Boards of Governors of the Bank and the Fund on the Transfer of Real Resources to Developing Countries. Country Based Scaling Up: Assessment of Progress and Agenda for Action."

———. 2007c. "Spain (2007) DAC Peer Review." OECD.

———. 2009. "Ireland (2009) DAC Peer Review." OECD.

———. 2010. "United Kingdom (2010) Peer Review." OECD.

———. 2011a. "Spain (2011) DAC Peer Review." OECD.

———. 2011b. "United States (2011) Peer Review." OECD.

———. 2012. "Annual Aggregates Database." OECD.

Development Committee. 2006. "Joint Ministerial Committee of the Boards of Governors of the Bank and the Fund on the Transfer of Real Resources to Developing Countries. Statement made by Richard Manning."

Duvendack, Maren, and others. 2011. "What Is the Evidence of the Impact of Microfinance on the Well-Being of Poor People?" *Systematic Review.* UK Department for International Development (www.dfid.gov.uk/r4d/PDF/Outputs/SystematicReviews/Microfinance 2011Duvendackreport.pdf).

Easterly, William. 2006. *The White Man's Burden: Why the West's Efforts to Aid the Rest Have Done So Much Ill and So Little Good*. New York: Penguin.

Easterly, William, and Laura Freschi. 2009. "Why Does British Foreign Aid Prefer Poor Governments over Poor People?" *Aid Watch* (blog) (http://aidwatchers.com/2009/03/why-does-british-foreign-aid-prefer-poor-governments-over-poor-people/).

Filmer, Deon. 2004. "If You Build It, Will They Come? School Availability and School Enrollment in 21 Poor Countries." Policy Research Working Paper 3340. World Bank.

Government of Ireland. 2002. *Report of the Ireland Aid Review Committee* (www.irishaid.gov.ie/Uploads/irlaidreview.pdf).

Hartmann and others. 2013. 'Scaling Up of Programs for the Rural Poor: IFAD's Experience, Lessons, and Prospects." Working Paper 49. Global Economy and Development, Brookings.

Interaction. 2008. "Transformational Diplomacy: The 'F Process.'" Policy brief (www.interaction.org/sites/default/files/1/POLICY%20REPORTS/FOREIGN%20ASSISTANCE%20BRIEFING%20BOOK/Sec9_InterAction_Foreign_Assistance_Briefing_Book.pdf).

Kharas, Homi. 2010. "The Hidden Aid Story: Ambition Breeds Success." Brookings (www.brookings.edu/research/opinions/2010/02/19-foreign-aid-kharas).

Linn, Johannes F., and others. 2010. "Scaling Up the Fight against Rural Poverty: An Institutional Review of IFAD's Approach." Working Paper 43. Global Economy and Development, Brookings (www.brookings.edu/~/media/research/files/papers/2010/10/ifad%20linn%20kharas/10_ifad_linn_kharas.pdf).

MCC (Millennium Challenge Corporation). 2011. *Annual Report: A Gateway to Opportunity.* Washington.

OECD. 2012a. "Aid to Developing Countries Falls Because of Global Recession" (www.oecd.org/development/developmentaidtodevelopingcountriesfallsbecauseofglobalrecession.htm).

———. 2012b. "StatExtracts."

Park, Kang-Ho. 2011. "New Development Partners and a Global Development Partnership." In *Catalyzing Development: A New Vision for Aid,* edited by Homi J. Kharas, Woojin Jung, and Koji Makino. Brookings.

Pritchett, Lant. 2010. "Lant Pritchett on What Obama Got Right about Development." Aid Watch blog (http://aidwatchers.com/2010/09/lant-pritchett-on-what-obama-got-right-about-development).

Sachs, Jeffrey. 2005. *The End of Poverty: Economic Possibilities for Our Time.* New York: Penguin.

UK (United Kingdom). 2008. "Working Together to Make Aid More Effective." House of Commons, International Development Committee. Ninth Report of Session 2007–08.

———. 2009. "Promoting Social Transfers: DFID and the Politics of Influencing." Working Paper 32. Department for International Development.

———. 2011. House of Commons, International Development Committee. Third Report. Department for International Development Annual Report & Resource Accounts 2009–10.

UN (United Nations). 2002. "Monterrey Consensus on Financing for Development" (www.un.org/esa/ffd/monterrey/MonterreyConsensus.pdf).

———. 2005. *Investing in Development: A Practical Plan to Achieve the Millennium Development Goals.* Millenium Project.

———. 2010. "The Global Partnership for Development at a Critical Juncture." MDG Gap Taskforce Report.

———. 2011. "The Global Partnership for Development: Time to Deliver." MDG Gap Taskforce Report.

————. 2012. "Integrated Implementation Framework: Tracking Support for the MDGs" (http://iif.un.org).

UNAIDS. 2012. "Factsheet: Getting to Zero" (www.unaids.org/en/media/unaids/contentassets/documents/epidemiology/2012/201207_FactSheet_Global_en.pdf).

UNDP. 2006. "UNDP/Spain Millennium Development Goals Achievement Fund Framework Document."

UNICEF. 2012. "2012 Progress Report on Committing to Child Survival: A Promise Renewed."

USAID. 2005. "U.S. Overseas Loans and Grants." Greenbook.

————. 2008. "U.S. Overseas Loans and Grants." Greenbook.

————. 2012. "U.S. Overseas Loans and Grants." Greenbook.

U.S. Department of State. 2010. "The First Quadrennial Diplomacy and Development Review (QDDR): Leading through Civilian Power."

Uvin, P., P. S. Jain, and L. D. Brown. 2000. "Think Large and Act Small: Toward a New Paradigm for NGO Scaling Up." *World Development* 28, no. 8): 1409–19.

Woolcock, Michael. 2009. "Global Poverty and Inequality: A Brief Retrospective and Prospective Analysis." Working Paper 78. Manchester: Brooks World Poverty Institute.

4

Scaling Up Impact:
Vertical Funds and Innovative Governance

DAVID GARTNER AND HOMI KHARAS

The challenge of scaling up for development requires innovative institutions with the capacity to leverage the contributions of diverse stakeholders, to support truly country-driven strategies, and to closely link financing to results. This chapter addresses the question of whether large-scale development impact can be achieved by channeling aid resources through vertical funds and, if so, what properties of vertical funds are critical to enabling this success. Vertical funds with more participatory governance structures and a closer link between performance and funding seem to be demonstrating more success in the areas of resource mobilization, learning, and impact. In this chapter we highlight the dramatic expansion of vertical funds over the last decade and analyze institutions in the areas of global health, education, and agriculture.

Vertical funds are global programs for allocating official development assistance that focus specifically on an issue or theme. According to the World Bank's definition, they are "partnerships and related initiatives whose benefits are intended to cut across more than one region of the world and in which the partners: (a) reach explicit agreement on objectives; (b) agree to establish a new (formal or informal) organization; (c) generate new products or services; and (d) contribute dedicated resources to the program."[1] They contrast with more traditional channels for development assistance, which focus on the needs of

1. World Bank (2004a, p. 2).

each partner country through country-based, horizontal, funding allocations. Although vertical funds have a long history, only since the late 1990s have they become the international community's funding vehicle of choice. There are now approximately twenty-seven multilateral vertical funds, of which thirteen have been created in the last fifteen years. In addition, there has been verticalization within the assistance programs of several Development Assistance Committee (DAC) countries, most notably the President's Emergency Plan for AIDS Relief (PEPFAR) in the United States.

Proponents of vertical funds point to several explanatory factors: one, the innovations that can be introduced by a new agency unencumbered by out-moded bureaucratic processes; two, a results focus, which has a clear causal chain between resources, interventions, and outcomes and which rewards partner-country contributions and effectiveness; three, transparency; and four, an appeal to the public and to political leaders through clear goals.[2] But vertical funds also have detractors, who view them as contributing to the fragmenta-tion of the international aid architecture and as increasing coordination costs for partner countries. With the clear focus of these funds on specific areas, their success at resource mobilization is sometimes viewed as coming at the expense of draining resources from other areas.

Amidst this ongoing debate between proponents and skeptics of vertical funds, there is relatively little analysis of the comparative advantages among vertical fund institutions. In this chapter we examine vertical funds across three sectors: global health, education, and agriculture. Significantly, the institutions we focus on vary in terms of their institutional home and degree of autonomy, their level of partic-ipation in governance, and their adoption of performance-based approaches. In the global health context, the Global Fund for AIDS, Tuberculosis and Malaria combines a governance structure that includes diverse stakeholders with a fairly strong country-driven process and a close link between financing and perfor-mance on program objectives. In the realm of global education, the Global Part-nership for Education includes a global structure of diverse stakeholders but is hosted within the World Bank, is working to strengthen its country-level pro-cesses, and is in the early stages of implementing a closer tie between performance and results. Within the field of agricultural development, the International Fund for Agricultural Development (IFAD) is an institution established in an earlier era within the United Nations, while the Global Agriculture and Food Security Program (GAFSP) is a new institution, housed in the World Bank, which incor-porates more inclusive governance but not performance-based funding.

The next section reviews the literature on global funds and documents the dramatic emergence of a new generation of vertical funds over the last decade.

2. Isenman and Shakow (2010).

In a later section we analyze the innovative governance structures of these institutions. Following that, we compare the performance of vertical funds in health, education, and agriculture in scaling up development impact.[3] Performance is reviewed along three dimensions: the mobilization of money, institutional learning and innovation, and impact on the ground. We argue that performance on each of these dimensions is in turn influenced by novel features of recent vertical funds, particularly the engagement of civil society in governance structures, the strength of country-based planning mechanisms, and the link between financing and results. The purpose of this chapter is to examine how well different vertical funds have performed given the challenges that they were established to address. We do not examine whether the goals for each vertical fund are themselves properly specified but rather focus on the links between specific features of these funds and their ability to deliver results in line with their core mission.

The Emergence of Vertical Funds

Vertical funds have a long pedigree and some notable successes. One of the first vertical funds was the Consultative Group on International Agricultural Research (CGIAR), a body established in 1971 as a partnership of fifteen agricultural research centers around the world to apply cutting-edge science to foster sustainable agricultural growth to benefit the poor. After the success of public-private research partnerships to achieve food self-sufficiency in developing countries (the Rockefeller and Ford foundations had established centers in Mexico, Colombia, India, and the Philippines), CGIAR was set up to scale up and sustain the impact of these bodies by transmitting the research to other countries while providing a more sustainable funding basis for existing research centers and broadening the number of research centers that would be supported.[4] CGIAR was born out of a strongly felt need to solve a critical global problem, namely a shortage of food and the prevalence of poverty, hunger, and famine in developing countries, especially in rural areas. In the same vein, a new generation of vertical funds has emerged, as the international community confronts a range of global challenges.

Global funds became the vehicle of choice when donors looked for mechanisms to implement the Millennium Development Goals (MDGs). In health, education, agriculture, and climate change, for example, the MDGs created a focal point for plans and resources needed to achieve the targets. Vertical funds

---

3. Climate is the other sector where important vertical funds are now operating. But the largest and newest of these, the Clean Technology Fund and the Strategic Climate Fund, only came to scale in 2010 and are too new to be evaluated in any meaningful way.

4. The most famous success was the Green Revolution, which was brought about by Norman Borlaug's development of semidwarf, high-yielding wheat varieties.

Figure 4-1. *Vertical Fund Commitments as a Share of ODA Commitments and Country Programmable Aid, 2000–10*

Percent

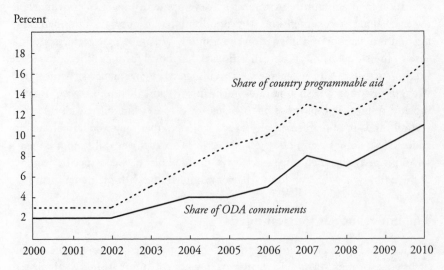

Source: Global Fund (2005); IFAD (2010a); OECD (2012b, table 3a); CTF (2009); SCF (2009); CGIAR (2004, 2010); EFA FTI (2007, 2010a); GAVI Alliance (2001–06); GAFSP (2011a); OECD (2012a).

provided a verifiable mechanism for implementation of these plans and for the allocation of donor money for specified purposes. Such earmarking could not be achieved by using the traditional channels represented by international financial institutions because these use horizontal, country-based, allocation models, rather than sector-specific funding allocations. With country-based allocations, it is not possible to accurately predict how much money would actually be allocated to any sector, such as health or education, for example.

The growing importance of these vertical funds in the broader development universe has been quite striking. At an aggregate level, the top ten global funds now account for around 14 percent of total country programmable aid.[5] The share has grown rapidly, from an insignificant proportion of 3 percent of total country programmable aid from DAC members and multilateral institutions in the year 2000 (figure 4-1).[6] Nine of the largest vertical funds now each account for over $500 million in official development assistance (ODA) annually (table 4-1).

5. Country programmable aid (CPA) is a concept introduced by DAC to denote those elements of aid actually available for country programs and projects (as opposed to items like debt relief, student loans, and refugee assistance in donor countries that are part of ODA but not of CPA).
6. DAC comprises twenty-three of the largest bilateral donor countries and the European Union.

Table 4-1. *Commitments of Major Vertical Funds, 2000–10*
Millions of U.S. dollars

Vertical fund	2000	2001	2002	2003	2004	2005	2006	2007	2008	2009	2010
CGIAR	331	337	357	381	437	452	458	506	542	603	657
CTF	...	...	...	...	...	...	...	...	...	216	1,889
SCF	...	...	...	...	...	...	...	...	...	287	1,750
EFA FTI	...	...	...	...	49	86	486	421	393	245	322
GAFSP	...	...	...	...	...	...	...	...	...	...	643
PEPFAR	...	...	...	...	1,730	2,358	2,745	3,794	5,191	5,680	5,826
IFAD	410	365	317	361	369	429	436	534	520	569	720
GAVI	..	26	113	132	198	182	208	968	748	501	783
GEF	485	459	395	499	619	583	557	1,062	814	711	530
GFATM	...	...	...	993	822	1,452	1,767	2,510	2,233	4,168	3,128
Total	1,226	1,188	1,181	2,365	4,224	5,542	6,656	9,795	10,441	12,981	16,247

Source: Global Fund (2005); GEF (2000); IFAD (2010a); OECD (2012b, table 3a); PEPFAR (2012); CTF (2009); SCF (2009); EFA FTI (2007, 2010a); GAVI Alliance (2001–06); GAFSP (2011a).

Quality of Vertical Funds

Vertical funds generally perform quite well in cross-donor comparisons of aid effectiveness.[7] Table 4-2 is an assessment of the quality of official development assistance. Aid quality is divided into four dimensions: maximizing efficiency, fostering institutions, reducing the transactional burden on recipients, and transparency and learning. The table shows the average scores of bilateral and multilateral funds and, within the multilateral category, the scores of vertical funds, development banks, and other aid agencies.[8]

In each dimension, thirty-one donor countries and large multilateral agencies are ranked against each other, based on a variety of criteria. The table shows that multilateral institutions generally outperform bilateral institutions across all categories, while vertical funds do better than many other multilateral agencies on average. They not only score high marks on criteria such as specialization but also perform well in terms of the share of funds going to well-governed countries and to projects with low administrative costs. However, vertical funds score poorly on criteria like the significance of the aid relationship and the share of aid being recorded on government budgets. Overall, the data suggest that vertical

7. Birdsall, Kharas, and Perakis (2011).
8. Scores are presented as the number of standard deviations away from the mean. That is, a negative score implies that an agency performs less well than the average for all donors.

Table 4-2. *Average Rankings by Donor Type for Each Aid Quality Dimension, 2009*

Donor type	Maximizing efficiency	Fostering institutions	Reducing burden	Transparency and learning
Bilateral	−0.03	−0.06	−0.09	0.01
Multilateral[a]	0.15	0.15	0.42	−0.08
Vertical funds	0.24	−0.01	0.57	−0.28
Multilateral banks	0.43	0.33	0.96	0.04
Other	−0.18	0.05	−0.19	−0.09

Source: Birdsall, Kharas, and Perakis (2011, table 11).

a. The vertical funds in this analysis are the International Fund for Agricultural Development; the Global Fund to Fight AIDS, Tuberculosis, and Malaria; GAVI (formerly the Global Alliance for Vaccines and Immunization); and the Global Environment Facility. Multilateral banks include the Asian Development Fund; African Development Fund; International Development Association (World Bank); Inter-American Development Bank Special Fund; International Monetary Fund Trust Fund; Organization of the Petroleum Exporting Countries' Fund for International Development; and Nordic Development Fund. Other agencies include two EU agencies and five UN agencies.

funds do well in terms of efficiency but somewhat less well on responsiveness to country priorities. That accords with anecdotal evidence of a focus by vertical funds on short-term results instead of on long-term institutional dimensions.

Similar conclusions emerge from the multilateral aid review conducted by the UK's Department for International Development (DFID). In that review, multilateral donor agencies were scored in absolute terms as to their strengths and weaknesses. Among the indicators used by DFID are some that are loosely linked to the development contribution made by an agency (link to international objectives, focus on poor countries, contribution to development results) and others that are linked to the organizational strength of the agency (cost and value consciousness, strategic management, transparency and accountability). We averaged these indicator scores for a dozen vertical funds and seven other multilateral financial institutions (figure 4-2).[9] Vertical funds do very well in terms of their contribution to development (especially the newer ones), and some also do well in terms of organizational strength. For the most part, international financial institutions show the reverse: stronger performance in terms of organizational strength than in terms of contribution to development (they lie to the right of the forty-five-degree line in figure 4-2).

9. DFID uses a four-point scale, with 1 = unsatisfactory; 2 = weak; 3 = satisfactory; 4 = strong. Note that DFID also includes other indicators that do not fall into these broad categories. These are excluded from figure 4-2.

Figure 4-2. *Quality of Vertical Funds and International Financial Institutions*

Mean contribution to development score

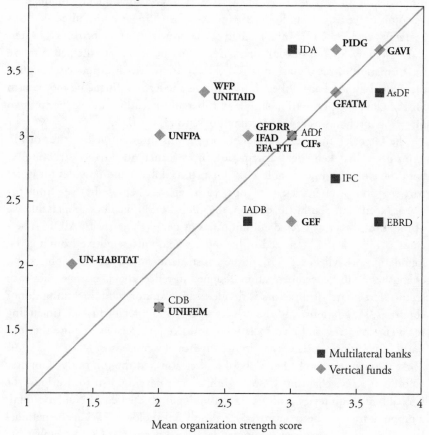

Source: Authors' estimates, based on DFID (2010).

Comparing Vertical Funds across Sectors

Modern vertical funds have experimented with new governance structures at both the global and local levels that have contributed to their performance. This section reviews the key characteristics of those structures in order to better assess their potential role in shaping the divergent performance outcomes of these vertical funds.

Global Fund to Fight AIDS, Tuberculosis, and Malaria

The Global Fund to Fight AIDS, Tuberculosis, and Malaria was launched in 2002 in response to calls for a comprehensive global response to the AIDS crisis from diverse quarters. The earliest steps toward the creation of such a fund were catalyzed by a bipartisan effort in the U.S. Congress in response to civil society proposals for a new fund to combat AIDS. The G-8 subsequently highlighted its commitment to expanding access to AIDS treatment and United Nations Secretary General Kofi Annan called for action in advance of the UN General Assembly Special Session on AIDS. This special session helped catalyze the formation of the Transitional Working Group, which ultimately designed the Global Fund. Today, the Global Fund is the leading financing mechanism for the global response to malaria and tuberculosis and is among the top two financing mechanisms in the global response to HIV/AIDS.

The Global Fund went further than previous international institutions in terms of multistakeholder participation in its formal governance structures at both the global and national levels.[10] First, the Global Fund provides for wider participation of civil society groups, with separate representatives from the global North and South. In addition, the Global Fund includes a representative of the most directly affected communities of people living with AIDS, tuberculosis, and malaria.[11] Instead of having a single representative from a given foundation or civil society group, the constituency model of the Global Fund establishes a full-fledged delegation designed to reflect the diversity within each sector. The board of directors is divided into a donor bloc (including donor countries, foundations, and the private sector) and a recipient bloc (including recipient countries and civil society groups). Major decisions require the support of two-thirds of each group in the absence of a consensus.

At the national level, the Global Fund established the innovative Country Coordinating Mechanism (CCM). Unlike most development institutions, the Global Fund requires a country seeking funding from the Global Fund to submit a proposal that has been approved by a multistakeholder CCM at the national level. The fund's secretariat recommends that 40 percent of CCM membership consist of nongovernmental organizations, and its guidelines explicitly require that CCM members "be broadly representative of a variety of stakeholders, each representing an active constituency with an interest in fighting one or more of the three diseases."[12] Within the Global Fund's structure the CCM is responsible for developing and submitting proposals that reflect the country's needs, for nominating a principal recipient to lead implementation efforts, and for providing oversight of the implementation of the grant. Although much of the Global Fund's financing is channeled through national institutions, significant financing is also channeled through nongovernmental organizations (NGOs).

10. Bartsch (2007).
11. Bartsch (2007, p. 152).
12. Global Fund (2005, p. 2).

The Global Fund has thus far had impressive success in opening up participation in its country-level processes to diverse nonstate actors. Of the 130 countries funded by the Global Fund, 82 percent had nongovernment actors, representing at least two-fifths of the CCM; 80 percent had at least one private business representative serving on the CCM. NGOs accounted for nearly a quarter of the average membership of these bodies, and people living with the diseases (PLWD) that are the focus of the fund accounted for 8 percent of the average membership. Taken together, NGO, PLWD, faith-based organizations, and the education sector accounted for nearly half of the membership of these bodies.

To ensure independence among these diverse stakeholders, the Global Fund requires that all CCM members representing nongovernment constituencies be selected by their own constituency through a transparent process developed by the constituency itself. Recent case studies of the functioning of the CCMs find that in many countries these institutions contributed to a redefinition of the relationship between civil society and government in the health sector, and in some cases the CCM chair may not be a Ministry of Health official. In Peru, for example, the CCM has evolved through the creation of regional bodies and the development of a conflict-of-interest guide, leading one participant to characterize the national-level process as generating "a dialogue that never before took place."[13] Case studies of forty countries find that the greater the substantive participation of NGOs, the better the CCM performed.[14] This is at least in part because of the seriousness with which the Global Fund supports an inclusive CCM process. For example, in Senegal, the marginalization of civil society in the early years led the fund to threaten to withdraw its funding in 2005.[15] But in less extreme cases, such as South Africa and Gambia, a divided or noninclusive CCM has weakened performance.

Global Partnership for Education

In 2002, at the Kananaskis Summit in Canada, the G-8 committed to creating "a new focus on education for all" and pledged to significantly increase support for basic education.[16] The G-8 also helped to catalyze the creation of a new global partnership based at the World Bank: the Education for All Fast-Track Initiative (FTI). Like the Global Fund, the FTI from the outset sought to establish new country-level coordination mechanisms. Over time it has increasingly sought to leverage the contributions of diverse stakeholders. The FTI's initial approach reflected the principle of rewarding high-performing countries, but only recently has the institution sought to more fully integrate

13. For the guide, see Buffardi, Cabello, and Garcia (2011, p. 8).
14. Global Fund (2008).
15. Cassidy and Leach (2010, p. 37).
16. Kananaskis Summit (2002).

performance-based financing into its work. In 2011 the FTI was renamed the Global Partnership for Education. The Global Partnership for Education provides financing primarily for basic education to countries with endorsed national education plans. It provides financing directly through its Catalytic Fund and contributes indirectly by encouraging other donors to support countries with endorsed plans.

The original framework for the Education for All Fast-Track Initiative provided for governance through a partnership that included donors, recipient countries, nongovernmental organizations, and UN agencies.[17] In 2009 the FTI formally established a board of directors with a composition more heavily weighted toward the donors. An independent midterm evaluation highlights an imbalance between donors and country partners in the governance of the initiative.[18] In 2010 the FTI shifted to equal representation for donors and partner countries and expanded representation for nonstate actors, to include the private sector, the foundation community, and teachers.[19]

The Global Partnership for Education has also relied on country-level processes to guide its work from the outset. The charter of the partnership requires that each country establish a local education group (LEG), which can comprise governments, donors, multilateral agencies, civil society organizations, and other actors working in support of the education sector. With the help of the partnership's support for capacity building, the number of civil society national education councils participating in LEGs increased from eighteen in 2009 to thirty-one in 2011. However, national governments hold the primary responsibility for implementation, and other actors are viewed as serving in a support role.[20] In addition, a local donor group (LDG) for education, composed solely of donors, evaluates government strategy and provides recommendations to the partnership.

The midterm evaluation of the partnership finds that its implementation at the country level was uneven—that the partnership had "remained more of a donor collaboration than a genuine partnership."[21] Reflective of this dynamic, in a number of countries LEGs and LDGs were seen to be indistinct, and in many countries LEGs were not involved in key decisions regarding endorsing the national plan. A more recent evaluation by the secretariat, based on surveys of sixty-one countries, finds that most countries were engaged in some form of joint planning between government ministries of education and the donors on effectiveness targets. However, few countries were working together in monitoring these targets through a joint sector review. A separate review finds that

17. World Bank (2004b).
18. EFA FTI (2009, p. 21).
19. EFA FTI (2010b).
20. Global Campaign for Education (2011, p. 29).
21. EFA FTI (2009, p. xxi).

consultations were generally held only with government ministries of education and finance, but that meaningful participation often did not extend outside the government sphere to nonstate actors.[22]

International Fund for Agricultural Development

At the 1974 World Food Conference in Rome there was agreement that "an International Fund for Agricultural Development should be established immediately to finance agricultural development projects primarily for food production in the developing countries."[23] The World Food Conference itself had been organized in response to the droughts, famines, and food insecurity that had afflicted parts of Africa and Asia in preceding years. The International Fund for Agricultural Development was established in 1977 as an international financial institution within the United Nations system to mobilize resources for agricultural and rural development. This mission emerged from recognition among World Food Conference participants that food insecurity was driven by structural problems associated with rural poverty rather than simply by failures in food production systems.

Unlike some more recently established vertical funds, the International Fund for Agricultural Development (IFAD) does not have formal structures to include nongovernmental organizations in its governance process. IFAD was formed as a partnership between developed countries, OPEC member states, and developing countries, with each of them forming one section of its tripartite membership structure. IFAD's Governing Council currently comprises the 167 IFAD member states, with voting rights partially weighted by contributions to IFAD's operations; approximately one-third of votes are assigned to developing-country members. The second core governance structure is the executive board, with members elected from each of three categories of members according to each bloc's overall share of votes. The executive board has authority over program and project approval, budgetary decisions, and matters relating to policy, pending approval of the Governing Council.

To enhance global-level strategic dialogue with stakeholders in rural development, in 2005 IFAD began working with representatives of small farmers' and rural producers' organizations to create the Farmers' Forum. The forum held its first meeting in 2006 and provides a biennial opportunity for global-level consultation and dialogue with IFAD's stakeholders, to coincide with every second convention of the IFAD Governing Council. Representatives at the forum have observer status during the meetings of the IFAD Governing Council and are invited to deliver a synthesis of their deliberations to a session of the council.

22. Bashir (2009).
23. IFAD (1976, p. 3).

However, IFAD's own evaluation of its partnership with farmers' organizations has identified this relationship as unsatisfactory, because there "is still a lack of organized and ongoing feedback from the meetings between IFAD staff and farmers' organizations at country or regional level." This leads to a key weakness of the forum, namely that "the agenda of the global meeting in conjunction with the Governing Council and the selection of participants are developed late and in an ad hoc manner instead of building upon a continuous process."[24]

At the national level, the Country Strategic Opportunities Programme (COSOP), which was developed by IFAD staff in consultation with government and other stakeholders, frames IFAD's goals and project work. It provides the framework for strategic dialogue on IFAD's operations with key country-level stakeholders in rural development. The COSOP process is intended to ensure that there is wide consultation on opportunities for IFAD-financed projects, to deliver strong project management for results, to ensure that IFAD's operations support the country's own development strategies, and to identify potential synergies and strategic partnerships with other multilateral and bilateral development partners. COSOP also seeks to promote continuous learning through reflection on previous IFAD operations in the country and on lessons learned from wider evaluations of IFAD projects.

Internal evaluations show that IFAD has increased the range and depth of its in-country partnerships with civil society organizations, particularly famers' and rural producers' organizations, which IFAD has identified as key partners.[25] These groups were involved in 81 percent of COSOPs that occurred in the years 2008–09. In 61 percent of COSOPs, they were partners in organizing specific workshops or sat as full members of the country program management teams. In 52 percent of new projects over this period, farmers' or rural producers' organizations were involved as implementing agencies or service providers. However, IFAD has yet to systematize farmers' and rural producers' organization involvement across projects that are not specifically focused on agricultural production or marketing. Areas with lower farmer and producer engagement include projects on rural infrastructure, community development, rural finance, and business services—despite these projects having a significant impact on agricultural development.

Global Agriculture and Food Security Program

The Global Agriculture and Food Security Program (GAFSP) was established following the G-20 meeting in Pittsburgh in September 2009, which sought a multilateral mechanism to assist in the implementation of pledges made at the

24. IFAD (2010b, p. iii).
25. IFAD (2010b, p. i).

G-8 summit in L'Aquila in July 2009. GAFSP's mission is to assist medium- to long-term strategic investments in national and regional agriculture productivity and food security systems—and to do so with greater speed and flexibility than bilateral assistance.

There are two GAFSP financing windows, one that funds public sector projects and another that supports private sector activities. As of June 30, 2011, $897 million had been pledged for the public sector window and $75 million for the private sector window, with pledges made by Australia, Canada, Ireland, South Korea, Spain, the United States, and the Gates Foundation.[26] The public sector financing window is focused on investment and technical assistance projects as part of programs that emerge from sectorwide national or regional consultations. In the case of Africa, such consultations and strategies should be consistent with the framework of the Comprehensive Africa Agriculture Development Programme. GAFSP seeks to foster civil society participation and includes clear and verifiable evidence of stakeholder participation in project design as well as evidence of government commitment to the objectives of the proposal in the form of financial commitments and reform of the policy environment.

GAFSP is organized as a financial intermediary fund administered under the trusteeship of the World Bank. Investments are administered and appraised by supervising entities responsible to GAFSP's Steering Committee, which has formal authority over public window funds. The committee is composed of an equal number of voting members from donor and recipient countries. There are also nonvoting members, who are drawn from potential supervising entities (World Bank, AfDB, ADB, IADB, IFAD, FAO, WFP), the IFC, CSOs (two from Southern CSOs and one from a Northern CSO), and the Special Representative of the UN Secretary General for Food Security and Nutrition. The Steering Committee's decisions are informed by an independent Technical Advisory Committee, which evaluates country proposals according to established assessment criteria and provides recommendations to the Steering Committee. So far, there is little data on the impact of GAFSP's investments. However, GAFSP has allocated 2.5 percent of pledged contributions to in-depth impact evaluations for public sector window investments.[27] The in-depth evaluations will cover about 30 percent of public sector window investments and take place under the auspices of the World Bank's Development Impact Evaluation Initiative.

The International Finance Corporation manages the private sector financing window, under the authority of the GAFSP Steering Committee. Contributors to the window are responsible for investment decisions, which are informed by

---

26. GAFSP (2011a, p. 8).
27. GAFSP (2011b).

a consultative board composed of representatives from academia, civil society, private financial institutions, and development agencies. The private sector window provides short- and long-term credit guarantees, loans, and equity to the private sector intended to support innovative initiatives to enhance agriculture development and food security. Private sector window investments are evaluated through the IFC's internal monitoring and evaluation process.

Assessing the Performance of Vertical Funds

Among vertical funds, there is significant divergence in performance across sectors and across institutions. For example, the DFID review finds the vertical fund for urban development, UN-HABITAT, to be weak in many respects, while a number of global health institutions were given consistently high scores. To gain insight into the dynamics that shape the performance of these institutions, this section compares the performance among vertical funds, with a focus on the health, education, and agriculture sectors. It looks at three indicators of performance: the ability to raise money, learning and innovation, and impact and development results. These indicators reflect the capacity of these institutions to leverage financial commitments for their mission, to adapt and foster improvements in their own work, and to deliver on their ultimate mission in terms of generating results.

Ability to Raise Money

How important are vertical funds in raising money for each sector? Figure 4-3 disaggregates the three sectors. It looks at vertical fund commitments (see table 4-1) compared to commitments in each sector from all DAC donors and multilateral agencies. In health, the comparison is to the sum of two categories provided separately by DAC: health and population programs and reproductive health programs. In education, the comparison is to basic education. Agriculture comprises agriculture, forestry, and fishing.

The results are striking. In health, three vertical funds—the Global Fund for Aids, Tuberculosis and Malaria, the U.S. President's Emergency Plan for AIDS Relief (PEPFAR), and the Global Alliance for Vaccines and Immunization (GAVI)—have become dominant funding channels, now accounting for about 60 percent of all health ODA. Vertical funds have been the key driver of the expansion of global health funding over the last decade. Overall, DAC global health funding nearly quadrupled between 2002 and 2010, and vertical funds accounted for two-thirds of that growth. From a base of less than $1 billion in 2002, global health vertical funds expanded to over $10 billion by 2010. This dramatic expansion was largely driven by new commitments to invest in

Figure 4-3. *Sectoral Commitments of Vertical Funds as a Share of CPA in That Sector, 2000–10*

Percent

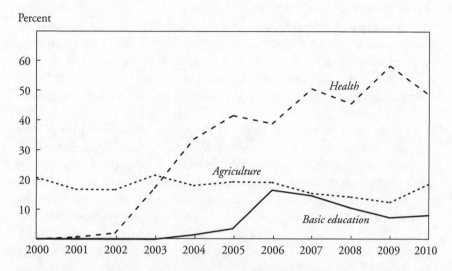

Source: PEPFAR (2012); CTF (2009); SCF (2009); CGIAR (2004, 2010); EFA FTI (2010a); EFA FTI (2007); GAVI Alliance (2001–06); GAFSP (2011a).

combating AIDS and other leading infectious diseases, such as malaria and tuberculosis. The leading multidonor vertical fund was the Global Fund.

By contrast, in education (the Education for All Fast-Track Initiative, which is now the Global Partnership for Education) and agriculture (CGIAR, IFAD, and GAFSP), vertical funds have remained relatively modest, with between 10 percent and 20 percent of sectoral resources flowing through them. Also, education and agriculture have not experienced anything like the growth trajectory of health vertical funds in absolute terms. Over the past decade, donor commitments to basic education have more than doubled, from just under $1.5 billion to nearly $4 billion by 2010, but so have total aid commitments by DAC countries. If anything, the share of basic education in total aid has slightly declined. Within basic education, the share channeled through vertical funds initially increased, but it peaked at 16 percent in 2006 before declining again to around 8 percent in 2010. Unlike the trajectory in health, the postpeak period reflects a steady decline in commitments to vertical funds for basic education. However, it is possible that the most recent replenishment of the Global Partnership for Education in 2011 may be a precursor to a reversal of this long-term trend. A similar pattern holds for agriculture. Although aid commitments to agriculture rose to $9.8 billion in 2010, the share of aid going to agriculture has remained unchanged over the last decade, staying constant at around

5.9 percent. Despite the creation of GAFSP and generous replenishments of IFAD, the share of agricultural aid being channeled through vertical funds has been slowly falling.

What accounts for the difference in performance in mobilizing the resources of these institutions? One likely reason, highlighted in the previous section, is the divergent approaches to governance adopted by the various vertical funds and the role of diverse stakeholders in catalyzing resource mobilization. Funds that have strong civil society advocates, based on participation in governance, have done better than those without such advocates.

Another likely reason is the clarity of the mission that vertical funds have been able to articulate. Although health delivery is a complex issue even within advanced countries, with substantial disagreement among countries on appropriate public policy, the messages around health aid through vertical funds have been systematically simplified and clarified. Communication strategists suggest that mass campaigns cannot start with a complex problem and solution but need an "escalator to complexity," with a simple entry point on which results can be visibly delivered, creating trust that then permits more complex challenges to be addressed later. In health, that simple message has been about lives saved, through vaccinations, immunizations, antiretroviral treatments, and insecticide-treated bed nets. In the case of health, there is a clear results chain beginning with the inputs bought by aid and progressing to number of lives saved in an easily understood way. Such a clear connection builds confidence that foreign assistance will have the desired impact. Critically, health vertical funds have not tried to address all issues in the health sector, which would have required very complex messaging, but have selected a subset of communicable diseases, where treatments are known and results can be measured.

It has proven harder to apply these same communication principles to other areas, such as agriculture. The issues in this sector are complex and interrelated with many other development issues. A simple causal chain between aid money and lower rural poverty and reduced hunger lacks credibility given the widely differing contexts across developing countries. Most problems, like raising smallholder productivity levels to advanced country levels, cannot be readily solved in the medium term, and identification of the binding constraint on agricultural productivity is not easy nor broadly agreed upon among professionals, with the raging debate over genetically modified food being just one contentious issue.

In agriculture, even technocrats agree that, at best, aid can only be a small part of any solution. For example, IFAD has directly invested $12.0 billion in 860 programs and projects through low-interest loans and grants since beginning operations in 1978. During this time it has used its investment to leverage an additional $19.6 billion of investment in projects, with $10.8 billion coming from project participants, governments, and other actors in the recipient country and $8.8 billion of cofinancing from other donors. Even if all cofinancing were attributed to IFAD activities, the total average investment in agriculture would still amount to less than $1 billion a year, much less than the $20 billion for agriculture that the international community agreed was needed.

So even if the moral imperatives to address illiteracy and hunger are as strong as those in health, the ability to communicate a message that the most cost-effective solutions are as dependent on aid has been far weaker. One important conclusion is that vertical funds are most likely to have a dramatic impact on fundraising when they can be focused on specific development outcomes that are critical to achieving international goals, when the causal chain from resources to outcomes is well accepted, and when such aid can effectively provide a development solution at scale. These challenges in term of messaging are accentuated when the structure of vertical funds fails to foster ownership on the part of civil society actors and other key stakeholders in support of resource mobilization within their home countries. These nonstate actors are often the most successful in generating a more compelling framing of key global challenges.

In the aftermath of the global recession of 2009 and the austerity measures being implemented by all DAC donors, the business model for vertical funds has been challenged, and continued success is by no means assured. In its most recent replenishment, the Global Fund received donor pledges of $11.7 billion, including pledges of over $1 billion from seven countries.[28] This figure was 20 percent higher than the fund's previous replenishment between 2007 and 2010. Despite this success relative to peer institutions, the fund has recently suffered from less reliability in the donor community in delivering on its pledges, leading it to postpone the next round of new grants.[29] Although the fund will provide for a "transitional funding mechanism" to prevent any disruption in existing programs before 2013, its financial outlook changed markedly over the past year. While donors had previously honored 100 percent of their pledges, this figure went down to 80 percent in 2010 and is lower still for 2011 amid the deepening economic crisis in Europe. As a result, confirmed pledges for 2011–13 have shrunk, along with the amount of funds available for financing any new round of proposals.[30]

The Global Partnership for Education also faces resource mobilization challenges, despite recent progress. The most recent replenishment in late 2011

28. Over the past decade, the Global Fund has received donor commitments of nearly $10 billion from the United States, $4 billion from France, and over $2 billion each from the United Kingdom, Germany, and Japan.

29. Jack (2011).

30. Rivers (2011). Some donor countries have highlighted issues related to the fund's oversight based on auditing of grants by the independent inspector general. The audits have revealed $17 million in fraud.

resulted in pledges from donors of $1.5 billion for the period 2011–14. The most significant pledges were from the United Kingdom ($352 million) and Australia ($278 million). Only two other countries, the Netherlands and Norway, pledged more than $100 million. Nearly two-thirds of pledged resources came from just these four countries. Although these numbers are still quite modest, they nonetheless reflect some improvement over the early efforts at resource mobilization and a broadening of the donor base. Between 2006 and 2009, just two countries contributed over 60 percent of the core Catalytic Fund's total resources, and many countries provided only token amounts. From its inception until 2010, the partnership has channeled approximately $1.2 billion to partner countries for financing the expansion of primary education, a tiny fraction of estimated global needs.

A new round of replenishments for IFAD, for the period 2012–14, has also just been concluded, with an announced $1.5 billion target for replenishments.[31] This represents a 25 percent increase over the previous round but will still leave IFAD as a small agency in the agricultural aid sphere. Other agricultural funds, including GAFSP, are also facing funding difficulties. In the case of GAFSP, its allocation from the United States in the recent 2012 Omnibus Spending Bill was just $135 million, far short of the president's initial request for $350 million.

Several studies examine the issue of whether vertical funds are fungible or whether they truly add to the resources available to the sector. Concerns about the fungibility of donor resources for global health are mitigated by the dramatic scale of the increase in overall global health resources over the last decade. With vertical funds accounting for nearly two-thirds of that increase, the overall financing for global health still significantly outstripped these new investments in AIDS, malaria, and TB. It seems highly unlikely that this additional $10 billion would have been committed without the focused effort to combat these diseases, given the trajectory of donor funding for global health. Donor funding for malaria multiplied nearly tenfold between 2001 and 2009, and donor funding for tuberculosis increased to more than five times its 2001 base.[32]

A more challenging issue of fungibility arises with respect to the investments of national governments in the health sector. Yet here again, the scale of the increases argues against the idea that donor investments in global health were mostly fungible. In Southern Africa health expenditures increased by 50 percent between 2002 and 2009, in West Africa these expenditures more than doubled, in East Africa they nearly doubled, and in Central Africa government health

---

31. IFAD (2011, p. 1).
32. Institute for Health Metrics and Evaluation (2011, p. 80).

spending nearly quintupled.[33] While recent studies find that donor financing for health had a significant negative effect on government health spending when provided to the public sector, such financing had a significant positive effect on domestic health spending when directed to the nongovernment sector, as was the case with much of the new AIDS funding.[34] However, such crowding out did not take place in many countries for which donor financing for global health increased.[35] Overall, there seems to be little evidence that donor health funding through vertical funds is fully fungible; more resources have undoubtedly gone into health programs supported by vertical funds.[36]

In terms of the fungibility of donor financing for basic education, the growth of overall financing for basic education has far outstripped the contribution to the Global Partnership for Education. In fact the 2010 commitments to the partnership by all donors represents less than 13 percent of the overall increase in donor financing for basic education, suggesting that vertical fund investments did not displace other assistance to basic education. In terms of recipients, it is more difficult to ascertain whether donor financing crowds out domestic investment, as there is little evidence on the extent to which aid replaces public funding.[37] While a previous study finds that education aid is fungible and does not add to public spending, a recent study finds that donor financing for education is not fully fungible, which could be expected in a sector in which domestic governments provide between 80 percent and 90 percent of all financing.[38] Education spending increased sharply in eighty developing countries between 1995 and 2007—to twice the amount of health spending and a larger share of total government spending.[39] Anecdotal evidence from some of the initial wave of countries endorsed for funding by the Global Partnership suggests that any crowding-out effect has been somewhat limited. In Gambia and in Ethiopia, for example, the share of the budget earmarked for education increased by a third in the three years after their respective endorsements.[40]

Agriculture is another sector that has historically been susceptible to fungibility concerns. Several studies find no evidence that aid to agriculture increases public spending in that sector in Africa. However, the same studies may show a reverse causation; public spending on agriculture crowds in more aid, perhaps because of

33. Institute for Health Metrics and Evaluation (2011, p. 95).
34. Lu and others (2010).
35. Ooms and others (2010).
36. Van de Sijpe (2010, p. 35).
37. Fredriksen (2008, pp. 6–7).
38. Fredriksen (2008, p. 15). For the fungibility finding, see Van de Sijpe (2010, p. 35). The earlier study is Feyzioglu, Swaroop, and Zhu (1998).
39. Gupta (2010).
40. EFA FTI (2010b).

better overall country performance on poverty reduction.[41] Within agriculture, of course, dedicated funds may well increase spending in certain categories, such as research, but that then comes at the expense of other sectoral priorities.

In sum, it is only health vertical funds that seem to have indisputably raised additional resources for the sector as a whole, as well as for their particular subsectoral priorities. In both basic education and agriculture, the presence of important vertical funds failed to increase the sector's prominence in aid commitments as a whole.

Learning and Innovation

Several vertical funds have joined together into the Global Programs Learning Group to share best practices to improve aid effectiveness and ensure that programs are implemented in a way that accords with the Paris Declaration principles on aid effectiveness.[42] Vertical funds are cognizant of the fact that their programs work best when complemented by strong policy and institutional environments in the sectors in which they operate, but they face difficulties in operationalizing several of the Paris principles.

Among the weaknesses of vertical fund programs are the sometimes weak links between their country strategy and coordination mechanisms with formal government institutions. Unlike traditional donors, who have tended to play an influential ex ante role in the preparation of country strategies and plans, vertical funds have instead sought to facilitate bottom-up leadership. The Global Fund refers to a "radical passivity" in its approach, waiting for country programs to emerge on their own. Vertical funds are forced to adopt such a strategy because of the absence of a strong country presence (one reason for their low administrative costs), but it also reflects an alternative approach based on learning and performance-based funding. Rather than laying out detailed strategies in advance, the vertical funds have tried to focus more on results, with countries free to make adjustments to programs during implementation, as they see fit. The key accountability and incentive mechanism is then a strong linkage between results and the size of funding.

The Global Fund has characterized itself as a learning organization since its founding. One of its most significant features is the extremely demanding level of transparency that it requires of itself and the incorporation of regular independent evaluations in order to foster a culture of continuous improvement.[43] Disclosing its failures is clearly a strength in terms of organizational learning.[44] But this characteristic has also exposed the fund to external critics in ways that

41. Devarajan, Rajkumar, and Swaroop (1999).
42. Isenman (2007).
43. *Lancet* editorial (2011).
44. Dare (2010).

most vertical funds or international institutions have not.[45] Since its creation a decade ago, independent experts have conducted eight evaluations of the fund, each of which has inspired further reforms. Most recently, the Comprehensive Reform Working Group adopted new policies to strengthen accountability and partnerships, improve governance, and adapt the fund's business model.[46]

One of the significant areas of innovation by the Global Fund is in drug procurement. In 2009 the fund adopted the Voluntary Pooled Procurement Initiative to encourage grant recipients to collectively procure drugs and related commodities at lower prices. This effort builds on the fund's important market intervention with respect to malaria treatment: soon after its creation, the fund utilized its large-scale purchasing power to create a sufficient market for the supply of new malaria treatments. Later, in 2004, the fund accelerated the shift to an improved artemisinin-based combination therapy, which expanded the availability of these medicines by dramatically reducing their pricing and reshaped the treatment of malaria.[47]

Another important area of innovation by the Global Fund and other vertical funds for health is their contribution to the development of innovative financing mechanisms. The Global Fund pioneered new forms of collaboration with the private sector to raise resources through a voluntary branding program, which dedicated a fixed percentage of consumer spending to the fund. It greatly expanded the use of debt swaps for global health and worked closely with UNITAID, which is financed through an airline-ticket levy. Other global health funds were the central institutions for innovations in predictable long-term financing; the Global Alliance for Vaccines and Immunizations worked through both the front-loaded International Finance Facility for Immunizations and the Advanced Market Commitments Initiative.

The Fast-Track Initiative has less of a defined track record as a learning organization. However, the FTI did engage in regular reviews of its structure and governance, which led to several different substantial reforms since its creation. Its Steering Committee sought outside experts to evaluate its internal structures and offered a range of options based on comparisons with other vertical funds.[48] The most recent reform of the partnership's governance, and the expansion of the range of actors who can oversee disbursement at the national level, reflect a surprising openness to structural reform.

---

45. In 2009 the Office of the Inspector General publicly disclosed findings of misappropriated funds in Mauritania, Mali, and Zambia, and the Global Fund subsequently suspended and terminated a number of its grants. Relatively few international institutions or bilateral development agencies match this level of transparency and sanctions following evidence of misappropriation.

46. Global Fund (2011).

47. Sabot (2012).

48. Buse (2005).

Another important dimension on which the FTI contributed to cross-country learning is through its shared leadership of the School Fees Abolition Initiative (SFAI). The conventional wisdom within the World Bank for many years was that user charges were an important financing mechanism for education, but this perspective lacked a clear understanding of what user fees were doing on the demand side. The FTI supported the perspective that eliminating primary school fees was important to expanding primary enrollment, and SFAI sought to share the lessons of early experiences in East Africa and develop best practices for governments seeking to abolish school fees. Through multiple workshops that brought together governments across the continent of Africa and beyond, and through guidance materials developed in partnership with UNICEF and the World Bank, the initiative contributed to South-South learning in an area of major policy change over the last decade.

Both IFAD and GAFSP are committed to learning. GAFSP has aggressively called for in-depth impact evaluations using experimental or quasi-experimental design methodologies for up to 30 percent of its investments. IFAD has explicitly focused on innovation in its strategic statements and practices, and among the noteworthy innovations it has introduced is support for grassroots farmer organizations. Many of these consultation processes have generated new ideas for good practice, but one recent review suggests that IFAD did not sufficiently scale up successful innovations to maximize impact.[49] It concludes that IFAD needs to focus on certain domains "where there is a proven need for innovative solutions and where IFAD has (or can develop) a comparative advantage to promote successfully pro-poor innovations that can be scaled up."[50] In response to the review, IFAD has amended its COSOP guidelines to enhance the role of monitoring and evaluation and increase focus on the drivers, spaces, and constraints that shape pathways to bring activities to scale. This is intended to form part of a move to more programmatic and less project-focused country operations.

Impact and Results

A strong linkage between performance and funding became one of the core founding principles of the Global Fund. The approval of all follow-up funding is linked to an evaluation of the performance of the principal recipient in meeting the agreed-upon program objectives. This approach allows for the redeployment of urgently needed resources to countries and recipients that are better placed to use them and creates strong incentives for national governments and other actors to overcome bottlenecks and improve performance. It also requires flexibility in procedures to permit the shifting of resources to programs that

49. IFAD (2010c, p. 60).
50. IFAD (2010c, p. 75).

have a successful track record. Some scholars have suggested that the fund is the paradigmatic example of a public-private partnership that is "managing for strategic results."[51] A recent analysis of the fund's tuberculosis portfolio finds that successful evaluation that leads to continued funding predicts higher performance in grants for tuberculosis.[52] Analyses of the fund's evaluation of programs demonstrates that the fund's grants performed better over time, so that the second and third round of grants were higher performing overall than the initial round.[53] At the same time, the diversity of the fund's implementers has enabled its efforts to scale up quickly. Civil society groups, the private sector, and multilateral recipients received higher performance evaluation scores than government implementers.[54]

Almost all vertical funds have clear statements of impact. For example, perhaps the best measure of the Global Fund's impact can be seen in the programmatic results it has achieved over the past decade. Over this period the fund has provided antiretroviral treatment to 3.2 million people, tuberculosis treatment to 8.2 million people, and bed nets to prevent malaria to 190 million people. The fund estimates that it prevented 830,000 deaths as a result of its malaria interventions alone. Estimations of the fund's expected impact on its target diseases (before the recent funding shortfall) projected that by 2015 it would provide antiretroviral treatment to over 5.5 million people, reach more than 60 percent of the global target on tuberculosis control, and distribute approximately one-third of the bed nets required to meet global goals against malaria in sub-Saharan Africa.[55] With the Global Fund providing approximately two-thirds of all donor financing for malaria, the overall progress against the disease in recent years gives further evidence of the fund's impact. In Africa malaria deaths decreased by more than one-third over the past decade, while malaria deaths worldwide were down more than one-quarter over that period. The most widespread intervention against malaria, providing insecticide-treated bed nets, is demonstrating impressive success. A recent survey finds that in homes with at least one insecticide-treated bed net there was a 23 percent reduction in child mortality.[56] Based on these results, DFID determined that the Global Fund offers "very good value for money," the highest ranking available.[57]

Nonetheless, there are calls from diverse quarters for the fund to further improve its approach to performance-based funding. Although the *Lancet* has

51. Kaul (2006).
52. Katz and others (2010).
53. Radelet (2007).
54. Radelet (2007, p. 1809).
55. Katz and others (2011).
56. Lim and others (2011).
57. UK (2011a).

praised the fund's general approach to measuring performance and acting on these findings, the journal has recently called for independent verification of the fund's evaluation of the performance of its grant portfolio.[58] The former executive director of the fund, Richard Feachem, has suggested that the fund must do more to "truly become the performance-based funding institution it aspires to be" and has joined others in calling for evaluation to be more focused on outputs or impact indicators rather than on inputs.[59]

In terms of impact, the Global Partnership for Education is harder to analyze than some other institutions, because much of its financing is channeled through national budgets. Therefore, the success of the countries that the partnership finances is often attributed to the partnership itself, but it remains difficult to disaggregate the relative contributions to that success. Nonetheless, there is evidence that partnership countries receive greater assistance for basic education and have expanded enrollment and improved primary completion rates more rapidly than nonpartner countries.

The Global Partnership for Education was not explicitly founded with the principle of performance-based financing. However, there was a clear ambition from the beginning to support only strong country plans as a way of building on countries' readiness for success. The most important dimension on which the fund is seeking to learn and borrow from other funds is to more closely link performance with financing. Reviews of the countries endorsed and funded by the partnership do not reveal a greater focus on managing for results in the education sector than elsewhere in a given country.[60] However, there is evidence that the initial countries selected to join were identified based on good performance rather than an assessment of need or other metrics, and few fragile and conflict-affected states have received support.[61] More recently the partnership has been working to develop a results framework to allow it to strengthen the link between flows of financing and performance measurements. Although more than three-quarters of the countries taking part in the partnership's 2011 monitoring exercise use results-oriented frameworks to monitor their national education plans, the partnership itself is still developing its approach to better link these results with financing.[62]

Significant progress has been demonstrated in the forty-three countries financed by the partnership. In these countries the average net enrollment rate increased from 66 percent to 81 percent between 2000 and 2008.[63] The pri-

---

58. *Lancet* editorial (2010).
59. Feachem (2011); Oomman, Rosenzweig, and Bernstein (2010, p. 41).
60. Bashir (2009).
61. Rose (2005).
62. EFA FTI (2010b).
63. Global Partnership for Education (2011).

mary completion rate in partner countries increased from 60 percent in 2002 to 72 percent in 2009. Partner countries in sub-Saharan Africa that are compared to nonpartner countries demonstrate significantly faster progress in expanding access to primary schooling. In terms of enrollment, partner country enrollment rose by 48 percent, compared to 28 percent for nonpartner countries. In terms of primary completion rates, the yearly percentage point gain was twice as large in partner countries as in nonpartner countries. These data, however, cannot be taken to trace a clear causal relationship between the partnership and improved education results. A strong element of self-selection (partner countries more committed to education are more likely to join the partnership) is also likely to be present.

Neither IFAD nor GAFSP explicitly links performance and funding. IFAD, unlike other vertical funds, has a country-allocation funding model, in which performance is one factor, and works through government processes. As DFID notes, IFAD "is a trusted partner of developing countries and the strong sense of ownership is demonstrated through contributions to projects. IFAD works through government processes, scoring highly against the Paris indicators."[64] GAFSP considers country needs and the strength of the country plan in determining its allocations, although it indicates it will consider performance in the future. In its approved monitoring and evaluation plan, GAFSP notes that "the allocation of budget resources for the following year, in normal circumstances, should be heavily influenced by the results and performance of the project during the current year, as recorded by the M&E system."[65]

GAFSP has committed to a transparent-results framework, with indicators to be updated every six months. It has outlined its quantitative objectives as reaching 7.5 million beneficiaries in twelve low-income countries, yielding aggregate annual income improvements of over $100 million, based on pledged commitments of $971 million.[66] IFAD also has a results and impact-monitoring system but does not attempt to develop aggregate quantitative goals attributed to its own operations. As a relatively small organization given the scale of the challenge of agriculture and rural development, IFAD explicitly recognizes the importance of catalyzing development processes to maximize the impact of its investments through developing innovative practices and scaling up projects.

A review of IFAD's results and impact shows that IFAD projects are rated highly for relevance and that increased focus on supporting market access and private sector development has increased their effectiveness.[67] IFAD projects' impacts on rural poverty are generally satisfactory, but results are weaker in

64. UK (2011b, p. 5).
65. GAFSP (2011a, p. 6).
66. GAFSP (2011b).
67. IFAD (2010a, pp. 18–21).

terms of the impact on natural resources and the environment. This is in part due to the limited attention paid by these projects to the risks and opportunities for natural resources and the environment; it is also partly due to the poor performance of natural resources and environment project components.[68] One key area of weakness identified in evaluations of IFAD's impact is project sustainability: 35 percent of projects evaluated between 2007 and 2009 were rated as moderately unsatisfactory or worse, with 43 percent rated moderately satisfactory and 22 percent satisfactory.[69] No projects were evaluated as highly satisfactory. The review finds that sustainability of results was linked to projects that exhibited the following characteristics: strong alignment with government priorities, policies, and programs; integration of project management units into existing institutional frameworks; strong community ownership and contributions; long-term support for grassroots organizations; and effective alignment of and links between project-created organizations and existing institutions.[70]

Assessment of Vertical Funds

Table 4-3 offers our summary assessment of the performance of vertical funds in health, education, and agriculture in each key performance dimension of resource mobilization, learning, and impact. The health funds stand out, with significant success in resource mobilization, in learning and innovations for effective impact, and in specifying and monitoring quantitative goals. In education, while there has been some contribution to new learning, the effect of the FTI on either resources or educational learning seems low. In agriculture there has been moderate success in mobilizing new resources through vertical funds, but specific global outcome targets are nebulous and poorly measured, so the impact to date on reducing global hunger and improving food security at a global level seems to be only modest. Some success has also been achieved in learning and innovations, especially in the involvement of local bodies in program design and implementation and in the spread of better seeds and farming practices.

In terms of resource mobilization, none of the funds outside of health examined here has mobilized more than $1 billion in a single year. While each of the agricultural funds has generated commitments in excess of $500 million for a single year, the Fast-Track Initiative never achieved even this level of donor commitment. However, the most recent replenishment of the more participatory Global Partnership for Education was roughly comparable to the most

68. IFAD (2010a, p. 22).
69. IFAD (2010a, p. 31).
70. IFAD (2010a, p. 32).

Table 4-3. *Assessing Vertical Funds' Performance*

	Health	Education	Agriculture
Resource mobilization	High	Low	Medium
Learning	High	Medium	Medium
Impact	High	Low	Low

Source: Authors' estimates.

recent IFAD replenishment, with each generating commitments of $1.5 billion over three years. Strong resource mobilization in health contrasts sharply with the modest success in agriculture and the limited success in education. Further evidence for the relative success of these funds can be found in the overall share of assistance in each sector that was channeled through vertical funds. In health this share has grown to more than 40 percent; in agriculture it has generally hovered around 20 percent, while in education it has only rarely broken past the 10 percent level.

In terms of learning, the health funds receive the highest rankings on multiple assessments, but both the agricultural and education funds also demonstrate some capacity. The most straightforward comparison is between the Global Fund and IFAD, because in two different assessments the Global Fund was found to perform much better. In the quality-of-aid index for transparency and learning, the fund scored 0.8, compared to –0.35 for IFAD.[71] In the DFID multilateral review, the Global Fund was found to be likely to change, while IFAD was ranked lower as uncertain to change. On this metric, the FTI ranked alongside the Global Fund as likely to change, which may reflect its capacity for institutional reform in recent years. While GAFSP has a more ambitious approach to learning, it is still too early to tell how it will work in practice, and it was not included in these evaluations. Therefore, on learning, our summary ranking across sectors is health, followed by education and agriculture.

In terms of impact, the strongest evidence of impressive outcomes is being generated in the health sector, with much weaker evidence of a transformative impact by vertical funds in the agricultural and education sectors. In the DFID multilateral review, only the Global Fund achieved the "very good" value for money ranking, while both IFAD and FTI received a "good" evaluation. Within this analysis, IFAD did outperform FTI and performed comparably with the Global Fund in terms of its contribution to results. However, if one looks at the overall sectoral impact there is not much evidence of results in agriculture,

71. Birdsall, Kharas, and Perakis (2011).

Table 4-4. *Structural Features of Vertical Funds*

Feature	Health	Education	Agriculture
Institutional home	Independent	World Bank	UN/World Bank
Participation	High	Medium	Low/medium
Performance based	High	Low	Medium/low

Source: Authors' estimates.

compared with steep declines in malaria and significant progress against other leading infectious diseases.

This summary assessment suggests that not all vertical funds are equal in terms of their contribution to development. The implication is that scaling up may not be a feature of the verticality of the funding channel but rather of other structural characteristics possessed by the more successful global funds. Global health, education, and agriculture funds have diverged in important ways in terms of their institutional homes and autonomy, their adoption of broadened participation, and their utilization of performance-based financing. Table 4-4 highlights the different structural features of vertical funds in health, education, and agriculture.

The three sectors vary significantly in terms of the primary institutional home and degree of autonomy among vertical funds. While the Global Fund to Fight AIDS, Tuberculosis and Malaria and other leading vertical funds for health are independent institutions, vertical funds in education and agriculture are closely linked to the World Bank or the United Nations. The Education for All Fast-Track Initiative was historically embedded within the World Bank, and despite movement toward greater autonomy for the relaunched Global Partnership for Education, the secretariat's staff formally remain World Bank employees. In the agricultural sector, IFAD is a specialized agency of the United Nations, while GAFSP is housed within the World Bank despite having its own governance structure. Thus, while vertical funds for global health have great autonomy, vertical funds in education and agriculture have historically been more closely tied to and more constrained by their institutional homes in larger multilateral institutions.

The three sectors also diverge significantly in terms of the level of participation by civil society and other nonstate actors in their respective governance structures at the global and national levels. While the Global Fund has strong participation by these actors in its country-coordinating mechanisms as well as its global structures of governance, there has been less robust participation in the education and agricultural sectors. Although reforms in education and the launch of GAFSP have shifted these sectors toward more inclusive governance at the global level, there are not yet strong enough institutions for meaningful country-level participation in shaping national strategies within either education or agriculture. IFAD, as the only UN agency, is an outlier among these funds, which allows for minimal participation by nonstate actors at the global, as well as the national, level. While independent institutions generate the highest level of participation, the World Bank–affiliated institutions are now a middle case, with the UN agencies offering the most limited formal participation for nonstate actors.

On the dimension of performance-based financing, the gap between health funds and education and agricultural funds remains significant. While the Global Fund and other health funds incorporated performance-based financing into their core business model, this approach was much slower to be integrated into funds within the other sectors. Interestingly, IFAD has moved further along in adopting reforms to emphasize performance in its decisionmaking over financial allocations, but it remains constrained by its country-allocation formula. Both the Global Partnership for Education and GAFSP are currently seeking to strengthen this dimension of their work, but neither has gone as far in implementing such an approach. Thus in terms of performance-based financing, independent institutions are the furthest along, and World Bank–linked institutions are the furthest behind.

It is quite striking that the more independent, more participatory, and more performance-based vertical funds are outperforming the less independent, less participatory, and less performance-based vertical funds on the dimensions of resource mobilization, learning, and impact. These variables seem to be closely linked such that the institutional home can be a key factor in shaping the degree of inclusive participation in the governance of a given fund. Less-independent institutions are less likely to involve nonstate actors in governance, and UN agencies are the least likely to do so. Participation, in turn, seems to play an important role in shaping resource mobilization within these funds and in contributing to effective implementation at the country level.

The success of the Global Fund in scaling up and sustaining resource levels, even in the face of recent challenges, reflects strong ownership and sustained advocacy by nonstate actors in donor countries. Similarly, the recent success of the GAFSP in securing even modest resources from the U.S. Congress in an extremely challenging period was enabled by a targeted effort by key civil society actors involved in its governance, who invested heavily in its success but did not similarly invest in IFAD's recent replenishment. While the education sector has been the least successful of the three in mobilizing resources, the recent reforms of the governance of the Global Partnership for Education (which broadened the involvement of nonstate actors) likely contributed to its somewhat more promising replenishment last year. Yet the institutional home may also have independent effects on resource mobilization, as donors can more easily separate the clear focus of a given vertical fund from the political controversies that sometimes hinder financing for the World Bank or United Nations and reduce concerns over the fungibility of resources within these much larger institutions.

The variation in learning among the sectors also reflects the degree of participation in governance to the extent that it contributes to more robust transparency within these vertical funds. Yet the institutional home and degree of autonomy is also likely a significant factor in shaping the level of transparency within these funds, with independent institutions the most transparent, and UN agencies often weaker than World Bank–linked institutions in terms of transparency. Performance-based financing also likely plays a role in learning, as it provides a built-in feedback loop on the consequences of past practices, which can generate innovation and foster the wider dissemination of key lessons learned.

Finally, in terms of impact, both agricultural and educational vertical funds have yet to demonstrate major impact in reshaping their respective sectors. Impact is ultimately shaped by the success of these funds in terms of resource mobilization and learning. The limited impact of a number of these funds reflects their failure to reach adequate scale through effective resource mobilization in contrast to global health. Yet the modestly greater success in resource mobilization within the agricultural sector compared to the education sector did not lead to substantially greater impact. Different levels of learning within these funds might help account for the limited impact of funds with greater resources. Modestly better learning within the education sector also did not translate into greater impact than in agriculture. It is likely that both resource mobilization and learning are necessary components of generating substantial impact. Only the heavily resourced and learning-driven health sector generated high impact. Thus it seems there is an interaction between resource mobilization and learning that contributes to impact.

Concluding Remarks

Across a number of sectors vertical funds are emerging as an extremely important element of international development assistance and demonstrating significant promise for effectiveness when it comes to resource mobilization, learning, and impact. Vertical funds now represent approximately one-seventh of all programmable aid, and in some important sectors these funds account for over half of all donor commitments. Most of these new-generation vertical funds emerged in response to specific global challenges in the twenty-first century in the wake of the launch of the Millennium Development Goals. Overall, vertical funds demonstrate significant results in terms of institutional efficiency and learning, despite ongoing concerns that they are often less responsive to the priorities of recipient governments. The most innovative of these funds have adopted mechanisms that seek to foster country-driven, rather than merely government-driven, strategies and performance-based financing, but these approaches are not well developed within many vertical funds. The design of vertical funds is a key dimension of their relative success in catalyzing effective global responses to challenges in areas such as health, education, and agriculture.

There is significant divergence in the apparent effectiveness of these vertical funds across sectors and institutions. Although much of the debate has been over whether vertical funds represent the best way of scaling up development impact, this may be the wrong issue. Verticality appears to be only one element of success, defined as scaling up development impact and improved outcomes on a global scale. The most successful sector to date has been global health, and it is in global health that vertical funds are the most participatory and the most advanced in linking performance with financing. Because of this performance, a few select institutions have also taken on a leadership role in their sector, which has allowed them to galvanize innovations in funding and intervention modalities.

One of the less successful sectors is education, where the institutional architecture has only recently become more participatory and where progress in linking performance with financing has been much slower. Nonetheless, there are some initial indications that a recent overhaul of the education architecture may be helping its resource mobilization, and its potential embrace of performance-based financing could improve its impact. Similarly, the mixed performance by vertical funds in agriculture may be improving with the launch of a more participatory institution in recent years and could improve still further with the adoption of performance-based financing. However, a striking contrast remains in that neither education nor agriculture yet has autonomous free-standing vertical funds. Instead, both sectors maintain funds that are housed in the World Bank and, in the case of IFAD, in the United Nations. These institutional homes allow for less autonomy, appear to limit the boundaries of participation by nonstate actors, and contribute to the slower adoption of performance-based financing.

It is clear that vertical funds are not a panacea for all global challenges. Some challenges lend themselves more easily to a framing that catalyzes global action, particularly donor financing. Global issues are more successful in terms of verticalization and scaling up when they can be framed in terms of focused, simple, and compelling outcomes (such as lives saved) and when expanded resources can make a visible transformational change when closely linked to outcomes. Broad participation in the governance structures of these vertical funds can leverage key nonstate actors in donor countries to become champions for the fund and solidify the credibility with beneficiaries of the interventions at the country level. Further research is needed to evaluate the impact of vertical funds across a wider range of sectors, and this would be helped if there were an independent audit model for presenting results. Nonetheless, the important contribution of these funds to the challenge of scaling up is reflected both in their innovative approaches and in the rising share of development assistance that is channeled through these funds. While not all vertical funds have succeeded in scaling up, they may have done better than traditional approaches to development on some dimensions. Where they have not, the obstacles are often the result not of the vertical approach but of the barriers to participation and innovation that remain when funds are not truly independent. More independent, more participatory, and more results-focused vertical funds pose a challenge to traditional approaches to development, and a wide range of institutions is now seeking to adopt the best practices of many of these vertical funds.

References

Bartsch, Sonja. 2007. "The Global Fund to Fight AIDS, Tuberculosis and Malaria." In *Global Health Governance and the Fight against HIV/AIDS,* edited by Wolfgang Hein, Sonja Bartsch, and Lars Kohlmorgen. Palgrave Macmillan.

Bashir, Sajitha. 2009. "Catalyzing Country Ownership and Aid Effectiveness: Role of the Education for All Fast Track Initiative." *Prospects: Quarterly Review of Comparative Education* 159: 39.2.

Birdsall, Nancy, Homi Kharas, and Rita Perakis. 2011. "Quality of Official Development Assistance Index." Center for Global Development and Brookings Institution (www.cgdev.org/section/topics/aid_effectiveness/quoda).

Buffardi, Anne, Robinson Cabello, and Patricia Garcia. 2011. "The Chronicles of CONAMUSA: Institutional Strategies to Overcome Shared Governance Challenges." Paper prepared for annual convention, International Studies Association. Montreal. March.

Buse, Kent. 2005. "Review of the Governance and Management Structures" (www.odi.org.uk/resources/docs/1993.pdf).

Cassidy, Rebecca, and Melissa Leach. 2010. "Mediated Health Citizenship: Living with HIV and Engaging with the Global Fund in Zambia." In *Globalising Citizens,* edited by John Gaventa and Rajesh Tandon. Zed Books.

CGIAR. 2004. *Financial Report 2004* (www.cgiar.org/pdf/cgiar_finreport_2004.pdf).
———. 2010. *Annual Report 2010* (www.cgiar.org/pdf/2010_CGIAR_Financial_Report.pdf)

CTF (Clean Technology Fund). 2009. *Financial Statement 2009* (www.climateinvestment funds.org/cif/sites/climateinvestmentfunds.org/files/CTF%20Financial%20Statements_December%2031%202009.pdf).

Dare, Lola. 2010. "Independent Evaluations of the Global Fund." *Lancet* 375: 1694.

Devarajan, Shantayanan, Andrew Sunil Rajkumar, and Vinaya Swaroop. 1999. "What Does Aid to Africa Finance?" Policy Research Working Paper 2092. World Bank Development Research Group (http://elibrary.worldbank.org/content/workingpaper/10.1596/1813-9450-2092).

DFID (Department for International Development). 2010. "Multilateral Aid Review."

Doctors without Borders. 2011. "MSF Response to Global Fund Board Meeting." Press release, November 22 (www.doctorswithoutborders.org/press/release.cfm?id=5630&cat=press-release).

EFA FTI (Education for All Fast Track Initiative). 2007. Global Partnership. *Catalytic Fund Pledges and Support* (www.globalpartnership.org/media/Misc./Annex%201.pdf)

————. 2009. "Mid-Term Evaluation of the EFA Fast Track Initiative" (www.educationfast track.org/newsroom/focus-on/mid-term-evaluation-of-the-efa-fast-track-initiative/).

————. 2010a. *Annual Report 2010* (www.globalpartnership.org/2010-annual-report).

————. 2010b. "Revisions to the FTI Governance Partnership Document" (www.global partnership.org/news/187/61/Revisions-to-the-EFA-FTI-Governance-of-the-Partnership-Document/).

Feachem, Richard. 2011. "The Global Fund: Getting the Reforms Right." *Lancet* 378: 1764.

Feyzioglu, Tarhan, Vinaya Swaroop, and Min Zhu. 1998. "A Panel Data Analysis of the Fungibility of Foreign Aid." *World Bank Economic Review* 46: 12.1.

Fredriksen, Birger. 2008. "The Evolving Allocative Efficiency of Education Aid: A Reflection on Changes in Aid Priorities to Enhance Aid Effectiveness" (http://siteresources.world bank.org/EDUCATION/Resources/278200-1099079877269/547664-1099079993288/Allocative_Efficiency_Edu_Aid.pdf).

GAFSP (Global Agriculture and Food Security Program). 2011a. *Annual Report 2011* (www.gafspfund.org/gafsp/content/global-agriculture-and-food-security-program).

————. 2011b. "Global Agriculture and Food Security Program: A Transformational Approach to Development Assistance" (www.aideffectiveness.org/busanhlf4/images/stories/hlf4/eposters/ePoster60_en.pdf).

GAVI Alliance. 2001–06. "GAVI Commitments and Disbursements" (www.gavialliance.org/country/all-countries-commitments-and-disbursements).

GEF (Global Environment Facility). 2000. "Project Performance Report 2000" (www.thegef.org/gef/sites/thegef.org/files/documents/C.17.08.pdf).

Global Campaign for Education. 2011. "Regional and National Civil Society Education Fund 4th Progress Report" (www.campaignforeducation.org/docs/csef/reports/csef%20 4th%20progress%20narrative%20report-Nov%202011_final.pdf).

Global Fund. 2005. "Revised Guidelines on the Purpose, Structure, and Composition of Country Coordinating Mechanism Guidelines and Requirements for Grant Eligibility" (http://aidspan.org/documents/globalfund/5_pp_guidelines_ccm_4-en.pdf).

————. 2008. "Lessons from the Field: A Report on the Country Coordinating Mechanism Model."

————. 2011. "Report of the Comprehensive Reform Working Group." Twenty-third Global Fund board meeting (www.theglobalfund.org/documents/board/23/BM23_13 ComprehensiveReformWorkingGroup_Report_en/).

Global Partnership for Education. 2011. "The Case For Investment, 2011–2014."

Gupta, Sanjeev. 2010. "Correspondence." *Lancet* 376: 593.

IFAD (International Fund for Agricultural Development). 1976. *Agreement Establishing the International Fund for Agricultural Development* (www.ifad.org/pub/basic/agree/e/!01agree.pdf).

————. 2010a. *Annual Report on Results and Impact of IFAD Operations Evaluated in 2009.*

————. 2010b. "IFAD and Farmers' Organizations: Partnership in Progress 2008–09 (www.ifad.org/farmer/2010/doc/prgrep_e.pdf).

————. 2010c. "IFAD's Capacity to Promote Innovation and Scaling Up" (www.ifad.org/evaluation/public_html/eksyst/doc/corporate/innovation2.pdf).

————. 2011. "Chairperson's Summary: Consultation on the Ninth Replenishment of IFAD's Resources." Fourth Session, Rome (www.ifad.org/gbdocs/repl/9/iv/e/REPL-IX-4-INF-3.pdf).

Institute for Health Metrics and Evaluation. 2011. "Financing Global Health 2011: Continued Growth as MDG Deadline Approaches" (www.healthmetricsandevaluation.org/sites/default/files/policy_report/2011/FGH_2011_full_report_high_resolution_IHME.pdf).

Isenman, Paul. 2007. "The Learning Group of Global Programs: Actions for Aid Effectiveness" (http://siteresources.worldbank.org/ACCRAEXT/Resources/4700790-121000 8992554/4968817-1218029841627/Learning-Group-Final.pdf).

Isenman, Paul, and Alexander Shakow. 2010. "Donor Schizophrenia and Aid Effectiveness: The Role of Global Funds" (www.ids.ac.uk/files/dmfile/Pp5.pdf).

Jack, Andrew. 2011. "A Stretched Safety Net." *Financial Times,* November 25.

Kananaskis Summit. 2002. *A New Focus on Education for All* (www.g8.utoronto.ca/ summit/2002kananaskis/education.html).

Katz, Itamar, and others. 2010. "Factors Influencing Performance of Global-Fund Supported Tuberculosis Grants." *International Journal of Tuberculosis and Lung Disease* 1100.

———. 2011. "Scaling Up toward International Targets for AIDS, TB, and Malaria: Contribution of Global Fund Supported Programs." *PLOS One* e17166.

Kaul, Inge. 2006. "Exploring the Policy Space between Markets and States: Global Public-Private Partnerships." *New Public Finance: Responding to Global Challenges* 219.

Lancet editorial. 2010. "The Global Fund: Replenishment and Redefinition in 2010." *Lancet* 375: 865.

———. 2011. "Five Reasons to Fund the Global Fund." *Lancet* 387: 1198.

Lim, Stephen, and others. 2011. "Net Benefits: A Multicountry Analysis of Observational Data Examining Associations between Insecticide-Treated Mosquito Nets and Health Outcomes." *PLOS One* e1001091.

Lu, Chunling, and others. 2010. "Public Financing of Health in Developing Countries: A Cross-National Systematic Analysis." *Lancet* 375: 1375.

OECD. 2012a. *Country Programmable Aid* (http://stats.oecd.org/).

———. 2012b. *Total Commitments.* (http://stats.oecd.org/).

Oomman, Nandini, Steven Rosenzweig, and Michael Bernstein. 2010. "Are Funding Decisions Based on Performance?" Center for Global Development (www.cgdev.org/ files/1424030_file_CGDPerformance_based_funding_FINAL.pdf).

Ooms, Gorik, and others. 2010. "Crowding Out: Are Relations between International Health Aid and Government Funding Too Complex to Be Captured in Averages Only?" *Lancet* 375: 1403.

PEPFAR. 2012. "Funding Fact Sheet 2004–2012" (www.pepfar.gov/press/80064.htm).

Radelet, Steven. 2007. "Global Fund Grant Programmes: An Analysis of Evaluation Scores." *Lancet* 369.

Rivers, Bernard. 2011. "The Most Important and Difficult Board Meeting Ever." AllAfrica. Com. November 21.

Rose, Pauline. 2005. "Is There a Fast Track to Achieving Education for All?" *International Journal of Educational Development* 385: 25.4.

Sabot, Oliver. 2012. "One More Reason to Fund the Global Fund." *Lancet* 379: e25.

SCF (Strategic Climate Fund). 2009. *Financial Statement 2009.* (www.climateinvestment funds.org/cif/sites/climateinvestmentfunds.org/files/SCF%20Financial%20Statement %20_December%2031%202009%20.pdf).

UK. 2011a. Department for International Development. "Multilateral Aid Review: Assessment for International Fund for Agricultural Development" (www.dfid.gov.uk/Documents/ publications1/mar/IFAD.pdf).

———. 2011b. Department for International Development. "Multilateral Aid Review: Taking Forward the Findings of the UK Multilateral Aid Review" (www.dfid.gov.uk/Documents/ publications1/mar/Taking-forward.pdf).

Van de Sijpe, Nicolas. 2010. "Is Foreign Aid Fungible? Evidence from the Education and Health Sectors" (2www.feb.ugent.be/nl/Ondz/wp/Papers/wp_10_688.pdf).

World Bank. 2004a. "Addressing the Challenges of Globalization: An Independent Evaluation of the World Bank's Approach to Global Programs" (http://lnweb90.worldbank.org/oed/oeddoclib.nsf/DocUNIDViewForJavaSearch/762997A38851FA0685256F8200777E15/$file/gppp_main_report_phase_2.pdf).

————. 2004b. "Education for All Fast-Track Initiative: Framework Paper" (www.educationfasttrack.org/media/library/FrameworkNOV04.pdf).

5

Incentives and Accountability for Scaling Up

JOHANNES F. LINN

The scaling up of successful development interventions involves an iterative cycle of innovation, knowledge management, and expansion or replication.[1] Experience shows that successful scaling up requires driving forces (drivers) that push the process forward and the creation of spaces—or the removal of obstacles—so that successful innovative initiatives can be expanded and replicated.[2] Among the drivers of scaling are the innovative idea or model, leaders and champions who have a clear vision of scale to be achieved, external events or influences (economic crisis, external aid), and incentives and accountability for the actors involved.

A 2008 study considers incentives (and accountability) a particularly important driver for the scaling-up process and explores it briefly in its review of the literature and experience with scaling up.[3] The German aid agency GIZ (formerly GTZ) in its guidelines for scaling up also addresses incentives as an important factor facilitating scaling up, including financial incentives (such as subsidies), competitions, transparency, and peer-to-peer learning.[4] An exemplary case study of the scaling-up experience of the Mexican national conditional cash-transfer program, Progresa-Oportunidades, stresses the importance

1. Linn and others (2010).
2. Hartmann and Linn (2008).
3. Hartmann and Linn (2008).
4. GTZ (2010).

138

of appropriate incentives and accountabilities in explaining the scaling-up success of this program.[5] A recent institutional scaling-up review carried out by a Brookings team for the International Fund for Agricultural Development (IFAD) systematically looks at how IFAD's operational incentive and accountability mechanisms (its operational strategy, policies, processes, and instruments, as well as its budgetary practices and management practices) support the scaling up of successful interventions.[6] Another 2010 study explores options for providing incentives for scaling up successful interventions in fragile states by modifying donors' country-allocation rules for aid.[7]

Beyond these few sources, I find no systematic consideration of incentives as a driver in the scaling-up literature, although incentives are mentioned in passing in various documents dealing with the scaling-up challenge, and useful evidence can be gleaned here and there. For example, in developing its comprehensive framework for scaling up, one study mentions the need for incentives in connection with managing implementation and coordination.[8] The World Bank, in its report on the major conference it organized with the Chinese authorities in 2004 in Shanghai on scaling up poverty reduction, summarizes the example of China's successful strategy for scaling up, which allows insights into the incentives provided by the Chinese approach.[9] The World Bank's exploration of scaling up in agriculture and rural development mentions the role of "financial incentives of donors and governments" for supporting scaling up.[10] And the World Bank's report that calls for large-scale action on nutrition notes that incentives are needed for implementers, including performance monitoring and linking aid disbursement to performance.[11] The official review by the UK government, "Scaling Up Innovation in the Public Sector," repeatedly notes the importance of "rewards, incentives and recognition" for effective scaling up by the public sector.[12]

All these documents have one thing in common: while postulating that incentives and accountability are important for scaling up, none of them provide any detailed analysis of or guidance on what incentives are needed by whom, for whom, and when, what incentives actually work, why, and how, and so on. The purpose of this chapter is to begin to fill this gap with a special focus on what innovative approaches and tools are available and should be further explored to support the scaling-up process in development.

5. Levy (2006).
6. Linn and others (2010).
7. Gelb (2010).
8. Cooley and Kohl (2005).
9. Wang (2005).
10. World Bank (2003b, p. 42).
11. World Bank (2006).
12. H.M. Civil Service (2011).

In doing so, the chapter draws on a related strand of literature regarding effective service provision and sustainability of aid. The World Bank, in its report on public service delivery, provides a useful analytical framework for considering incentives and accountability in public service provision, although it does not specifically focus on the scaling-up challenge.[13] An earlier study considers incentives in an in-depth review carried out for the Swedish aid agency SIDA, with a view to how incentives support sustainability, which is closely related to scalability.[14] Indeed, this quote summarizes well why it is important to look carefully at incentives: "A successful approach to the problem of development must focus on how to generate appropriate incentives so that the time, skill, knowledge, and genuine effort of multiple individuals are channeled in ways that produce jointly valued outcomes. . . . Unless development aid properly addresses the incentives of underlying collective-action problems, it will likely be ineffective or, worse, even counterproductive."[15]

Finally, a 2011 study provides a very helpful inventory and categorization of incentives in development assistance and explores the opportunities, constraints, and pitfalls that donors and recipients face in dealing with incentives (and disincentives) in connection with aid.[16] However, as with the other studies, the author does not explore the implications for scaling up.

I first present a framework for analyzing incentives and accountability for scaling up and how this framework can be applied to scaling-up initiatives pursued by national authorities in developing countries. I then adapt the framework to a context where aid supports countries' development efforts and consider options for improving incentives and accountabilities for scaling up with aid. In a concluding section I summarize the main implications and recommendations of the preceding analysis.

Before proceeding, a word of caution is needed. There is no blueprint for successful scaling up, and, there are no silver bullets for the design of appropriate incentives and accountabilities.[17] Moreover, this chapter is only a start in addressing this complex set of issues, with a limited set of experiences to draw on and only a preliminary set of conclusions and recommendations. However, the chapter confirms the view that careful consideration of incentives and accountabilities is critical for the design of an effective scaling-up process, and it provides an analytical approach and some empirically based insights for the design of appropriate incentive and accountability mechanisms.

13. World Bank (2003a).
14. Ostrom and others (2001).
15. Ostrom and others (2001, pp. xiii–xiv).
16. Savedoff (2011).
17. Hartmann and Linn (2008).

Incentives and Accountability at the Country Level

Let us start with definitions: "An incentive is the promise of a reward (or the fear of a punishment) that encourages certain behaviors and discourages others."[18] And according to Merriam-Webster's, accountability is the "obligation or willingness to take responsibility for one's actions."[19] An incentive will be effective only if the incentive provider lives up to the promise made and the recipient exhibits, in return, the agreed-on behavior.

Framework of Analysis

In exploring the role of incentives and accountability for scaling up, I draw on the framework developed by the World Bank for the analysis of incentives and accountability in public service delivery.[20] This framework looks at the triangular relationship among the state, service providers, and citizens (figure 5-1). The state, represented by politicians and policymakers, contracts with service providers (government departments, provincial and local governments, public and private enterprises, and NGOs) for the delivery of services to its citizens.

Two routes of incentives and accountability from citizens to providers assure effective service delivery: one, the "long route," by which citizens and their interest groups elect (or otherwise influence) the politicians and policymakers and with their taxes support the state budget, while the state contracts with, pays, and holds accountable the providers for the delivery of services; and two, the "short route" by which citizens directly provide incentives for and hold accountable the service providers. This can involve payment for services by consumers, empowerment of communities to demand access, expansion of services, and improvements in services. In any case, transparency and widely available information about the activities of all actors, the results of their interventions, and of the costs and benefits of the service provided make both short and long routes function better.

Many complexities could be added to this simple picture. For example, multiple agencies of the state and among providers may be involved in the provision of particular services. Or in federal states or in countries with empowered local governments, multiple governmental layers and relationships would need to be added. Finally, and very importantly, as shown in figure 5-1, within

---

18. Savedoff (2011, p. 2).
19. See www.merriam-webster.com/dictionary/accountability.
20. World Bank (2003a). Ostrom and others (2001) also provide a framework for analyzing incentives for sustainability of development interventions, which is similar to that of the World Bank in that it links the interactions among donors, donor agencies, contractors, and recipient governments, their agencies, and the ultimate beneficiaries.

Figure 5-1. *Incentives and Accountabilities for Donors and Recipients* [a]

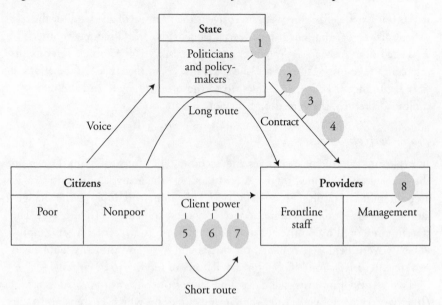

Source: Adapted by author from World Bank (2003a).
a. Numbers in bubbles refer to incentive and accountability instruments discussed in the text.

provider institutions one needs to distinguish between the management of the organization and the frontline staff, who actually deliver the services.

In a context where the long and short routes of incentives and accountability work well, they provide powerful drivers for scaling up. If some citizens have access to services but others do not, those with lack of access to services will pressure the state to contract with providers for the extension of services along the long route, while at the same time consumers of services will put pressure on the providers along the short route. If an innovation offers the prospects of enhanced services, information will flow through the system to make sure that all actors are aware of it and provide incentives to introduce the innovation systemwide.

Problems of Incentives and Accountability

Unfortunately, much can go wrong in the long and short routes of accountability. For the long route, a misalignment of incentives between principals and agents is pervasive, with principals (citizens, state, provider management) having different interests from agents (politicians and policymakers, provider management, and frontline staff) and limited or no accountability of the latter to the former. In underdeveloped democratic systems, citizens, and especially poor and underserviced people, often have a weak voice in influencing and holding accountable politicians and policymakers, and weak legal systems limit the incentives (and ability) of policymakers to effectively represent citizen interests in contracting with providers. In democratic systems, electoral politics often reward shifts in priorities and discontinuities in programs from one elected government to another, as politicians promise different initiatives from those pursued by their predecessors.

Even where the state has the interests of the citizenry at heart, it may not have the capacity or the will to implement effective national plans and budgets or to design and enforce effective contracts with providers. Interagency fragmentation and competition, lack of effective monitoring and evaluation of programs, and corrupt channels of transmittal of funding lead to programs of limited effectiveness, sustainability, and scale. A common story is the leakage of education funds in the transmission from the national budget to local providers.[21] And then there is the problem of providers' weak institutional capacity, including ineffective and corrupt management of frontline staff without appropriate incentives and accountabilities: the stories of underpaid teachers not showing up to teach are well known, as are those of public health doctors serving private patients rather than the public at large.

In short, the short route is nonexistent or hardly functions in many countries: the systems of user fees are underdeveloped, communities are weakly empowered to negotiate with utilities, and information on the plans, budgets, and service quality of providers is generally kept out of the public domain. As a result of these breakdowns in the system of incentives and accountabilities, service is not extended to the poor. Further, innovations, while they may be introduced locally, are not scaled up, since the actors do not have an incentive to do so. This tendency is reinforced by the fact that in a public sector environment, where decisions are made on political and bureaucratic grounds, there are strong biases against replication and scaling up. Instead, incentives are geared toward trying different approaches from those of one's political or bureaucratic predecessor or from the agency one competes with. While innovation is writ large in many development institutions as the key goal, systematically evaluating whether the new ideas actually work and then systematically building on those that do work is given little political support, managerial attention, or financial incentives.

Contrast this with a private, competitive market provision of goods and services. Although the state may have a role in regulating and taxing the private transaction, the short route dominates in a market setting, with multiple providers competing for an empowered consumer. In essence, only the short route needs to be considered and the alignment of incentives and accountabilities. The provider has every reason to respond to the needs of the citizen consumer and will be held accountable if he does not. Promising innovations will be scaled up,

---

21. World Bank (2003a); Birdsall and Savedoff (2011).

since they yield additional profits either to the innovator or to his competitors, who will find it in their interest to copy the innovation. In fact, in order to give adequate incentives to private innovators, patent protection is needed.

Of course, there are also reasons that the simple private model doesn't work in many social and infrastructure service areas: the public goods nature of the services involved, such market failures as lack of competition, and the inability of poor populations to pay for commercial access to public services. For these reasons, state engagement in the provision of public services is common and appropriate. And so the question of how to provide effective incentives and accountabilities for public goods and service provision remains critical.[22]

Examples of Incentives and Accountability

Despite the rather gloomy perspective on the long and short routes of incentives and accountability in the preceding paragraphs, there are examples of the system working relatively well, where ways have been found to align incentives and accountabilities to ensure the effective scaling up of successful development interventions. Perhaps the most powerful example for successful scaling up is the Chinese development experience since the early 1980s. Key elements of the Chinese approach relevant to the current discussion include the following:[23]

—Clear goal setting at the national level in terms of overarching growth and poverty-reduction objectives.

—Monitoring and rewards for political and bureaucratic leaders at provincial and local levels in their achievement of these goals.

—Encouragement of piloting of new initiatives with systematic learning and evaluation of impacts and scaling up of successful interventions.

—Decentralization of decisionmaking to local and firm levels with competition among jurisdictions and actors.

—Participation of poor households in poverty program design and implementation.

This approach resulted in strongly aligned incentives along the long and short routes of accountability in support of effective scaling up and development. In the words of one commentator, "China is able to align incentives for central, provincial, and local government officials with its development goals, and implement a merit system with accountability for civil servants."[24] Specific programs reflect the general approach; for example, the South-West Poverty Reduction Project and the Loess Plateau Watershed Rehabilitation Project were both large-scale, comprehensive rural poverty reduction programs, which

22. Ostrom and others (2001) provides a comprehensive list of potential sources of government and market failure that are grounded in misalignment of incentives.

23. Wang (2005).

24. Wang (2005, p. 75).

benefited millions of poor Chinese farmers.[25] Of course, there are also risks involved in China's scaling-up strategy, resulting from the way growth-oriented incentives are working in practice. For example, the detrimental environmental impacts of industrialization and urban development tend to be neglected, and in their pursuit of unbridled expansion municipal leaders have had strong incentives to expand urban boundaries without due regard to the interests of established farming communities. In the case of the Loess Plateau project and other rural development programs, overuse of water resources was encouraged according to an evaluation by the World Bank, which supported these programs.[26]

A second example is the Mexican Progresa-Oportunidades program. Over a period of ten years, this program was gradually expanded to provide substantial cash benefits to most poor Mexican households, or almost 25 million people, as long as they sent their children to school and for regular health checkups and provided them with nutritional supplements. In his comprehensive evaluation of the scaling-up approach of this program, its chief architect, Santiago Levy, stresses the importance of strong leadership by Mexico's presidents and a clear vision of the ultimate scale of the program desired.[27] Levy also notes that effective incentives and accountabilities were key to the success of the program:

—The conditionality of the cash transfers (regarding schooling, health, and nutrition), combined with recipients' sense of empowerment.

—The scaling up of efficient delivery of the funds to households by the newly created central administrative unit, which has exclusive responsibility for the implementation of the program, bypassing all ministries and state and local authorities.

—Clear rules of operation, systematic program evaluation, and transparency in ensuring accountability of all actors.

—Unassailable evidence of the success of the program and delinking it from the political process, ensuring accountability of the government in general and that parliamentarians and political administrations would continue the program across electoral cycles.

As a result of the careful design of this program, traditional obstacles to scaling up effective antipoverty programs in Mexico could be kept in check, including the tendency to introduce new programs with each new presidential administration and the lack of incentives among governmental agencies at national, state, and local levels to cooperate.[28]

The case of basic education reform in Uganda reflects a number of key incentive and accountability dimensions. In 1996, during the first democratic

25. Wang (2005).

26. World Bank (2007).

27. Levy (2006).

28. As Levy (2006, p. 95) puts it: "incentives . . . for 'starting a new initiative,' 'creating a new program,' and 'designing a new approach.'"

election in Uganda since a military takeover in 1986, one of the presidential candidates promised to introduce universal free primary education. He won, and his government abolished school fees and within five years dramatically scaled up primary school enrollment from about 3.5 million to about 7 million. Three key factors accounted for this outcome:[29]

—Democratic accountability: the election and subsequent reelection of the president could be directly linked to his promise of universal free primary education and his subsequent success in delivering on this promise.

—Financial incentives: the abolition of school fees provided a key incentive (or removal of disincentive) for parents to enroll their children, combined with a sustained shift in budget resources toward education.

—Information and transparency: the government regularly published information on monthly school district transfers, providing incentives for more effective pass-through by provincial and local authorities and thus dramatically reducing the share of transfers "lost in transit" from 80 percent to 20 percent, which contributed to the successful scaling up of education services.

The community health program of Brazil, which was piloted in the state of Ceará in the late 1980s and early 1990s and later expanded to the rest of Brazil, resulted in 170,000 community health workers serving 80 million people by 2001 and in notable improvements in health conditions.[30] The program involved five incentive elements:

—Community involvement: health agents were selected from the communities, and community representatives participated in program evaluations.

—Incentive grants to municipalities: municipalities receive national and state matching grants in support of the expansion of the local community health program.

—Special awards to mayors: mayors who are actively engaged in the programs receive a special (nonmonetary) "seal" of recognition from their state government.

—Monitoring and evaluation: program implementation is actively monitored and evaluated.

—Information dissemination: information on programs and their impact is widely circulated to provide incentives and accountability for politicians and bureaucrats.

Instrumentalities for Incentives and Accountability

Let us now take a brief and partial look at selected instrumentalities for creating incentives and accountabilities at the country level. First, I consider the long route in figure 5-1 and, in particular, how effective incentive alignment and accountability can be created between the state and providers. I then also explore the same issue for the short route. The number of each instrument refers to the numbered identifiers in figure 5-1.

29. World Bank (2003a).
30. World Bank (2003a).

1. NATIONAL AND SECTORAL STRATEGIES. These are one way national governments aim to ensure alignment between national development goals and the actions of specific line agencies, reinforced by budget allocations as incentive and accountability mechanisms. However, national planning and strategy exercises—including growth and poverty-reduction strategies, often supported by aid donors—in practice tend to be weak instruments, not least because they rarely set priorities in line with resources and tend not to be linked to specific modalities for ensuring implementation at the agency level. In particular, they tend not to be linked to specific annual budget processes, which in turn tend to have a short-term perspective, rather than linking to long-term objectives, which would include developing scaled-up national programs from successful pilots, to annual resource allocation decisions. Sectoral and subsectoral strategies can be more effective mechanisms for linking long-term goals with short-term resource allocation and implementation modalities. Indeed, these strategies are increasingly the preferred way for donors to link their own resources to those of nationally supported initiatives.

2. INCENTIVE GRANTS. Implementation of national development goals generally takes place in a decentralized, multilayered governmental structure, where provincial and local governments have some degree of independent planning and budget authority. Incentive grants by higher-level governments to subnational authorities or providers are a common method for generating desired institutional behavior, including pursuit of the scaling-up objective, by agencies in charge of public goods and service delivery. This type of grant, also known as a matching grant, where local cost sharing is required, is a well-known instrument of intergovernmental fiscal relations. However, it has a mixed track record.[31] For these grants to be effective, monitoring of the providers' activities is required to ensure that the conditions of grant release are met. Only if the grant-making agency is willing to enforce the conditions, including nonrelease of grants where providers have not acted appropriately, will this grant mechanism act as an effective incentive and accountability mechanism. In the case of urban programs, higher-level governments do not have a good track record in this regard.[32]

3. CONTRACTS. A special form of conditional relationship between higher-level government and providers involves the development of formal contracts. These are particularly relevant when the provider is a private or nongovernmental entity. For example, in the case of public health reform in Costa Rica in the 1990s, the government introduced performance contracts for hospitals and private health cooperatives, resulting in significant expansion and improvements

31. Bahl and Linn (1992).
32. Kharas and Linn (forthcoming).

of health delivery conditions and outcomes.[33] A similar approach was followed in Cambodia beginning in the late 1990s.[34] There, a distinctive feature was that parallel systems of contracting out to private providers, "contracting in" (getting private managers to assist public providers), and traditional public provision were implemented and evaluated in terms of their impacts. Contracting out was found to have the best results in terms of scaling up and health outcomes. Contract-based arrangements require careful design, effective management, and transparent monitoring of inputs and outputs. Not surprisingly, this has created difficulties in institutionally weak environments, where the legal and regulatory framework for contracting may be poorly developed and where both contracting parties are subject to lack of institutional capacity, political interference, or corruption. Dissatisfaction with the traditional contracting methods has led some to argue for outcome-based contracting (also known as cash on delivery).[35]

4. COMPETITIONS OR TOURNAMENTS. Grants and contracts between the state and the providers may be structured as competitions among providers. Such competitions may involve financial rewards or penalties for the "winners" or nonmonetary rewards or recognition. They may involve simple certification of performance at some threshold level, or there may be a true competition, where only the top tier of performers receives a reward.[36] The seal of recognition for Brazilian mayors is such a nonmonetary certification. In the case of the Peru highlands poverty program true competitions with financial rewards were used to allocate community development funds across participating highland communities in developing local antipoverty and job-creation programs.[37] Competitions are effective ways of aligning incentives between principals and agents, according to theory and evidence.[38] They are inherently instruments for achieving desired provider behavior at a large scale, since by definition they cover a multitude of agents. There is indicative (case study) evidence that competitions achieve positive outcomes. However, they need to be transparent, tailored to the specific circumstances, and carefully monitored and evaluated.

5. SUBSIDIES AND OTHER FINANCIAL INCENTIVES. Turning then to the short route of accountability between the providers and the citizens, let us first look at subsidies and other financial incentives for beneficiaries, which are a

---

33. Moreno-Dodson (2005).
34. World Bank (2003a).
35. Birdsall and Savedoff (2011).
36. Mixed approaches are also possible, such as when the top tier takes the main prizes and others who meet certain minimum standards receive a consolation prize.
37. Linn and others (2010).
38. Zinnes (2009).

common way of creating demand for the public goods and services that a government wants to scale up. The cash grants under the Progresa-Oportunidades project in Mexico and the free primary school admission in Uganda are cases of using financial incentives to create and scale up the demand for public services. Financial incentives have two common risks: they may be set too high and create wasteful use and excessive demand for a scarce commodity requiring rationing (such as public utilities); and they tend to run into fiscal constraints. In the case of Mexico, the latter problem was avoided by eliminating other subsidy programs judged to be less effective.[39] In the case of Uganda, the combination of rapid economic growth and effective macromanagement helped avoid a fiscal constraint.[40] However, a recent review finds that the lack of financial sustainability is a key constraint for urban service expansion in aid-supported programs.[41]

6. COMMUNITY EMPOWERMENT. Another very prominent means for improving the short route of accountability for scaling up is community empowerment. This can take many forms, including the active engagement of community representatives in the planning, budgeting, management, and evaluation of provider activities. The EDUCO program in El Salvador is a particularly successful case of community involvement in the education sector. This program involved an agreement between the ministry of education and an elected executive committee for each school (consisting mostly of parents) for the delivery of education funding and the hiring and firing of teachers. The initiative developed from a pilot into a nationwide program with a strong positive impact on access to education.[42] Another successfully scaled-up program based on community engagement is the Kecamatan Development Program in Indonesia, which involved the large-scale provision of local infrastructure investments in poor rural (and later urban) areas. This was funded by a national agency but was fully under the control of local communities. A similar community-based approach was followed in the Peruvian highlands in support of local agricultural development and off-farm employment creation.[43]

A common feature of all these community-based programs is that they have the capacity to engage poor and remote communities not just one at a time but rather along a scaling-up pathway, driven by the active participation, experimentation, and own-resource generation of the communities concerned. This effect is reinforced by the demonstration effect of the successful participating communities on nonparticipant communities. However, for these programs to succeed,

39. Levy (2006).
40. World Bank (2003a).
41. Kharas and Linn (forthcoming).
42. World Bank (2003a).
43. Linn and others (2010).

persistent, supportive, and low-key engagement by the public agencies over the long haul is required, often with the support of civil society organizations, as was the case in the Peru highlands program. But the key ingredient is effective incentives and accountabilities at the community level along the short route.[44]

7. WIDELY ACCESSIBLE INFORMATION. Another form of citizen engagement is more arm's length, involving widely accessible information. This information might be about the number of school transfers (as in the case of Uganda). Another example is the use of citizen report cards, initiated in Bangalore, India, but later replicated in other Indian cities and in other countries.[45] These report cards rate the performance of service providers based on surveys, interviews, and complaints received. They have led to greater responsiveness by utility managers and local politicians to citizen concerns. Critical for the report cards to succeed is their repeated use and the engagement of the media and civil society in publicizing the findings of the reports and using them to press the political establishment and bureaucracies for effective and lasting change.

8. INTERNAL MANAGEMENT. Finally, an important element of the incentive and accountability loop is what goes on within provider organizations. A common weakness of public providers is that internal management practices do not offer effective incentives and accountability between top management and frontline staff. The problem may lie in a lack of internal controls or otherwise poor and unstable management, in a lack of staff motivation and of a performance-based culture, in salaries that are too low, or all of the above. Simple activities, such as requiring teachers to send dated cell phone pictures from school or student and parent involvement in monitoring teacher presence and performance, can serve as incentive mechanisms. But more general reform of civil service and provider institutions may be required if these institutions are to be effective at scaling up.

Incentives and Accountability in Aid Agencies

When one adds aid donors as key actors in many developing countries, the picture of incentives and accountability gets further complicated.

Framework of Analysis

As shown in the left-hand side of figure 5-2, the donor side of the picture is also characterized by a triangular set of actors: the government of the donor country,

---

44. For an in-depth treatment of community-driven scaling up of poverty programs, see Binswanger-Mkhize and others (2009).
45. World Bank (2003a); Hartmann and Linn (2008).

Figure 5-2. *Incentives and Accountability with Aid Donors*[a]

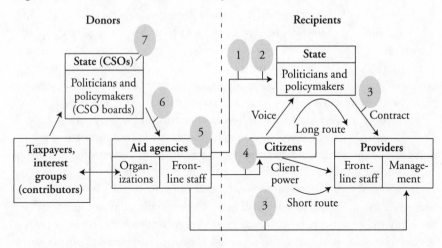

Source: Adapted by author from World Bank (2003a).
a. Numbers in bubbles refer to incentive and accountability instruments discussed in the text.

the aid agency, and the national taxpayers and their interest groups. Here the long route of accountability runs from taxpayers through the government to the aid agency; there is also a short route, in that some taxpayer groups (such as advocacy NGOs) try to influence aid agencies directly. And through provision of information and appeals, aid agencies may directly try to motivate taxpayers for greater support.[46] In addition, there are the linkages between donor agencies and recipient countries, as funding flows from the aid agency either to the recipient country's government, to the providers, or to citizens directly. Many bilateral donors, vertical funds, and civil society organizations (CSOs) bypass the government and contract directly with providers (either existing local organizations or new project implementation units).[47] Some aid donors, especially smaller CSOs, work directly with recipients' communities in providing their financial support. Multilateral development banks, in contrast, tend to work directly with governments, especially in their programmatic and budget support, although they also often work with, or set up, providers, especially freestanding project implementation units, in the actual implementation of their projects and programs.

46. Applied to nongovernmental donors (CSOs), figure 5-1 reflects the triangular relations among the contributors, boards, and agencies of the CSO donors.
47. Vertical funds are special-purpose funding agencies set up by donors to provide financing for specific areas of intervention, especially in the health field (such as the Global Fund for AIDS, Tuberculosis, and Malaria and the GAVI Alliance for Vaccines and Immunization).

Problems of Incentives and Accountability

As documented by the many critics of development aid, the incentives and accountabilities for effective delivery of aid are often absent, because the problems with the long and short routes of accountability in recipient countries are reinforced by problems with the long and short routes of accountability in donor countries and with the problems introduced by aid flows themselves.[48] For example, special interest groups among donor taxpayers may skew aid along the long or short route in ways serving these special interest groups. Or political control over aid agencies may be weak, fragmented, or inconsistent across electoral cycles, and the management of aid agencies may have difficulty in providing incentives to their frontliné staff for ensuring effective delivery of aid. And there are the usual principal-agent problems along the chain of actors. In each of these cases, incentives and accountability for scaling up successful development interventions are likely to be particularly weak, since each actor in the system tends to pursue special interests and operates with short time horizons and limited information.

Additional problems of incentives and accountability arise in connection with the aid flows themselves. Aid that flows directly to the government can, in principle, support the strengthening of national institutions, policy reforms, and nationwide programs and thus support large-scale interventions or scaling up of successful innovations at the national level. However, such aid also tends to undermine the role of citizens in influencing governments in recipient countries and to weaken the accountability of governments to their citizens, since citizens do not have to pay taxes to mobilize resources (as in the case of resource-rich countries). Aid flows that bypass governments may undermine national institutional capacity and miss opportunities for strengthening the institutional, policy, and regulatory environment, which is a critical aspect of scaling up. Aid that flows directly to citizens and their communities is likely to be small in size and difficult to scale up. Since the donor community is highly fragmented, with hundreds of bilateral and multilateral official agencies and thousands of nongovernmental entities providing aid and with a rising number of projects at ever smaller median size, the problem of lack of scale in donor interventions is further reinforced.[49]

Strengthening Incentives and Accountability

Let us now look at various ways to improve incentives and accountability for scaling up with aid. Seven specific instrumentalities are developed in the following paragraphs and referred to in figure 5-2 with the numbered call-out identifiers.

48. See for example Ostrom and others (2001), World Bank (2003a), and Birdsall and Savedoff (2011) for summaries of and references for these critiques.
49. Kharas (2007).

1. CASH ON DELIVERY. The idea for cash-on-delivery (COD) was developed in recent years by experts in the Center for Global Development.[50] They argue that the best way to empower aid recipients is for the aid agency to enter into a contract with the recipient government, in which the aid donor agrees to provide a determined annual amount of aid for a period of five years (and more, if the contract is renewed) if specified outcomes (increase in school enrollment, for example) have been achieved, as verified by independent third-party monitors. The argument for this approach is that rewarding outcomes (rather than inputs or outputs) is preferable, since it is then left entirely up to the recipients how they will achieve these outcomes. Furthermore accountability of aid agencies to their political masters and taxpayers is improved, and these actors have greater incentives to support aid because they can see demonstrated improvements in outcomes. The center's study specifically envisages using the COD approach in support of a long-term scaling-up pathway and offers the example of COD aid payments for primary school enrollment. The authors somewhat counterintuitively argue that the approach is especially well suited for aid to fragile states.

The simplicity of the COD approach and the apparent alignment of interests across key actors is attractive, but it raises various concerns, including

—The realism of the approach in terms of the ability of aid agencies and recipient governments to identify relevant simple, achievable, and monitorable outcome indicators.

—Recipient governments' ability to implement programs to attain the outcomes without support for specific inputs and outputs.

—What happens when external factors beyond government control either impede or enhance the achievement of the outcomes.

—Aid agencies and their political masters' willingness to adopt a hands-off approach (including absence of measures to prevent corruption or environmental harm in the use of the aid flows).[51]

The center's study largely dismisses these and related concerns, but it does recognize the need for careful design, experimentation, and monitoring, as COD approaches are developed in practice. Until such time as donors and recipients have tried out the approach, COD remains a hypothesis in political economy waiting to be tested.

50. Birdsall and Savedoff (2011).
51. See de Renzio and Woods (2008). The negative response of some critics in the NGO community to the World Bank's program for results (P4R)—which embodies some elements of the COD approach but retains many fiduciary, social, and environmental safeguards—is instructive about the acceptance of COD among some key constituencies in the donor countries. For an example of a such a critique of P4R, see Alexander (2011). The recent response of the governing body of the Global Fund for AIDS, Tuberculosis, and Malaria to allegations of fraudulent use of some of its funding in recipient countries, which led to a tightening of ex ante fiduciary controls, is another example of the difficulty that aid donors have with hands-off fiduciary controls.

2. PROGRAMMATIC AID. The COD approach is an extreme version of programmatic aid, where aid agencies provide support not for specific projects but in support of recipient country governments' national policy reforms, budgets, or sectoral reform and strategies. The history of such aid goes back to the U.S. Marshall Plan for European reconstruction after World War II, but it was revived by the World Bank in the 1980s with its "structural adjustment lending" and associated policy conditionalities, later transformed into "development policy lending," "sector program loans," and most recently, "program for results" (P4R) lending. While practices vary across donors and programmatic instruments, all these programmatic approaches have certain features in common:

—They aim to support scaled-up interventions by the government through policy and institutional reform with broad national impacts. They do this by funding general budgets or sector-expenditure programs that have a broad impact of national or sectoral significance. Increasingly, they pool the financial resources of multiple donors, therefore providing explicit and potentially strong incentives to governments to pursue scaling-up approaches.

—They monitor key input and output metrics (such as budgetary expenditures, policy and institutional reforms, and program output deliveries) and disburse against progress in these metrics.

—They impose strong fiduciary control requirements and social and environmental safeguards.

Programmatic approaches have been criticized because of their conditionalities, which are seen to reduce recipient governments' empowerment to decide on how to achieve desired development outcomes and which are often honored in the breach.[52] These approaches are thought to weaken the accountability of recipient governments to their own citizens. In addition, donor assistance for policy and institutional reform may be misguided or ineffective, and standards of fiduciary controls and social and environmental safeguards may be inappropriate for the development stage of recipient countries.

The World Bank's recent P4R initiative represents an effort to build a bridge in its programmatic financing to the COD approach.[53] The key feature of this new instrument is to identify outcome (rather than input and output) metrics and to disburse against the achievement of agreed outcomes. As such it reflects both some of the strengths and some of the weaknesses of the COD approach. However, judging from the World Bank's P4R documentation, the approach differs from COD in several ways:

---

52. Birdsall and Savedoff (2011).
53. World Bank (2011).

—P4R engages the World Bank in detailed assessments of recipient institutional capacity, in support for institutional capacity building, and in monitoring progress in this regard.

—P4R requires extensive fiduciary, social, and environmental safeguards.

—P4R does not in general require independent verification.

The P4R approach will continue to involve significant encroachment by the World Bank on recipient independence and authority, which has been criticized by the protagonists of the COD approach.[54] It remains to be seen whether the P4R approach is a significant improvement over the previous programmatic approaches in creating effective performance incentives and accountabilities.

At the sectoral level, donors have increasingly linked a programmatic approach with support for sectoral and subsectoral strategies developed by government, usually with donor assistance, as a way to support a sectorwide scaling up of initiatives. Three approaches have emerged:

—Under the first option global sectoral or vertical funds are set up, such as the Global Fund to Fight AIDS, Tuberculosis, and Malaria and the Global Alliance for Vaccines and Immunization. These funds have generally been found to serve as excellent platforms for helping to scale up narrowly defined sectoral (or subsectoral) initiatives by aligning goals and incentives across the whole spectrum of agents involved in the formulation and implementation of country-based strategies.[55]

—The second option involves global initiatives in support of specific sectoral goals, such as Education for All, the Comprehensive Africa Agriculture Development Programme (CAADP), and Scaling Up Nutrition (SUN). Since these initiatives lack a clear commitment mechanism to bundle donor resources at the global level in support of national sectoral goals, their incentive effect has been unclear, and they appear to have a weaker track record to date than vertical funds.

—The third option involves coordinated support at the country level by donors for specific sectoral strategies. This support has increasingly taken place under the umbrella of so-called sectorwide approaches (SWAps). Again, coordination under these umbrellas has had mixed success, since incentive and accountability mechanisms are relatively weak.[56]

3. COMPETITIONS. Aid donors can support the development and implementation of competitive grants, certifications, and competitions (as described

---

54. Gelb and Savedoff (2011).
55. Linn (2011).
56. See for example Cabral (2010) for an assessment of the performance of SWAps in agriculture.

earlier) in connection with country-based incentive schemes. A review of the principles and practices of countries and aid donors in regard to such schemes concludes that they are well suited to align incentives and interests not only within countries but also between donors and recipient.[57] The study cites two specific cases of relevance.

One case is that of the World Bank's assistance for a competitive grant system supporting reform across Russian provincial governments, a competition that not only was successful in its limited form but also led to a continuation and scaling up by the Russian authorities, strengthening decentralized decision-making around agreed-upon broad objectives of improved provincial management. The other specific case is the U.S. Millennium Challenge Corporation, which combined a process of allocation decisions of U.S. bilateral aid funds against stringent country performance measures thresholds but then allowed great freedom to national authorities in the use of the funds. In effect, these two cases show a competitive form of programmatic financing. Other cases involve donor support for competitions among providers, such as IFAD support for community competitions in the Peru highlands poverty program.

A special form of competitive scheme of financial rewards was set up by the World Bank in the late 1990s to stimulate and reward innovative initiatives in development solutions. The Development Marketplace invited submissions of promising ideas, which were then vetted and short-listed by experts for presentation at events at which winners were selected and rewarded with cash prizes.[58] Similarly, in the early 2000s, the UK's Department for International Development set up various challenge funds that provided competitive grants for innovative business initiatives in developing countries. A principal focus of these funds was assisting start-ups to overcome the initial hurdles of taking innovative ideas to market, rather than scaling up successfully launched initiatives.[59]

A similar approach could be pursued by setting up replication funds.[60] These funds would reward those initiatives that are being successfully scaled up. In effect, USAID already incorporates this idea in its Development Innovation Ventures (DIV) initiative.[61] DIV was set up in 2010 and, according to its website, "aims to identify, develop, test, and scale innovative approaches to achieve cost-effective, scalable solutions to development challenges that correct market

57. Zinnes (2009).

58. See the special World Bank website, http://wbi.worldbank.org/developmentmarketplace/.

59. For a description of the Africa Enterprise Challenge Fund, see www.dfid.gov.uk/work-with-us/funding-opportunities/countries-and-regions/aecf/. For an evaluation of the Business Linkage Challenge Fund, see Deloitt (2004).

60 Hartmann and Linn (2008)

61. For a description of DIV, see http://idea.usaid.gov/div/div-model-detail.

and government failures while accelerating promising solutions with a proven impact." It grants funding for these public and private sector initiatives competitively. The website lists three stages that the DIV supports: "Stage 1: the development needed to support proof of concept and feasibility; Stage 2: implementation of the project at large scale with rigorous impact testing; Stage 3: transition of innovations to widespread adoption throughout one country and/ or additional adoption in other countries. The most successful projects from the DIV portfolio are expected to be mainstreamed around the world or at least throughout a continent." This incentive-based initiative deserves careful monitoring for possible replication elsewhere.

4. DEMOCRACY DEVELOPMENT AND COMMUNITY EMPOWERMENT. Aid agencies have also provided support for the strengthening of citizen voices through democracy development and for the empowerment of communities in dealing with providers, thus trying to enhance both the short and long routes of accountability in public goods and service provision. Much of this support is provided by CSOs such as the Open Society Institute, by political foundations such as the institutes affiliated with national parties in Germany and the United States, and by bilateral official donors. While CSOs generally do not directly support the scaling up of specific governmental programs in recipient countries, the underlying notion is that a citizenry with a stronger voice in political discourse and a community able to look after its own needs improve access to, and quality of, public goods and service provision.[62] However, efforts from outside to support democratic and community empowerment (or even domestic efforts along these lines) can lead to negative reactions by national and local political elites, if they feel threatened by the strengthening of bottom-up accountability mechanisms.

5. INTERNAL INCENTIVES AND ACCOUNTABILITIES. So far we have considered how aid agencies can support scaling up by the recipient. But most aid agencies actually do not systematically pursue a scaling-up agenda.[63] This is for two reasons: either management does not buy into the agenda or frontline staff do not have incentives to support scaling up. For example, an evaluation of municipal development programs supported by the European Bank for Reconstruction and Development (EBRD) shows that EBRD project managers are rewarded with bonuses for each loan project processed, which leads to the proliferation of many city-specific projects rather than the bundling of projects under a multicity program. At the same time, EBRD's internal review process

62. World Bank (2003a).
63. Linn (2011).

discourages the replication of support for successful programs on the grounds that it does not create additional benefits.[64] This is reflective of similar, if less explicit, incentives for staff in most aid agencies, who see career rewards from managing many small projects rather than working in teams on larger operations, and who are discouraged from supporting replication projects.[65]

One recommendation is that aid agencies carry out "institutional scaling up reviews," which assess the corporate mission, strategy, operational policies, processes, and instrumentalities, as well as staff incentives and budget management, to see whether they reflect a scaling-up agenda and support or discourage scaling up by the frontline staff.[66] One such review was recently carried out by a Brookings team for IFAD.[67] It concludes that although scaling up is enshrined in IFAD's corporate mission and strategy statements, the agency has operational policies, processes, instrumentalities, staff incentives, and budget practices that do not encourage, and in some regards actively discourage, frontline staff from pursuing a scaling-up agenda. It is therefore not surprising to find that, while IFAD has a number of cases of successful support for the scaling up of programs, in many more cases scaling up was not systematically pursued. Specific recommendations for strengthening internal management incentives and accountabilities for a more systematic scaling-up effort by IFAD have been published.[68] Based on this experience, I conclude that systematic reviews of institutional scaling up need to be carried out by all donor agencies that wish to be active participants in scaling up aid-supported programs.

One study recommends a specific mechanism for improving resource availability and incentives for scaling up successful projects in fragile states.[69] It notes that performance-based approaches, commonly used by the multilateral development banks and other donors for allocating aid resources across countries, tend to bias allocations against fragile states with weak governance and institutional capacities—and in fact provide disincentives to agency staff for engaging in these countries. Noting, however, the special assistance needs of fragile states and the fact that there are examples of successful development initiatives in these countries, it argues that a special fund ought to be set aside from the overall resource pool and allocated separately for support of scaling up successful initiatives in such countries, based on objective evaluations of project success and scalability.

64. EBRD (2010).
65. I experienced this firsthand as a vice president in the World Bank responsible for operations in the Europe and Central Asia region between 1996 and 2003.
66. Hartmann and Linn (2008).
67. Linn and others (2010). Ostrom and others (2001) provides an in-depth institutional review of incentives for sustainability in the case of the Swedish aid agency SIDA. Many of the incentive issues highlighted in that exemplary institutional analysis also apply to the scaling-up objective.
68. Linn and others (2010).
69. Gelb (2010).

Box 5-1. *Introducing Scaling Up as a Core Feature of JICA's work*

The creation of the newly restructured JICA in 2008 represented a far-reaching organizational change in Japan's development cooperation system. JICA is now responsible for all three of Japan's main development cooperation tools: loans, grants, and technical cooperation.

JICA's new mission statement stressed "scaling up" as one of the agency's top priorities, and its leader, President Sadako Ogata, personally stressed scaling up as a key institutional goal. With these commitments in play as incentives for managers and staff, the agency has institutionalized scaling up by combining various tools brought together by the merger.

First, important procedures were introduced to strengthen the agency's operational strategies and to maximize the merger's synergistic effects, including the introduction of Analytical Works (AWs). AWs are JICA's countrywide analysis and assistance strategy papers, which serve as a basic framework to guide the agency's engagement with partner countries. These show how different aid tools (loans, grants and technical cooperation) can be employed in unison and help staff from previously separate agencies to work cooperatively under one roof. The AWs are also expected to be used as a communication tool among other agencies in Japan and with their partner countries.

Second, at the operational level, the natural direction of the agency's efforts was to link technical cooperation with financial facilities in support of scaling up. One example is a loan project, signed in 2012, with the government of Bangladesh for maternal and child health care improvement. This project and parallel technical assistance aim to scale up the achievements of an earlier technical cooperation project called the Safe Motherhood Promotion Project (2006–11), which resulted in a major increase in the use of health services for expectant mothers.

Third, along with efforts to achieve synergies of its operational tools, the Japanese aid agency is looking for fresh partnerships with nongovernmental organizations and the private sector. One example of JICA's move in this direction is a $65 million loan in 2011 to Pakistan for a polio vaccination program—aimed at capitalizing on the success of a series of earlier polio-related technical and grant projects conducted in Pakistan since 1996. This loan also represents JICA's attempt to link up with new partners. In a new arrangement for JICA, and one that provides a special incentive for effective scaling up, the aid agency signed an agreement for a "loan conversion" with the Bill and Melinda Gates Foundation. Under this, the foundation will repay the credit to JICA on behalf of the government of Pakistan, if the project is implemented successfully.

Source: Prepared by Hiroshi Kato, JICA Research Institute.

Finally, box 5-1 presents a snapshot of how a particular bilateral aid agency, Japan International Cooperation Agency (JICA), has approached the scaling-up agenda in a systematic manner following a major organizational restructuring.

6. EVALUATION PRACTICES. It has become best (although not universal) practice for governing boards of aid agencies to commission systematic and independent evaluations of the programs they support. However, these evaluations

generally focus exclusively on whether projects have been successful in achieving their goals and not on whether the agencies supported the scaling up of successful projects, either by continued financial engagement in follow-up programs or by systematically handing off to other partners for expansion or replication.[70] The exceptions known to me are IFAD and UNDP, as they have recently amended their evaluation guidelines to systematically assess their own scaling-up performances. As long as the governing boards of aid agencies (or ministers, in the case of bilateral agencies) do not require that evaluations assess the scaling-up performance of agencies, a potentially significant incentive and accountability mechanism is missing. Introducing this mechanism is undoubtedly one of the easiest ways to help get aid agencies focused on the scaling-up agenda.[71]

7. INTERNATIONAL AID ARCHITECTURE. Two contrasting trends are at work in the international aid architecture that are relevant for scaling up. On the one hand, ethical, political, and economic interests in donor and recipient countries alike have led to a proliferation of aid actors, of special funding mechanisms and trust funds, and of aid-funded projects with declining median sizes. This proliferation, combined with aid volatility, has led to an ever-worsening fragmentation of effort, with increasing difficulties and costs of coordination and cooperation among aid donors and recipient entities and a pronounced lack of a scaling up of successful interventions.[72] On the other hand, the international community has made intensive efforts over the last ten years to achieve more effective cooperation among donors, the alignment of donor programs with country priorities, and enhanced effectiveness in the delivery of aid. This is reflected in the Paris Declaration and in the Accra Agenda for Action, which were both reconfirmed and reinforced recently by the Busan Partnership for Effective Development Cooperation. By agreeing on such measures—elimination of project implementation units, use of country procurement and financial management missions, recipient-country leadership in aid coordination and harmonization, and commitment to transparency—donors and recipients have tried to create incentives and accountabilities for all development partners.[73]

Many of the specific measures agreed in Paris and Accra are consistent with and supportive of an agenda for scaling up successful development initiatives, but in neither of the declarations and their monitoring metrics is there an explicit reference to the idea of scaling up as a concept that needs to be systemically

70. Linn (2011).

71. A recent self-evaluation of the World Bank's Independent Evaluation Group unfortunately failed to note that scaling up is not addressed by World Bank evaluations. See Linn (2012).

72. Kharas (2007).

73. See OECD-DAC (www.oecd.org/document/3/0,3746,en_2649_3236398_41297219_1_1_1_1,00.html).

introduced and pursued in the development debate. At Busan scaling up was a topic of discussion in side events, and the concept did find its way into the Busan Declaration in the form of occasional references to scaling up and in the notion that leverage and catalytic effects are important. While it would have been preferable for the scaling-up idea to have a more central role in defining appropriate incentives, actions, and metrics, this represents progress. There was also progress in Busan in the explicit recognition that the proliferation of aid channels and special funds needs to be reversed, with a commitment to reach agreement by the end of 2012 on the principles and guidelines to achieve this goal.[74]

In short, the High Level Forum on Aid Effectiveness produced useful incentives for the scaling up of successful development interventions, even though the idea of scaling up could have played a more central role and more specific actions in support of scaling up could have been included. In any case, however, the incentive and accountability impact of these high-level agreements in changing donor and recipient behavior on the ground has been weak, as evaluations of progress using performance metrics reveal only limited progress. The key therefore in the future will have to be to carry the good intentions of Paris, Accra, and Busan more directly into an assessment of incentives and accountabilities of each of the organizations that are supposed to implement the declarations. This is entirely consistent with the intent of this chapter, which has considered the need for a careful analysis of institutional incentives and accountabilities and ways to improve them, with a view to effectively implementing a scaling-up agenda.

Conclusions and Recommendations

Let us now summarize the main conclusions and principal recommendations of the discussion in the preceding sections.

Conclusions

This chapter started with the proposition that incentives and accountability are an important driver for scaling up. With few exceptions, this dimension of the scaling-up agenda has not been given adequate attention, a gap that this chapter can only begin to fill. Much of the literature on scaling up deals with the question of what to scale up, and too little with the question of how to scale up.

In the private marketplace incentives are, if anything, skewed toward rewarding the successful replicators and against innovation that is unprotected by patents. By contrast, in the public and not-for-profit sectors incentives are skewed in the opposite direction, with political and bureaucratic incentives

---

74. See "Busan Partnership of Effective Development Co-operation" (www.busanhlf4.org).

overwhelmingly encouraging and rewarding the new and the different while, if anything, discouraging systematic and sustained replication, expansion, and scaling up over the long haul.

The framework of accountability along the long and short routes (figure 5-1) can usefully be adapted to analyze the incentives and accountabilities for scaling up, both in countries' own programs and in donor-supported initiatives. In practice, however, the short and long routes often do not work well due to an absence of effective incentives and accountabilities in the weak institutional and governance environments of developing countries.

The review of successful country cases of scaling up demonstrates that incentives and accountability played an important role in these examples, and I identify a number of instrumentalities that could serve to enhance the long and short routes of accountability, including incentive grants, contracting, and competitions for strengthening the long route; and subsidies and other financial incentives, community empowerment, information provision, and improved internal management among providers for strengthening the short route.

In considering incentives and accountability for aid agencies, I find that not only is there a lack of systematic attention in most aid agencies to the scaling-up agenda but also that incentives and accountability for scaling up are missing or insufficiently developed. Donors can support scaling up with various instruments, such as COD, programmatic financing, support for competitive approaches, and aid for democracy development and community empowerment. In addition, however, aid donors need to focus on their own incentive and accountability mechanisms, by carrying out institutional scaling-up reviews, by systematically incorporating the scaling-up dimension in their evaluations, and by bringing the scaling-up perspective explicitly into the top-down reforms of the global aid architecture (as is beginning to take place now with the Busan Declaration). Aside from mainstreaming incentives for scaling up into their core business, donors can also set up special funding mechanisms in support of scaling up. These mechanisms would operate in parallel to their main programs. However, the latter is no substitute for the former.

Recommendations

Rather than developing a detailed list of recommendations for the design and implementation of each incentive and accountability instrument, my recommendations focus on overarching innovations and on the no-brainers and easy wins. One overarching recommendation stands out:

—Governments and aid donors need to focus systematically on the scaling-up agenda, in general, and specifically on ensuring effective incentives and accountabilities in support of scaling up.

There are three no-brainers and easy wins:

—Governments and aid agencies should systematically collect and transparently publicize information on development and aid expenditures and their outputs and outcomes.

—Aid agencies (and governments) should incorporate scaling-up dimension explicitly into the evaluations of their activities.

—Aid agencies should carry out institutional scaling-up reviews, which assess the corporate goals, strategies, operational policies and processes, staff incentives, and budgetary practices in terms of whether they support a scaling-up agenda and provide the right incentives and accountabilities.

In addition, I offer three recommendations for experimental initiatives:

—Aid agencies should experiment with COD initiatives specifically focused on creating incentives for the long-term scaling up of desired development outcomes.

—Aid agencies and governments should experiment with setting up replication funds, which would provide financial incentives on a competitive basis to those agencies and individuals who effectively support scaling up.

—Aid agencies should experiment with structuring their aid-allocation mechanisms to provide incentives for better performance in aggregate and in fragile states should allocate resources earmarked for the scaling up of successful and scalable interventions.

References

Alexander, Nancy. 2011. "The World Bank's Proposed Program for Results (P4R): Implications for Environmental, Social, and Gender Safeguards and Corrupt Practices." Washington: Heinrich Böll Stiftung North America.

Bahl, Roy W., and Johannes F. Linn. 1992. *Urban Public Finances in Developing Countries.* Oxford University Press.

Binswanger-Mkhize, Hans P., Jacomina P. de Regt, and Stephen Spector, eds. 2009. *Scaling Up Local & Community Driven Development (LCDD): A Real World Guide to Its Theory and Practice.* World Bank.

Birdsall, Nancy, and William D. Savedoff. 2011. *Cash on Delivery: A New Approach to Foreign Aid.* Washington: Center for Global Development.

Cabral, Lidia. 2010. "Sector-Based Approaches in Agriculture." Briefing Paper 58. London: Overseas Development Institute.

Cooley, Larry, and Richard Kohl. 2005. "Scaling Up—From Vision to Large-Scale Change: A Management Framework for Practitioners." Washington: Management Systems International.

Deloitt Emerging Markets Group. 2004. "BLCF: Assessing Achievements and Future Directions." London.

De Renzio, Paolo, and Ngaire Woods. 2008. "The Trouble with Cash on Delivery Aid." Washington: Center for Global Development.

EBRD. 2010. "Municipal and Environmental Infrastructure Operations Policy Review." Special study. London.

Gelb, Alan. 2010. "How Can Donors Create Incentives for Results and Flexibility for Fragile States? A Proposal for IDA." Working Paper 227, October. Washington: Center for Global Development.

Gelb, Alan, and William D. Savedoff. 2011. "A New Instrument to Advance Development Effectiveness: Program for Results Lending." Comments on concept note. Washington: Center for Global Development.

GTZ. 2010. *Scaling Up in Development Cooperation: Practical Guidelines.* Eschborn.

Hartmann, Arntraud, and Johannes Linn. 2008. "Scaling Up: A Framework and Lessons for Development Effectiveness from Literature and Practice." Working Paper 4. Wolfensohn Center, Brookings.

H.M. Civil Service. 2011. "Scaling Up Innovation in the Public Sector." Final report of the Capability Building Programme Project Group. London.

Kharas, Homi. 2007. "Trends and Issues in Development Aid." Working Paper 1. Wolfensohn Center, Brookings.

Kharas, Homi, and Johannes F. Linn. Forthcoming. "Metropolitan Government Finances in Developing Countries." In *Financing Metropolitan Governments in Developing Countries,* edited by Roy W. Bahl, Johannes F. Linn, and Deborah L. Wetzel. Cambridge: Lincoln Institute of Land Policy.

Levy, Santiago. 2006. *Progress against Poverty: Sustaining Mexico's Progresa-Oportunidades Program.* Brookings.

Linn, Johannes F. 2011. "Scaling Up with Aid: The Institutional Dimension." In *Catalyzing Development: A New Vision for Aid,* edited by Homi Kharas, Koji Makino, and Woojin Jung. Brookings.

———. 2012. "Evaluating the Evaluators: Some Lessons from a Recent World Bank Self-Evaluation" (www.brookings.edu/opinions/2012/0221_world_bank_evaluation_linn.aspx).

Linn, Johannes F., and others. 2010. "Scaling Up the Fight against Rural Poverty: An Institutional Review of IFAD's Approach." Global Working Paper 39. Brookings.

Moreno-Dodson, Blanca. 2005. "Observations at the Country Level." In *Reducing Poverty on a Global Scale,* edited by Blanca Moreno-Dodson. World Bank.

———, ed. 2005. *Reducing Poverty on a Global Scale.* World Bank.

Ostrom, Elinor, and others. 2001. "Aid, Incentives, and Sustainability: An Institutional Analysis of Development Cooperation." Main report. Workshop in Political Theory and Policy Analysis, Indiana University.

Savedoff, William D. 2011. "Incentive Proliferation? Making Sense of a New Wave of Development Programs." Washington: Center for Global Development.

Wang, Yan. 2005. "Development as a Process of Learning and Innovation: Lessons from China." In *Reducing Poverty on a Global Scale,* edited by Blanca Moreno-Dodson. World Bank.

World Bank. 2003a. *World Development Report 2004: Making Services Work for Poor People.*

———. 2003b. "Scaling-Up the Impact of Good Practices in Rural Development." A working paper to support implementation of the World Bank's Rural Development Strategy.

———. 2006. *Repositioning Nutrition as Central to Development: A Strategy for Large-Scale Action.*

———. 2007. "People's Republic of China: Second Loess Plateau Watershed Rehabilitation Project." Report 4122. Independent Evaluation Group, project performance assessment report.

———. 2011. "A New Instrument to Advance Development Effectiveness: Program-for-Results Financing." Operations Policy and Country Services, July 18.

Zinnes, Clifford F. 2009. *Tournament Approaches to Policy Reform.* Brookings.

6

Angel Investment: Enterprise Solutions to Scale

CHRIS WEST

W hen Shell Foundation (SF) was established in 2000 we had ambitious objectives to catalyze scalable and sustainable solutions to global development challenges. We set about doing this in ways that were new at the time, by pioneering an enterprise-based approach and concentrating our efforts on tackling social and environmental issues, in which the energy industry has a particular responsibility. We also sought to test whether we could harness value-adding links to our corporate parent to maximize charitable benefit.

Since then we have learned a lot about how to target scale and sustainability. This chapter outlines some of the key lessons emerging from our successes and failures and the evolution of our approach as applied to sustainable solutions to urban mobility, supporting the growth of the SME sector (small and medium-sized enterprises), enhancing access to modern energy, reducing indoor air pollution, and facilitating a pro-poor ethical trade.

Importance of Scale

The magnitude of global poverty and development problems requires solutions that reach billions of people. Exactly how difficult this is to achieve is evidenced by the varied progress made in achieving the UN Millennium Development Goals. To succeed we need new solutions that can be scaled across countries and replicated throughout regions in ways that benefit large numbers of people. As financial resources available to tackle these vast problems will always be limited, we started with the view that we needed to design solutions that were lasting and could exit a financial dependency on ourselves.

Much thought has been dedicated to the subject of how foundations and social investors can be more effective in scaling up the solutions they support in order to increase the impact of their work. We remain convinced that going to scale is an important objective, not just because it can increase impact and reach but also because it avoids the need for hundreds of parallel efforts to solve essentially the same problem—so-called islands of excellence—leading to a more efficient allocation of resources.

From the outset we took the view that, while public-sector programs, community-based initiatives, multilateral agreements, and traditional charity can certainly be effective, by far the greatest opportunity to achieve scale rests in the creation and growth of enterprise-based solutions. Our experience over more than a decade of trying to implement such solutions reinforces this view.

We believe that many development challenges result from a market failure of some sort. To try and solve such problems requires, in our view, two types of expertise. First is the need for what we label development DNA, which enables an understanding of the particular needs and characteristics of those affected. This expertise is traditionally well developed in the NGO and donor sectors. But we believe that to achieve scale and sustainability there is a critical need for another kind of DNA, and that is business DNA. Business DNA enables an understanding of how to develop and execute viable models to deliver products or services to customers in ways that they value due to being affordable, accessible, appropriate and adaptable.

With our own mixed backgrounds in the development sector and private sector, coupled with our links to a major corporation, we deliberately looked to harness both sets of DNA to identify such models and to deploy a blend of support (based on the provision of funding, business skills, and market linkages) that would help our partners achieve scale and sustainability.

Assessing Our Performance

In seeking to assess our performance, we found no widely used or accepted criteria for assessing the impact of grants with respect to achieving scale and sustainability. In short, scale means different things to different people. As such, we developed our own set of criteria, which we believe are simple to use and help us avoid the risk of over-reporting success.

Methodology

For our purposes we chose to define the achievement of scale as delivering cost-efficient solutions that benefit large numbers of poor people in multiple locations in ways that are ultimately financially viable. Grants judged to have achieved scale were deemed to meet the following criteria:

—Large-scale development outcomes (measurable)
—Multiple country or regional operations (measurable)
—Earned income derived from the market (measurable)
—Leverage that matches or exceeds our grant contribution (measurable)
—Management team competence to execute the venture (subjective)

While we recognize that such an approach is not academically rigorous, we believe it is sufficiently robust and light in touch to be fit for purpose. For example, we evaluated development outcomes against targets pre-agreed with our partners, with our definition of *large scale* varying according to the specific development challenge we sought to meet. Using these five criteria enabled us to adopt a simple system for scoring success and allowed us to self-assess performance since our inception (figure 6-1).

Evaluation

While our mission to achieve scale has always remained unchanged, our strategy to achieve it has evolved considerably as a result of being able to examine our own performance over the last decade.

In total, SF has committed almost $111.9 million in grant funding since its inception, $88.9 million of which was committed to initiatives that targeted achieving scale from the outset and were completed by the end of 2009. Of this amount, 66 percent achieved scale according to our evaluation criteria, 19 percent were implemented successfully but showed no evidence of going to scale, and 15 percent failed to achieve intended outcomes. But underlying these percentages are considerable changes in performance over time that resulted from us adapting our strategy in response to the lessons we learned. This becomes more evident when we examine our operational history across three distinct phases.

PHASE 1: 2000 TO 2002. During our inception phase we adopted the traditional open request-for-proposals (RFP) methodology for selecting not-for-profit organizations and providing them with short-term (less than three-year) grants of up to $300,000. While we have no reason to believe that our selection process was any more or less efficient or effective than that applied by others adopting the RFP approach, our impact was low. Of all the initiatives we

Figure 6-1. *Shell Foundation Performance, Global Development, 2000–09*

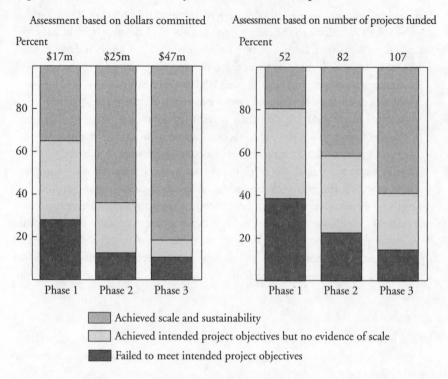

Assessment based on dollars committed   Assessment based on number of projects funded

Achieved scale and sustainability

Achieved intended project objectives but no evidence of scale

Failed to meet intended project objectives

Source: Shell Foundation, "Enterprise Solutions to Scale Report, 2010."

supported in our inception phase, 80 percent failed to achieve any evidence of scale or sustainability (figure 6-2).

Of the 38 percent of projects that failed to even achieve their basic stated objectives, almost half (45 percent) did so due to poor execution by the partner. The other main reason for failure was the inability of partners to meet the needs of their customers and market: in other words, the inability to ascertain whether people either wanted or valued a particular service or product. This issue, rather than the nature of the product or service, was often behind the failure of several of our energy projects in being able to scale up.

We quickly learned to appreciate early on the importance of understanding the needs of the poor and of avoiding eternal dependency on subsidy. But we equally recognized that our own approach, based on time-limited funding that was not always linked to close, hands-on, business-skills support to partners, also contributed to these failures. The conclusion we reached at the end of our inception phase

Figure 6-2. *Failure Rate, Traditional Philanthropy, and New Shell Foundation Model*

Traditional philanthropy	Shell Foundation model
Multiple activities	Sector focus
Existing short-term projects	Innovative long-term partnerships
Small investment, low risk	High investment, high risk
NGO focus	Social enterprises
Poor as beneficiaries	Poor as consumers
Financial support	More than money
Subsidy dependence	Financial viability and exit
80% failure	80% success
(2000 to 2002)	(2002 to 2008)

was that a spray-and-pray approach—based on backing a multitude of short-term, solely NGO-run projects that were not market based—was not likely to generate scale of impact or lasting change without a continued need for subsidy.

PHASE 2: 2003 TO 2005. We recognized that during our inception phase we had greater success when we focused our resources, both time and money, on developing new approaches with a few carefully selected partners or by supporting organizations with a clear market demand for the products or services they offered. This led us to a radical shift in strategy. From 2003 we began to focus on codeveloping and implementing new business models by working very closely with a few strategic partners (both NGOs and emerging social enterprises) that we ourselves sought to identify.

This more proactive, closed approach contributed to a direct increase in the success of our grants. During this period we shifted to piloting a number of strategic partnerships, either as the sole investor or together with other investors.

PHASE 3: 2006 TO PRESENT. During this period we restructured our operations to better support a small number of strategic partners. We made greater efforts to recruit staff with entrepreneurial flair, business acumen, and the skills and ability to work collaboratively in long-term and close joint-venture type relationships with our selected strategic partners. In addition, we shifted our financial management systems to be able to report the deployment of all our resources, including staff and financial and not simply grant expenditure.

The results have been significant: after changing the way we work we now find that 80 percent of our grants meet our criteria for having achieved scale or sustainability.

Evidence of Scale

Over the last ten years SF has focused on a limited number of global development challenges aligned to the energy industry and the expertise of our corporate founder. We have learned that the path to achieve scale is not easy, predictable, or short. We have also had to act swiftly to adapt our ways of working in response to our own experience. This has involved learning from failure as a necessary stage in improving our strategy and overall performance. We have applied principles of sound corporate governance to enhance internal knowledge and learning processes, develop better key performance indicators (that now enable us to assess progress against projected targets), and put in place a reporting framework to our board of trustees that drives accountability and makes it easier to explain variations in performance.

Our strategy today is based on both the lessons learned from these past failures and the lessons learned during the successful scaling up of an increasing number of our strategic partners. These partners deserve the accolades, as without their vision, commitment, and perseverance none of the outcomes we report would have been achieved. But as we look out across quite a diverse set of partnerships, each striving to achieve scale and sustainability, we are beginning to see some common features underpinning their success, features that we believe are of general relevance for others seeking to achieve scale. Below we provide an overview of three of our strategic partners to illustrate how the same enterprise-based model can be deployed to tackle markedly different development challenges.

Case Study 1, GroFin: SME Sector Development in Emerging Markets

Small and medium-sized enterprises are critical to economic development. In developed countries formal SMEs account for over half of annual contributions to GDP and nearly two-thirds of employment. By contrast, formal SMEs in low-income countries contribute less than 20 percent to economic growth and employment. Emerging markets are missing out on an important engine of economic growth and sustainable job creation.

IDENTIFYING THE MARKET SOLUTION. SF has sought to find a scalable and financially viable solution to the "missing middle" since 2002. The perceived wisdom has always been that formal SMEs struggle to grow in emerging economies because they cannot access capital, largely due to a lack of collateral or track record. The level of funding required by most formal SMEs exceeds that of microfinance, yet they are seldom able to access finance from banks or private equity. Our view was that there was a need for a new intermediary that could provide both business development assistance and risk capital to viable start-up and growing enterprises in ways that could generate net returns to investors.

PARTNER SELECTION. In 2002 we met Jurie Willemse, a serial entrepreneur from South Africa who ran an energy business and, through links to a U.S.-based NGO, had a track record of providing skills and finance to African SMEs. We shared a vision of creating a scalable and financially viable business that focused solely on supporting start-up and growing SMEs that were otherwise unable to access the necessary skills and finance required to succeed. Between 2002 and 2004 we codeveloped and then piloted a new business model through establishing an SME fund in South Africa. We were able to learn and increasingly adapt and improve the business model. In 2004 we helped Willemse establish GroFin, an African-based specialist finance company providing both business support and risk capital to viable start-up or growing businesses.[1]

GROFIN'S BUSINESS MODEL. GroFin is a specialist intermediary that raises funds, invests in the SME sector, and delivers both financial and social returns to investors. The company provides pre- and post-investment business support to entrepreneurs through local teams of investment experts. Those identified as viable (capable of sustained growth) are provided with mezzanine finance between $50,000 and $1 million in local currency (which can be increased up to $1.5 million, depending on performance). Throughout the financing term, close business support is provided by GroFin to help enterprises achieve their growth objectives.

BUSINESS PERFORMANCE AND DEVELOPMENT IMPACTS. GroFin now has over a hundred staff working in local offices in South Africa, Kenya, Tanzania, Uganda, Ghana, Rwanda, Nigeria, Zambia, Oman, Jordan, Egypt, Iraq, and Dubai, with a total of $320 million under management (across four SME funds) from a wide range of investors (including the International Finance Corporation, the African Development Bank, the UK development finance institution, CDC, and the Dutch development finance institution, FMO). The $160 million GroFin Africa Fund is the world's largest fund targeting the under-one-million-dollar SME sector.

GroFin has to date provided integrated business and financial support to 397 enterprises across Africa, creating and maintaining over 12,100 sustainable jobs, which in turn benefit a further 192,000 people through impacts on households and indirect employment. In total, nearly $116 million has been invested

1. For more on this company, see www.grofin.com.

(24 percent into start-ups) with an average deal size of $324,000 over an average term period of fifty-eight months. Their performance to date demonstrates both the strong market demand from local SMEs and the robustness of the business model under different market conditions.

The organization aims to have $1 billion under management and to scale its operations beyond Africa to over twenty-five emerging economies worldwide by 2020.

ANGEL INVESTMENT. Investing in the SME sector has traditionally proven challenging because of weak managerial capacity, high transaction costs, few exit opportunities, and wider business environment risks. As a consequence the few organizations in this space are typically heavily subsidized, with those providing subsidy usually giving greater weight to maximizing developmental returns rather than financial returns. GroFin and SF deliberately set out to be different by designing a model that would be self-sustaining. SF brought expertise in growing start-up businesses, "smart subsidies" to enable GroFin to hire good staff and develop effective operating systems from the outset, "patient capital" to help the organization grow, and its market linkages and Shell brand to help secure investors.

Over the period 2002–09, SF committed $11.5 million as grant funding toward recruiting and training staff, setting up local offices across Africa and establishing operational systems to support them. GroFin was a significant co-contributor toward these set-up costs. This enabled GroFin to expand operations to the scale needed to make the whole business viable.

Acting as an anchor investor, SF committed a further $8 million in the form of risk capital contributions over the same period (with all returns to be reinvested in scaling up) and in 2008 invested $15 million in the GroFin Africa Fund. We then leveraged our networks and the Shell brand to open doors to major development finance institutions, selected foundations, and several African commercial banks.

Case Study 2, EMBARQ: Sustainable Solutions to Urban Mobility in Megacities

Forty percent of the world's population lives in megacities with populations over 10 million. These megacities are typically the engines for economic growth in developing countries, but they are stifled by the problems of congestion and pollution associated with rapid urbanization and the explosive growth in vehicle ownership. Poor people in the developing world suffer particularly from the economic impact of traffic congestion, which causes air pollution and lengthy commutes to work where public transport is inadequate. Transport is responsible for 25 percent of global greenhouse gas emissions, with road transport the most significant cause.

IDENTIFYING THE MARKET SOLUTION. SF recognized that transport problems in cities are essentially a result of market failures: transport decisions by city administrators and providers are too often supply led rather than demand driven, leading to suboptimal solutions. Having market-tested the idea of creating a global center for sustainable transport, we collaborated with leading planning experts to identify a specialist partner that could deliver practical, action-oriented solutions to city authorities.

PARTNER SELECTION. In 2002, following a restricted tender, we selected the World Resources Institute (WRI) as a strategic partner. WRI is an internationally respected environmental NGO that shared our desire to build a sustainable transport network that focused on in-country expertise and multiple stakeholder engagement. SF worked closely with WRI to co-create EMBARQ and helped recruit a core team of multi-disciplinary experts (including engineers, policy advisers, health and safety experts, and environmental specialists) headed by Nancy Kete, herself previously a senior environmental and trade adviser to the U.S. government.[2] Together we developed a plan for scaling up based on the creation of sustainable regional centers of excellence.

EMBARQ'S BUSINESS MODEL. EMBARQ works with cities to diagnose their mobility problems, identify cost-effective market solutions, and leverage funding (both public and private) to implement them. Its goal is to allow cities to serve their populations' mobility needs in a financially sustainable way. It achieves this by engaging with city decisionmakers and their stakeholders to identify and implement solutions that reduce unnecessary travel, for example through efficient transport routing and urban planning; high-capacity, efficient, and affordable modes of transport such as bus rapid transit (BRT) corridors; and safe infrastructure for nonmotorized transport (such as cycling and walking).

The goal is to establish a locally run transport center in major client cities, enabling EMBARQ to expand its remit to influence other cities and transport policy in the country as a whole. By working in this way, EMBARQ aims to deliver measurable improvements in transport.

BUSINESS PERFORMANCE AND DEVELOPMENT IMPACTS. EMBARQ now operates in multiple locations, with a focus on Latin America and Southeast Asia through five regional centers in Mexico, Brazil, Peru, Turkey, and India.

2. For more on this company, see www.embarq.org.

EMBARQ's team of experts now provides support for sustainable transport projects in fifty-eight cities across the world and has leveraged over $2.9 billion investment into these projects. In Mexico City EMBARQ developed Metrobus, a sixty-seven-kilometer BRT corridor, serviced by 284 articulated buses that carry more than 620,000 passengers each day, cutting travel times by 53 percent and reducing carbon dioxide emissions by 100,000 tonnes a year. In 2007 the network played a key role in establishing the world's first intercontinental BRT corridor, across the Bosphorus Bridge in Istanbul, linking Europe with Asia. This forty-one-kilometer route serves 800,000 people a day, saving each commuter an average two hours in travel time and some 100,000 tons of carbon dioxide a year. Across all its projects EMBARQ improves the lives of over 3.8 million people each year and has saved nearly 2 million tons of carbon dioxide emissions from entering the atmosphere. The organization has built a significant international reputation as a result of both its transport expertise and its ability to deliver real solutions on the ground, which has been key to securing other strategic funding partners.

Through delivering success on the ground in cities, EMBARQ has also begun to foster replication at city and regional levels and to embed policy change at a national level, particularly in Mexico (where they are advising the government on further BRT systems throughout the country) and in Brazil (leading to the adoption of vehicle inspection legislation that will remove unsafe vehicles from the roads and significantly reduce emissions).

ANGEL INVESTMENT. Since 2002 SF has invested $16.5 million as grant subsidy toward establishing a strong management team, a center of core expertise in Washington, D.C., and the phased establishment of EMBARQ's network of Centers for Sustainable Transport, which deliver in-country projects.

In 2006, the Caterpillar Foundation became a global strategic partner through a contribution of $7.5 million. On the back of this support, EMBARQ has leveraged additional funds from other regional and national supporters, increasing year on year. In 2009 it secured a five-year, $30 million commitment from Bloomberg Philanthropies.

SF has provided strategic advice, analysis, and governance to help EMBARQ renew its organizational structure to be fit for the purpose of scaling up and to manage talent and knowledge across its network. We are currently working closely with EMBARQ's senior management team, with assistance from a team of pro bono consultants from Shell, to help EMBARQ identify opportunities to diversify its revenue stream and progress opportunities for earned income so that it can reduce reliance on grant funding. These may include charging for transport policy and planning advice or technical consultancy, for example, to help provide revenue that can be deployed in poorer areas where urgent action is required.

*Case Study 3, Envirofit: Design, Distribution,
and Sale of Improved Cookstoves*

Indoor air pollution (IAP) results from toxic smoke created by using wood, charcoal, or other biomass to cook on open fires or with inefficient stoves in poorly ventilated homes. It is arguably the greatest energy-poverty issue in the world, affecting the lives of over 3 billion people and leading to the premature death of over 1.9 million every year, 85 percent of whom are women and children under the age of five.

IDENTIFYING THE MARKET SOLUTION. It is widely acknowledged that the most viable way to reduce IAP at scale is for people to use clean cookstoves or clean fuels that reduce both emissions and fuel use. By 2007, SF had invested over $15 million in nine pilots with a range of IAP-specialist NGO partners across the globe. While this resulted in significant sales of improved cookstoves, no pilot showed the potential for scaling up or sustainability. As a result, we changed strategy and sought a global strategic partner with a proven track record in product design, coupled with commercial experience in the marketing, distribution, and sale of consumer durables.

PARTNER SELECTION. Envirofit International, a nonprofit organization based in the United States, was selected as our global strategic partner following a restricted tender in 2007.[3] While Envirofit had no prior experience in producing clean cookstoves, it had a strong track record in engineering environmental solutions for application in developing countries (enhanced by its close links to Colorado State University), and its chairman and CEO, Ron Bills, had managed several for-profit companies involved in product development, distribution, and sales.

ENVIROFIT'S BUSINESS MODEL. To achieve the desired global health, environmental, social, and economic impact of tackling IAP, hundreds of millions of clean cookstoves need to be sold. From the outset, SF and Envirofit worked together to develop a viable business model, conduct voice-of-the-customer market research, undertake groundbreaking research and development, and establish distribution and sales networks with an initial focus on southern India. Envirofit subsequently produced a line of durable clean cookstoves that currently retail for between $15 and $30 in India. Compared to traditional cooking fires, these cookstoves reduce emissions, improve fuel efficiency, and reduce cooking time significantly. In 2011 the organization launched a clean

3. For more on this company, see www.envirofit.org.

charcoal-burning stove, which is now sold in nine African countries through multiple distribution partnerships.

BUSINESS PERFORMANCE AND DEVELOPMENT IMPACTS. Envirofit has succeeded in creating a sustained and growing market for its clean cookstove products, becoming a market leader in the sale of improved stoves. Aggregate sales to date of more than 475,000 stoves benefit an estimated 1.9 million IAP-affected people in India, Africa, and Latin America.

With a durability of three to five years, depending on the model, stoves sold to date are predicted to save over $30 million for India's lowest-income consumers through fuel saving, to save over 600,000 tons of wood, and to prevent 1 million tons of carbon from entering the atmosphere. The business has also fostered enterprise development and created more than 500 local jobs through the growth of its network of manufacturing, sales, and distribution channel partners.

In spring 2012 the business opened its first African manufacturing operation in Nairobi, to serve demand in East Africa. As market growth continues, Envirofit will shift further toward localized assembly and manufacture so as to continue efforts to lower end-user costs. As with many other types of consumer durable products aimed at the bottom of the pyramid, it takes a long time for this high-volume, low-margin business to reach a tipping point, whereby sales growth is generated largely through brand awareness. Although Envirofit is still dependent on grant funding to finance its continued efforts to develop markets and improve stove performance and affordability, its earned-income flows and gross margins are improving steadily and, on current projections, will achieve financial breakeven in 2013.

ANGEL INVESTMENT. Over the period 2007 to late 2012, Shell Foundation committed $15.6 million as grant funding toward the development of a range of clean cookstoves as well as building up the capacity and operational systems of both Envirofit International and the organization's operations on the ground in India and Africa.

We have developed and piloted a range of activities to raise awareness and develop new routes to market. These include a local and national IAP-awareness-raising campaign in rural villages in Karnataka state in India and a number of effective distribution channels through partnerships with microfinance institutions, local retailers, cooperatives, and rural NGO networks. We also support Berkeley Air Monitoring Group to conduct independent monitoring of the performance of the stoves.

More recently, we have been working together to capitalize on the carbon-saving aspects of Envirofit stoves by generating and selling carbon credits. This effort could become a key enabler for the clean cookstove industry by driving down prices and making stoves more affordable. Pilot programs were initiated in core African countries (Kenya, Ghana, Nigeria, South Africa, Côte d'Ivoire, Tanzania, Uganda, and Cameroon) in 2012. SF has also harnessed its value-adding links to Shell by securing pro bono advice from Shell Trading to help Envirofit develop a robust carbon strategy.

Emerging Lessons

Our experience to date of helping different partners to achieve scale and sustainability in tackling diverse global development challenges points to five particular lessons.

Lesson One: Be Disruptive!

We find it striking that all of the strategic partnerships we have supported that have achieved verifiable scale (according to our own defined criteria) are organizations that we have helped create and that all pioneer new business-based solutions to old challenges. Despite our best (and continuing) efforts, we remain unsuccessful in supporting any well-established not-for-profit organization with an existing track record and diverse funding sources to effect a shift toward greater scale or sustainability.

While we never set out with a specific intent to be disruptive or catalytic, we consistently find that our greatest success and impact comes when we act like an angel investor would in the commercial world, namely, playing a high-risk, early-stage, pivotal role in identifying innovative market-based solutions and deploying both skills and capital to establish new ventures and support them as they test and develop their models during the early stage.

We have found that our "disruptive" behavior has taken different forms, such as deploying our own entrepreneurial thinking to identify the need for a different blend of support to deliver a service or product that was otherwise missing (as evidenced by the integrated service provision offered by EMBARQ and GroFin) or the need for new partners, with different skills sets and greater commercial experience to deliver new services or products successfully at scale (as evidenced by the founders of GroFin and Envirofit). We started to realize that traditional approaches were not necessarily best suited to scale or sustainability. For example, we dismissed from the outset the idea of creating an expendable, grant-based "technical assistance" facility to offset the costs of GroFin providing business skills support to SMEs, because we believed this would not build the core capacity of GroFin, that it risked a nonalignment between social and financial return objectives, and that it created the potential for subsidy dependency that was ultimately unsustainable.

Lesson Two: Social Enterprise as a Driver of Scale

A commonality underpinning all our most successful partnerships is that the senior executive is either someone with prior commercial experience (GroFin, Envirofit) or with a history of innovative thinking and practice in the social sector (EMBARQ). We therefore find that, while they may not class themselves as such, all our successful partnerships are led by social entrepreneurs who have entrepreneurial flair and business acumen and place value on achieving both developmental and financial returns. These core characteristics—as opposed to whether a social enterprise is structured as a for-profit or as a not-for-profit business—we find to be the common differentiators underpinning success.

PARTNER SELECTION. But despite the growing recognition and emergence of social entrepreneurs, finding quality partners remains hard and, in our experience, unlikely to occur through an open reactive process of soliciting applications. This is partly because such entrepreneurs, especially those coming from the private sector, are not naturally attuned to seeking support from foundations and other donors. It is also because such essential networks that might connect them are still maturing. A key success factor in our ability to be disruptive or catalytic is therefore our ability to not just think of new solutions but to proactively find partners who share these goals and with whom we could collaborate. We have benefited from our own personal networks generated through work in both the private sector and the development sector, but we have also had to invest our own time and energy into conducting in-depth market surveys to try and source prospective partners. We have consistently found this resource-intensive, hands-on approach to be far more effective in the long term than other reactive ways of finding partners (such as through RFP exercises or third-party-led market analyses).

Over time we have implemented increasingly rigorous partner selection criteria. Rather than assessing written proposals, we invest time in meeting and assessing the lead people involved, using criteria such as the following:

—Personal alignment with the importance of achieving verifiable social benefit through solutions that can be delivered at scale and sustainably

—Evidence of being able to execute a venture both at the start-up and during its growth stages (substantiated by prior personal track record)

—Ability to draft a business plan and openness to receive skills support to shape and refine this ability

—Commitment to focusing 100 percent on the venture and sharing risks with us in trying to achieve success

—Understanding and accepting the need to comply with our business principles

BUILDING A SHARED VISION. Starting up and growing any new venture is hard. But starting up a social enterprise offering a new service or product in an emerging economy is even harder. Where we have partnered with individuals or organizations who did not share an early ambition to achieve scale, we found it virtually impossible to "retrofit" the subsequent capacity needed to achieve it. "If you build small it's difficult to upscale. You need to devise a plan from day one that provides the platform for going to scale, notably by recruiting the best staff and developing robust operating systems even before the market is fully tested," says GroFin's Jurie Willemse.[4]

EMBARQ is a good example of strong mutual understanding of the desire to achieve scale. As Nancy Kete, EMBARQ's former managing director, notes, "We understood early on that we needed to achieve significant change in at least three to five developing countries, as this was required to create a multiplier effect. The world is a big place and there are hundreds of cities that require sustainable transport solutions. By starting in Mexico City and demonstrating success we were able to generate sufficient traction to replicate these solutions in other places." She concludes: "That was always the golden apple—achieving success in iconic places so that we could trigger replication in other places. Now we see many more cities in Mexico and other countries around the world wanting to work with EMBARQ."[5]

Our experience with Envirofit reiterates this point. "You can't solve a problem that affects half the world's population one village at a time," notes Ron Bills, Envirofit's managing director. "We had to ramp up the plan from focusing on the lowest hanging fruit in India and Africa to moving to a sustainable business model, with in-country business opportunities and local staff."[6]

Lesson Three: Plan for Financial Viability

A strong market-based and value-chain approach underpins all the social enterprises we have supported that have gone to scale. This has reinforced our belief that only an offer of good-quality products or services that the poor value and can afford can achieve the financial viability that is essential for lasting and scalable solutions. While our strategic partners comprise both nonprofit and for-profit enterprises, they all share a common mindset about cost efficiency, customer service, and revenue generation. We have found that a disciplined focus from the outset on financial returns and earned income is a critical part of a planned exit strategy to avoid subsidy dependency.

4. Personal communication, 2010.
5. Personal communication, 2010.
6. Personal communication, 2010.

Performance against agreed key performance indicators (KPIs) is measured, documented, and reported on a regular basis to ensure an accountability mind-set from the beginning. We select a few (usually three to five) KPIs that make sense for the organization itself to collect in order to measure its own progress toward achieving its goals. Typically KPIs cover both financial and developmental measures that are specific to each organization. Wherever possible, we try and agree on "smart" ratios that can be tracked over time (such as cost per job created, ratio of fixed overhead to service delivery cost, or cumulative subsidy per clean cookstove sold).

An example that captures this learning is the evolution of our program to reduce IAP through the sale of improved cookstoves. The majority of the early pilot projects we supported were unsuccessful, as they were based on the limited and inefficient production of often poor-quality, nondurable products that generated no real consumer demand. By contrast, Envirofit was able to rapidly become the market leader in the sale of improved cookstoves in southern India because it designs and manufactures high-quality and durable products at prices poor people can afford. In addition, despite being a nonprofit, it takes a commercial approach to sales and distribution.

With our partner GroFin, we aimed from the beginning to develop a financially viable model based on the integrated provision of skills and finance to African start-up and growing enterprises. GroFin set out to be self-sustaining by generating income through management fees and returns on investments, coupled with being rigorously cost efficient and financially disciplined. To date, every grant dollar that SF has invested into building GroFin's operations in Africa has leveraged over $20 in risk capital contributions from others. The fact that GroFin has succeeded in having over $320 million under management means that it can operate in its current markets with no further need for subsidy provision. Thus a virtuous circle is born, whereby targeting financial viability leads to increased leverage, and increased leverage ensures financial sustainability and an exit from subsidy.

Similarly, EMBARQ has been able to leverage over $2.9 billion from public and private investors into new BRT systems based on its financial strength. For example, Bloomberg Philanthropies joined Shell Foundation and Caterpillar Foundation as a new global strategic partner of EMBARQ in January 2010, with a five-year commitment of $30 million. This will allow EMBARQ not only to fund its existing solutions-based approach to urban mobility but also to scale up its activities. It also allows for relationship leverage by connecting EMBARQ with the other grantees of Bloomberg's $125 million global road-safety initiative (including the World Health Organization, the World Bank, the Global Road Safety Partnership, and the Johns Hopkins Bloomberg School of Public Health). EMBARQ will now lead work to measure the air quality, health, and road safety impacts of urban mobility projects and build the case for future large-scale investment to achieve these benefits across the transport sector. Nancy Kete recognizes the importance of early business-based advice from Shell Foundation: "We would not have seen such strong appetite from the likes of Bloomberg Philanthropies if it wasn't for our clear business-based model, our robust financials, and KPI reporting, all of which were driven by Shell Foundation."[7]

Our successful partnerships have demonstrated that scale and sustainability are critically dependent upon financial viability and its associated linkage to securing investment from the financial sector. Demonstrating the acumen to be able to render development solutions commercially viable has also proven critical in establishing the credibility of the solution, the venture, and the management team.

Lesson Four: Building for Scale

Our experience leads us to believe that social enterprises require three critical inputs to help them achieve scale, namely: core funding, business skills support, and access to market linkage.

CORE FUNDING. Creating scalable and sustainable enterprises requires building core capacity, slick operational systems, and a robust infrastructure. This means recruiting the best staff and developing efficient operating systems from the start. Without these, being able to manage complex, multiple-location operations, as scale requires, becomes extremely difficult. Equally, the early adoption of efficient systems and procedures (information technology, management information systems, human resources, and communications) that automate and reduce the cost of day-to-day operations significantly enhances the potential for scale.

Our early experience was that short-term, project-based funding helped neither us nor our partners achieve these objectives. Indeed it led us to believe that to achieve scale and sustainability we had to change strategy and move away from supporting time-limited activities, which we see as akin to buying services from a partner to deliver pre-agreed outputs. Instead, we have shifted toward building viability by providing long-term core funding and support to our partners, to build capacity for business plan–related milestones and KPIs. We believe that our operational experience with our partners reflects this. Only through providing long-term core funding support to EMBARQ was it possible for them to recruit quality staff, develop a network of regional centers, and have the staying power necessary to build trusted relations with city partners. All of

7. Personal communication, 2010.

these were essential to their long-term expansion and scale-up. As Nancy Kete explains, "You have to use initial grant finance to build capacity. Only once we had a credible, established business model and were recognized in a number of key markets as an independent entity could we really deliver a customer-value proposition."[8] She also points out, "Only through this could we ultimately begin to think about how to diversify EMBARQ's revenue by developing some earned-income streams that would enable the business to progressively move away from grant dependency."

BUSINESS SKILLS SUPPORT. Building viable partners takes more than money. Our view is that few development problems of any kind are solved permanently by money alone. While all of our partners have their own key strengths, all have equally testified to the benefit received from some form of business support or advice from staff in SF. This could be broad business planning, participation at the governance level, specific support on issues such as product marketing, strategy review exercises, or enhancing communications.

This requires us to be able to deploy a broad range of business planning guidance and challenge to our partners. It means that we work in a very active and close way with our partners, similar to that of a joint venture relationship (although unlike a joint venture, we lack any equity stake in our partners). As necessary and appropriate, we have also been able to leverage other, typically specialist, pro bono support from Shell (such as marketing, supply chain management, human resources, and information technology).

While this approach requires us to spend a lot of time with our partners in places where they operate, it has the benefit that we fully understand the challenges they face and are therefore better positioned to restructure our support as and when required. Both we and our partners have found this true partnering relationship to be far more effective than more traditional relationships between funders and grantees, which typically resemble contractual relationships based on monitoring progress against pre-agreed objectives.

MARKET LINKAGES. Social enterprises can enhance their ability to scale through being able to make effective links to others in the market or value chain, be these investors, sources of business, route-to-market partners, or others with close links to local communities. To this end, we continuously seek to use our networks to facilitate such connections for the benefit of our partners and, in some cases, have provided direct support to others (for example, route-to-market partners and NGOs involved in social awareness campaigns) to test and develop such market linkages.

8. Personal communication, 2010.

Since our establishment we sought to leverage our "independent yet linked relationship" with our corporate parent. We have tried to test whether we could, where appropriate, harness links with Shell that add value either to us directly or to our partners in achieving our charitable objectives. This was a radically new approach back in 2000 and one based on the premise that, as a multinational company with over 100,000 employees in over 150 countries, our corporate founder offered a potentially rich and diverse range of resources for us to tap into.

Our success to date has been mixed. However, without doubt our common brand has been of tremendous and consistent value in leveraging support from others. It has been recognized by our partners as having the ability to convene power and facilitate access. GroFin's Jurie Willemse acknowledges that the brand facilitated access to financing institutions that may not otherwise have been receptive. "We used the Shell brand a lot to get introduced to other investors. It's very different when they know you have the backing of the corporate. It gave us credibility and leveraged access."[9]

Lesson Five: Scale-Up Is Not Linear

No matter how good the selection of partners or the deployment of blended assistance, we have never as yet encountered an easy, predictable, or linear path to scale in any of our partnerships. This should come as no great surprise, as the success of any new venture is fragile, hard to maintain, and vulnerable to change, and these risks become magnified when considering new business models applied by social enterprises in emerging markets. Our own experience is that achieving scale takes patience, flexibility, persistence, and funding.

Bringing any new product or service to market requires considerable investment in building consumer understanding and stimulating demand. For example, with EMBARQ, considerable time and effort was required to establish the best options for enhancing sustainable transport while also navigating the political complexities of cities and gaining the trust and confidence of multiple stakeholders. But once this tipping point was reached (through the perseverance of EMBARQ staff, coupled with our flexibility and patient subsidy) it was demonstrated that the urban poor were willing and able to pay a higher price to use a new bus rapid transit system than alternative modes of transport. Customer surveys proved that this was because the urban poor placed a value on the enhanced quality of life associated with using fast, safe, reliable, and clean buses.

We have found it to be essential to place early emphasis on the marketing and pricing of any new product or service offering, particularly when these products or services are not related to immediate income-generating opportunities for the user.

9. Personal communication, 2010.

Our experience has shown that the complexity of catalyzing enterprise-based solutions to global development challenges requires a lot of time, patience, and money—often substantially more than is initially foreseen. Achieving scale and sustainability is not a linear progression. We have invested between $10 million and $20 million of grant support in each of our core partners, but in our experience, while it takes a good three to five years to reach the tipping point for delivering significant development returns, it can take six to nine years to achieve real scale and sustainability. We believe it's very difficult to fast-track scale—and it's not for the fainthearted.

With GroFin, for example, we provided $11.5 million in grant funding over nine years, with most of this being invested before a significant increase in developmental impact could be verified. To try and measure the developmental impact of our support to GroFin to date, we draw on an emerging methodology to calculate social return on investment.[10] Figure 6-3 shows that, using various reliable donor metrics, the estimated monetary value of social impacts achieved to date by GroFin in Africa is between $15 million and $30 million, thus exceeding our total disbursed grant support of $11.5 million (even under quite harsh sensitivity weighting). Equally, the figure shows that considerable subsidy was provided before any significant developmental returns were generated, again emphasizing the need for substantial up-front investment in core funding if one wants to achieve long-term, significant, sustained, and growing social impact.

With our partner Envirofit we have invested similar time and money—$15.6 million over five years—and we have witnessed a similar pattern. As Envirofit's CEO Ron Bills acknowledges, "Success in mass production takes time. It's complicated and requires a robust understanding of many different processes—the purchase of raw materials, production and manufacture, shipping and transportation, distribution and the entire value chain. You don't do it with an Excel spreadsheet. It takes an advanced system like SAP, where we use expensive software and detailed order-management systems to track everything from orders to accounts payable, and inventory management. So it also takes significant money."

It's not just the operational building process that takes time. Building brand equity also requires significant patience. Ron Bills points out that processes

10. We calculate the cumulative social return on investment as the number of jobs created or maintained multiplied by $1,400 (average income, per World Bank), plus the number of employment dependents (using independent DBSA/IDC metrics), multiplied by $1,400, plus the number of indirect jobs created (using independent DBSA/IDC metrics), multiplied by $1,400. We generated two SROI estimates (using sensitivity weightings of 30 percent and 10 percent retrospectively to employment dependents and indirect jobs, recognizing that only a fraction will benefit from jobs created or maintained). We then compare the two cumulative SROI estimates with the cumulative grant funding by SF to GroFin over the period 2003–11.

Figure 6-3. *Social Return, GroFin in Africa, 2003–11*

Millions of U.S. dollars

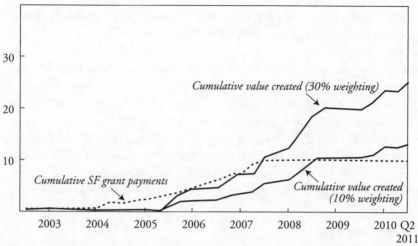

Source: Shell Foundation internal reporting.

alone don't sell products. Brand visibility is critical but cannot be built overnight. Shell Foundation is now working with Envirofit on raising brand awareness through market research and structured marketing and sales and follow-up. "But it's not easy," says Bills. "There are multiple value propositions to be articulated—why buying an improved cookstove is good for health reasons, financial reasons, fuel saving, and so on."

With a pro-poor social enterprise, where the route to market doesn't already exist and where you still need to show bottom-line impact, commercial success can take much longer than a traditional for-profit initiative. Envirofit works with a highly inefficient supply chain, one that doesn't even exist for the last mile. As a result, the program is effectively trying to create a supply chain infrastructure from scratch for a single product category in a very untested space. Patience is of the essence, and the jump from pilot to enterprise is usually a considerable step change, with some rather steep learning curves.

Conventional businesses struggle with numerous, common start-up challenges, but when there is also a specific social purpose or developmental goal, these are compounded. We have learned that we need to be flexible and adaptable. While several of SF's partners are now achieving large-scale impact in ways that are sustainable, in each case this growth has taken longer than originally expected and required adaptation of the original business model. This has required our staff to constantly engage with partners, understand the issues faced and new approaches required, and maintain a commitment to continuous improvement. We have learned that it takes far longer than we ever anticipated to achieve scale and sustainability.

Our staff use their experience in growing start-up enterprises and close working knowledge of our partners' businesses to assess the projected viability of the enterprise and the growth of the new market. If the likelihood of meeting mutual objectives for scale and self-sufficiency is improbable—either because of the model itself, because of execution by management, or through an insurmountable adverse change in the marketplace—then SF will exit promptly. Despite this, many of our former partners have continued to operate successfully within a more limited market at a state or national level.

We have also found it necessary to engage with a small number of partners for whom the objective is not to achieve scale but rather to catalyze wider systemic change on a time-bound basis through research, awareness raising, or advocacy—although this remains a very small percentage of our grant-making total.

Angel Investment

Our experience over the last decade has taught us the following:

—Social enterprises offer tremendous promise to be the most viable organizations capable of delivering development outcomes at scale.

—Social enterprises require access to a blend of core funding, business expertise, and market linkages in order to prove their business models and become financially viable.

—Only at this stage can social enterprises attract sufficient levels of further investment to deliver sustainable impacts on a global scale.

Despite the emergence of a growing class of social entrepreneurs and impact investors, our experience and that of many of our strategic partners is that there are still very few foundations or donors willing or able to provide the level and duration of subsidy required to build the core capacity of such organizations—in particular for-profits—that aim to pilot and scale up solutions to development challenges. All too often our experience, and that of our partners, has been that such concessional funding is drip fed into the venture, with significant restrictions, delays, and conditions. Such behavior can frustrate the chances of a partner achieving scale and sustainability, since it may prevent the recipient from investing in high-quality institutional infrastructure that can support taking a solution to scale and having a broad impact. Without effective angel investment to test new solutions and build the up-front capacity of partners, we see a risk that the growing number of social investors or impact investors may not be able to help their investees fully achieve their scale-up potential.

Figure 6-4 illustrates the point by examining the growth stages of any enterprise from start-up to sustainable growth. A growing number of impact investors

Figure 6-4. *Growth Stages of Enterprises, from Start-Up to Sustainable Growth*

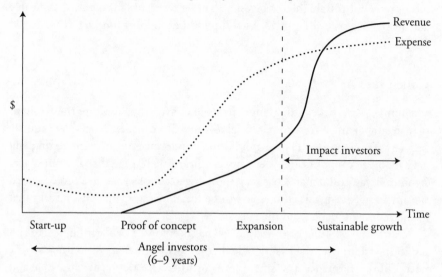

Source: Shell Foundation.

are seeking to finance social enterprises offering blended financial and developmental returns. But in our experience, the majority of these impact investors remain relatively risk-averse and seldom finance start-ups. This is where smart subsidy, deployed in ways similar to angel investing, can play a hugely important role in providing core funding to social enterprises during their start-up and early growth stages, such that they have the capacity, systems, and track record to enable them to leverage support from others.

As an angel investor, SF believes it can help social enterprises bridge this gap and reach scale through the following four means:

—Identifying disruptive market-based opportunities with the potential for high impact

—Providing early-stage (patient, flexible) smart subsidy, business skills, and market linkages to support these enterprises to pilot business models and achieve financial viability

—Accelerating the quality and quantity of opportunities for impact investors

—Signaling these investments to the wider development community as viable destinations for cost-effective, low-risk use of social investment capital

Acting as an angel investor differs radically from the approach adopted by donors who promote an incentives-based approach to scaling up, whereby funds are released on the basis of results delivered (akin to a cash-on-delivery model). Our experience is that the real obstacle faced by social enterprises seeking to achieve scale and sustainability is not simply access to finance over defined periods of time but the absence of investors willing to take high risks, act in flexible and adaptable ways, and provide vital support beyond just funding.

Conclusion

In summary, we believe that angel investors have a hugely important role to play in supporting efforts to resolve global development challenges. We equally believe that the current debate around the importance of impact investing will help mobilize capital from other sources toward these shared goals. But a very significant gap still remains between those organizations that give project-based subsidy to not-for-profit entities and those social investors that seek returns that are both developmental and financial.

As a relatively young organization, SF has been on a steep learning curve and has learned a lot over the past decade that has helped it chart its journey for the next. Our performance assessment leads us to believe that achieving scale and sustainability is fostered by the ability to perform three tasks:

—Catalyze disruptive change through angel philanthropy

—Provide critical inputs to enable sectoral pioneers to create new solutions to old problems

—Ensure an exit from subsidy and a transition to earned income and financial independence

After ten years, however, we have come to realize that, even though assisting any one partner to achieve scale and sustainability is a hard task, it is not enough by itself. No matter how successful our partners are at pioneering new business-based solutions to development challenges, they will never fully solve any one global development challenge. The world is too big, the numbers of poor affected too large, and the need for constant innovation too pervasive. To have a real impact on world poverty an even greater ambition is needed.

In each of the new markets we have created there is a need for wider system change to promote replication and overcome market barriers. We recognize that, as our partners grow, so too will our role have to advance beyond day-to-day operational support and into market development and broader advocacy. We have made some tentative steps toward sectoral reform, but we are only starting our efforts to address wider ecosystem change. This will require us to acquire new skills and create new partnerships. Doubtless we will learn more through our successes and failures. But fundamentally, we feel that organizations that are closest to market and have the practical experience of tackling real barriers to growth must be positioned at the heart of any effort to effect wider sector reform.

7

Scaling Up through Disruptive Business Models: The Inside Story of Mobile Money in Kenya

PAULINE VAUGHAN, WOLFGANG FENGLER,
AND MICHAEL JOSEPH

The M-PESA mobile money service was launched in Kenya in 2007 to provide basic financial services to a largely unbanked population. Reaching 50 percent of Kenyan adults in less than two years, M-PESA experienced an unprecedented rate of adoption, with 10,000 new customers registering for the service daily. Five years on, mobile money is ubiquitous in Kenya but is yet to scale in other countries. Similar applications were introduced earlier elsewhere; what made M-PESA special was the focus on scale. It was introduced as part of a medium-term business strategy with the aim of building brand loyalty rather than that of short-term financial reward. More than one in two mobile money transactions worldwide are carried out in Kenya.[1] Mobile money has radically reduced the cost of low-value financial transactions and lowered the barriers of entry to the financial system in Kenya. It is emerging as a powerful and innovative tool in the fight against poverty.

Introduction

Mobile money in Kenya (M-PESA) allows people to move money at the speed of a text message.[2] Kenyans no longer need to travel long distances to the nearest

---

1. GSMA (2012).
2. M-PESA is the trademark of Safaricom Kenya Ltd.'s mobile money transfer service, introduced in March 2007.

bank branch to send money nor queue for hours to pay school fees and electricity bills. Transfers to relatives in rural areas can be done safely and securely. By the end of 2011, M-PESA had signed up 15.2 million customers.[3] Together with the services of other providers, four in five Kenyan adults have access to mobile money. Mobile money represents a culmination of the telecommunication revolution in Africa, and it demonstrates that Africa can be exporters of global innovations.

How does mobile money work? To register for M-PESA customers need an ID document and their Safaricom mobile phone: the "e-wallet" account created is associated with the mobile phone number. Customers can deposit funds with an M-PESA agent and receive an equivalent value of funds in their mobile money account (a cash-in transaction). They then use their mobile phone to give secure instructions to the service provider to transfer funds to any other phone number, transactions that are carried out in a matter of seconds (figure 7-1). The recipient can then "cash out" from any of the 35,000 M-PESA agents across Kenya. M-PESA is short-message-service-based and works on any mobile phone handset.

This chapter follows the origin of the M-PESA mobile money service. It shows how learning from a pilot led to the national launch of a simple, relevant service that has been adopted en masse. We analyze the scaling up of mobile money and recount the decisions taken when M-PESA was launched in Kenya. We then explore reasons that M-PESA has become such a dominant force in Kenya in comparison with other countries. Looking forward, we see that mobile money is being used by a growing number of organizations as a payment method of choice, and we examine how this will extend the reach of formal financial services to the unbanked. Finally, we explore the next frontiers in mobile-money-related services.

Kenya's Information and Communications Revolution

As in most of Africa, the telecommunication revolution took hold in Kenya in 2000. At the close of the 1990s, less than 3 percent of Kenyan households owned a telephone, and less than 1 in 1,000 Kenyan adults had access to mobile phone services. By 2011 the number of phone subscriptions exceeded 26 million, which is more than the country has adults. Internet users also climbed to 12.5 million, which indicates that the data revolution is now in full swing (figure 7-2). Mobile money has been adopted even more rapidly. After five years of operation, there are some 18 million mobile money users in Kenya.

---

3. Customer and agent statistics are those of December 2011, according to Safaricom. These statistics to April 2011 are published at www.safaricom.co.ke/personal/m-pesa/m-pesa-resource-centre/statistics. Figures beyond this were obtained from the company.

Figure 7-1. *How Does Mobile Money Work?*

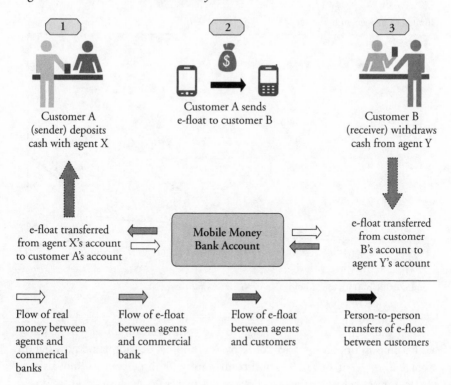

Source: World Bank (2010).

A combination of local and global factors explains the telecommunication revolution in Kenya, which has a number of similarities with other successful African countries. First, with rapid population growth and urbanization, Kenya developed scale economies that allowed for the development of new business models and products. Second, the global revolution in cell phone technology and low-cost production in Asia generated the arrival of affordable phones. Third, Safaricom was among the first telecommunication companies targeting the middle and bottom of the pyramid. The shift from postpaid to prepaid services turned out to be a tipping point in Kenya's adoption of mobile phones, and Safaricom offered units of airtime purchases for as low as 20 cents. Given the ubiquity of mobile phones, Africa's internet revolution is now happening through mobile devices. Cheaper smart phones and social networking applications with both Internet and mobile interfaces are proving increasingly popular, especially among urban youth.

Figure 7-2. *Kenya's Mobile Money Revolution, 1999–2011*

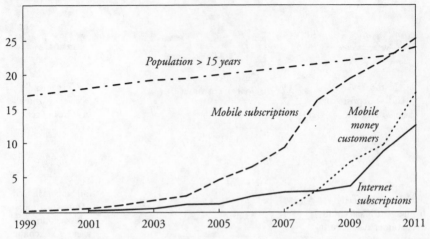

Number of persons in millions

Source: Communication Commission of Kenya; World Bank (2011).

Over the last decade the information and communication technology sector has become an important driver of Kenya's economic development, growing on average 20 percent since 2000 and contributing a full percent to Kenya's economic growth, which has averaged around 4 percent over this period (that is, a small sector of the economy has contributed a quarter of its growth). In Kenya, scaling up and the mobile revolution happened not only vertically (from small numbers to ubiquity) but also horizontally (spreading into related areas). For example, Kenya's information and communication technology sector generated mobile banking, linking mobile money with personal bank accounts, mobile credit, and mobile insurance. These innovations are expanding the reach of financial services to the previously unbanked population (figure 7-3). However, horizontal scaling up does not happen automatically, as the partial success in Kenya's mobile savings innovation demonstrates.

How Mobile Money Came About

M-PESA was not the product of a top-down plan.[4] No one ever set out to create mobile money. Rather, it emerged out of a process of private initiative that

4. The M-PESA pilot is covered in Hughes and Lonie (2007). Nick Hughes is the Vodafone executive who championed the mobile money concept and obtained the initial seed capital in 2003. Susie Lonie is the e-commerce expert who went to Kenya in 2005 to develop the pilot operation.

Figure 7-3. *Scaling Up Mobile Innovation, Kenya*

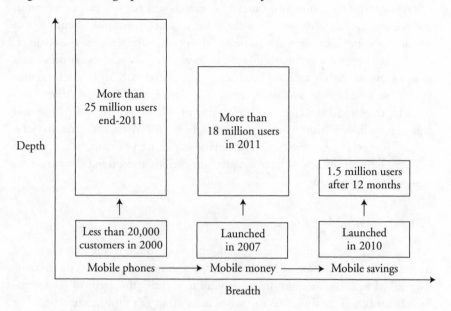

Source: Authors' compilation.

evolved over time in response to consumer demand, after an initial contribution from a donor innovation fund.

DFID's Innovation Fund

In 2000 the UK government established the Financial Deepening Challenge Fund (FDCF) through its Department for International Development (DFID). The fund made available £15 million for joint investments with the private sector to improve access to financial services for the unbanked. In mid-2003 Nick Hughes, a Vodafone executive with a social innovation remit, developed a proposal for using the mobile phone to deepen financial access and built up support within the company. Hughes notes that the "entrant of a telecom company into a funding competition for the financial services sector took a few of the FDCF proposal team by surprise," but nonetheless the company was awarded funding of nearly £1 million, which was matched by Vodafone.[5]

At the point at which the funds were awarded, the concept of mobile money had not taken shape. Hughes explains that the proposal consisted largely of "a preliminary needs assessment and not a functional specification of a new product." Vodafone then conducted a series of open workshops in 2004 in Nairobi

5. Hughes and Lonie (2007).

and Dar-es-Salaam to consult with banks, microfinance organizations, technology service suppliers, nongovernmental organizations involved in microcredit, and telecommunications and financial sector regulators to think about ways in which they could increase access to financial services. After much brainstorming, the idea emerged of a partnership between Safaricom (a Vodafone associate and Kenya's largest mobile telecommunications company), a Kenyan microfinance institution called Faulu, and the Kenya-based Commercial Bank of Africa. Specifically, they decided to develop a platform to allow customers to receive and repay microfinance loans using a phone handset, with payments made via Safaricom's prepay airtime resellers.[6] The service was conceived entirely as a way of improving the efficiency of microfinance institutions and extend their reach to more customers and in more remote locations.

Piloting Mobile Money in Kenya

A pilot steering committee was created, and Vodafone installed an executive within the Safaricom team in Nairobi to set up and run the project. The committee worked with the partners on the ground to identify the needs of the microfinance customers and the microfinance institution (Faulu): the functionality required, the infrastructure design, and different distribution network options.

The system was given the name M-PESA, with *m* for mobile and *pesa* meaning money in Swahili. It was launched on a pilot basis in October 2005 with just 500 microfinance clients, who were given mobile handsets and enrolled as customers able to perform limited functions:

—Deposit cash at participating outlets and use this credit to repay their loans via a group treasurer

—Withdraw any excess funds as cash at participating outlets[7]

—Send money to other enrolled customers (which was easily added to the product suite and expected to be useful among people within the same microfinance client group)

—Perform account administration tasks, like registration, checking account balance, and changing a personal identification number (PIN)

Once the pilot was under way the team focused on ensuring that customers were well educated in how to use the service, what challenges they experienced,

6. The Kenya mobile phone market is predominantly prepay, with very little credit information available on customers. Less than 3 percent of Safaricom's customers have contract phones, instead purchasing airtime credit as and when they can afford to. Prepaid airtime is typically sold using vouchers, which are distributed nationwide through a network of resellers and are readily available at retail stores.

7. For the pilot, eight Safaricom prepay airtime resellers were used in Thika and Nairobi, near the location of microfinance institutions.

and what opportunities for improvement existed. By attending Faulu group meetings, spending time with pilot retail outlets, observing customer behavior, and soliciting feedback, the team was able to recommend changes to both the pilot and the commercial service that followed.

Experience and feedback led to some simple modifications to the pilot service, including the ability of customers to buy Safaricom prepaid airtime with their M-PESA credit. While retrospectively this seems an obvious addition to a mobile phone operator's service, the need was highlighted through interaction with pilot users, who felt it would increase the utility of the service if they could use their M-PESA account to buy airtime at their convenience without having to withdraw the cash first. Another change made during the pilot was for some customers to receive their loan disbursal via M-PESA, rather than having it paid into a bank account. This was also requested by pilot users, who preferred the added convenience of not having to visit a bank branch.

It was then discovered that M-PESA transactions were taking place among the microfinance clients for a wide variety of purposes not intended by its creators:

—Repaying the loans of others in return for services or cash

—Trading between businesses

—Using M-PESA as an overnight safe after banks closed

—Using it to secure money while journeying (depositing cash at one end and withdrawing it at the other)

—Sending airtime directly to relatives in rural areas

—Sending money to others for various ad hoc reasons (for example, one lady whose husband had been robbed sent him money for his bus fare home)

The innovative uses that customers made of M-PESA during the pilot, which ran through October 2006, convinced Vodafone and Safaricom that there was a market for M-PESA far beyond its narrow use for microfinance transactions—in particular for domestic remittances, a common phenomenon in Kenya and many other African countries. (Urbanization means that often family members migrate to work in the cities, sending home money to support their rural families.)

The pilot customers embraced M-PESA more enthusiastically than the microfinance institution involved. Faulu was burdened with inflexible, bureaucratic, and lengthy processes and was slow to innovate in integrating mobile money as a loan repayment method. As a result, Safaricom decided to offer M-PESA to all its customers and worked with Vodafone to prepare for a national launch.

Turning a limited, low-risk pilot into a commercially viable system involved scaling up technology, developing internal processes and a distribution network to support scale, ensuring that appropriate security measures were in place, and enhancing reporting and audit functions. That mobile money was so new meant that close attention to risk management was required, with internal and independent risk audits. Not least, Safaricom required a buy-in from the Central Bank of Kenya as the regulatory body for banking and payment services.

Early Investment in Mobile Money

DFID and Vodafone provided funding for the M-PESA pilot; both parties were interested in how technology could be used to deepen financial access, with Vodafone having the added incentive of the benefit of such services to its core business. At the pilot's conclusion Vodafone and Safaricom debated on how to proceed with a commercial service. While related, the two companies were separate, and their objectives and roles in M-PESA differed. As the technology provider, Vodafone anticipated sharing the cost of developing and hosting the technology across a number of deployments, expecting that Kenya would be the launching pad of a service that could also be sold in other countries. Return on investment would come from service fees from Safaricom and other networks.

Safaricom management saw M-PESA as an opportunity to extend a service to its existing customers, recognizing that the majority of them did not have bank accounts and would value the ability to transfer funds to other mobile users. In an increasingly competitive market, such a service could translate into strong loyalty from existing customers, protecting Safaricom's market share and reducing customer churn.[8] Safaricom therefore launched M-PESA as a loyalty driver, intending to cover operating costs with service fees and not expecting to turn a profit. Safaricom was in fact investing in customer acquisition.

Vodafone and Safaricom entered a managed service agreement, under which each party covered the costs over which it had control (table 7-1). They also signed a corresponding revenue-sharing agreement. A single organization would have struggled to justify the full spending required to support the early scale-up of M-PESA. Without this agreement, M-PESA's growth would have been throttled.

Adoption of Mobile Money

M-PESA was launched in March 2007. Within the first month of operation, 20,000 customers signed up, exceeding the expectations of all involved. Within one year M-PESA had more than 2 million customers. Within three years there were almost 10 million customers—some 50 percent of Kenya's adult population—and the agent network grew equally fast (figure 7-4). M-PESA enjoyed the most rapid adoption of innovation in the developing world ever. The volume of mobile money transfers exceeded all expectations as well (figure 7-5). In many cases, full

---

8. According to Safaricom senior management, customer churn rate was over 20 percent; more than one in five customers exit the network each year. Much of this is internal churn, with the customer purchasing another Safaricom subscriber identity module (SIM) later. This presents acquisition costs to Safaricom that can be avoided if the churn is curbed. (Authors' personal communication with Safaricom officials.)

Table 7-1. *Financial Investment by Key M-PESA Stakeholders, from Pilot to Year 1*

Party	DFID	Vodafone	Safaricom
Role	Provide seed funding for proof of concept through pilot Advocate as an independent party pushing the inclusion agenda	Design and operation of M-PESA pilot Develop and host M-PESA technology	Acquire mobile network customers and operation of the service in Kenya
Investment, pilot to first year of operations	£1 million through Challenge Fund	£4–5 million estimated	£4–5 million estimated
Main use of investment	Matched funding for pilot	Matched funding for pilot Technology platform	Customer acquisition (marketing, sign-up fees, and SIMEX to support M-PESA)[a] Customer care Develop distribution
Return on investment	Deeper financial access	Revenue through license fees or revenue/profit share on transaction fees	Increased customer loyalty and customer acquisition Revenue from transaction fees

Source: Authors.

a. See text for description of exchange of SIM cards for existing customers to support the M-PESA application.

application of new tools lags with lower income groups, which tend to remain inactive even after they have signed up to a new service. But in 2011, M-PESA transacted an estimated $7 billion, which is equivalent to 30 percent of Kenya's GDP and substantially larger than Western Union's total operation in Africa.[9]

Mobile money is attractive to Kenyans because of the low barrier to entry and high accessibility compared to formal financial services. It offers a way for people to perform low-value transactions, making it possible for those at the middle and bottom of the income pyramid to access financial services. The penetration of M-PESA across the Safaricom subscriber base is high: some 80 percent of lines are registered, higher than any other value-added service outside of short-message services (SMS).

9. Fengler, Joseph, and Mugyenyi (2011).

Figure 7-4. *M-PESA Growth in Customers and Agent Outlets, 2007–11*

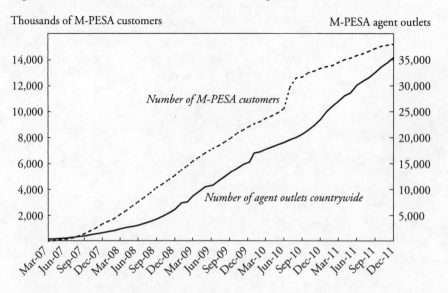

Source: Safaricom (www.Safaricom.co.ke).

Figure 7-5. *M-PESA Person-to-Person Transfers, 2007–11*

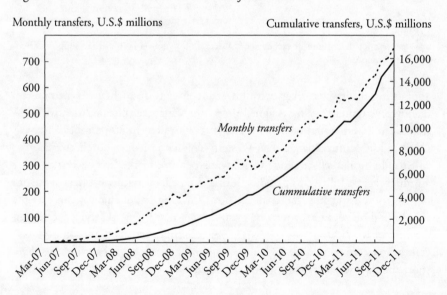

Source: Safaricom (www.Safaricom.co.ke).

In just three years M-PESA helped grow financial access in Kenya from 26 percent in 2006 to 40 percent in 2009, one of the highest levels in the developing world. This growth has continued, with some estimates of financial access being as high as 75 percent.

Keys to Scaling Up

In all examples where technology scales up, the network effect plays an important part, with positive word of mouth driving adoption and usage. Positive word of mouth is driven by positive experience. The scaling up of M-PESA benefited from several factors and early decisions, most of which are replicable across industries.

Strong Distribution Network

A key factor in the success of mobile money is the distribution channel that gets the service to the customers. M-PESA established a strong network of agents, rapidly expanding its points of presence from mainly urban areas to points of presence that serve the majority of the population. Only a very large network of agents could deliver on M-PESA's promise to "send money home."

The role of the M-PESA agent is to register new customers and to facilitate cash-in and cash-out transactions. The agent receives a small commission for each transaction. He also serves a vital role in educating customers when they sign up for mobile money. Safaricom realized that to gain the trust of new customers, agents would need to provide excellent service, and the company invested heavily in training the agents to achieve this. To cope with the rapid expansion, it outsourced agent training.[10] Trade development representatives delivered set-up kits to new agents, activated their agent handsets, trained their staff, branded their shops, and ensured that the shops could carry out the required transactions. They then visited each agent on rotation, at least weekly. This close contact allowed Safaricom to disseminate information efficiently, constantly retraining the agents and gathering information. It is likely that the bond between Safaricom and its agents kept M-PESA agents loyal to Safaricom when other mobile payment providers entered the market.

During the pilot, Safaricom realized that an efficient way of growing the distribution network would be to recruit organizations that already had a network of outlets. M-PESA was designed with this in mind: an organization signs up through a head office, to which its outlets are attached. The head office is responsible for float management, among other things, and can move electronic

10. Agent training was initially outsourced to Top Image, a local experiential marketing firm. As the network of agents grew, other firms were employed to share the workload.

value between its outlets via SMS or web instruction. With this structure, M-PESA targeted three types of outlet:

—Airtime dealers. These dealers are exclusive to Safaricom; they buy airtime and sell it to retail outlets through regional outlets of their own. Safaricom invited dealers to add M-PESA to their portfolio of products, and because of their existing relationship some dealers agreed to try the new service in some of their shops. As the service gained popularity, Safaricom was easily able to add new outlets, with minimal effort by M-PESA.

—Networked organizations. The fuel retailer Caltex and Group 4 Securicor courier services were among the initial agents. Both had nationwide coverage, providing presence in forty or fifty locations with a single contract. Supermarket chains, dry cleaners, and banks followed suit when they recognized the benefit M-PESA provided their customers. The independent ATM network Pesa Point signed up in 2009, making M-PESA withdrawals possible at 110 ATMs in Kenya.

—Stand-alone shops. Some strategic outlets were signed up without being part of a network. These either provided coverage where networked organizations were not present, or they had the potential to serve many customers (for example, hospitals, restaurants, and large retail outlets).

To start with, Safaricom had to "sell" the idea of M-PESA to prospective outlets. It did so based on the premise of additional revenue, more feet through the door, and value-added service to their customers. Requirements were an existing business of good repute and sufficient cash to invest in an M-PESA float. As M-PESA's popularity grew, the agent proposition strengthened, with outlets earning healthy commission. Safaricom was flooded with requests for agency. Requirements were strengthened to ensure that the agents chosen would provide the most convenience, customer comfort, and the best service to customers.

Beyond agent availability, mobile money requires agent quality if the customers are to trust the service. Once a sufficient network was built, Safaricom focused on building quality and loyalty among its agents. Its methodology includes continued training, agent promotions, agent forums, and quality audits. One of the biggest challenges an agent faces is maintaining the right liquidity: the correct mix of cash and e-value (or float) is required. Over time, initiatives to ease the balancing of liquidity have been taken, like recruitment of banks as M-PESA super-agents, where an agent can go with a mobile handset to exchange cash for float, and vice versa. With the number of outlets in the country growing to 39,000 within five years, M-PESA has managed to build up the most extensive distribution network of any financial service in Africa, with availability penetrating to the most rural areas.[11] By 2009 the mean distance

11. Safaricom March 2012 annual statistics (www.safaricom.co.ke).

to the closest M-PESA agent for Kenyans was just 3 kilometers.[12] As M-PESA agent numbers swell, there have been dramatic improvements in agent density across the entire distribution of households. For the bottom 20 percent of surveyed households in terms of agent access (the households situated furthest from their closest agents), household distance to the closest agent fell by 40 percent between 2008 and 2009.

Starting Simple

Built as a payments platform that allowed value transfer between any two accounts, Safaricom had the option of marketing a more sophisticated bouquet of services that would allow customers to make and receive payments to multiple organizations, interact with banks, and even receive international remittances. Safaricom chose instead to focus on one service—domestic remittance—and the account management tools to support this. By starting simple, Safaricom was able to

—Concentrate its resources on communicating one message well, rather than multiple messages across different segments

—Familiarize customers with how the service worked before adding more complicated functionality

—Test and refine operational procedures to support domestic remittance at scale, before adding more actions to complicate operation

—Gain the buy-in of the Central Bank of Kenya for a single feature and over time build its confidence in Safaricom's ability to operate at scale and add new features

Once a critical mass of customers had started to use M-PESA with confidence and growth had become self-perpetuating, Safaricom added new functionality, including

—Pay bill. By choosing "Pay Bill" on the M-PESA menu instead of "Send Money," a customer can send money to an M-PESA partner organization, for example to pay the national electricity provider or an e-commerce merchant. The customer enters a business number, to identify the partner organization, and then an account number, to identify him to the partner organization.

—Bulk payments. These payments allow an M-PESA partner organization to send money to multiple customers anywhere in Kenya—for example, to pay low-value wages and social benefits.

—International remittance. This choice allows people living in the diaspora to send money to Kenyans directly into their M-PESA accounts. The international remittance service is operated in partnership with organizations like Western Union, which is licensed for money transfer in the sending markets.

12. Jack and Suri (2010). Data exclude the sparsely populated North Eastern Province.

These new options are value-added services that improve the proposition for existing customers and are designed to give them more reasons to transact rather than a reason to sign up for M-PESA.

Removing Barriers to Entry

Customers will normally only make one attempt to sign up for or use a service; if their experience is poor, they are likely to be lost. Safaricom made it as easy as possible for a customer to register and use M-PESA. Some examples are

—Minimal account-opening requirements. With no regulation for m-wallet accounts in place, Safaricom proposed appropriate know-your-customer (KYC) rules for M-PESA, rules agreed to by the Central Bank. Typically, financial institutions require onerous documentation for account opening; given that Safaricom would not be providing any loans to customers, less information about the customer was needed. All Kenyans over the age of eighteen are issued a national ID card, and this was chosen as being the only KYC required beyond the customer's mobile phone number, making it possible for all adults to sign up using a document that they already carry daily. In countries where no national ID exists, KYC becomes a significant challenge. Nonstandard documentation must be allowed, and even then some people will not meet the minimum requirements.

—Free registration. By fully absorbing the cost of account opening, Safaricom was able to advertise its free account opening. Even a small cost to open an account can put off potential users.

—Free and simple SIM exchange (SIMEX). M-PESA is a proprietary application embedded on the Safaricom SIM card, which for security reasons is placed on the SIM by the manufacturer. Five months before launching M-PESA, Safaricom included the application on all new SIM cards, but by the launch of M-PESA there were still 6 million mobile subscribers who had an old-generation SIM card without the M-PESA application. These customers had to do a SIMEX before they could use the service. This was the biggest barrier to signing up for M-PESA. Safaricom fully absorbed the cost of SIMEX, at over $2 per customer—a huge investment but one that paid off, as customers would very likely have shied away from paying for an unrelated upgrade to access M-PESA.

—Simple user experience. Early on the team realized that a reduced and simple menu of options would increase adoption. A simple, intuitive, user interface was designed for the pilot, and this is still used by customers and agents today. The M-PESA application guides users step by step through a menu, with the only entries required being numerical: the recipient phone number, the amount to be sent, and the secure M-PESA PIN. Users can choose between English or Swahili.

Achieving Familiarity

With any new service, the key is to gain a critical mass of customers who will educate other customers on its benefits and usage. This can be very difficult, and some approaches that contributed to early adoption of M-PESA are

—Free deposits. Customers need credit in their account before they can transact. Ensuring that there was no cost of getting it there removed this barrier.

—Low-risk airtime top-ups via M-PESA. Entrusting their cash to Safaricom via the M-PESA agents was something new to customers and a big step to take. The average money transfer is around $40, a huge amount for the average Kenyan to deposit for an initial transaction. The only transaction possible at launch, other than money transfer, was a Safaricom airtime top-up. This allowed a customer to deposit the minimum of KSh 100 (around $1.30 at the time) and immediately use it to purchase airtime. This boosted customers' confidence and familiarized them with M-PESA menus.

—Experiential communication. To complement the advertising in newspapers and on radio and television, Safaricom invested heavily in experiential advertising. By talking directly to target customers at public venues, sales people gave customers the opportunity to try out the service and ask questions.

—Promotions. Mobile phone companies are well known in Kenya for running massive promotions to reward their customers for loyalty, often giving free airtime to randomly selected subscribers. Within twelve months of M-PESA's launch, Safaricom chose to use M-PESA to give out cash rather than airtime. Some 240,000 Safaricom users were sent between $7 and $35, an amount significant enough to incentivize registration by people not already registered for M-PESA.

—Limited usage without registration. A customer who is registered for M-PESA can send money to any other mobile phone in Kenya. If the recipient is not registered for M-PESA, he can still collect at an agent's outlet; at this point, the agent could register the recipient. In the initial stages, when customers were few, this contact was very important in driving the network effect; if customers were limited to sending only to other customers, then growth would have been slow.

Making Information Accessible

Customers need information to be readily accessible to them, particularly for financial services, which can be confusing to people without prior experience. By providing information through various channels, Safaricom built customer confidence:

—Free twenty-four-hour call center. The center provides general information as well as addressing queries on specific transactions.

—Tariff information. This information is provided at all agent outlets at a minimum, to ensure that pricing is completely transparent, with no room for arbitrary charges by agent staff.

—Training of agents. M-PESA agents are the location for cash in and cash out, which account for two of three transactions. M-PESA agents are therefore the customer's first point of query and are trained to be able to educate customers.

—Locating other agents. In the days before general access, it was important to know where to locate an agent as it was uncertain if the recipient of the transaction was close to another agent. The agents had a full list and schedules of all the agents in the country.

Thinking Big

How we do something is partly determined by the scale at which it needs to be done. Will something that works for 100 work for 100,000? If we plan to bring lots of people into a program over time, then from the outset processes, budgets, and targets ought to be designed for the larger scale. Even if initial numbers will be low, the question must be asked, How will this work for the future, when everyone is on board? The result is likely to be a simpler, more customer-focused, means of doing things.

Safaricom planned to make mobile money available to all customers, so the implementing team knew they needed to design for scale. Before launch, acquisition targets were set at some 300,000 sign-ups within the first twelve months, which the team was reasonably confident of achieving. Within days of launch, the CEO realized just how important the network effect would be to mobile money and raised the bar threefold by demanding 1 million customer sign-ups within a year. To meet this would require higher budgets, which were not withheld, and highly efficient processes. The team focused on getting things right from the beginning—aware that customer escalations would place huge demands on customer-service staff, due to the sheer number of queries, and that to fix things later would be near impossible, when millions of users were involved.

The human psyche responds well to realistic targets, and people innovate to find ways of meeting ambitious goals. In the event, there were over 2 million customers registered for M-PESA within one year. The team celebrated milestones along the way, reinforcing the importance and attainability of the goals. As more customers signed up and started using the service, the effort taken to streamline processes early on paid off, as resources could not be increased proportionally.

Thinking big challenges how we do things. Had the Vodafone team, looking to use mobile money to facilitate financial services, used traditional banking services as a benchmark, the service they developed would have looked quite different from mobile money today. It is because they looked further than the existing banked customer numbers—to embrace all Kenyans—that mobile money as we know it today evolved.

Why Did M-PESA Work So Well?

An often-asked question is why M-PESA has been so much more successful in Kenya than many other mobile money deployments that have been launched worldwide in the ensuing years. There is no single, simple answer: M-PESA scaled up so successfully because of a combination of factors that came together. Rather than being the result of a perfect storm, many of these factors were constructed, are replicable, and can provide important lessons in social innovation.

It is critical to develop the right distribution network to make a service available and trusted by customers. Early in 2007 Safaricom had some 55 percent share of the Kenyan mobile phone market. The company was looking for ways to increase customer loyalty to combat increasing competition with the entry of new players. As market leader it had the benefit of strong airtime distribution in place for M-PESA to draw from and build on; it also has a substantial customer base of 8 million to target with the new service. By recruiting airtime sellers and other outlets as M-PESA agents, Safaricom succeeded in building a strong enough network of outlets to drive customer confidence and usage of the new service.

Safaricom's strong market share and the resultant trust in the Safaricom brand undoubtedly contributed to the success of mobile money in Kenya. While Safaricom took other actions to drive retention and growth of its customers since 2007, this success is evidence that M-PESA was a major contributing factor in the growth of Safaricom's total base and market share.[13] All mobile network operators have subsequently launched mobile money: Zain (now Airtel) launched Zap in February 2009, Yu launched Yu Cash in December 2009, and Orange launched Orange Money in November 2010. Safaricom's strong market share was helpful in scaling up mobile money, but many other factors contributed to its success. In the following sections we explore the main factors that made mobile money successful in Kenya.

Meeting a Need

Kenyans send money home. Before M-PESA they did so by mostly informal means, using friends and family or the public transport system to carry cash, methods that were slow and prone to leakage (figure 7-6 and box 7-1). Taking to market a solution that met a recognized need better than the current solutions

---

13. Safaricom launched a loyalty program in January 2007 as well as other value-added services during the year. The continuous reduction in cost of both mobile handsets and minutes of call time has allowed entry of new subscribers to mobile usage.

Figure 7-6. *Replacement of Traditional Fund Remittance with Mobile Money, Kenya, 2006 and 2009*

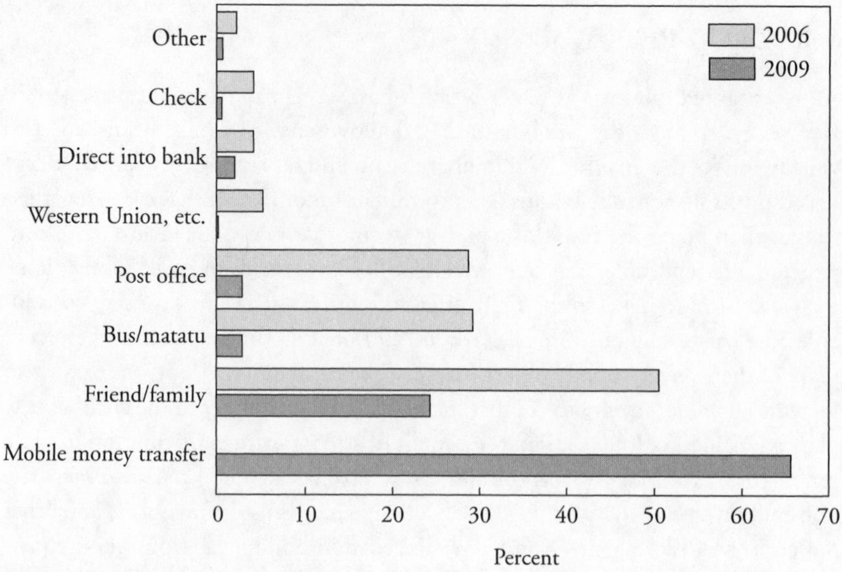

Source: World Bank (2010).

was an attractive alternative, which the Kenyan public was willing to try out. The marketing message, "Send money home with M-PESA: fast, safe, and convenient," hit the spot, especially for those who had lost money in the past.

Domestic remittance has been identified as the "killer" application that drove customers to sign up for mobile money in Kenya. This was not evident from the pilot, which focused on microfinance transactions. Having ruled out microfinance as an initial application, Safaricom held a workshop to derive the go-to-market messaging for M-PESA. As participants expressed why they might personally use the service, the overriding purpose was for sending money across distances, generally to support members of the family or the rural homestead: the send-money-home theme was born. This worked well as an acquisition message, and once customers experienced the convenience of the service, they expanded their usage for other purposes. Research quantifying the reasons people send money now would likely show that "home" is a minority destination, as M-PESA has become a tool for a wide array of payment transactions.

Mobile money services in other countries are struggling to find their killer application to drive adoption. With domestic remittance not so predominant continent-wide, no single payment service provides the "I need to use that" factor to drive mass sign-ups.

Box 7-1. *Impact of Mobile Money at an Individual Level*

Stephen works as a security guard in Nairobi; he supports his parents, who live in Kerio district, about 300 kilometers from Nairobi. Previously, Stephen saved his money and would travel home to visit them every second month, carrying around $60 cash for them. The trip would take him around two days and cost him $15 in bus fare. Sometimes he could not spare the time to travel, meaning that his parents missed out on their remittance. On one such occasion he sent the cash with a friend, who "lost" the bulk of the remittance and only delivered $20. Since using M-PESA, Stephen is able to send his parents $20 every two weeks. They now know to expect the transfer and are able to plan their expenditure and buy extra food with the additional money that Stephen is able to send them by saving on his cost of transport.

Source: Authors.

A Business Case for All: Win-Win Situations

All too often, clever technology fails to find a foothold as one or more stakeholders have no reason to adopt it. M-PESA is a good example of technology being put to use in an innovative way to deliver a new business model, ensuring that each and every participant will benefit from its introduction (table 7-2). Safaricom's long-term business strategy of serving the mass market with relevant and affordable products; the development vision of the donor community; and the Kenya government's reform commitment converged to improve financial services offered to the Kenya public.

In this example it is clear that all stakeholders had an incentive for progressing mobile money. Often, even when there is good reason for cooperation, it still does not occur or does not have the required intensity of commitment required for progress at scale. Important for the evolution of M-PESA was the involvement of DFID, represented on the pilot Steering Committee through FSD Kenya. Spurred by its interest as cofunder of the pilot and having knowledge in financial policy and access, DFID acted as a broker between various stakeholders. Together with other public sector bodies, such as the World Bank, and philanthropic organizations, such as the Bill & Melinda Gates Foundation, DFID was able to provide support—in particular to the Central Bank of Kenya.[14] This was through targeted advisory and coordinated research into the impacts and challenges of mobile money.

14. CGAP (Consultative Group Acting for the Poor) under the World Bank has a keen interest in deepening financial services for the poor (www.cgap.org). More information on the Financial Services for the Poor of the Bill & Melinda Gates Foundation can be found at www.gatesfoundation.org.

Table 7-2. *Role and Rationale of M-PESA for M-PESA Stakeholders*

Stakeholder	Role	Rationale
Kenyan public	Potential customer for mobile money; source of revenue as fees are charged to transact	Mobile money provided a faster, safer, cheaper, and more convenient way to move money long distances than existing informal methods.
Telecommunication company (Safaricom)	Mobile network operator in Kenya	In an increasingly competitive market, mobile money was expected to boost loyalty and attract new customers to core business of Voice and SMS. The aim was to strengthen the Safaricom brand to reduce churn. Secondary was the transaction revenue to be used to cover the costs of operations.
Retail outlets recruited as M-PESA agents	Register customers and provide cash-in and cash-out services	Agents earn a commission for each transaction. Safaricom targeted existing businesses, often airtime resellers, for whom incremental revenue would come at little extra cost. It also sold the idea that M-PESA would bring extra customers to the shop's core business.
Commercial banks	Hold the M-PESA float	The pool account holding the cash equivalent to the combined balance of all M-PESA participants (customers plus agents plus Safaricom) became a large and growing business through which banks could mediate, a core business for a bank. In the launch service, Commercial Bank of Africa held the M-PESA float. For diversification of risk, the funds are now held by a number of local banks, and some are placed in treasury bills.
Central Bank of Kenya	Regulator responsible for oversight of banks and payment systems in Kenya	The Central Bank has a double remit: ensuring stability of the financial systems and deepening financial access. M-PESA was positioned as a financial service for the unbanked, with the promise of providing secure financial services to a larger population and hence increasing the amount of money in the financial system.
Vodafone	Safaricom's major shareholder and M-PESA technology provider	With operations in multiple developing countries, Vodafone is always seeking methods to grow its business and retain customers through attractive value-added services. As a service for the unbanked, M-PESA had the potential to touch base with large numbers of their mobile subscribers.

Stakeholder	Role	Rationale
Donor community	Provided pilot funding through DFID's FCDF	Provided DFID with an innovative approach to meeting its objective of providing more and better services for the poor, an important tool in the fight against poverty.
Faulu (limited to pilot)	Microfinance institution whose customers were repaying loans via M-PESA	Integrating mobile money into microfinancing has the potential of cutting costs through reduced cost of cash, fraud, and operational efficiencies. Though this was not realized in the pilot, these objectives still stand for integrating mobile money into microfinance.[a]

Source: Authors' compilation.

a. Musoni, a new microfinance institution based in Nairobi, is attempting to do just that by removing cash from its operations and working only with mobile money for all loan disbursements and repayments (www.musoni.co.ke).

However, the success of M-PESA was made possible by the joint vision and drive of the operator and the regulator (especially the Central Bank of Kenya and the Ministry of Information and Communication), which became champions of M-PESA.

Experimentation

Many product trials focus on technical and operational readiness, or act to fine-tune aspects such as customer pricing, and can be thought of more as soft launches. This is particularly the case if a similar product or service exists elsewhere, with providers wanting to tweak the service or customer communication for their market rather than reinvent the wheel. Vodafone could have chosen this approach, looking to earlier mobile money deployments in the Philippines as a basis.[15] However, copying an idea will not necessarily work; it is the intricacies of getting it right for that market that will make it successful.

The M-PESA pilot was different in that the objectives were broadly about testing the feasibility of using mobile for financial services: they were not specifically to test the incorporation of mobile phones into microfinance. At the end of piloting there was the luxury of multiple options: proceed with minor service adjustments, rewrite the book from what had been learned, or walk away.

15. Mobile money was launched in the Philippines before Safaricom's launch of M-PESA in Kenya.

As the money from DFID's FDCF covered a pilot for a substantial period, there was the luxury of being able to really test customer usage as well as the technology—something not often possible in private organizations, when the race to recover costs starts early. A substantive pilot was run for a year to test the business and to ensure that the design of customer touch points met their needs. Using customer feedback during the pilot, significant modifications were made to shape the final service, and the book was rewritten to address the needs of Safaricom's large subscriber base. Here there is perhaps an element of chance: had Faulu played ball and had M-PESA continued along the course it started, it would have failed to scale up and be relevant to the majority of Kenyans because the target base would have been limited to microfinance customers.

Another important benefit from the extensive trial is that operational challenges were identified up front, meaning that procedures could be molded for efficiency at scale before M-PESA was nationally launched. The significance of this cannot be overstated: remembering that the devil is in the details is critical for scaling up—if the details are not resolved, then process issues may well diminish customer experience and impair adoption. The power of social networking to spread negative experiences is strong, stronger than for spreading positive news, and recovering from process setbacks can be a major hurdle.

As with most technical trials, the pilot period also highlighted challenges with technology and local infrastructure, like frequent Internet outages. These were identified and accommodated, although as with technology worldwide M-PESA still experiences occasional technical hitches, particularly during peak periods of usage.

Regulation after Innovation

An important factor in the success of mobile money in Kenya is the progressive role of Kenya's regulators, especially the Central Bank. Mobile money entered a regulatory vacuum. At the time that M-PESA was piloted, no regulations existed for e-money initiatives nor for the involvement of mobile phone operators in any kind of financial transactions. The operator kept the Central Bank updated on developments, inviting critique and suggestions through the pilot.

In preparation for a commercial launch of mobile money, Safaricom sought approval from the Central Bank. Safaricom and the Central Bank worked together to address key aspects of payment system regulation including product functionality, legal compliance, stability and redundancy of the technical platform, prudential controls, and consumer protection. The Central Bank consulted with relevant governmental and policy bodies, including DFID through its local FSD representative. In parallel, Safaricom lobbied the government and notably gained the support of the permanent secretary in the Ministry of Information and Telecommunication.

Once the Central Bank was confident in the legal structures and controls implemented by Safaricom and Vodafone, the acting governor at the time issued a letter of "no objection." This set the spirit of working together going forward as regulation was developed. Most important, Safaricom was required to report regularly, thereby setting the standard for regular consultation. The Ministries of Finance and of Information and Telecommunication jointly launched M-PESA at a ceremony attended by many officials, and the government of Kenya's support for deepening financial access was confirmed.

The Kenyan government allowed regulation to follow innovation, while reassuring the market of its oversight. The regulator agreed that M-PESA agents needed limited restrictions to enter the business, as they were not providing banking services, while the operator behaved as if it was regulated and reported financial data as regularly as banks do. Stakeholders worked together in good faith, allowing service providers to proceed, as they could see the potential benefit of a domestic remittance product for the average Kenyan.

As the popularity of mobile money grew in Kenya, there was an attempt by traditional banks and parts of government to stop M-PESA, and the minister of finance requested the Central Bank to audit the service. In January 2009 the Ministry of Finance published a notice in the national dailies on the M-PESA money-transfer service incorporating the results of this audit, further driving public confidence in mobile money (box 7-2).

The volume of mobile money transfers made it also an important macroeconomic variable, and the monitoring of mobile money flows helped the Central Bank to monitor money circulation better than before. As money was moved from "mattresses to the market," money circulation increased, and velocity declines gave the Central Bank more flexibility in monetary policymaking.[16]

Focus on Execution

The technologies used for mobile money had matured sufficiently to pose no major technology risk at launch: secure SMS, SIM tool kit applications on SIM cards, and direct charging of airtime for a top-up. A small development team delivered the pilot system. The team was totally focused on M-PESA and was able to react quickly to changing needs, leading to innovative solutions.

Safaricom decided very early on that if M-PESA was to succeed, it should not be given to an existing department to manage. With such small initial revenue forecasts, it stood the risk of being sidelined by people with mainstream revenue responsibility. Once the decision to launch was made, a separate department was created, with its own sales, marketing, legal, and technical staff. This was, in hindsight, a fundamental and wise decision, as it allowed a network of agents to

16. Ndung'u (2011).

Box 7-2. *Reflections by Michael Joseph on M-PESA's Critical Moments*

I firmly believe that the decision to allow Safaricom to go ahead with M-PESA was, first, because no one really realized or anticipated the phenomenal success that M-PESA would achieve and the scale of the adoption, and second, because all parties, particularly the Central Bank, wanted to support innovation and agreed that regulation should follow innovation.

The real key to the success of the M-PESA rollout and acceptance was the number and geographic spread of M-PESA agents. Not many people, either within or external to Safaricom, understood the concept and the necessity of the number and spread of M-PESA agents. Thus the necessity of getting regulatory approval for the management and appointment of agents was not sought as rigorously as for the product itself. It was only after the initial success and the concerns that were raised by the traditional banks that attention was then given to getting regulatory "approval" of the agent structure.

The joint launch of M-PESA by both finance and telecommunications ministries, the support by the Central Bank governor, and the genuine innovative culture of Kenyans, in both the Central Bank and Safaricom, were the basis of the huge success of M-PESA and the subsequent defense of M-PESA by treasury, when the traditional banks belatedly realized the potential impact on their own business.

Personally, I was determined to learn from some of the lessons of the past, when I had launched a new product but had not given it sufficient resources or attention to make it succeed. Launching new value-added services of such magnitude requires dedication, passion, commitment, and imagination, even if you are not expecting (as we were) success on the scale we achieved and even if the business plan tells you that you are crazy!

---

be recruited separately from airtime dealers, with their own legal contracts and management processes and procedures. This permitted a very strict management style from the beginning. This created a behavioral pattern for M-PESA agents and a clear management structure that could also withstand the scrutiny of the regulator.

Keeping the team delivering M-PESA to market small and dedicated allowed it to be totally focused—sometimes a difficult task in a large organization where shifting priorities can often change the goals. That the team believed strongly in the potential for positive impact instilled a passion in their activities, and passion is a great seed for getting things done well. Safaricom and Vodafone management provided critical support. Once the pilot funding was over, the respective M-PESA departments became part of the regular corporate budgeting process. Vodafone spent millions of pounds getting the technology to a commercial stage, and Safaricom spent an equal amount to take it to market.

Table 7-3. *Improvement in Agent Service and Trust, Rounds 1 and 2*
Percent

Problem	Round 1 (2008): nearest agent	Round 2 (2009): last 2 transactions
Unable to withdraw money (due to agent liquidity)	16	5
Unable to deposit money (due to agent liquidity)	7	4
Asked by agent to show ID	77	95
Trust agent	65	95

Source: Jack and Suri (2010).

Trust

Trust in a financial service is normally built up over time. Expecting relatively unsophisticated people to entrust their hard-earned money to a mobile service, which is also new and unproven, is not something you might expect. Such trust is even rarer when the average transaction values (around $40) are high when compared to the average Kenyan income (sometimes the money deposited in M-PESA would be all a customer had). But Safaricom had built a strong Kenyan brand over the past seven years, and because of this trust that Kenyans had in Safaricom, there was little resistance from the early adopters of M-PESA. Empirical research carried out among early users of the system confirms this—and that this trust existed at two levels: in the service provider and in its agents.[17]

The design of the system's platform and its operational processes required 100 percent integrity: nobody should risk losing money due to system failure or agent fraud. This is fundamental: mobile money could not afford a "run on the bank" because of lost money or extended system downtime. These standards, although difficult to implement and adhere to in the early days, were emphasized over and over, driving the resulting culture of trust.

Managing many external agents poses challenges both with the integrity of the thousands of people servicing customers and with the quality of service. Through management practices and constant customer communication, however, Safaricom increased the trust in its agents between 2008 and 2009 (table 7-3).

What Next for Mobile Money?

We have seen how technology enables the birth and growth of services like M-PESA. In the same way, M-PESA itself is spawning other services by providing a means for customers from all over Kenya to make low-value payments

17. Morawczynski and Miscione (2010).

Box 7-3. *Paying for Clean Water*

Access to clean, affordable water benefits a household immensely. Especially in rural areas, people rely on collecting water from open sources that are susceptible to pollution, carrying it long distances home for drinking, cleaning, and even agriculture. Grundfos Lifelink has developed a new model for servicing community water needs by providing a way for them to pay over time for a borehole. The community obtains financing for a borehole that is installed and maintained by Grundfos. People in the community purchase water credits via M-PESA, which are loaded to a key fob that they use to draw the water they need from a tap. The funds collected in the community's M-PESA account are then used to pay back their loan. Grundfos has so far installed three such systems in rural Kenya, affecting over 10,000 households. While this initiative appears to be struggling to scale rapidly, it is a good example of how having an effective means of collecting money from customers allows service providers to innovate in service delivery.

for goods and services. Nairobi is becoming a new Silicon Valley as innovators develop services for the poor (box 7-3).

More Reasons to Transact

Today more than 500 organizations use M-PESA to pay bills and conduct transactions. Companies also use M-PESA to make payments for items as varied as social support and dividends and salaries. This number is growing rapidly as businesses and integrators become more adept at incorporating the new payment method into their supply chains. It is likely that governments will adopt mobile money to cost-effectively deliver benefits such as pensions to people without bank accounts.

Businesses that use mobile money to make and receive payments come from a cross-section of industries. They are of varied size, with small and medium businesses arguably standing to gain the most benefit through increased productivity and ability to widen their customer base. Some examples are as follows:

—Utility service providers. These include the national electricity provider and city water providers.

—Health providers. A number of new medical schemes allow customers to save for medical costs via ongoing payments by M-PESA.

—Banks and microfinance institutions. These institutions mobilize savings and loan repayments and process withdrawals from customer deposit accounts.

—Microinsurance providers. Organizations like Syngentia, working with insurance companies, provide crop insurance to smallholder farmers and automatically pay farmers based on weather reports.

—Online commerce sites. These sites now have a way to receive payment for goods and services.

—Airlines ticket sales. Those airlines that process sales over the phone or the Internet can now guarantee seats following remote payment.

—The entertainment industry. Safaricom provides mobile ticketing services through select M-PESA agent outlets.

—School fees. By partnering with the banks that service schools, Safaricom provides an alternative to banker's drafts. Many schools also informally accept mobile money transfers direct to teachers; paying in small regular amounts is more manageable for many parents than one-off payments and avoids children being sent home for lack of fees.

To Safaricom, with 80 percent of its subscribers using M-PESA, growth is coming from additional transactions per customer, hence their focus on more "reasons to use" mobile money and on expanding the number of organizations with which it partners. Over time, with further economies of scale and increased circulation of value within the mobile money system (reducing the cost of commission paid to outlets for cash in and cash out), the cost to use will be reduced, enticing customers to use mobile money more frequently for their lower value transactions (which are still mostly satisfied using cash). A tariff revision in March 2012 is the first evidence of this happening: the minimum amount that can be sent via M-PESA was reduced to KSh 10, or around 10 cents; charges were adjusted to vary according to the amount sent. By lowering the cost of sending small amounts, Safaricom hopes that customers will increase their transaction frequency and do more of their low-value transactions on M-PESA.

Integrating with Formal Banking

Mobile money in Kenya has had significant impact on access to basic financial services like money transfer and payments. But the fact that Safaricom is not a bank prevents it from offering services like savings and credit. Financial institutions have adopted the use of "Pay Bill" to receive payments and deposits from their existing customers, and "Bulk Payments" to facilitate a withdrawal from a bank account to an M-PESA account, but this requires manual involvement and comes with risks and operational challenges that inhibit scaling up. Furthermore, this choice only extends to existing banked customers.

Integrating mobile money with the traditional banking environment to facilitate seamless transactions between the formally banked and people that "bank" by mobile money is the next step. Once customers can move money conveniently from bank accounts to mobile money accounts, and vice versa, mobile money will further facilitate formal financial services—allowing banks to offer such conventional services as savings and loans to more customers. Small and medium-sized enterprises could benefit from this too: being able to interact

Box 7-4. *The Transition to "Real" Financial Services*

In May 2010 M-PESA partnered with Equity Bank (Kenya's biggest retail bank in terms of customer and branch network) to launch the M-Kesho bank account.[a] A customer signs up for the account at an M-Kesho agent and, once the application is approved by Equity Bank, the customer's new M-Kesho bank account is linked to her M-PESA account, allowing him to move money easily between them using the M-PESA menu. Money in the bank account earns the customer interest, and the customer becomes eligible for microcredit after having the account for six months. Within six months of launch, M-Kesho had registered 600,000 customers, equivalent to about 10 percent of Kenya's total bank accounts.

M-Kesho suffered from process hitches in its early days, with customer recruitment and sign-ups often being delayed. The service was not seamless either, with transactions between M-PESA and M-Kesho accounts taking a few minutes to be completed, detracting from customer confidence. Because of this, marketing efforts by Safaricom and Equity Bank have been reduced, resulting in a growth slowdown. However, the rapid adoption of M-Kesho early on clearly illustrates the appetite of consumers for integrating banking and mobile money. It is clear that people want more from a savings account than an "e-wallet" such as M-PESA can provide.

a. For more details on M-Kesho's challenges, see Demombynes and Thegeya (2012).

via mobile money with their customers and yet enjoy the advantages of a bank account to sweep funds into—or withdraw funds from.

Safaricom advertisements in December 2011 demonstrate that the majority of banked customers in Kenya can choose to transfer value to and from their bank accounts by using M-PESA. Both locally based banks (such as Equity and Postbank) and multinationals (such as Barclays and Standard Chartered) have embraced mobile money to deliver added convenience to their existing customers (box 7-4).

Global Scaling Up

Mobile money can change the world the way cell phones have already changed lives in most emerging economies. The success of mobile money in Kenya can be replicated in other countries, many of which often have better starting conditions than Kenya had in 2007. As with other innovations, succeeding replication will be easier and could also result in variations of the original model. Many poor and emerging economies have high mobile phone penetration and low access to traditional banking facilities, which makes mobile money an ideal tool for financial inclusion.

Figure 7-7. *Potential Impact of Mobile Money, Top Ten Countries*

Millions of individuals

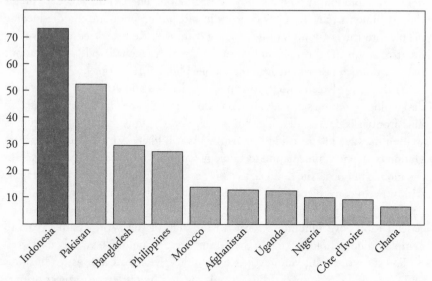

Source: World Bank estimates.

Thanks to cheaper handsets and to the switch to prepaid payment systems, large numbers of poor and middle-class citizens became part of the global mobile revolution but are yet to access financial services. This mobile money access gap represents hundreds of millions of people. Four of the five most promising countries for mobile money are in Asia: Indonesia, Pakistan, Bangladesh, and Philippines (figure 7-7). All these large countries have ubiquitous cell phone service, but relatively few of their citizens own a bank account.

Conclusion

We live in exponentially changing times. Technological changes are reshaping our lives much faster than ever before, and mobile money is one prominent example of these rapid changes. Development practitioners would love to find quick solutions to poverty reduction that could reach scale and have lasting impact. In many areas this dream remains elusive, as it requires deep social and political change, such as reforming the judiciary in a country or enhancing a country's skill level. All of these will take years, even if education is reformed. However, in some areas positive change can come much faster than anyone would have thought possible just a decade ago.

After decades of experimentation, the development community is still grappling with access to finance, which many studies identified as an important hindrance to rapid and sustainable poverty reduction. The lack of adequate financial instruments remains a key concern in integrating poor and middle-income people into the economies of developing countries. Kenya solved this development conundrum through mobile money, which reached scale within about two years, much faster than even the mobile phone it relies on.

As the cost of technology continues to decline and Africa is increasingly developing economies of scale, market adoption will accelerate further. Africa's next frontier is data retrieval, and there are already signs that this revolution is well on its way. The next big breakthroughs will likely come through the integration of the new information technology economy into the old economy, with the mobile phone as the main channel (even countries that are not poor grapple with ways to conveniently and securely transfer small amounts of money). Poverty analysis is another area where breakthroughs should be expected. In the past, it took governments (often with the help of the World Bank) years to complete a household survey. In the future, surveys could take merely days.

The story of mobile money in Kenya holds five broad lessons for business and economic development. First, think big and be restless. A project or program will only be truly successful if it can be scaled up and ultimately reach a multiple of the initial target population.

Second, management matters more than technology. In fact, good management generates technology and business innovation. In Kenya the focus was on scale and building a wide distribution network. The management of its agents and ensuring healthy rewards for all participants was critical to its success factor.

Third, development partners and business can generate strong synergies and play complementary roles. In a new model of aid effectiveness, development partners do not fill gaps but plant the seeds. This provides catalytic investment for innovation, which is then scaled up by business or other partners.

Fourth, utilize available technology and management tools. M-PESA is a low-cost transaction platform that was customized to meet local needs at a low enough cost to deliver profitable services.

Fifth, go for the medium term. In a world where business is increasingly driven by short-term profits, medium-term investment still pays off. Social profit is a strong driver: successful companies and institutions build a trusted brand and make their clients happy by positively having an impact on customer welfare. A long-term perspective needs to be complemented with a tight management system and a determined focus on results.

References

Demombynes, Gabriel, and Aaron Thegeya. 2012. "Kenya's Mobile Revolution and the Promise of Mobile Savings." Policy Research Working Paper 5988. World Bank.

Fengler, Wolfgang, Michael Joseph, and Philana Mugyenyi. 2011. "Mobile Money: A Game Changer for Financial Inclusion." In *What Matters, McKinsey on Society.* McKinsey & Company.

GSMA. 2012. "State of the Industry: Results from the 2011 Global Mobile Money Adoption Survey." April.

Hughes, Nick, and Susie Lonie. 2007. "M-PESA: Mobile Money for the 'Unbanked': Turning Cell Phones into 24-Hour Tellers in Kenya." *Innovations: Technology, Governance, Globalization* 2, no. 1–2: 63–81.

Jack, William, and Tavneet Suri. 2010. "The Adoption and Impact of Mobile Money in Kenya: Results from a Panel Survey." Sloan School of Business, MIT (www.mit.edu/~tavneet/MPESA_Slides2.pdf).

Morawczynski, O., and G. Miscione. 2010. "Trustworthy Mobile Transactions: A Longitudinal Study on M-PESA in Kenya." In *Trust and Technology in a Ubiquitous Modern Environment: Theoretical and Methodological Perspectives.* IGI Global.

Ndung'u, Njuguna. 2011. Keynote address, Fifth Joint CMA/CBK/RBA/IRA Board Members Retreat, October 13 (www.bis.org/review/r111025c.pdf).

World Bank. 2010. "Kenya at the Tipping Point? With a Special Focus on the ICT Revolution and Mobile Money." Kenya Economic Update, December.

———. 2011. "Navigating the Storm, Delivering the Promise." Kenya Economic Update, December.

8

Meeting the Demand of the Poor: Two Cases of Business-Led Scaling Up at the Base of the Pyramid

HIROSHI KATO AND AKIO HOSONO

The base-of-the-pyramid (BoP) perspective has been gaining influence in business and international development circles since C. K. Prahalad and S. L. Hart and other proponents articulated it.[1] Underlying this trend is the belief that firms can identify innovative, commercially viable solutions to respond to the needs of the poor. Numerous studies and research have sought to identify effective strategies and business models with which private firms can break into these markets.[2] This chapter is an attempt to contribute to the existing literature by examining two cases of BoP businesses that have achieved scale.

In this chapter, *BoP business* is loosely defined as interventions that involve either the private sector only or a commercial partnership between the private and public sectors, and that provide the poor with goods and services to which they otherwise do not have access, such as education, health, finance, and energy. *The poor* refers broadly to people in the poorer segments of society rather than to a particular income threshold.

The first case is the scaling up of long-lasting insecticide-treated mosquito nets (LLINs) through the development and propagation of the Olyset net

The authors would like to thank Tatsuo Mizuno and Atsuko Hirooka of Sumitomo Chemical Co. Ltd. and Atsumasa Tochisako of Micromanos for providing valuable information. The authors are responsible for all the errors that may remain.
1. Prahalad and Hart (2002).
2. See, for example, Prahalad (2010).

developed by Sumitomo Chemical. With the remarkable effects that have been demonstrated in malaria control, the introduction and mainstreaming of LLINs is one of the most outstanding recent achievements in global health. It is therefore of considerable interest to look at this case from a scaling-up perspective.

Second, we look at the international remittance and microfinance business Microfinance International Corporation (MFIC). As a business with a wide range of enthusiastic customers, it is attracting the attention and support of many mainstream financial institutions and socially minded corporations. This case also provides us with useful insights into what constitutes a scalable business model.

Analytical Perspective

Our analysis is based on the understanding that scale is not merely a desirable target for BoP businesses but that it constitutes an essential condition for their success. This is because BoP businesses are different from normal commercial businesses for a variety of reasons:

—BoP businesses are inherently challenging. Even a successful scaling up cannot ensure profits due to the limited purchasing power of low-income customers and the cost of doing business in low-income environments. In other circumstances, private firms protect their innovative products and business models with patents, thus guaranteeing them a certain market share. But in BoP markets, firms cannot use patents to set higher prices, as these will not be acceptable to customers. Furthermore, by limiting competition, patents may slow the process of scaling up and thus limit development impact.

—BoP businesses require particularly high levels of up-front investments, because in many cases products are new and businesses are unfamiliar with the low-income market. Investments can help BoP businesses develop their products and understand the low-income market. Scale can only be achieved when these fixed costs can be financed and when low variable-cost models have been identified and tested.

—BoP businesses often involve presenting poor customers with goods and services that they have not previously purchased or used. Building these markets requires the development of trust between the buyer and seller, a process that entails educational efforts by the BoP business and also acceptance by the users (for instance, when the product is contraception). An individual company is often unwilling to take on this burden, given the costs and the potential for other companies to free ride.

Of the above points, the first presents the most fundamental challenge: How can BoP businesses be profitable and pro-poor at the same time? If an innovative product or business model is to be pro-poor, it should be made available to the poor at low prices or at no charge—and as rapidly as possible. In other words, it should be provided as a public good or good that everyone can afford.

But the private sector will only be interested in operating in these markets if a commercial opportunity can be found.

Scaling up can be one way to reach commercial viability. With scale, low unit rates of return or profit margins can be compensated for by sales volume. Because of this, we argue that scale is essential for the success of BoP businesses. As Prahalad states, "Scale of operations is a prerequisite for making an economic case for the BoP. Given a stringent price-performance equation and low margins per unit, the basis for returns on investment is volume."[3]

However, reaching scale is no easy feat. Competition can prevent firms from achieving large sales volume. Moreover, low profit margins are unlikely to cover the sunk costs incurred in product development, market testing, and developing consumer trust, so many ventures are unlikely to get off the ground, let alone reach scale. This chapter focuses on how these challenges can be overcome. Prahalad claims that multinational corporations are "ideally suited for this effort."[4] But we contend that, with the appropriate business model in place, other players can overcome these challenges as well. In both our case studies, success hinges on the establishment of strategic partnerships, committed leadership, and innovative approaches to finance and delivery.

Case 1: Making Insecticide-Treated Bed Nets Available to the Poor: Sumitomo Chemical

Despite some controversies over their effectiveness and alleged negative side effects—such as insecticide-resistant mosquitoes—insecticide-treated nets (ITNs) are one of only two safe and cost-effective options to prevent malaria transmission in large parts of Africa.[5] In order to meet the target of universal access, the World Health Organization (WHO) recommends that one LLIN be distributed for every two persons.[6]

Sumitomo Chemical played a pioneering and central role in the scaling up of LLIN distribution by inventing the Olyset net. In 2001, this LLIN became the first WHO-recommended mosquito net.

Scaling-Up Pathway

The process through which the LLIN came to be mainstreamed started with an initiative by scientists working at Sumitomo Chemical. These scientists, along with their international partners, brought the LLIN into worldwide use.

3. Prahalad (2010, p. 56).
4. Prahalad (2010, p. 56).
5. WHO says that LLINs are one of the two most powerful and most broadly applied interventions, along with indoor residual spraying. World Health Organization (2011).
6. World Health Organization (2011).

START-UP PHASE. Founded in 1913, Sumitomo Chemical is one of Japan's major multinational chemical companies. Starting in the 1960s, Sumitomo's insecticides were used for malaria control, but the company was not particularly active in malaria control at that time.

During the 1980s, several scientists published papers arguing for the effectiveness of insecticide-treated mosquito nets. Inspired by these findings, two engineers, Takaaki Ito and Takeshi Okuno, of Sumitomo Chemical and their team started developing an ITN whose effects could withstand continual washing. The team aimed to develop an ITN with the following characteristics:
—Long-lasting efficacy (at least five years)
—Wide mesh size (allowing good airflow)
—Durable
—Safe

In the meantime, the company had accumulated technologies and expertise in insecticide-treated products such as insect-resistant nets for use in industrial facilities. Ito's team continued working on the development of LLINs, capitalizing on this knowledge and technology and repeating meticulous experiments and research.[7] By 1992 the first prototype of a long-lasting insecticide-treated mosquito net was in place.[8] The Olyset net uses a hybrid polymer and insecticide technology. A chemical substance called permethrin is incorporated inside the Olyset fibers to create a bed net guaranteed to last at least five years.[9] Permethrin is a synthetic insecticide with a chemical structure similar to natural pyrethrins, which come from a species of chrysanthemum. Because it poses minimal toxic risk to humans, the Olyset net is particularly suited to the protection of babies and small children.

After the product was developed, Sumitomo started distributing Olyset nets to Africa, Southeast Asia, and Latin America, to test consumer interest.[10] The remaining challenges were to reduce the product's cost and establish its distribution systems so that it would be marketable in developing countries, especially in Africa.

EARLY DEVELOPMENT PHASE. Subsequently, several international movements arose that drove the mainstreaming of LLINs. The first was the policy of international organizations regarding malaria. In 1998, WHO, UNICEF, the World Bank, and the UNDP launched a campaign, Roll Back Malaria (RBM), with a target of halving the number of deaths caused by this insect-borne disease by 2010. WHO's initial strategy was to use ITNs. Soon, however, it became apparent that the suitability of scaling up ITNs was diminished by their need

7. Ito and Okuno (2006).
8. Nihon Kokusai Koryuu Center (2009).
9. Sumitomo Kagaku (2011).
10. Tatsuo Mizuno of Sumitomo Chemical, interview with authors, October 1, 2012.

for reimpregnation. In 2000, two years after the launch of RBM, WHO modified its strategy and decided that LLINs should be used, instead of traditional ITNs. This decision was possible because information on the effectiveness of the Olyset net was widely circulated by that time, thanks to a marketing effort by the company.[11] The Olyset net became the first WHO-recommended LLIN under the WHO Pesticide Evaluation Scheme (WHOPES) in October 2001.

In April 2000, fifty-three African leaders gathered in Abuja, Nigeria, to translate the RBM's overall goal into practical actions. This summit meeting was planned and hosted by President Obasanjo of Nigeria, with support from RBM. The participating leaders committed to halving malaria mortality in Africa by 2010, and to ensuring that 60 percent of the at-risk population would sleep under insecticide-treated nets. Included in the Abuja Declaration were some practical actions, such as the reduction of tariffs and taxes imposed on mosquito nets, netting materials, and insecticides to lower retail prices.[12]

The second favorable movement for Sumitomo's Olyset net was the establishment of the Global Fund to Fight AIDS, Tuberculosis, and Malaria in January 2002. This move prompted a massive inflow of funds into developing countries to fight these diseases. Driven also by WHO's decision to adopt LLINs, the demand for LLINs by the governments of developing countries and international agencies increased sharply.

Under these circumstances, Sumitomo expanded its production capacities for the Olyset net. In 1999, production started in Changzhou, China, with an initial capacity of 20,000 nets a year. WHO, which came to believe that increasing the supply of LLINs to Africa was indispensable if the fight against malaria was to be effective, requested that Sumitomo Chemical increase the production of the Olyset nets and, at the same time, suggested that production be transferred to Africa. Sumitomo accepted this offer, as it also believed that cost reduction through overseas production was the only way to increase the use of the Olyset net.

To accomplish this plan, WHO created a consortium of interested organizations, the Olyset Consortium, in which seven public and private organizations participated: A to Z Textile Mills, Sumitomo Chemical, Acumen Fund, Exxon Mobil, UNICEF, Population Service International, and WHO.[13] This plan was

11. Tatsuo Mizuno of Sumitomo Chemical, interview with authors, October 1, 2012.

12. Karugu and Mwendwa (2007).

13. A to Z was founded in 1965 as a family-run company. Initially producing garments for the local market, the company had grown into the largest African manufacturer of ITNs by the time the discussions began with Sumitomo. See Masum and others (2010). Acumen Fund was incorporated in 2001. Its mission is "to create a world beyond poverty by investing in social enterprises, emerging leaders, and breakthrough ideas" (www.acumenfund.org). Population Service International is "a global health organization dedicated to improving the health of people in the developing world by focusing on serious challenges like a lack of family planning, HIV/AIDS, barriers to maternal health, and the greatest threats to children under five, including malaria, diarrhea, pneumonia and malnutrition" (www.psi.org).

conceived by the WHO scientist Pierre Guillet and was subsequently developed with Steven Phillips at Exxon Mobil.[14]

The central plank of the plan was the royalty-free transfer of Sumitomo's technology to A to Z Textile Mills.[15] A to Z, located in Tanzania, was the largest conventional (non-long-lasting) bed net manufacturing company in Africa and was recommended by Acumen Fund as a potential partner for Sumitomo in the mass production of the Olyset net. At that time, A to Z was already producing six million conventional insecticidal nets annually and was a major supplier of bed nets to UNICEF. The company had acquired capacity in plastics, textiles, and production technology, in which Sumitomo, a chemical company, did not have a comparative advantage. Sumitomo also did not have access to the African market.[16]

The other members of the Olyset Consortium would facilitate the process according to their comparative advantage.[17] Sumitomo, in addition to sharing its production technology, trained A to Z technicians to help improve the company's efficiency. Acumen Fund lent $325,000 to A to Z for the initial purchase of equipment. A to Z agreed to purchase polymer from Exxon Mobil, and the latter, in turn, donated $250,000 to UNICEF, an amount equivalent to the value of the material needed to produce the nets. UNICEF purchased nets from A to Z for distribution in Africa, while Exxon Mobil agreed to sell nets through its Mobil Mart service stations in five African countries. Finally, Population Service International and UNICEF would support the marketing and distribution of the nets to users.

The Olyset Consortium ultimately dissolved, with those partners who had no ownership stake in the project bowing out. However, the consortium served an important role in creating a vision, without which the shift to local manufacturing would surely not have occurred.[18] With the transfer of Olyset LLIN technology to A to Z Textile Mills, trial runs began in 2003 with 300 bed nets. Production reached 1.5 million in 2005. By 2009 production had increased to 25 million nets a year.[19]

A further boost to the provision of LLINs occurred with the establishment of another public-private partnership: the Tanzania National Voucher Scheme (TNVS). Under this agreement, the government subsidized the cost of ITNs for the most vulnerable members of its population, with the support of a number of

14. Karugu and Mwendwa (2007).

15. Masum and others (2010).

16. Masum and others (2010) reports that A to Z's capacity for the delivery of products was one of its advantages.

17. Information on this point is based on Fast Company (2005).

18. Gradl (forthcoming).

19. Masum and others (2010).

large international NGOs. The scheme was launched in 2004 and expanded to the national level in 2006. Under this scheme, a voucher is given to each pregnant woman on her first visit to a reproductive and child health clinic; she can use the voucher as a partial payment for the purchase of an ITN. The voucher is worth about $2.50 against the purchase of a net, which sells for between $3 and $10, depending on quality and size.

The scheme also worked as a social marketing tool to disseminate knowledge about malaria and the importance of bed net use. This was critical; other than cost, the lack of knowledge about the value of antimosquito nets is believed to be the biggest obstacle to greater uptake. The TNVS is "arguably the most well established voucher distribution scheme" for bed nets.[20]

FULL-FLEDGED DEVELOPMENT PHASE. Encouraged by these developments, Sumitomo Chemical came to believe, by 2005, that the time had come for the Olyset project to become a for-profit venture. To scale up production, Sumitomo, together with A to Z, decided to set up a company solely dedicated to the production of the Olyset net, named Vector Health International.[21] The factory opened in 2007, with an initial production target of 300,000 nets a year. As of 2012 its annual production had reached 30 million. The company now provides twenty-three different types and sizes of nets, priced at $8 to $13. (This contrasts to an initial cost by Sumitomo Chemical of around $30–40 per net in the early 2000s.)[22] Vector Health International employs around 7,000 workers, 85 percent of whom are women. The company has 180 trucks to deliver the products to 7,000 delivery points around Tanzania.[23]

In addition, to meet the increasing demand for the Olyset net, Sumitomo established two new factories in China and Viet Nam in 2005. With these, the company currently has a production capacity of 60 million nets a year (29 million in Tanzania, 19 million in Viet Nam, and 12 million in China).[24]

Meanwhile, due to global initiatives to achieve universal coverage, the market for LLINs has expanded considerably. Attracted by the expanding consumer base, more firms entered into the market, and the number of suppliers of LLINs with recommendations by WHO increased from three in 2007 to ten in 2011.[25] The total number of ITNs supplied annually (mostly LLINs) increased from

---

20. Sexton (2011).

21. This project was financially supported with a loan of $5.8 million from the Japan Bank for International Cooperation.

22. See www.fasid.or.jp/_files/seminar_detail/H21/187_r.pdf.

23. Government of Japan (2012).

24. Sumitomo Kagaku (2011).

25. Bahl and Shaw (2012).

5.6 million in 2004 to 145 million in 2010.[26] This scaling up of the market and increasing competition among suppliers is pushing down the price of the nets, making them more affordable for final users.

At the same time, some challenges to successfully achieving scale have arisen.[27] In Tanzania, the TNVS initially succeeded in both expanding access to LLINs and spurring competition. However, expansion of the voucher scheme in 2009 hurt domestic competition by creating a monopoly in the supplier market (the result of a government tender) and eliminating the wholesale market (by requiring nets to be tracked with bar codes). Simultaneous campaigns to distribute bed nets freely further eroded the retail market. This undermined much of the work done to foster a commercial, competitive market for nets in Tanzania by organizations such as PSI. Vector Health International is now shifting its focus to other countries, such as Kenya, where stronger commercial opportunities exist.

This relates to broader concerns regarding sustainability. The dissemination of LLINs has been accelerated by donor funding, which has, until now, effectively guaranteed that demand will meet supply at a given price. The slowdown in the growth of global aid volumes, vividly reflected in the cancellation of the 2011 replenishment of the Global Fund, suggests that such a guarantee may no longer hold in the future.

Observations

Looking at the history of the mainstreaming of LLINs, we can identify several dominant factors that enabled the successful scaling up. First, the invention of the Olyset net by Sumitomo Chemical was an indispensable technological breakthrough at the core of the scaling up process. It was a major technical innovation that resolved the problems that traditional ITNs could not overcome. A second critical factor was WHO's decision to mainstream LLINs as a means to fight malaria. A third factor was the partnership of a range of actors as represented by the Olyset Consortium. This partnership (involving Sumitomo, A to Z, international organizations, the private sector, and NGOs) was vital to making this technological innovation scalable. By subsidizing the upfront costs of relocating production to Africa, where production would ultimately be cheaper, the consortium increased affordability and facilitated distribution. A fourth factor was the mobilization of national and international resources and attention to fighting malaria, including the initiative for universal bed net coverage, which ultimately subsidized the cost of purchasing nets for poor customers and accelerated the take-up of bed nets. This initiative also subsidized the cost of social

---

26. WHO reports that this figure is likely to have ended lower in 2011. World Health Organization (2011).

27. Gradl (forthcoming).

marketing to the target population, enhancing beneficiaries' understanding of the value of bed nets.

In view of the categories of scaled up models discussed in chapter 1 of this book, Sumitomo Chemical's scale-up of Olyset nets represents a case of the subsidy model. Even with an increasing number of private firms participating as product suppliers, a large part of provision of nets to end users is done free of charge or with substantial subsidy by international organizations and NGOs.

Three points are worth noting here. The first is that the scaling-up process was not driven by the public sector; it was actually initiated by the private sector, and later facilitated by partnership with the public sector. Second, the integration of subsidy-based and market-based approaches is not without challenges, as demonstrated by the deleterious effect of the 2009 subsidies and bed net giveaway to the formation of a competitive market and the harnessing of market forces. Third, though the enterprise is currently heavily subsidy-dependent, there are moves toward a more for-profit-oriented business in the sale of LLINs. Sumitomo Chemical has expressed its intention to explore a commercially viable market, with further cost reduction and diversification of products.[28]

Case 2: Making Financial Services Available to Immigrant Workers: Microfinance International Corporation

In spite of high real and potential demand, neither public institutions nor private companies have succeeded in supplying tailored financial services to low-income immigrants. The Microfinance International Corporation (MFIC) sought to fill this gap in the market with the launch of its international remittance business in 2003. MFIC has continuously scaled up its activities in the last ten years. MFIC is seen as a forerunner of the "remittance revolution."[29]

Worldwide, foreign workers sent an estimated $501 billion in remittances to their home countries in 2011, of which $372 billion was remitted to developing countries. This is more than double the level of official development assistance provided to the developing world. Remittances are expected to grow between 7 percent and 8 percent a year, exceeding the pace of economic growth in nearly all countries.

Around 60 percent of the 21 million immigrants from Latin America in the United States make periodic remittances to their families. These remittances amount to approximately $650 million a year. However, most of them are made

---

28. Government of Japan (2012).

29. Nikkei BP (2011). The *Harvard Business Review* regards MFIC as an outstanding global for-profit social enterprise. See Isenberg (2008). Atsumasa Tochisako, the founder of MFIC, has received numerous awards for his groundbreaking social entrepreneurship from, among others, the Schwab Foundation, *Businessweek, Newsweek Japan,* and Ashoka.

by informal means, such as the postal service and friends traveling to their home countries. The cost of remittances is therefore very high: on average, around 10 percent of the value of the remittance, but often considerably more. It should also be noted that most of these immigrants do not have access to formal banking services.[30]

The international remittance business developed by MFIC has radically reduced the cost of low-value international remittances and increased immigrants' access to the financial system in the United States and elsewhere. This system is emerging as a powerful tool in the fight against poverty.

Scaling-up Pathway

MFIC's unique remittance business began with a pilot plan focused on remittances from Washington, D.C., to El Salvador. The model was scaled up to ten destinations in less than five years and has been further extended since. MFIC ultimately became an effective model compared to conventional remittance modalities. Its system is now used by a growing number of organizations.

START-UP PHASE. Atsumasa Tochisako spent twenty-seven years in various operational and representative positions with the Bank of Tokyo–Mitsubishi. This includes twelve years as a manager and officer in Mexico, Ecuador, Peru, and Panama. He retired from the company as chief representative of its Washington office. During his twelve years working in Latin America Tochisako learned that many immigrants have no access to banking services, including access to loans; that they cannot provide money to families in their home countries; and that hardly any microfinance or microcredit infrastructure existed in the countries where he worked, despite extremely high demand. In the United States, documents such as a credit history, social security number, and a personal identification card are necessary to open a bank account. Immigrants who are not eligible for these documents, or "unbanked immigrants," amount to more than 30 million, which is over 50 percent of the total Hispanic population in the United States.[31]

Tochisako envisaged an innovative Internet-based remittance system to address this situation. For this system, a new payment platform called Arias was developed. As its basic operation system, Arias uses COBIS, a core banking system commonly used by banks for their daily business. Compared with the conventional remittance platform, SWIFT, Arias enables more rapid and inexpensive transfer of remittances. Furthermore, Arias has implemented a com-

---

30. JICA/Global Partnership (2007, p. 54).
31. JICA/Global Partnership (2007, p. 62).

pliance check against money laundering, which automatically refers to the list of individuals prohibited from making remittances.[32]

MFIC's new business consisted of two components: a system for international remittances, which includes a wholesale processing service for financial institutions; and a retail financial service network for customers who require face-to-face service.[33] For the latter, MFIC planned to introduce a one-stop shop for financial services for unbanked immigrants who use the new remittance system.

MFIC's first step was to launch a pilot project for remittances from the United States to El Salvador. This country was selected because El Salvador immigrants were the most populous immigrant community in the three states surrounding Washington, D.C.; El Salvador's currency was the U.S. dollar, eliminating the risk of exchange rate variations; and a number of efficient microfinance institutions were operating for poor people in the country.[34]

One of the first steps in launching MFIC's business with El Salvador was to select microfinance institutions with which MFIC would connect to send money from the United States. The selection criterion was that they had branches or agents that the immigrants' families could easily access. MFIC consulted advisers and experts from the Inter-American Development Bank in El Salvador regarding the selection. In many cases, Tochisako himself visited preselected institutions to confirm their eligibility, especially in terms of relationship with customers, financial balance, and their training of employees. Later, MFIC established a system for lending money to these partner microfinance institutions. Tochisako also contacted high-level officials in the government of El Salvador to request their support for the activities of MFIC in the country. The vice president of El Salvador, Ana Vilma Escobar, attended the launch ceremony of MFIC in San Salvador in 2004.

EARLY DEVELOPMENT PHASE. In less than five years, the activities of MFIC were extended to cover twelve countries—Mexico, Brazil, Argentina, Colombia, Peru, Ecuador, Bolivia, the Dominican Republic, and four Central American countries. It was thus able to scale up horizontally within a relatively short period. MFIC diversified its activities after establishing the remittance system. After a few months, it began providing small loans to Hispanic immigrants in the United States. In 2005, MFIC began to grant loans to three microfinance institutions in El Salvador so that they could provide microcredit to their customers. At the same time, it amended the selection criteria for partner institutions slightly to include large banks if they recognized the importance of

32. The list is compiled by the Office of Foreign Assets Control, in the U.S. Treasury Department. See Tochisako (2012, p. 135).

33. Tochisako (2012, p. 7).

34. JICA/Global Partnership (2007, p. 64).

microcredit. HSBC in Mexico, BancoSol in Bolivia, and Banrural in Guatemala were the first such partners.

In this early development phase, MFIC became firmly established not only as a new unique international remittance entity but also as a multiservice microfinance institution for immigrant workers from Latin America in the United States. The number of one-stop shops (called Alante Financial) increased to seven and offered a full spectrum of financial services for immigrants: low-cost and speedy remittance; microcredit (the credit history builder's loan and the remittance loan); affordable exchange of checks for cash (1 percent charge, compared to 3 percent at other financial institutions); medical and life insurance; and transnational family housing loans.

The loans were innovative and unique. The credit history builder's loan assured borrowers that MFIC would register their repayment record with credit bureaus. With this system, for the first time, borrowers were able to obtain a credit history, an important document for gaining access to the formal banking system in the United States. The remittance loan was for financing remittances when immigrants needed to send money to families in their home country in an emergency. The transnational family housing loan was for financing the purchase of houses and cars for borrowers' families. These innovative financial measures were an important breakthrough for previously unbanked immigrant workers.

FULL-FLEDGED DEVELOPMENT PHASE. Although the expansion of MFIC's activities was made possible through its own capital, financial support from public or semipublic institutions that recognized the importance of MFIC's initiatives enabled it to scale up faster and to reach a more advanced phase of development. The Overseas Private Investment Corporation provided $4 million to MFIC in 2006.[35] Other financial institutions then followed: the Netherlands Development Finance Company in 2008 and Global Brain, a Japanese venture capital firm, in 2009.

A decisive expansion was assured in 2008, when MFIC agreed to partner with the United Arab Emirates Exchange. The reciprocal use of the remittance network by the two companies enabled MFIC's expansion to Asia, Europe, Africa, and the Middle East. Major destinations such as India and the Philippines were particularly significant.[36] Another important milestone in MFIC's development was its 2008 merger with San Diego–based El Camino Transferencias, a remittance company with distribution networks in twenty-two countries and state money transfer licenses in California, Texas, Washington, and Oregon.[37]

35. JICA/Global Partnership (2007, p. 67).
36. Tochisako (2012, p. 156).
37. Lazo (2008).

Further, in 2009 MFIC entered into an agency agreement with INES, a Japanese company specializing in system building, to facilitate the adoption of the Arias system in Asian countries. This was very timely, because a new international payment law was enacted in the same year in Japan. This agreement enabled the introduction of Arias in Asia, most notably for Asian migrants working in Japan.[38] At the same time, MFIC's business model was gaining recognition as the most efficient international remittance model. Moreover, its high level of compliance with money laundering legislation was also highly valued.

The Federal Reserve Board of the United States adopted MFIC's Arias by 2010 for its FedGlobal project, which was designed to facilitate U.S. banks' handling of immigrants' remittances.[39] This partnership with the Federal Reserve was a significant milestone for MFIC.[40] In 2010 the World Savings Banks Institute, CECA (Confederación Española de Cajas de Ahorros, the Spanish confederation of savings banks), and Money Express (a remittance company in Africa) adopted Arias to support fair-value remittances and the financial inclusion of the unbanked.[41]

MFIC has also strengthened its services through the use of mobile payments. In 2010, MFIC and KDDI, one of the largest telecommunication companies in Japan, announced their new partnership to promote a global remittance and payment platform for telecommunications carriers. As a first step, they allowed remittance payments using the international telephone cards of KDDI's U.S. subsidiary. In 2011, NTT DoCoMo, another major telecommunications company in Japan, decided to use the Arias remittance platform for a new international remittance service using cellular phones. The service, called DoCoMo money transfer, cuts more than 50 percent off the cost of remittances.[42]

Because of these accomplishments, Tochisako was selected as one of the hundred most influential people in Japan by Nikkei Business in 2011.[43] One of the major public TV broadcast companies, NHK, broadcast a one-hour documentary program on MFIC on July 27, 2010. MFIC's dynamic scaling-up pathway is illustrated in figure 8-1.

Observations

Several factors are behind the success of MFIC. First is the identification of innovative solutions to bridge the gap between the demand and supply of financial services for BoP customers, including inexpensive and reliable overseas

---

38. Tochisako (2012, p. 157).
39. Nikkei BP (2011, p. 29). Arias was chosen instead of SWIFT.
40. Tochisako (2012, pp. 181–82).
41. Tochisako (2012, p. 183).
42. Nikkei BP (2011).
43. Nikkei BP (2011).

Figure 8-1. *Scaling Up of MFIC, 2003–12*

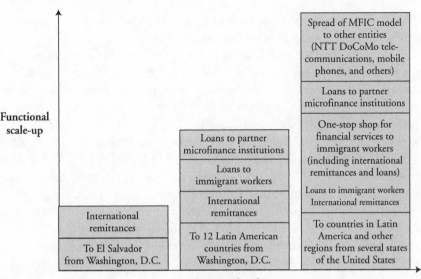

Source: Authors.

transmission and microloan services. Second are the partnerships with and support from public institutions, as well as socially oriented private institutions. Third is the strong leadership of the initiator/entrepreneur. And fourth is close and constant interaction with both clients (in this case, poor immigrant workers) and partner microfinance institutions.

It is interesting to compare the scaling up strategies of MFIC with the strategy of M-PESA (see chapter 7). M-PESA is a payment platform that allows value transfers between any two mobile, prepaid accounts. Safaricom, a Vodafone associate and Kenya's largest mobile telecommunications company, could have opted to market a more sophisticated service that would allow customers to make payments to and receive payments from multiple organizations, interact with banks, and even receive international remittances. However, Safaricom chose instead to focus on one service—domestic remittances—and on the account management tools to support this. And it was only after a critical mass of customers began to use M-PESA with confidence—and its growth had become self-perpetuating—that the company started adding new functions, including international remittances. In contrast, MFIC began as an international remittance platform, expanded at a very early stage to provide multiple services to its clients, and its application to mobile phones was achieved later, through its subsequent partnership with KDDI and NTT DoCoMo.

Summary and Conclusion

The two case studies provide us with some important lessons that could be applied to the scaling up of other BoP businesses.

First, cases were successful because they tapped into the latent demand of the target market. Demand for an effective bed net for fighting malaria and user-friendly financial services for immigrants has always existed, waiting for the arrival of the Olyset net and MFIC—or their equivalent. Second, in order to tap into this latent demand, innovative business models were needed. A point worth noting is that technological innovation alone is often insufficient to allow a business to be scaled up, as illustrated in the LLIN case study. Third, close communication with the client is an essential factor behind successful scaling up, as illustrated by both cases. Fourth, in supporting BoP businesses, selective partnerships, in particular those between the private and public sectors, are a critical factor. And fifth, the role of visionary leadership cannot be overstated. Indeed, it is debatable whether either venture could have occurred in the absence of the individual pioneers that led them to success.

One factor that sets these two case studies apart from other accounts of scaling up is their innovative approach to delivery. In the case of the Olyset bed nets, the relocation of production to Africa brought the product closer to its beneficiaries. Furthermore, the consortium facilitated the initial process of scaling up by cleverly separating responsibility for production and distribution, based on an efficient division of labor. In the case of MFIC, the Internet provided an accessible platform for migrant workers to administer remittance transfers, while local microfinance institutions offered a convenient route to workers' families and friends in their home countries.

While these lessons are derived from business-led case studies of scaling up, they are pertinent not only for entrepreneurs with similar business plans and aspirations but also for public sector efforts. The factors that determine the success or failure of scaling up development projects do not appear to differ significantly between public and private sector approaches.

References

Bahl, Kanika, and Pooja Shaw. 2012. "Expanding Access to LLINs: A Global Market Dynamics Approach." (Results for Development Institute).

Fast Company. 2005. "Net Profit" (www.fastcompany.com/55317/net-profit).

Government of Japan. 2012. Interview with Tatsuo Mizuno of Sumitomo Chemical on October 1, 2012 (www.cao.go.jp/noguchisho/info/mrmizunointerview.html).

Gradl, Christina. Forthcoming. "Sumitomo Chemical and the Fight against Malaria Using Bed Nets: A Case Study." Harvard Kennedy School Corporate Social Responsibility Initiative.

Isenberg, Daniel J. 2008. "The Global Entrepreneur." *Harvard Business Review.* December: 107-11.

Ito, Takaaki, and Takeshi Okuno. 2006. "Development of 'Olyset Net' as a Tool for Malaria Control." *Sumitomo Kagaku 2006*, no. 2.

JICA (Japan International Cooperation Agency) and Global Partnership. 2007. "Micro-finance ni kansuru beikoku ni okeru kanmin no doukou" [The trend of public-private partnership regarding microfinance in the United States]. Tokyo.

Karugu, Winifred, and Triza Mwendwa. 2007. "A to Z Textile Mills: A Public-Private Part-nership Providing Long-Lasting Anti-Malaria Bednets to the Poor." UNDP.

Lazo, Alejandro. 2008. "Microfinance Firm Extends Its Reach to Western U.S." *Washington Post,* April 7.

Masum, Hassan, and others. 2010. "Africa's Largest Long-Lasting Insecticide-Treated Net Producer: Lessons from A to Z Textiles." *BMC International Health and Human Rights 2010* 10 (supp. 1).

Nihon Kokusai Koryuu Center. 2009. "Chikyuu kibo kansensho (pandemic) to kigyo no sekinin" [The challenges of global pandemics and corporate social responsibilities].

Nikkei BP. 2011. "Game Changers" (in Japanese). *Nikkei Business* 1614: 29.

Prahalad, C. K. 2010. *The Fortune at the Bottom of the Pyramid: Eradicating Poverty through Profits.* Revised ed. Upper Saddle River, N.J.: Prentice-Hall.

Prahalad, C. K., and S. L. Hart. 2002. "The Fortune at the Bottom of the Pyramid." *Strategy+Business* 26: 2–14.

Sexton, Alexis R. 2011. "Best Practices of an Insecticide-Treated Bednet Distribution Pro-gramme in Sub-Saharan Eastern Africa." *Malaria Journal* 10: 157.

Sumitomo Kagaku. 2011. "CSR Report 2011" (www.sumitomo-chem.co.jp/csr/report/docs/csr_highlight2011.pdf).

Tochisako, Atsumasa. 2012. "Sekai 40 oku nin wo yuryo kokyaku ni suru: Honto no kin-nyu wo motomete tsukutta shikumi" [Making 4 billion people good customers: A system established through seeking real financial system]. Tokyo: Nikkei BP.

World Health Organization. 2011. *World Malaria Report 2011.*

9

Scaling Up South-South Cooperation through Triangular Cooperation: The Japanese Experience

AKIO HOSONO

I n recent years, many developing countries, particularly emerging donors, have become more actively engaged in development cooperation. South-South cooperation (SSC) was recognized as an important form of development cooperation in the Busan High Level Forum on Aid Effectiveness, held in November 2011.[1] The "Busan Partnership for Effective Development Cooperation," the document adopted by the forum, proposes several measures to strengthen SSC. Specifically, it states: "We recognise that many countries engaged in South-South cooperation both provide and receive diverse resources and expertise at the same time, and that this should enrich cooperation without affecting a country's ability to receive assistance from others."[2] It goes on to list several ways of strengthening the sharing of knowledge and mutual learning:

—Scaling up—where appropriate—the use of triangular approaches to development cooperation.
—Making fuller use of South-South and triangular cooperation, recognising the success of these approaches to date and the synergies they offer.

1. South-South cooperation has been loosely defined as an exchange of expertise among governments, organizations, and individuals in developing nations, although it also has other components, including financial assistance.
2. See www.aideffectiveness.org/busanhlf4/images/stories/hlf4/OUTCOME_DOCUMENT_-_FINAL_EN.pdf.

—Encouraging the development of networks for knowledge exchange, peer learning and co-ordination among South-South cooperation actors as a means of facilitating access to important knowledge pools by developing countries.

—Supporting efforts to strengthen local and national capacities to engage effectively in South-South and triangular cooperation.

The Busan outcome document is important in recognizing the fact that the organization of SSC lacks institutions and mechanisms to scale up and often suffers from high transaction costs, fragmentation, small scale, and limited impact. This is also the conclusion of Hyunjoo Rhee, who suggests two hurdles to scaling up SSC: the limited financial capabilities of many emerging economies to expand their assistance, given their own continued needs to finance domestic development; and the lack of an easy, low-cost system for matching the supply of development solutions from emerging economies with the needs of other countries operating in similar, but not identical, environments.[3]

This chapter argues that, if properly designed, triangular cooperation (TrC) is one mechanism for scaling up SSC impact.[4] It uses a case study approach to illustrate how TrC can both provide resources for expanding knowledge exchange and support local capabilities to create and absorb knowledge to achieve impact at scale. Scaling up via TrC can be thought of as occurring in two dimensions. First, it strengthens the impact of SSC knowledge exchange through complementary capacity development and institution-building assistance. Second, it propagates SSC across countries by organizing, institutionalizing, and programming the replication of effective SSC interventions.

From this perspective, the scaling up opportunities provided by TrC differ from the mechanical increases in scale of SSC that are to be expected given the rise of emerging economies. The key research question addressed in this chapter, therefore, is how TrC can scale up the impact of SSC knowledge exchange.

This chapter focuses only on scaling up the knowledge component of SSC. It recognizes that SSC also has other components, including significant financial assistance, but those are not the subject of study here. The chapter also focuses on the experiences of Japan. While other advanced countries—notably Germany,

---

3. Rhee (2011).

4. Triangular cooperation is defined as "support provided by developed countries, international organizations and civil society to developing countries, upon their request, in improving their expertise and national capacities through triangular cooperation mechanisms, including direct support or cost-sharing arrangements, joint research and development projects, third-country training programs, and support for South-South centers, as well as by providing the necessary knowledge, experience and resources, so as to assist other developing countries, in accordance with their national development priorities and strategies." UN High Level Conference (2009, para. 15). See http://southsouthconference.org/wp-content/uploads/2010/01/GA-resolution-endorsed-Nairobi-Outcome-21-Dec-09.pdf.

Spain, and Canada—have significant TrC programs, Japan has the longest and most established experience with this form of development cooperation.

South-South Cooperation and Triangular Cooperation: Background

The concept and philosophy of SSC first came into the spotlight more than half a century ago.[5] Yet SSC never attracted the attention of either developing countries or donor countries in the manner that has occurred in recent years. Greater attention to SSC today is a reflection of the rapid expansion of economic activities of the South and the deepening of South-South relations. Developing countries now account for more than a third of global trade and nearly three-quarters of global growth.[6] At the same time, many developing countries, especially the so-called emerging donors, have become more active in providing international cooperation. Alongside this expansion of SSC, fiscal and financial problems among traditional donors may constrain their assistance in the near future.

The United Nations launched SSC-related initiatives forty years ago. In 1972 the Working Group on Technical Cooperation among Developing Countries (TCDC) was formed by the General Assembly. In 1974 the UN Development Program's (UNDP) Special Unit for TCDC was created. And in 1978, the first United Nations conference on TCDC was held, adopting the Buenos Aires Plan of Action (BAPA), now recognized as a milestone in the growth of SSC. In the same year, the United Nations General Assembly endorsed BAPA and called for the strengthening of the Special Unit for TCDC. It also arranged for a high-level meeting of representatives of all states participating in the UNDP to undertake an overall intergovernmental review of TCDC within the UN system. In 2004, the General Assembly replaced the term *TCDC* with *South-South cooperation*.[7] In 2008, on the occasion of the thirtieth anniversary of the adoption of BAPA, the General Assembly decided to convene a high-level UN Conference on SSC, which was held in Nairobi in December 2009 and gave a major political boost to SSC as the framework within which developing countries agree to work together.[8]

TrC also dates back to the 1970s. In 1975 Japan started triangular cooperation with a number of developing countries through the Third Country

---

5. The Colombo Plan was adopted in 1951. The Asia-Africa Conference at Bandung, Indonesia, was held in 1955. The Group of 77 was formed in 1964. On each of these occasions, the concept and philosophy of SSC were highlighted.

6. OECD (2010, pp. 18, 30).

7. For the evolution of SSC-related activities in the UN, see UN Joint Inspection Unit (2011, p. 3).

8. UN Joint Inspection Unit (2011, p. 4).

Training Program (TCTP). Japan has since constantly expanded its TCTP activities.[9] As Negash Kumar puts it, "Japan has emerged as an important pioneer in this direction, supporting SSC activities especially in capacity building in the Asia-Pacific region."[10] In 1994 Japan initiated a more systematic approach to TrC with the creation of its partnership programs, first with countries in Asia and subsequently with African and Latin American countries. In 2003 it approved a new ODA charter that identifies triangulation as an effective modality for promoting development cooperation.[11]

In Europe, Germany started its TrC initiative in the 1990s. Germany's commitment to triangular cooperation is embedded in the cooperation policy with fifteen so-called anchor countries.[12] Spain followed, also integrating TrC objectives into its development cooperation policy.[13] Nevertheless, key policy documents in Europe, such as the 2005 *Consensus on Development,* do not mention triangular cooperation as an operational or policy option.[14] Recently, other traditional donors have begun to introduce new TrC initiatives, such as the UK's Department for International Development's Global Development Partnership Programme. More recently, Germany announced its "Strategy for Development Cooperation with Global Development Partners, 2011–15."[15]

The Accra Agenda for Action (AAA) recognized in 2008 that SSC and TrC were effective aid modalities for capacity development in developing countries. In 2010, the Group of Twenty (G-20) issued its multiyear action plan on development, highlighting South-South and triangular cooperation as important and innovative tools for information sharing and domestic resource mobilization for sustainable development.[16] In 2011, the Busan High Level Forum on Aid Effectiveness (HLF 4) further emphasized the importance of SSC and TrC as methods for developing and advanced countries to achieve common goals.

9. In this chapter, TCTP is later referred to as triangular training programs (TTPs), which is more commonly used in international discussion.

10. Kumar (2008, p. 5).

11. According to the 2003 ODA charter, "Japan will actively promote South-South cooperation in partnership with more advanced developing countries in Asia and other regions. Japan will also strengthen collaboration with regional cooperation frameworks and will support regionwide cooperation that encompass[es] several countries." Ministry of Foreign Affairs (2003, p. 3).

12. Schulz (2010, p. 6).

13. Spain backed its bid for triangular cooperation by including the modality in its master plan of 2009–12, while exploring the opportunities to use triangular cooperation more broadly in the partnership frameworks with middle-income countries. Schulz (2010, p. 6).

14. Schulz (2010) also mentions that the 2008 backbone strategy, aiming to guide technical cooperation toward capacity development, does not embrace triangular cooperation as a possible driver for reform, even though related studies also suggest that national actors in partner countries often prefer South-South resources over North-South technical cooperation.

15. BMZ (2011).

16. In the same year, an UNCTAD document focused on Africa-South partnerships. UNCTAD (2010, p. 10).

These milestones suggest that SSC and TrC have significant political backing in principle. What remains is to translate that backing into specific mechanisms.

South-South Cooperation and Triangular Cooperation: Potential and Challenges

The Busan outcome document emphasizes the importance of SSC and TrC in terms of knowledge sharing for sustainable development: "The inputs to sustainable development extend well beyond financial co-operation to the knowledge and development experience of all actors and countries. SSC and TrC have the potential to transform developing countries' policies and approaches to service delivery by bringing effective, locally owned solutions that are appropriate to country contexts."[17]

The potential of SSC and TrC in knowledge sharing and mutual learning is high because the South has accumulated valuable experience in identifying and implementing development solutions and in overcoming difficulties and constraints. In addition, South and North can collaborate on knowledge creation, knowledge exchange, capacity development, and institution building to implement development solutions at scale.

The experiences of the South are diverse and can be divided into three types. First, there are experiences in tailoring programs for conditions in developing countries that share specific characteristics: landlocked, island, or fragile and post-conflict countries are examples. Second, there are experiences exclusively related to the South: experiences in this category include technologies for agriculture in tropical climates and the marketing of goods and services to poor consumers, the so-called bottom of the pyramid. Third, there are experiences that relate to managing new challenges of climate change adaptation and mitigation and prevention of natural disasters, areas where the South and North are learning together to arrive at appropriate solutions.

Scaling up SSC typically depends, first, on financing the often significant fixed costs incurred in developing and testing innovative technological interventions and, second, on keeping variable costs low so that an expanded scale of activities fits within the country's resource constraints. For example, progress and scaling up of tropical agriculture require years of efforts for achieving necessary innovations and for their dissemination to farmers with limited financial and technical capacity for assimilation of new techniques. SSC and TrC allow countries to share successful technical and process knowledge, including institutional and organizational innovations, achieved after years of effort and adaptation by pioneering countries of the South.

17. Fourth High Level Forum (2011, p. 9).

However, SSC still faces several challenges. The quality of information, results orientation, and alignment to national systems are, generally, not well developed in SSC, which is therefore more supply driven than demand driven. Moreover, according to a year-long study led by the OECD/DAC Task Team on South-South Cooperation, based on 120 cases of South-South technical cooperation, the number of projects and their size remain small. Exchanges are usually one-off and random and hence SSC is highly fragmented and unpredictable.[18] The study therefore recommends that SSC adopt more structured approaches; that TrC help Southern countries strengthen their capacities to match the demand and supply of development knowledge; and that SSC and TrC efforts are better coordinated to avoid fragmentation and overlap (including with traditional aid).[19]

Scaling Up through Centers of Excellence

While there is now a broad consensus on the importance of SSC and TrC, there are few operational models of how to scale up impact. In fact there are no universally accepted definitions, nor is there a clear understanding of concepts at the operational level, as the UN Joint Inspection Unit concludes.[20] Hence, it is now time to identify practical and operational approaches to the two cooperation efforts, having more clearly in mind both their potential and their challenges. Below, some lessons at the operational level for scaling up impact are drawn from successful cases of SSC and TrC.

One approach is to scale up through Southern centers of excellence that specialize in particular fields. The Nairobi outcome document of the High Level United Nations Conference on South-South Cooperation in 2010 encourages United Nations organizations to assist developing countries in enhancing or establishing centers of excellence in their respective area of competence.[21] Examples, further discussed below, include the Singaporean Productivity and Standards Board, the Brazilian Agriculture Research Corporation (EMBRAPA), the Faculty of Marine Sciences at Chile's Católica del Norte University, and Mexico's National Center for Prevention of Disasters (CENAPRED). These centers have been able both to share knowledge and to co-create knowledge and jointly find innovative solutions with partner countries.

The TrC scaling-up model is depicted in figure 9-1. The Northern partner (Japan in the cases described below) provides assistance in building a center of excellence in the South and in encouraging the Southern partner to become a new

18. Rhee (2011, p. 265).
19. OECD/DAC (2011).
20. UN Joint Inspection Unit (2011, p. 7).
21. United Nations (2011, pp. 17–18).

Figure 9-1. *Triangular (Third-Country) Training Program*

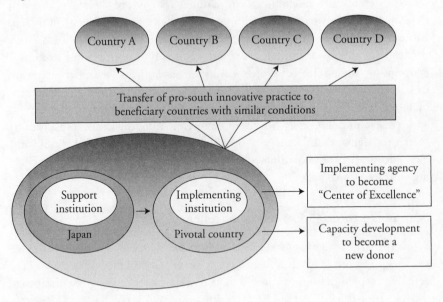

Source: Author.

donor. That center then provides further assistance to other developing countries with similar conditions. The concept is similar to that of training the trainers, as opposed to providing direct assistance to ultimate beneficiaries. The benefits come from the creation of knowledge by the center of excellence, from its adaptation of global knowledge to developing country conditions, and from cost savings when further assistance is extended by the center to other developing countries.

One variant on this model is when the support institution in the Northern country learns lessons from its engagement with a center of excellence and goes on to create further centers of excellence in other countries. In that case, scaling up does not happen through the training of trainers but through better understanding of the success factors involved in traditional North-South technical cooperation.

Case 1: Singapore's Productivity and Standards Board

The experience of Singapore is particularly relevant as a country that benefitted from North-South cooperation in enhancing its productivity and international competitiveness and that then shared its experience with other countries.

A country without natural resources and with a large number of unemployed persons at the time of independence, Singapore was one of the first Southeast Asian countries to promote export-led growth rather than import substitution-led growth. In the late 1970s, faced with rising competition from other exporters whose wage rates were lower, Singapore decided to transition from exports dependent on cheap labor into a knowledge economy based on skilled labor and higher value-added exports. In the process, Singapore overcame the middle-income trap to become one of the most competitive countries in the world.[22] To achieve this transition, increasing productivity was deemed essential.

"The shift to a knowledge-intensive industrial structure with strong international competitiveness is only possible through the human-resource development of 2.6 million people, the only resource Singapore has," said Prime Minister Lee Kuan Yew.[23] In April 1981 the Singaporean Committee on Productivity was formed by representatives of enterprises, workers' organizations, government officials, and academia. The committee reviewed the experiences of productivity movements in Japan, another country without natural resources but with abundant labor.[24] It then presented a report to the president of the National Productivity Board (NPB) of Singapore. NPB was designated as the main body for promoting productivity development in Singapore. In June 1983, the Singapore Productivity Development Project (SPDP) was launched with the support of the Japanese government.

Some 15,000 Singaporean engineers, managers, and other professionals participated in the project. Two hundred engineers, managers, and other professionals from Singapore took part in training courses in Japan. More than 200 Japanese experts were dispatched to Singapore. More than 100 textbooks and other training materials were prepared specifically for the project. During the period of SPDP and beyond, labor productivity in manufacturing industries improved by an annual average rate of 5.7 percent (1981–86), 3.0 percent (1986–91), and 4.8 percent (1991–96).

In 1990, when SPDP ended, 90 percent of workers in the country were involved in productivity development activities, compared with 54 percent in 1986.[25] In 2001, 13 percent of the total labor force was participating in quality-control circles, in comparison with 0.4 percent in 1983, when SPDP started.[26]

---

22. The middle-income trap is a concept introduced by Gill and Kharas (2007) to describe the difficulties faced by many middle-income countries in continuing to grow rapidly.

23. Remarks made by the prime minister when he visited Kohei Goshi, honorary president of Japan Productivity Center in June 1981. Japan Productivity Organization (1990, p. 1).

24. See for example Hosono (2009).

25. JICA/IDCJ/IDJ (2010, p. 16).

26. JICA/IDCJ/IDJ (2010, p. 22).

Quality control circles are considered the most effective vehicle for improving quality and productivity with the active participation of workers. Through this participatory approach, workers' ideas are incorporated into the production process with innovative solutions. Hence SPDP became one of the driving forces for productivity gains in Singapore.

NPB's activities gathered considerable momentum, progressing from the awareness stage (1982–85), in which it created widespread awareness of productivity among companies and the workforce, to the action stage (1986–88), when it translated awareness into specific programs to improve productivity in the workplace, and then to the follow-up stage (1988 to the present), in which it encouraged ownership of the productivity movement.[27] The NPB was merged with the Singapore Institute of Standards and Industrial Research in 1996 to create the Productivity and Standards Board (PSB), bringing together the soft skills and the technical aspects of productivity. The PSB was later strengthened and reorganized into the Standards, Productivity and Innovation Board (SPRING) in 2002.

NPB, PSB, and now SPRING became global centers of excellence in the field of productivity, quality, standards, and innovation. Other key factors that bolstered these institutions include the transition from a public-sector-led entity to a private-sector-led entity, active advocacy and publicity, human resource development inside and outside the institution, and the establishment of a skills development fund by the government.

In the initial phase, Japan played an important role in a deep-rooted, mutual learning process with Singapore. Low Hock Meng, the executive director of the Singapore Productivity Association, commented: "We Singaporeans have the experience of overcoming barriers of language and culture to absorb Japanese productivity and make it into our own thing."[28] The initial phase was therefore one of adaptation; Singaporeans and Japanese had very serious discussions about how to implement the project. Step by step, Japanese experts developed familiarity with Singapore's local context, while Singaporean experts had the chance to directly observe the Japanese system, gaining knowledge that allowed their companies to rapidly increase their productivity. Through this phase of mutual learning, with the strong ownership of the Singaporeans, a Singapore-style productivity movement was born.[29]

Singapore's productivity initiative was strongly encouraged by the country's senior leaders, especially Prime Minister Lee. Lee was strongly concerned with "how labor gets motivated and organized to really make the most of their

27. Ohno and Kitaw (2011).
28. JICA/IDCJ/IDC (2010, p. 43).
29. For details, see JICA/IDCJ/IDC (2010); Ohno and Kitaw (2011).

improved skill and modernized equipment."[30] He understood the need for institution building and the need to promote creativity and the capacity to innovate in order to sustain growth for Singaporeans.

The PSB entered a new phase to become a promoter of SSC in the 1990s. Botswana was the first example of such cooperation, in 1992, around the end of the SPDP. Singapore provided technical cooperation to Botswana geared to improving productivity. It continued this project until 2003, utilizing the lessons learned during implementation of the SPDP. A study team and experts were dispatched from Singapore to Botswana, while trainees were invited from Botswana to Singapore to take part in practical guidance, with an emphasis on displaying actual know-how in corporations.[31] Since then, the government of Singapore, through the Singapore Productivity Association, usually together with the Asian Productivity Organization, has provided SSC to numerous developing countries, including Hungary, South Africa, Kenya, and Botswana, as well as ASEAN countries.[32] In some of these initiatives, a TrC approach through Japan Singapore Partnership Program (JSPP) was adopted. Singapore thus continues to convey the know-how that was co-created with Japanese experts as well as knowledge created by themselves.[33] For its part, Japan has also learned lessons from the SPDP. Japan International Cooperation Agency (JICA) has cooperated with many other countries in the area of quality and productivity, or *kaizen:* Philippines, Thailand, and India in Asia; Brazil, Argentina, Paraguay, and Costa Rica in Latin America; and Tunisia, Egypt, Zambia, and Ethiopia in Africa, among others. As with Singapore, other centers of excellence were developed.[34]

Case 2: Brazil's EMBRAPA

The Cerrado biome, in the central plateau of Brazil, is a tropical savannah ecosystem with specific characteristics of soil, climate, vegetation, wildlife, ecology, and biodiversity. Brazil's EMBRAPA (Brazilian Agriculture Research Corporation), set up in 1973, established a research center dedicated to developing agricultural technology in the Cerrado, which at the time was a barren plateau. It

---

30. Lee Kwan Yew, *Memories,* cited in JICA/IDCJ/IDJ (2010, p. 30).

31. Regarding Singapore's cooperation to Botswana, see Kitaw (2011).

32. The author drew on several studies on Singapore's experiences and its South-South and triangular cooperation, among them JICA/IDCJ/IDJ (2010); JICA/GRIPS (2011); Japan Productivity Organization (1990).

33. Information in this paragraph is based on JICA/IDCJ/IDJ (2010, p. 43).

34. For details, see Ueda (2009). Other examples to build or strengthen centers of excellence include the King Mongkut's Institute of Technology Ladkrabang in Thailand, the Standard and Industrial Research Institute of Malaysia, and the Triangle of Hope Strategic Action Initiative for Economic Development in Zambia.

achieved innovations in soil improvement and developed new varieties of plants for the Brazilian tropical savannah, allowing Brazil to become the first tropical food-producing giant in the world. Mutual learning between Brazilian and Japanese researchers was one of the key factors for the successful initial phase of EMBRAPA's development. Before the major Brazil-Japan cooperation for agricultural development of the Cerrado officially started, bilateral cooperation for technological development was initiated by EMBRAPA through its Cerrados Agriculture Research Center, JICA, and JIRCAS (then Tropical Agricultural Research Center of Japan).[35]

Thanks to EMBRAPA, the Cerrado has become one of the most productive agricultural regions in the world. This remarkable transformation has become known throughout the world as the Cerrado miracle.[36] Norman Borlaug, the father of the Green Revolution and Nobel Prize laureate, told the *New York Times* that "nobody thought these soils were ever going to be productive."[37] Brazil had to find solutions to make the Cerrado productive. An important innovation involved soybeans. Traditional soybeans, a temperate-climate crop native to Japan, Korea, and China, are sensitive to changes of the hours of sunlight that prevail during the four seasons of the temperate climate. The breakthrough innovation by EMBRAPA was to create new varieties of soybeans suited to tropical climates.[38]

Plínio Itamar de Mello de Souza achieved the historical breakthrough innovation, developing the first variety of soybeans suitable for tropical climates. The variety was named *doko,* after Toshio Doko, a Japanese national who contributed greatly to strengthening Brazil-Japan economic relations and cooperation for many years.[39]

Research and development work for Cerrado agriculture had to begin almost from scratch. Eliseu Alves, known as the father of EMBRAPA, commented that "JICA-EMBRAPA exemplifies the joint-type cooperation, from which EMBRAPA, the cerrados, and Brazil profited very much."[40] In joint cooperation, "all the activities are jointly planned and carried out, as if there [were] an informal merging of the agencies in a unique institution for the purpose of the objectives of the cooperation project."[41] The World Food Prize, founded by Norman Borlaug, was awarded in 2006 to two Brazilians who contributed to the Cerrado miracle.

35. The official name of the Brazil-Japan cooperation is Japan-Brazil Cooperation Program for Cerrados Development (PRODECER).
36. "The Miracle of the Cerrado" (2010).
37. "Scientists Are Making Brazil's Savannah Bloom" (2007).
38. For details about Cerrado development, see Hosono and Hongo (2012).
39. Information on the Cerrado from Hosono and Hongo (2012); Inter-American Development Bank (2010).
40. Alves (2012, p. 13).
41. Alves (2012).

EMBRAPA was launched with the strong leadership of the president and central government ministers of agriculture and livestock. The institution developed very quickly. As its mission was the research and development of national agriculture and livestock, development of research capacity received particular emphasis. Two thousand researchers were sent abroad to study cutting-edge agricultural technology. The number of researchers possessing PhDs rose from 15 to 1,800 between 1974 and 2011. Today, EMBRAPA is one of the largest agricultural research institutes in the world and a center of excellence in tropical agriculture.

EMBRAPA established an organizational structure to undertake research for various grains and other crops across many regions of Brazil. Today, it has fifteen regional centers, sixteen centers for specific crops, and twelve centers for cross-cutting technologies. The institution was built to be flexible and sensitive to the needs of farmers. This principle was the key factor from the beginning, because leaders and managers were convinced that research and development that respond to the needs of farmers with innovative solutions was crucial for improving productivity. A new incentive system, geared especially toward researchers, was established. It featured a transparent meritocracy, making it very different from conventional systems for public entities. Because of this, EMBRAPA was considered a new model of public institution. The promotion of international cooperation and active public relations through the media were other crucial factors that ensured the success of EMBRAPA's institution building.

The experience, knowledge, and innovative solutions EMBRAPA acquired are now being extended to Mozambique through an innovative modality of triangular cooperation with Japan. Bill Gates includes it in his report to G-20 leaders:

> Brazil is working with Japan to help poor farmers in Mozambique grow soybeans, in a story that goes back 30 years. As part of a major technical assistance program in the 1980s, Japan helped adapt soybeans to Brazil's tropical savanna, the Cerrado. It became one of Brazil's most important crops. Now with Japanese financial support, Brazilians are helping Mozambiquan farmers in the Nacala corridor, an area with very similar climate and soil conditions. Meanwhile, the Japanese are looking to upgrade Mozambique's port and railroad infrastructure to make it easier for farmers to export beans.[42]

Other centers of excellence in agriculture and livestock technology include the Philippine Rice Research Institute, the Hanoi University of Agriculture, and the Faculty of Agriculture at Can Tho University in Vietnam, which have made great progress in rice production, including the development of new varieties. In Africa, the Jomo Kenyatta University of Agriculture and Technology in Kenya,

42. Gates (2011, p. 7).

the University of Zambia's School of Veterinary Medicine, and many other institutions have valuable experience in tropical agriculture and livestock. They are now outstanding centers of excellence in the global South and carry out the principles of SSC and TrC.

Case 3: Chile's Católica del Norte University

Católica del Norte University in Chile (specifically, its Faculty of Marine Sciences) is now one of the centers of excellence of shellfish aquaculture in Latin America. Aquaculture of Chilean scallops started in 1981. Within eight years, scallop aquaculture had become established as a new industry for the Coquimbo region, and Chile is now one of the three largest exporters of scallops in the world.

This achievement was made possible through a process of mutual learning and trust among Chilean specialists, Japanese experts, and local fishermen and industries. Together they established shellfish aquaculture technology appropriate for local conditions through innovations based on research and their application. At the same time, institution building was advanced. The Faculty of Marine Sciences emerged as a center of excellence. In 1988, it started SSC. In the twenty years through 2007, 400 aquaculture specialists selected from 1,200 candidates from sixteen Latin American countries participated in triangular training programs (TTPs, also called third country training programs) involving the faculty.

The mutual learning process of TTPs enabled Católica del Norte University to achieve a deep understanding of the state of aquaculture in partner countries and to establish a reliable network of specialists. Advanced SSC and TrC beyond the scope of TTPs was implemented, and several countries—including Peru, Ecuador, Brazil, Colombia, Venezuela, and El Salvador—began successful aquaculture projects. Chilean experts sent to these countries were able to cooperate smoothly with local professionals because Chileans already had significant country knowledge and could tap into a large network of local specialists created through the TTPs.

Case 4: The Mexican Disaster Prevention Center: CENAPRED

After the great earthquake of 1985, which affected the central region of Mexico, including its capital, Japan and Mexico started to cooperate in the area of earthquake disaster prevention. Using grant aid provided by Japan, the National Center for Prevention of Disasters (CENAPRED) was founded in 1988 to undertake research, training, and dissemination of earthquake disaster prevention technologies, ultimately as an independent organization. Its goal was to improve the earthquake disaster technology in Mexico and Central American and Caribbean countries.[43] CENAPRED is today one of the most important

43. Fukuta (2004, pp. 416–17).

research institutes of its kind. Many of its staff have benefited from training in Japan and the secondment of Japanese experts to the Center.

Earthquake-resistant houses are essential for preventing tragedies caused by earthquakes. However, for these houses to be introduced in slums and poor rural villages, innovative solutions are needed. Inexpensive and easily accessible local materials and appropriate design have to be tested. CENAPRED's large-scale structure-testing laboratory was used to study the seismic behavior of the frame and brick and adobe (locally available, low-cost material) structures common to Mexico, Central America, and the Caribbean. Research was also conducted on the repair and strengthening of damaged buildings, on building foundations, and on soil composition.

The technology and innovative methods developed by CENAPRED were widely used in the joint El Salvador-Japan-Mexico TAISHIN project, which promoted earthquake-resistant houses in El Salvador from 2003 through 2012. According to a study on two big earthquakes that affected El Salvador in 2001, 60 percent of the houses destroyed were those of poor people (those whose income was less than twice the minimum wage of the country). Houses made of improved adobe, soil cement, block panel, and concrete block were tested. The project also established technological standards for earthquake-resistant houses and increased the capacity of the government agency in charge of housing policy and construction permits.[44]

The Japan-Peru Center for Earthquake Engineering Research and Disaster Mitigation, located in the Peru National University, and other such centers in Chile, Turkey, and Romania are also examples of other centers of excellence that involve TrC and SSC in this field.

Scaling Up through Partnership Programs

To deal with the challenges of SSC and TrC, such as high transaction costs, fragmentation, supply-driven bias, and unpredictability, structured approaches and modalities are needed. One such approach is the partnership program (PP) carried out jointly by advanced countries and a number of pivotal developing countries. This approach provides a common framework within which a pivotal country and its development partner can jointly implement technical cooperation for beneficiary countries, while also allowing the two countries to share their knowledge and experience in aid management.

This approach was introduced in 1994, with the Japan-Thailand Partnership. Japan is now implementing PPs with twelve countries.

---

44. For details see Hosono (2012); Saito (2012).

PPs typically emerge from more modest cooperation arrangements. For instance, Japan and Brazil initiated triangular training programs in 1985, two years before the Brazilian Cooperation Agency (ABC) was established. Only after accumulating many years of experience was a Japan-Brazil Partnership Program (JBPP) developed in 2000. This then allowed more structured TrC. In 2010 a new initiative, Japan-Brazil Global Partnership, was introduced to JBPP to address specific issues on a global scale.[45]

Partnership programs have resulted in a more coordinated and systematic modality of knowledge transfer, due to joint planning and periodic consultation between the two countries and to a combination of cooperation schemes, such as triangular training programs, third-country experts, joint projects, and joint seminars and workshops (figure 9-2). They are particularly useful in addressing a specific challenge that is common to several countries. The case studies below illustrate how these kinds of approaches have been implemented in practice.

Case 5: Conservation and Monitoring of Tropical Rainforests

Tropical rainforests, which are very rich in biodiversity and function as huge reservoirs of carbon dioxide, are now endangered due to illegal logging. Indeed, significant losses have already occurred worldwide. One major reason that illegal logging is difficult to stop is because rainforests are both vast and hard to access and patrol. However, Brazil's National Institute for Space Research, the Brazilian Institute of Environment and Renewable Natural Resources, the Japan Aerospace Exploration Agency (JAXA), and JICA have together achieved a great breakthrough in patrolling using satellite monitoring.

Although the Brazilian satellite monitoring system was very advanced, since Brazil used optical sensors, observation was hindered by the heavy clouds often present during the rainy season, when most illegal logging took place. Since then, the observation system improved dramatically with the use of Pulsar radar mounted on an advanced land-observing satellite (ALOS) of JAXA, a system that is not affected by clouds and that operates twenty-four hours a day regardless of the weather. Japan's Aerospace Exploration Agency began providing satellite images to the Brazilian institute in 2007. The institute relays this information to the federal police and to the Chico Mendes Institute for Biodiversity Conservation, both of which are involved in monitoring and managing the Amazon. Thanks to improved real-time data, Amazon deforestation has been decreasing, reaching its lowest ever record during 2009–11.

Through the modalities of the Brazil-Japan Partnership Program, this experience and technology, developed in the Amazon, was shared with Indonesia, other East Asian countries, and several Latin American and African countries.

45. For details, see Sakaguchi (2012).

Figure 9-2. *Partnership Program: Advanced, or Structured,*
Approach to Triangular Cooperation

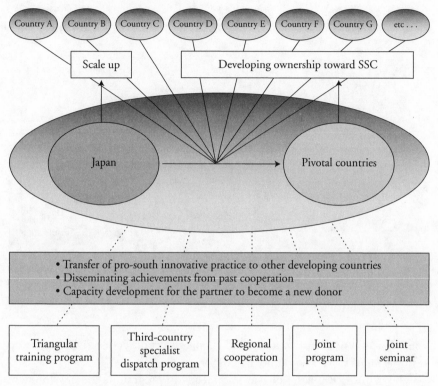

Pivotal countries of partnership are Thailand, Singapore, Philippines,
Indonesia, Chile, Brazil, Argentina, Mexico, Egypt, Tunisia, Morocco, and Jordan.

Source: Author.

JICA also supports the global networking of experts on rainforest conservation
and monitoring.[46]

Scaling Up through Regional Platforms

A third approach to scaling up SSC through TrC involves the establishment of
regional knowledge platforms supported by a Northern donor. One of the most
relevant examples of this approach is JICA's support for the establishment of
an ASEAN community and the Master Plan on ASEAN Connectivity, which

46. For details, see Aida and Kobayashi (2012).

Figure 9-3. *Asian Pacific Development Center of Disability (APCD) and a Stronger Regional Network*

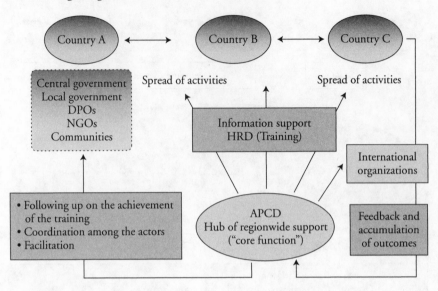

Source: JICA (2012a).

consists of physical, institutional, and people-to-people connectivity as vital to realizing an ASEAN community by 2015.

The main focus of the physical connectivity program is the development of East-West and Southern economic corridors and of maritime ASEAN economic corridors. Examples of people-to-people connectivity initiatives include the ASEAN University/Southeast Asia Engineering Education Development Network and the Asia-Pacific Development Center on Disability (APCD). The former program aims, inter alia, for improvement in the quality of research by member institutions. Through this modality more than 700 collaborative research projects have been undertaken.[47]

The APCD promotes disabled persons' empowerment and a "barrier-free society for all." UN ESCAP endorsed the APCD as a regional cooperative base for the Biwako Millennium Framework for an inclusive society in the Asia-Pacific Decade of Disabled Persons. More than a thousand people from ASEAN countries were trained by APCD (figure 9-3).[48]

47. JICA (2012a).
48. For details of AUN/SEED-net and APCD, see JICA (2012b). For APCD, see also Ninomiya (2010).

Another example of structured, regionwide SSC and TrC based on a regional integration system is the Central American Integration System (SICA).[49] The overall framework for this cooperation initiative was established in 2005 by the Tokyo Declaration of the Japan-SICA summit. It included region-wide cooperation in the fight against Chagas disease and in mathematics education, natural-disaster prevention, reproductive health, and productivity improvement.[50]

The Tokyo International Conference on African Development (TICAD) is another example of a regional approach to TrC. SSC promotion is one of the five areas covered by the Yokohama Action Plan of TICAD IV. The action plan lists Asia-Africa cooperation as a key element of the TICAD process, which progresses through mutual learning and sharing of best practices and technology between the two regions. One of the specific actions of the TICAD process is the Asia-Africa Knowledge Co-Creation Program. A project for total quality management for hospitals has been launched in fifteen countries in Africa. The project uses management tools such as *kaizen*.[51]

The Coalition for African Rice Development is another important case of innovative region-wide cooperation. The Alliance for a Green Revolution in Africa and JICA have taken the lead in developing this new cooperation architecture. Its aim is to set out an overall strategy and a framework for action to achieve an African Green Revolution through one increasingly important crop, rice. The coalition was launched during TICAD IV.

An association, Strengthening of Mathematics and Science Education in Western, Eastern, Central, and Southern Africa, is an initiative based on JICA's cooperation in establishing institutionalized in-service training for mathematics and science teachers in Kenya in 1998. The association was established in 2001 with thirty-three member countries. As of 2009, twelve projects were launched. It is expected that this kind of innovative SSC-TrC initiative will enable member countries to learn from their peers in Africa and to develop new ways of solving their own problems.[52]

Case 6: Combating Chagas Disease

Chagas disease, notorious as a silent disease and a disease of the poor, is caused by blood-sucking triatomine insects, euphemistically known as the kissing bug because of its method of transmission. But despite that benign designation, it has caused widespread death and destruction through South and Central America for centuries. Chagas disease is called the disease of the poor because this

49. Members are Belize, Costa Rica, El Salvador, Guatemala, Honduras, Nicaragua, Panama; Dominican Republic is an associate member.
50. Japan and Members of SICA (2005).
51. For details, see Honda (2012).
52. For details, see Ishihara (2012).

kissing bug lives almost exclusively in houses made of inexpensive materials such as adobe. It is also called the silent disease because of its long latent period of about ten years. It is estimated that there are 7.5 million patients in Latin America, of which 2.4 million are in Central America, equivalent to 9 percent of the population of this region.

Until recently, as many as 50,000 people, mainly poor and rural, were dying each year, while the number of new victims had reached 700,000 annually. The economic costs to Latin America were counted in billions of dollars, five times more harmful than malaria in the affected areas. JICA, working with the World Health Organization, the Pan American Health Organization, national governments, and local communities, has helped engineer a major turnaround in the fight against a disease that was largely ignored for decades by local and international organizations. From 1991 through 2014, JICA will allocate 2.26 billion yen to the Central American Initiative for Chagas Disease Control to help Guatemala, Honduras, El Salvador, Nicaragua, and Panama fight Chagas.

The results to date have been encouraging. In November 2008 WHO declared Guatemala as having, for the first time in the region, interrupted Chagas disease transmission via species introduced from South America that have more rapid disease transmission rates than native species.[53] In 2010 Honduras was also certified by WHO. In this fight against Chagas, the experiences, capacity development, and innovative solutions obtained in Guatemala were shared with other Central American countries.

The anti-Chagas campaign is now well organized and coordinated, with the number of new cases each year falling from around 700,000 to some 41,000 and the number of deaths from as many as 50,000 to around 10,000.[54]

Lessons Learned from Case Studies

The case studies provide some important lessons for scaling up. Most of the cases demonstrate how scaling up can take place when goals are clearly identified. Defining goals and targets clearly allows for the systematic programming of partnerships and the mobilization of resources that is needed for scaling up.

The first lesson, therefore, is for SSC and TrC to focus on areas where such approaches can uniquely add value, compared to traditional forms of assistance. The three categories of SSC identified earlier serve as a useful organizing framework for identifying potential areas of focus. But there may be value in narrowing down beyond this list to prioritize areas that are critical for improving welfare in developing countries. The G-20 Report of the Development Working

53. Sawaji (2009).
54. Information regarding Chagas disease is based on Hashimoto (2013); JICA (2011).

Group set out its views on priorities clearly in 2011: "We welcome the establishment of knowledge sharing networks or platforms in the areas of social protection, development of skills, and tropical agriculture technologies and productive system."[55]

The second lesson is that scaling up through TrC only takes place when there are effective SSC partners. That suggests that conventional development cooperation should also pay attention to capacity development and institution building in order to strengthen partners with whom scaling up can later occur. Investments in relationships with centers of excellence in the global South can be effective ways of scaling up by encouraging mutual learning. In this regard, triangular training programs (third-country training programs), as practiced by Japan and documented in some of the above case studies, may prove to be among the most practical modalities.

These training programs normally give the leading role in cooperation to centers of excellence. These centers share technical knowledge and the results of innovation as well as their experience in capacity development and institution building, ensuring relevant, high-quality cooperation. The programs create win-win-win processes for all three parties in triangular cooperation. Partner countries benefit from knowledge, innovation, and capacity development. Pivotal countries, the hosts of centers of excellence in the South, benefit from resources enhancing the scope and capacity of these centers of excellence. Traditional donor countries' most important benefit is the horizontal scaling up of their cooperation with pivotal countries to other developing countries in a more rapid, cost-effective, and efficacious way.

Training programs can therefore be considered a basic modality of TrC, where this is geared toward scaling up the impact of SSC. Because of these multiple effects, the programs can still produce an excellent return despite transaction costs, which are inherent in cases of cooperation among three or more parties. Because of this, the number of triangular training programs organized by JICA has increased steadily since they were first introduced in 1975. Participants have increased from fewer than 100 to 4,000 a year. Correspondingly, the number of participants from African countries has increased rapidly in recent years. The number of third-country specialists dispatched to partner countries within the framework of TrC has also increased. The case studies all identify long-term, sustained engagement of stakeholders and specialists, including traditional donors, as a key factor for success.

The case studies reveal that pivotal countries' centers of excellence can quickly become acquainted with the conditions, environment, and challenges of partner countries and establish stronger networks of professionals, researchers,

55. G-20 Development Working Group (2011, p. 13).

and practitioners. Thus this modality ensures mutual learning and trust among participants and their organizations. Training programs also frequently function as a starting point for more advanced or structured partnership programs.

The third lesson is that the capacity to internalize knowledge while adapting it to local context, and to create original knowledge, is crucial. This process of knowledge absorption, adaptation, and creation is enabled by capacity development, which is normally accompanied by institution building. Therefore, TrC should not be limited to mere knowledge sharing but should go beyond it to support capacity development and institution building. Each of the case studies shows how attention to capacity development or institution building was critical for success (box 9-1).

The fourth lesson is that in order to maximize the potential and minimize the risks of SSC and TrC, we need to think of ways to ensure adequate institutional, organizational, and programming innovations. The case studies suggest that specific institutional settings are instrumental in promoting the effectiveness of SSC and TrC. These include centers of excellence, triangular training programs based on these centers of excellence, structured SSC-TrC partnership programs, and established region-wide SSC-TrC programs having regional integration schemes as their platform. It has, however, proven difficult to scale up TrC rapidly using these institutional structures alone, and TrC remains a small element of the cooperation programs of most donors.

What is lacking is an intraregional or global system of SSC-TrC platforms through which knowledge exchange, peer learning, and coordination among SSC actors can facilitate access to important knowledge pools by developing countries. Hyunjoo Rhee argues that the platforms should be comprehensive, one-stop shops, encompassing the following four pillars: knowledge marketplace and networking, technical matching of demand for development solutions and supply of practical experiences, financial matching, and project advisory services.[56]

The United Nations Special Unit for South-South Cooperation's multilateral support architecture has been one of the most comprehensive global platforms for SSC-TrC. It consists of the Global South-South Development Expo and the Global South-South Development Academy, among others. In particular, the expo is the first ever solely from the South and for the South:

It showcases successful Southern-grown development solutions (SDSs) to address the need to meet Millennium Development Goals (MDGs). It is designed as a concrete response to the strong commitment made by the UN Secretary-General and the UNDP Administrator to help the global

56. Rhee (2011).

Box 9-1. *Capacity Development for Innovative Solutions*

In general, capacity development is the process by which people, organizations, and society as a whole unleash, strengthen, create, adapt, and maintain capacity over time, according to the widely cited definition from OECD/DAC.[a] Capacity development perceived as a mutual learning process demands that we shift our concept of what knowledge is and how it can be generated away from the traditional transfer-of-knowledge model toward a co-creation-of-knowledge model.

In this process, five factors are considered essential: stakeholder ownership, specific drivers, mutual learning, pathways to scaling up, and external actors.[b] Among the key drivers are group cohesiveness, the leadership of the top and middle ranks of organizations, the incentive system and structure of organizations, the commitment of high-level stakeholders such as central government ministers and local heads of government, and the engagement and long-term commitment of external actors.[c]

In most cases studied, the core of capacity development was a process of mutual learning to co-create the knowledge necessary to address the recipient countries' needs. This aspect is especially important in areas where development challenges must take account of constraints and difficulties different from those that advanced countries may be familiar with. The cases discussed in this chapter are examples of such areas, in which a simple transfer of knowledge or technology does not work, because relevant personnel in the North are not familiar with the conditions of the South. In these cases, an endogenous capacity development process was indispensable.

a. OECD/DAC (2006).

b. See Hosono and others (2011, pp. 182–83).

c. For the relationship between capacity development and institution building, see Fujita (2010).

South realize its shared aspirations for achieving sustainable and equitable development through the sharing and transfer of SDSs, with the support of the donor community and the multilateral system under innovative triangular and public-private partnership (PPP) arrangements. It also constitutes one of the Special Unit's three global and United Nations system-wide South-South support platforms.[57]

In this regard, the World Bank Institute is developing a South-South knowledge exchange "that focuses on South-to-South practitioner exchanges and plays a partnership and outreach role in raising the prominence of SSKE. . . . This

57. UNDP SU/SSC (2011).

unit is developing a series of operational support services, including the tools and instruments needed to play a more effective global connector role."[58]

Rhee argues that existing frameworks do not pay sufficient attention to the South-South matching process, so that SSC remains fragmented and unpredictable. She emphasizes that frameworks should be aimed at facilitating and brokering the matching process so as to ensure effective, feasible outcomes. The JICA-ASEAN Regional Cooperation Meeting (JARCOM) is such an innovation. It provides an innovative matching system of demand for technical cooperation and the supply of relevant experiences. Cambodia, Lao PDR, Myanmar, Vietnam, and Timor-Leste participate in JARCOM mainly as recipients, while Indonesia, Malaysia, the Philippines, Singapore, and Thailand (as well as Japan) participate mainly as providers. Successful matching increased substantially, from 28 percent in 2004 to 78 percent in 2007. As a result, eighty-six projects have been developed. The mobilization of resources from new providers was one of the unexpected achievements. A study conducted by UNDP and JICA highlights JARCOM's contribution to SSC aid-effectiveness synergies, such as alignment with national priorities, enhanced ownership, support for emerging donors, and a reduction in transaction costs for recipient countries.[59]

Based on the experience of JARCOM, the Japan-Southeast Asian Meeting for South-South Cooperation was created. It seeks to make regional SSC demand driven. Specifically, it aims to develop and implement well-prepared SSC, improve SSC quality, and maintain and enhance the network of JICA and the member agencies in Southeast Asia.

Concluding Remarks

To conclude, the following two points should be emphasized. First, while discussion of SSC and TrC flourishes on the philosophical and policy levels, evaluations of practical approaches at the operational level still seem scarce. Sharing practical experiences on the ground is truly needed for advancing mutual learning about the conditions required for promoting and scaling up effective SSC and TrC.

The second point has to do with an issue related to the substantive elements of development of SSC and TrC. We need to deepen our discussion on the particular domain of knowledge and skills for development, where SSC and TrC have a comparative advantage over traditional North-South cooperation. In a similar context, there is a need to closely examine the role of knowledge, learning, and innovation. In this regard, the Korean government's Knowledge Sharing Program appears to be very relevant. Without question, knowledge is a key

58. World Bank Institute (2011).
59. JICA and UNDP (2009).

component of development, and discussion around it should include knowledge sharing and, perhaps more important, knowledge co-creation and innovation.

To scale up SSC and TrC with further institutional, organizational, and programming innovations, the following actions are key:

—Identify specific and ambitious goals and targets in areas of greatest comparative advantage of SSC.

—Choose and invest in effective partners in the South, through identification and development of Southern centers of excellence.

—Develop long-term training and staff exchange programs.

—Invest in capacity development and institution building in partner countries.

—Develop regional and global platforms for knowledge exchange.

The case studies presented here suggest there is significant potential for scaling up SSC and TrC and ample rewards when this is successful. But some evaluations provide warning signals. The issue is not whether SSC can be scaled up but whether and how its impact can be scaled up. Practical innovations that could be taken to scale are still scarce, and in some cases effectiveness has still to be proven.

References

Aida, Yukiko, and Chiaki Kobayashi. 2012. "Towards Sustainable Rainforest Conservation in the World: International Course on Rainforest Monitoring." In *Scaling Up South-South and Triangular Cooperation*. Tokyo: JICA.

Alves, Eliseu. 2012. "JICA Cooperation: A Lesson on Institutional Building." Background paper. Tokyo: JICA.

BMZ (Federal Ministry for Economic Cooperation and Development, Germany). 2011. "Strategy for Development Cooperation with Global Development Partners, 2011–15."

Fourth High Level Forum on Aid Effectiveness. 2011. "Busan Partnership for Effective Development Co-operation."

Fukuta, Toshibumi. 2004. "JICA Technological Cooperation Projects on Establishment of Earthquake Disaster Prevention Research Organizations." *Journal of Japan Association for Earthquake Engineering* (special issue) 4, no. 3: 412–20.

Gates, Bill. 2011. "Innovation with Impact: Financing 21st Century Development." Report to G-20 leaders, Cannes Summit. November.

Gill, Indermit, and Homi Kharas. 2007. *An East Asian Renaissance: Ideas for Economic Growth*. World Bank.

G-20 Development Working Group. 2011. "The G-20 Report of the Development Working Group."

Hashimoto, Ken. 2013. *Way to Overcome "Shagas Disease," an Unknown Endemic Disease in Central America* (in Japanese). Tokyo: Diamond.

Honda, Shunichiro. 2012. "Inspired by Sri-Lankan Practice: Scaling-up 5S KAIZEN-TQM for Improving African Hospital Service." In *Scaling Up South-South and Triangular Cooperation*. Tokyo: JICA.

Hosono, Akio. 2009. "*Kaizen:* Quality and Productivity and Beyond." In *Introducing Kaizen in Africa*. GRIPS Development Forum.

———. 2012. "Climate Change, Disaster Risk Management, and South-South/Triangular Cooperation." In *Scaling Up South-South and Triangular Cooperation*. Tokyo: JICA.

Hosono, Akio, Shunichiro Honda, Mine Sato, and Mai Oto. 2011. "Inside the Black Box of Capacity Development," in *Catalyzing Development: A New Vision for Aid,* edited by Homi Kharas, Koji Makino, and Woojin Jung. Brookings.

Hosono, Akio, and Yutaka Hongo. 2012. "Cerrado: Brazil's Agricultural Revolution as a Model of Sustainable and Inclusive Development." Tokyo: JICA.

Inter-American Development Bank. 2010. *The Age of Productivity: Transforming Economies from the Bottom Up.*

Ishihara, Shinichi. 2012. "Network-type Cooperation: Strengthening of Mathematics and Science Education in Western, Eastern, Central, and Southern Africa (SMASE-WECSA) Network." In *Scaling Up South-South and Triangular Cooperation*. Tokyo: JICA.

Japan and Members of SICA (Sistema de la Integración Centroamericana). 2005. "Plan de Acción de la Declaración de Tokyo."

Japan Productivity Organization. 1990. "Singapore Productivity Improvement Project." Tokyo.

JICA. 2011. "The 'Kissing Bug.'" *JICA's World* (October): 11.

———. 2012a. "JICA's Regional Cooperation in ASEAN." Tokyo.

———. 2012b. "An Overview of South-South Cooperation and Triangular Cooperation." Tokyo.

JICA and GRIPS. 2011. "Handbook of National Movements for Quality and Productivity Improvement."

JICA, IDCJ (International Development Center of Japan), IDJ (*International Development Journal*). 2010. "Data Collection Survey on Strategy Formulation on Human Resources Development in Southeast Asia: Final Report. Part 4." Tokyo.

JICA and UNDP (United Nations Development Program). 2009. *Networking and Learning Together: Experiences in South-South and Triangular Cooperation in Asia.*

Kitaw, Daniel. 2011. "Botswana's Productivity Movement." In *KAIZEN National Movement: A Study of Quality and Productivity Improvement in Asia and Africa*. JICA/GRIPS Development Forum.

Kumar, Negash. 2008. "South-South and Triangular Cooperation in Asia-Pacific: Towards a New Paradigm in Development Cooperation." UN ESCAP Working Paper WP/09/05.

Ministry of Foreign Affairs, Japan. 2003. *Japan's Official Development Assistance Charter.*

"The Miracle of the Cerrado." 2010. *The Economist*, August 20, pp. 58–60.

Ninomiya, Akiie. 2010. *Wheelchairs in Asian Streets: Challenges of APCD* [in Japanese]. Tokyo: Diamond.

OECD (Organization for Economic Cooperation and Development). 2010. *Perspectives on Global Development 2010: Shifting Growth.*

OECD/DAC (TT-SSC). 2011. "Unlocking the Potential of South-South Cooperation."

Ohno, Izumi, and Daniel Kitaw. 2011. "Productivity Movement in Singapore." In *KAIZEN National Movement: A Study of Quality and Productivity Improvement in Asia and Africa*. GRIPS Development Forum.

Rhee, Hyunjoo. 2011. "Promoting South-South Cooperation through Knowledge Exchange." In *Catalyzing Development: A New Vision for Aid,* edited by Homi Kharas, Koji Makino, and Woojin Jung. Brookings.

Saito, Shinobu. 2012. "The *Taishin* Triangular Initiative in Central America: Cocreating Quake-Resistant Construction Methods for Popular Low-Cost Housing." In *Scaling Up South-South and Triangular Cooperation*. Tokyo: JICA.

Sakaguchi, Kota. 2012. "Japan-Brazil Partnership Program: A Framework for Triangular Cooperation." In *Scaling Up South-South and Triangular Cooperation.* Tokyo: JICA.

Sawaji, Osamu. 2009. "On the Trail of the Assassin Bugs." *Japan Journal,* October.

Schulz, Nils-Sjard. 2010. "Triangular Cooperation in the Context of Aid Effectiveness—Experiences and Views of EU Donors." Agencia Española de Cooperación Internacional para el Desarrollo. March 17.

"Scientists Are Making Brazil's Savannah Bloom." 2007. *New York Times,* October 2.

Ueda, Takafumi. 2009. "Productivity and Quality Improvement: JICA's Assistance in Kaizen." In *Introducing KAIZEN in Africa.* GRIPS Development Forum.

UNCTAD (United Nations Conference on Trade and Development). 2010. "South-South Cooperation: Africa and the New Forum of Development Partnership." Report 2010. Economic Development in Africa.

UNDP SU/SSC (United Nations Special Unit for South-South Cooperation). 2011. FAQ, May 18 (http://ssc.undp.org/faq/#irfaq_11_4f0e0).

UN High Level Conference. 2009. "Nairobi Outcome" (http://southsouthconference.org/wp-content/uploads/2010/01/GA-resolution-endorsed-Nairobi-Outcome-21-Dec-09.pdf).

United Nations. 2011. "The State of South-South Cooperation." Report of the Secretary General, A/66/229.

UN Joint Inspection Unit. 2011. "South-South and Triangular Cooperation in the United Nations System." JIU/REP/2011/3.

World Bank Institute. 2011. "The South-South Experience Exchange Facility."

10

Institutional Challenges to Scaling Up Learning in Kenya

TESSA BOLD, MWANGI KIMENYI, GERMANO MWABU,
ALICE NG'ANG'A, AND JUSTIN SANDEFUR

E ducation is a fundamental component of the development process, and
governments in developing countries invest heavily in education. Despite
this commitment, learning outcomes remain poor in low-income countries. In
Kenya, a highly publicized study by the advocacy organization Uwezo demonstrates the severity of the learning crisis, with only a third of grade three pupils
able to read simple sentences and very slow improvements in reading and math
skills as students progress to higher grades.[1]

To cite one example from the enormous policy literature on this learning
failure, the recent Africa Learning Barometer discusses the many reasons that
learning outcomes on the continent are inadequate. These include resource constraints such as books, facilities such as toilets and classrooms, and the quality
and number of teachers. But resources are just part of the story—the incentives
provided to parents, students, and teachers also matter, and these incentives are
shaped by curriculum design, testing systems, school governance structures, and
the types of mechanisms used to monitor school performance.

How can policymakers find out what works? Small-scale experiments provide a means to pilot innovative approaches to improve learning outcomes and
subject them to rigorous evaluation. In the United States, the Department of

---

1. Uwezo (2011).

Education's "What Works Clearinghouse" provides a catalogue of school management and teaching practices that have been shown to improve learning. In the developing world, research in Western Kenya has led the way in using randomized controlled trials (RCTs) to demonstrate the effectiveness of school-level reforms to incentives. This broad research program suggests a number of low-cost ways to improve learning in Kenyan primary schools, including tracking students by ability, offering merit-based scholarships as an incentive to students, and hiring teachers on fixed-term, renewable contracts.[2]

Although these and many other small-scale interventions to improve educational or other development outcomes have been found to be effective in a variety of settings, it is not quite obvious that such successes can be replicated when the interventions are scaled up to entire regions or even a country. We review a number of, by now, familiar concerns that must be addressed when extrapolating from small-scale experiments to forecast the impact of scaled-up policies.

We devote special attention to one obstacle to scaling-up experimental results that has received relatively less attention in the literature to date. This stems from the fact that, in many cases, the implementation of experimental pilots is undertaken by nongovernmental organizations. There are clear logistical and cost reasons for this. But there are also drawbacks to piloting with NGOs, especially considering that large-scale delivery of education and other social services is dominated by the government in most developing countries. Thus the most feasible and sustainable approach to scaling up successful interventions will necessarily be through government implementation. As we discuss in detail below, it cannot be assumed that implementation by NGOs and the government will yield similar outcomes.

We illustrate this point using our own prior work.[3] The idea is to explore, first, whether the results observed under small-scale interventions hold when scaled up and, second, whether the outcomes differ whether the intervention is by an NGO or the government. The results of the interventions reveal that indeed there are differences in outcomes between NGO and government implementation. The results suggest that we need to look beyond the intervention— the contract teacher—to the institutions of implementation. It is by getting a clear understanding of the dynamics of the institutions of implementation— political economy, so to say—that we can then know the conditions under which scaling up will succeed.

2. The program is summarized in Kremer and Holla (2009). See also Duflo, Dupas, and Kremer (2011, 2012); Kremer, Miguel, and Thornton (2009).

3. Bold and others (2012); this work attempts to replicate the results of the NGO project described in Duflo, Dupas, and Kremer (2012) in other contexts, using both NGO and government implementation.

Why Experiment? The Challenge of Internal Validity

Randomized controlled trials are ideally suited for measuring the causal effects of a particular policy in a particular setting at a particular time. Joshua Angrist and Jorn-Steffen Pischke give a useful definition of causal relationships and why we would like to measure them: "A causal relationship is useful for making predictions about the consequences of changing circumstances or policies; it tells us what would happen in alternative (or 'counterfactual') worlds. . . . The causal effect of schooling on wages is the increment to wages an individual would receive if he or she got more schooling."[4]

These trials (RCTs) estimate causal relationships by following medical trials in selecting a sample of participants and then randomly partitioning that sample into a treatment group (the units that will participate in the policy whose causal effect is to be estimated) and a control group (the units that will not participate). The causal effect of the policy is then measured by comparing the outcome of interest (for example, test scores in primary schools following a class size reduction, or employment rates following a job training program) in the treatment and control groups after a suitable time has passed.

The great advantage of randomized controlled trials is that they solve the selection problem that plagues policy evaluation based on nonexperimental data. If a researcher observes that, in a cross section of schools, test scores are lower in schools with larger class sizes, should she conclude from this that reducing class sizes would result in higher test scores? Not necessarily. Schools that have lower class sizes may systematically differ from schools with larger class sizes in ways that directly affect test scores. For example, head teachers that are more motivated may get a teacher vacancy filled more easily, but head teacher motivation may be an important determinant of test scores in itself.

The traditional response to this concern has been to attempt to measure all the dimensions along which schools with small and large class sizes differ and include them in the regression. If we could indeed measure all the relevant factors, then conditioning on them would solve the selection problem. Conditional on head teacher motivation (and possibly many other factors), we could claim that class sizes were as good as randomly assigned across schools and that the coefficient on class size measures the causal effect.

What do we mean by this exactly? The causal effect of class size answers the following question: If we gave school A an additional teacher and thereby reduced class size, how would test scores in school A increase? That is a counterfactual question: at a particular point in time we can observe school A either with small classes or with large classes, but never with both. We therefore have

---

4. Angrist and Pischke (2009, p. 3).

to find a counterfactual in the data; that is, we pick school B, which has small classes, and compare its test scores with those of school A. We would then claim that school B (conditional on head-teacher characteristics—that is, we pick a school B that has the same head-teacher characteristics as school A) makes a good counterfactual for school A. That is, if school B had the same class size as school A, it would have the same test scores, or if school A had the same class size as school B, it would have the same test scores.

The problem with this argument is that no matter how many variables we try to measure in the survey, we can never be sure that school B makes for a good counterfactual. There could always be variables that are not measured or are badly measured, which are correlated with class size and that affect test scores directly. Take for example parental interest in education. This would have a direct effect on test scores and may lead the school to employ more teachers. If we don't measure this variable, or measure it badly, then school B's test scores may be higher than school A's even if school B had the same class sizes as school A.

In practice, it may be impractical to measure all the dimensions, other than class sizes, along which schools differ and that potentially affect test scores (and are correlated with class size). Randomized controlled trials offer a simple solution to this. Because treatment is randomly assigned across treatment and control groups (in the case of the causal effect of class size, the researchers assign an additional teacher to the randomly selected treatment group but not to the control group) we can be sure that, at least on average, treatment and control groups are comparable across all other dimensions that matter for test scores. Hence we can be confident that the average test score in the control group school is a good counterfactual for what test scores would have been in the treatment school in the absence of an additional teacher, and vice versa. Therein lies the power of experiments.

This power of RCTs (and the difficulty of estimating causal effects from observational data) was first demonstrated by Robert LaLonde in a now classic paper comparing causal estimates of a U.S. job training program using experimental and nonexperimental methods.[5] Based on an experimental evaluation of the National Supported Work Demonstration, a temporary employment program designed to help disadvantaged and low-skilled unemployed workers to move into employment, LaLonde estimates that the program increased wages of women by $851 and those of men by $886.

The analysis is then repeated using nonexperimental methods. To do this, the author discards the experimental control group and instead compares the experimental treatment group to a carefully selected comparison group from the general population. In the nonexperimental setting, the treatment effect is

5. LaLonde (1986).

calculated by first estimating what determines participation in the program and then estimating the differences in observed earnings among participants and nonparticipants that are due to participating in the job training program.

Of course, there are many ways in which these regressions can be specified and therefore many treatment effects that could be estimated. LaLonde attempts a number of specifications and finds that the majority tend to overestimate the effects of the training program on women and underestimate the effects for men. Even though some of the estimates replicate the experimental results, this is small comfort since we have no way of knowing which one among a number of sensible nonexperimental specifications measures the effect that would be obtained in an experimental setting.

Paul Glewwe and colleagues provide another example of how misleading non-experimental results can be.[6] They compare the effect of increasing school inputs (in the form of flip charts) on test scores in an experimental study and a nonexperimental study in Western Kenya. While the flip charts are estimated to have a large positive effect (20 percent of a standard deviation), in the nonexperimental study, the effect is zero when they are randomly assigned to treatment and control schools, indicating that the observational results suffer from positive selection bias. That is, schools that elect to put more flip charts into their classrooms differ from those that don't in many other ways that also positively affect test scores.

Because RCTs can convincingly overcome the problem of selection bias and because nonexperimental studies have proven unreliable in the identification of causal effects, RCTs have rightly become the gold standard of policy evaluation.

Limits of Experimentation: External Validity Concerns

Critics of RCTs argue that randomized controlled trials can show the efficacy of a program ("It worked here") but that policy advice needs to be based on showing the effectiveness of a policy, forecasting its effect in a different context ("It will work there").[7] Others translate this into a critique of the relevance of the treatment effects estimated by randomized controlled trials; Angus Deaton, for example, argues that as soon as compliance with an intervention is imperfect, randomized controlled trials have to rely on stronger assumptions to estimate treatment effects.[8] In addition, they estimate treatment effects on the population that was induced by the randomization to participate in a particular program.[9] As Deaton points out, this is unlikely to be a random sample of the population of interest (even if the initial RCT sample was a random sample, which is often

6. Glewwe and others (2004).
7. Cartwright (2011).
8. Deaton (2009); Heckman (1991, 2010).
9. Angrist and Pischke (2010) call this the local average treatment effect.

not the case). The estimates therefore lack external validity and are inappropriate to make forecasts when a policy is scaled up.

James Heckman notes that randomized controlled trials are seldom based on structural policy models and argues that they may suffer from randomization bias:

> Proponents of randomized social experiments implicitly make an assumption: that randomization does not alter the program being studied. For certain problems and for certain behavioral models this assumption is either valid or innocuous. For other problems and models it is not. A major conclusion . . . is that advocates of randomization have overstated their case for having avoided arbitrary assumption. Evaluation by randomization makes implicit behavioral assumptions that in certain context are quite strong. Bias induced by randomization is a serious possibility.[10]

More concretely, randomization bias could take the form of changing the types of projects that are evaluated, especially when working with governments. In what follows, we discuss a study that attempts to overcome and measure this form of bias.

Scaling Up Contract Teachers in Kenya

The provision of contract teachers is one of the most successful, well-documented interventions to raise student learning in primary schools.

A study by Abhijit Banerjee, Shawn Cole, Esther Duflo, and Leigh Linden, presenting results from a randomized evaluation in urban India, shows that an NGO program hiring young women to tutor lagging students in third and fourth grades led to a 0.28 standard deviation increase in test scores.[11] It is unclear from this study, however, whether the program's success stems from the mere provision of additional human resources, the fixed-term contracts offered to the tutors, the profile of the teachers (younger and more predominantly female than existing teachers), or the focus on remedial education.

Karthik Muralidharan and Venkatesh Sundararaman help answer this question.[12] They evaluate a statewide program in Andhra Pradesh that provided one extra contract teacher to public primary schools. Notably, this study maintained a fairly business-as-usual environment within the treatment schools, with no demands that the extra teachers focus on remedial education or early grades. Results show an increase in treatment schools of 0.15 and 0.13 standard deviations on math and language tests, respectively. In both of the

10. Heckman (1991, p. 5).
11. Banerjee and others (2007).
12. Muralidharan and Sundararaman (2010).

cases—Banerjee and others and Muralidharan and Sundararaman—the additional teachers led to significant learning gains despite salary costs (a small fraction of civil service wages).

Finally, a study by Esther Duflo, Pascaline Dupas, and Michael Kremer shows that exposure to a contract teacher in government schools in Western Kenya raised test scores by 0.21 standard deviations relative to exposure to civil service teachers.[13] Furthermore, the experimental design allowed these researchers to attribute this effect to contract teachers per se rather than to the accompanying reduction in class size resulting from hiring an extra teacher.

In 2009 the Kenya Ministry of Education decided to launch a full-scale, national teacher internship program, employing approximately 18,000 trained teachers on fixed-term contracts. As a first step in implementing this scaled-up program, the government agreed to conduct a pilot phase that would assess the program's results in a variety of conditions in Kenya, spanning urban slums in Nairobi and nomadic communities in the remote Northeastern province. The pilot allowed for some contract teachers to be provided and monitored by the government, through the Ministry of Education, and others by the NGO World Vision through its local affiliates. The selection of schools for each "treatment" was randomly defined.

The pilot was designed to test the Ministry of Education's ability to implement a fairly close variant of the NGO project described by Duflo, Dupas, and Kremer and to replicate the results across diverse conditions.[14] The key difference was that for some schools the government selected, paid, and monitored the new teachers, while in the other group of schools these functions were performed by the NGO World Vision.

A pilot contract teacher program was implemented from June 2010 to October 2011 in fourteen districts spanning all eight Kenyan provinces; 24 schools were sampled from each province, yielding 192 schools in total. One contract teacher per school was randomly assigned to 128 out of the 192 sampled schools to teach second or third grade. Learning outcomes were measured through a standardized score on a math and English test administered to these pupils in 2009, before the program's inception, and in 2011, after its completion.

As noted in the introduction, a necessary step in scaling up any proven NGO education intervention in Kenya—as in many other settings—is a transition to working with the government as monopoly supplier of public education at the national level. The experiment was designed to address this central question of whether the Kenyan government could replicate the impacts reported by the NGO variant of the program. The results consistently suggest that the positive

---

13. Duflo, Dupas, and Kremer (2012).
14. Its results are detailed in Bold and others (2012).

findings of an overall effect of a contract teacher on learning outcomes was driven by the NGO program, where the presence of a contract teacher raised scores by 0.16 to 0.19 standard deviations. But for contract teachers hired by the government, no impact on learning was found.

What explains the performance gap between the government and NGO programs in the study by Bold and her colleagues? One obvious factor could be poor compliance; that is, the government may simply not have been able to recruit and fill the contract teacher positions. However, the random nature of our experiment allows one to differentiate between the effect of intending to hire a teacher and the effect of actually doing so. In both cases, students taught by the government contract teachers do not score discernibly higher than students with no contract teacher at all.

The Political Economy of Scaling Up

The history of the contract teacher program in Kenya, both in its pilot form and in the nationally scaled up version (where 18,000 teachers were employed nationwide), provides an interesting example of how experimentation and scaling up can be combined and how the seesaw effect identified by Daron Acemoglu played out in Kenya.[15]

As part of its Vision 2030, the government of Kenya committed to establishing "a Teachers Recruitment Programme that would employ an additional 28,000 teachers and ensure that schools would have adequate teachers."[16] The national union of teachers (KNUT) welcomed this but calculated the actual shortfall of teachers in Kenyan schools at 60,000. This would be the increase in net hiring needed to get average pupil teacher ratios down to forty children per teacher.

The Ministry of Education first began discussing plans for employing teachers on short-term contracts as part of this recruitment drive in 2008. The plans for both a scale-up (involving first 10,500 teachers and later 18,000) as well as an experimental evaluation of contract teachers became concrete in the spring of 2009, when a steering committee and technical committee consisting of a dozen high-ranking ministry officials and the authors was formed and tasked with the design of the research pilot as well as giving guidance on how the research could inform national policymaking.

At its inception, the contract teacher program had been envisioned as a way to standardize existing practices, in which communities hire teachers locally through funds raised by the School Management Committee (SMC) and the Parent Teacher Association (PTA). PTA teachers, who are employed at salaries

15. Acemoglu (2010).
16. Government of Kenya (2012).

far below Teachers Service Commission (TSC) teachers, make up a sizable proportion of teachers in Kenya. In the baseline study conducted by the authors as part of the experimental evaluation of contract teachers detailed above and in the sample of schools surveyed for this study, 83 percent of teachers were employed by the TSC and the remaining 17 percent by PTAs. TSC teachers earned an average of $261 a month in 2009, compared to just $56 a month for PTA teachers. The focus of the program and its rhetoric soon shifted toward the professionalization of the teaching corps. As in many other professions and countries (such as the *Referendariatssystem* in Germany and the trainee teacher and trainee doctor years in the United Kingdom), teacher trainees were supposed to be employed as teacher interns for two years before graduating into full civil service. This period was intended to be part of their professional training, and the fact that this would also allow the use of fully qualified but unemployed teachers was seen as a welcome by-product, but certainly not the main purpose, of the program. The program consequently became known as the teacher intern program.[17]

A topic that was hotly debated right from the start was what to do with the teachers following the two-year internship. Was this supposed to be a probationary period, and only teachers who performed satisfactorily would progress to full employment in the TSC? Would TSC employment be guaranteed for these teachers? Or only if a vacancy was available? How would the government assess that the teachers had performed satisfactorily? Another hotly debated topic was the salary of the teacher interns. Should this be modeled on the salary of PTA teachers (roughly 5,000 KSh at the time), or should it be closer to entry-level salaries of newly hired TSC teachers (close to 10,000 KSh at the time, but soon raised to 20,000 KSh)?

While the ministry preferred the teacher intern variant over the PTA variant for the national scale-up, it was nevertheless willing to experiment with both alternatives in the hope of producing experimental evidence that would help them make a political case for the technically preferred, but politically more contentious, design.

As a result, the research pilot in Bold and colleagues' 2012 publication introduced experimental variation in terms of both recruitment and hiring: half the schools were instructed to hire the teachers locally, with the SMC in charge of the hiring process; the other half were instructed to hire the teachers centrally, with the help of the district education officer, using the marginal rejects from the list of applicants for TSC employment. When teachers were hired locally, their salaries were transferred to the school's general purpose account, and the SMC was, in principle, in charge of disbursing the money. When teachers were

---

17. Technical Committee (2009).

hired centrally, the salaries were directly transferred to teachers' bank accounts, just as in the case of TSC teachers. The school therefore had much less oversight of its teachers. In addition, half the schools were instructed to hire teachers at 9,000 KSh, and half the schools received funds to employ teachers at 5,000 KSh. The local/central variation and the low salary/high salary variation were orthogonal to each other.

The ministry realized early on that its plan to employ teachers on short-term contracts would be controversial. In particular, employment of teachers on short-term contracts would put the ministry in violation of the TSC Act, which states that "the TSC and KNUT negotiate(s) the terms and conditions of service for teachers within the Teachers Service Remunerations Committee, and thereafter the employer is required to employ teachers under terms contained in the Schemes of Service as negotiated." Employing contract teachers therefore required the cooperation of the union.

Union cooperation was hard to come by, and in fact the union was quick to point out that there was no provision for employment of teachers on contract in the current schemes of service and that employment of teachers on contract was therefore illegal. The union also alleged that the government would be in violation of the TSA Act, which states that "an employer shall pay his employees equal remuneration for work of equal value," and the country's constitution, because contract teachers were subject to discrimination. The government tried to circumvent these legal issues by bypassing the TSC and putting the Ministry of Education directly in charge of recruiting and employing teachers on short-term contracts.

The summer of 2009 was a period of intense and increasingly acrimonious negotiations between the government and the teacher union, which culminated in the union filing a lawsuit against the government in August 2009. The court found in favor of the union and ordered the minister of education and the permanent secretary to "quash the decision to advertise for 10,500 vacant posts for Primary School Intern Teachers as posts for professional qualified teachers contrary to the law"; to "follow the law in their quest to recruit 10,500 vacant posts for Primary School Teachers as professional teachers"; and to "stop violating the law through their actions to recruit and/or employ 10,500 vacant Primary School Intern Teachers without involving the TSC."[18]

The judgment prevented the government from employing contract teachers. The deadlock persisted for almost a year.

In the summer of 2010, negotiations between the government and the union finally progressed, and the union agreed to withdraw its suit. According to internal union documents, the union acted in the belief that in exchange for

18. See "State Moves to Quash Order on Intern Teachers" (2009).

withdrawing the suit the government would commit not to employ teachers on short-term contracts. Instead, the government, under pressure from the Ministry of Finance to spend the funds, advertised 18,000 vacancies for two-year contracts at 10,000 KSh a month. The vacancies were filled and teachers employed by October 2010.

Almost immediately—during its annual congress in December 2010—the union began lobbying for permanent contracts for the 18,000. The topic was also discussed several times in Parliament, where opposition parties (such as Safina) took up the topic to score points against the government. After a flurry of ultimately inconclusive meetings between the union and government officials in June and July 2011, the union announced a national strike, with the explicit aim of making contract teachers permanent. After two days of strike action and nationwide teacher protests beginning on September 5, 2011, the government gave in to union demands and made the 18,000 contract teachers permanent.

Does this imply that scaling up the contract teacher program was doomed to failure from the start and that no general lessons about scaling up can be learned from the research pilot detailed in Bold and others' 2012 work? We believe not. First, the events surrounding the 18,000 contract teachers made it possible to measure some of the seesaw effects that would not have been present in a small-scale study and to "understand better the role of political economy factors in development."[19] Second, both theoretical and empirical literature observes that union hostility to performance-based pay and fixed-term contracts is a widespread phenomenon not specific to Kenya. There are good reasons for this.

When performance-based pay and fixed-term contracts are viewed through the lens of a principal-agent model, both are clearly ways to improve accountability by pushing risk from the school onto the teachers. Schools reduce the risk of teachers shirking, while teachers face increased risk of being punished (or rewarded) unfairly. If, for instance, teacher performance is based on subjective evaluations by head teachers, these local school officials wield enormous discretionary power, raising legitimate fears about inconsistent treatment across schools and arbitrary penalties or dismissal. If, instead, teacher performance is based on more objective criteria like test scores, teachers will inevitably suffer (and benefit) from test score fluctuations that are completely unrelated to their own effort.

Moreover, while contract teachers in the form envisaged in the pilot could not become national policy, the idea of performance-based contracts for Kenyan teachers is by no means dead. Plans were under way in 2012 to introduce three-year, performance-based contracts for head teachers.

19. Acemoglu (2010, p. 28).

Does Scalability Require Experimenting at Scale?

Development economists often cite the randomized impact evaluation of Mexico's national social insurance program, Progresa, as the advent of experimental methods to our discipline. Beginning in 1997, Mexican president Ernesto Zedillo inaugurated a conditional cash transfer program, providing between 70 and 135 pesos per month per child on the condition that parents keep their school-age children in school.[20] The International Food Policy Research Institute was contracted to evaluate the program, using village-level randomization of program eligibility.

Progresa had a positive enrollment effect for both boys and girls in primary and secondary school.[21] Estimates from a difference-in-differences model controlling for household and community characteristics show increases in enrollment at the primary level of up to 1.07 percentage points for boys and up to 1.45 for girls (enrollment rates had previously ranged from 90 to 94 percent). At the secondary level, where baseline enrollment rates were much lower, average enrollment increased by up to 5.8 percentage points for boys and 9.3 for girls.

As most readers are well aware, the success of Progresa-Oportunidades has had an enormous and far-reaching effect on social policy in the developing world. Twenty-eight conditional cash transfer programs were counted worldwide in 2009, with almost every country in Latin America adopting some form of the program.[22] This global influence highlights the ambiguity of the phrase "at scale." The most important outcome of the experimental evaluation of a nationwide program in a country of over 100 million inhabitants was arguably not, first and foremost, its effect on the design or continuation of that program within Mexico but rather a demonstration effect, encouraging adoption of similar programs worldwide.

But Progresa's demonstration effect may have been more about the political economy of scale than the economics of schooling. Although the conditions associated with conditional cash transfers often have limited economic importance, they may do much to win broader public sympathy for social safety net programs by emphasizing responsible behavior among beneficiaries.[23]

These findings highlight the enormous international public good provided by rigorous, large-scale, impact evaluations conducted by governments, which extend beyond their contribution to policymaking domestically in the short term. Nevertheless, the expectation that new policy proposals be piloted on the

20. Schultz (2000).
21. Schultz (2000).
22. Fiszbein and Schady (2009).
23. Das, Do, and Özler (2005).

scale of Progresa would impose huge costs, radically curtail the range of new solutions that could be tested, and thus stifle innovation.

One way to minimize this burden and to address a number of external validity concerns would be to encourage a greater focus on replication in the development literature. An initiative of the U.S. Agency for International Development known as Development Innovation Ventures attempts to do this by funding multiple stages of replication and scaling up, starting with demonstration projects and working up to larger trials. Replication allows researchers to test for heterogeneity of effects across settings and to confront the organizational and institutional issues that proved to be central in our work with contract teachers in Kenya.

Another route would be to focus research narrowly on the binding constraints to scaling up, which may not be at the school or clinic level but instead relate to bureaucratic incentives at a higher level, even national political dynamics. For instance, the government treatment arm in Bold and others' earlier study may have failed due to poor monitoring by district-level officials at the Ministry of Education or to a lack of credibility in teacher contracts within the context of national action by the teachers' union.[24] Research to address these issues need not wait for the program to go to scale.

Conclusion

In experimental research, results are deemed externally valid if the same experiment can be reasonably expected to produce the same result in a different context. This essay explores the relationship between the concept of external validity in experimental research and policy discussions about scaling up successful, small-scale NGO development projects.

Typically, when researchers worry about experimental validity, they worry about moving from one geographic place to another. Our goal has been to shift focus away from worrying primarily about geographic space, and toward worrying more about institutional context. The results of our earlier work in Kenya suggest that, when considering education interventions, extrapolating results from an NGO project to a government policy may be more problematic than extrapolating from one province to the next. Contract teachers were exclusively effective in schools where they were hired by an international NGO, more or less without regard to the baseline conditions in the school. Effects were significantly smaller and indistinguishable from zero in schools where the same program was administered by the Ministry of Education.

---

24. Bold and others (2012).

Our concern with institutional context is particularly salient when considering scaling up. As economists adopt the methods of randomized trials, we enhance our knowledge of what might work but gain little knowledge of what might work at scale. Development reforms are often politically contentious and, to operate at scale, must be implemented by public sector bureaucracies in weakly governed states. The fate of Kenya's contract teacher program is a reminder that, in many cases, institutions are not broken by accident. Our discussion suggests that many of the obstacles to smooth implementation of the program by the Ministry of Education were not a function of low capacity or inherent bureaucratic inefficiency but a result of the endogenous political economy response to a program that threatened vested interests.

Going forward, we would advocate for more experimental work that grapples directly with these institutional challenges, working hand in hand with the government institutions that are, in most cases, ultimately responsible for taking development innovations to scale.

References

Acemoglu, Daron. 2010. "Theory, General Equilibrium, and Political Economy in Development Economics." *Journal of Economic Perspectives* 24, no. 3: 17–32.

Allcott, Hunt, and Sendhil Mullainathan. 2012. "External Validity and Partner Selection Bias." Working Paper 18373. National Bureau of Economic Research.

Angrist, Joshua David, and Jorn-Steffen Pischke. 2009. *Mostly Harmless Econometrics: An Empiricist's Companion.* Princeton University Press.

———. 2010. "The Credibility Revolution in Empirical Economics: How Better Research Design Is Taking the Con out of Econometrics." *Journal of Economic Perspectives* 24, no. 2: 3–30.

Bold, Tessa, and others. 2012. "Interventions and Institutions: Experimental Evidence on Scaling Up Education Reforms in Kenya." Draft (www.cgdev.org/doc/kenya_rct_web draft.pdf).

Cartwright, Nancy. 2011. "A Philosopher's View of the Long Road from RCTs to Effectiveness." *Lancet* 377, no. 9775: 1400–01.

Das, J., Q. T. Do, and B. Özler. 2005. "Reassessing Conditional Cash Transfer Programs." *World Bank Research Observer* 20, no. 1: 57–80.

Deaton, Angus. 2009. "Instruments of Development: Randomization in the Tropics, and the Search for the Elusive Keys to Economic Development." Working Paper 14690. National Bureau of Economic Research.

Duflo, Esther, Pascaline Dupas, and Michael Kremer. 2011. "Peer Effects, Teacher Incentives, and the Impact of Tracking: Evidence from a Randomized Evaluation in Kenya." *American Economic Review* 101, no. 5: 1739–74.

———. 2012. "School Governance, Teacher Incentives, and Pupil-Teacher Ratios: Experimental Evidence from Kenyan Primary Schools." Working Paper 17939. National Bureau of Economic Research.

Duflo, Esther, Rema Hanna, and Steven P. Ryan. 2012. "Incentives Work: Getting Teachers to Come to School." *American Economic Review* 102, no. 4: 1241–78.

Fiszbein, Ariel, and Norbert Schady. 2009. *Conditional Cash Transfers: Reducing Present and Future Poverty.* World Bank.

Glewwe, Paul, and others. 2004. "Retrospective vs. Prospective Analyses of School Inputs: The Case of Flip Charts in Kenya." *Journal of Development Economics* 74: 251–68.

Government of Kenya. 2012. "Vision 2030: The Social Pillar—Investing in the People of Kenya" (www.vision2030.go.ke/index.php/pillars/index/social).

Heckman, James J. 1991. "Randomization and Social Policy Evaluation." Technical Working Paper 107. National Bureau of Economic Research.

———. 2010. "Building Bridges between Structural and Program Evaluation Approaches to Evaluating Policy." *Journal of Economic Literature* 48, no. 2: 356–98.

Kremer, Michael, and Alaka Holla. 2009. "Improving Education in the Developing World: What Have We Learned from Randomized Evaluations?" *Annual Review of Economics* 1: 513–42.

Kremer, Michael, Edward Miguel, and Rebecca Thornton. 2009. "Incentives to Learn." *Review of Economics and Statistics* 91, no. 3: 437–56.

LaLonde, Robert J. 1986. "Evaluating the Econometric Evaluations of Training Programs with Experimental Data." *American Economic Review* 76, no. 4: 604–20.

Muralidharan, Karthik, and Venkatesh Sundararaman. 2010. "Contract Teachers: Experimental Evidence from India." University of California, San Diego.

Schultz, T. Paul. 2000. "Final Report: The Impact of PROGRESA on School Enrollments." Washington: International Food Policy Research Institute.

"State Moves to Quash Order on Intern Teachers." 2009. *Daily Nation* (Kenya). August 19.

Technical Committee for Teacher Internship Program. 2009. Minutes of meeting, April.

Uwezo. 2011. "Are Our Children Learning: Annual Learning Assessment Report" (www.uwezo.net/wp-content/uploads/2012/08/KE_2011_AnnualAssessmentReportSummary.pdf).

11

Scaling Up in Education: School-Based Management in Niger

SHUNICHIRO HONDA AND HIROSHI KATO

The implementation of a school-based management (SBM) policy in Niger offers ample lessons pertinent to the debate on scaling up development impact. The case involves the adaptation of an institutional model of primary school management to the specific and difficult environment of Niger; a goal of reaching national scale; supportive donor engagement and broad participation of national and local stakeholders; an effective learning process, in which alternative institutional models were tested and evaluated; and implementation of the preferred approach consistently over a decade and beyond.

The government of Niger officially adopted an SBM policy in 2002 as the core of its national education sector reform program. SBM is a popular policy worldwide, intended to improve the efficiency and effectiveness of school management, especially in low-income countries. At the core of the policy is the establishment of school councils (Comités de Gestion des Établissements Scolaires, or COGES) and the delegation of various responsibilities and decisionmaking to these councils.[1]

COGES were established in practically all primary schools throughout the country and continue to function reasonably well, having survived Niger's

---

1. In 2012 COGES was renamed CGDES (Comités de Gestion Décentralisée des Etablissements Scolaires), with a ministerial decree on February 2012 (EPT 2012). However, here we use COGES, as this is the name used throughout the period covered by this chapter.

political turmoil since the coup in 2010. Although it is too early to fully evaluate Niger's SBM, its achievements so far in Niger's extremely difficult environment must be judged as remarkable, and Niger's policy and institution-building process should be of general interest to the international development field.

Our analysis provides insights on such issues as how a policy of foreign origin was adapted and later scaled up regionally and nationally; how institutional and capacity constraints were overcome; and how various actors including the government, communities, NGOs, and external donors interacted with one another for mutual learning and knowledge creation. While none of the individual components of the SBM initiative in Niger presents an innovation per se, the overall process of introducing, systematically adapting, and rapidly scaling up a policy and institutional approach that had previously not been pursued in this fragile state represents a significant and innovative achievement.

The case in Niger is also an interesting study for education professionals. While many developing countries have tried to replicate SBM policy, with El Salvador's EDUCO seemingly the most successful model, experiences are mixed in terms of both implementation and educational impact.[2] The achievement in Niger could provide us with useful insights for improving the feasibility of the model in difficult conditions.

We base our analysis on an analytical framework for the scaling up of development policies and interventions developed and applied by Arntraud Hartmann and Johannes Linn.[3] Accordingly, we define the concept of scaling up as the process of "expanding, adapting, and sustaining successful policies, programs, or projects in different places and over time to reach a greater number of people." Critical in this framework is the notion of scaling-up pathways, which are defined as "the sequence of steps that need to be taken in the innovation–learning–scaling up cycle to assure that a successful pilot or practice is taken from its experimental stage through subsequent stages to the scale ultimately judged to be appropriate for the intervention pursued."[4] Along with these pathways, the process of scaling up should be looked at to see if factors such as the following are appropriately addressed:

—Defining the desired scale

—Focusing on key drivers (the forces that push the scaling-up process forward) and spaces (the opportunities that can be created, or potential obstacles that need to be removed to open up the space for interventions to grow)

—Defining intermediate results

—Selecting operational modalities for scaling up

2. Caldwell (2005); Bruns, Filmer, and Patrinos (2011).
3. Hartmann and Linn (2008).
4. Quotations from Linn (2012, p. 4).

—Putting monitoring and evaluation (M&E) in place for effective learning

—Avoiding the risks of paying inadequate attention to scaling up.

In applying this framework to the case of SBM in Niger we emphasize certain factors, such as dimensions, learning, key drivers and spaces, incentives and accountability, and institutional capacity, for which the Nigerien case can provide relevant lessons.

The following section provides a general description of SBM policy in Niger. In subsequent sections we explore the pathways of Niger's SBM scaling-up policy and the achievements of the policy in terms of the scaling-up process and outcome and in terms of the factors driving the scaling-up process and the spaces that were created, following the Hartmann and Linn framework. A final section presents a summary and conclusions.

Niger's Education Sector in Context

Niger is a landlocked, largely arid Sahel country. The country context is challenging in every respect: it is one of the least-developed countries, with a GNI per capita around $360 in 2011.[5] The country is at the bottom of the UN Development Program's human development index, with most indicators below average for sub-Saharan Africa.

The majority of the population subsists on rain-fed agriculture. The external economy relies heavily on the export of uranium; this product is easily affected by the volatile international market, one of the causes of the economic crisis in the 1990s. The combination of a challenging economic structure and weak capacity in domestic resource mobilization has long made Niger highly dependent on aid: a large part of development expenditures, including those in the education sector, has been externally financed, while domestic revenues are mostly used to pay the salaries of public employees.

Niger's population of 14 million is growing rapidly, though with a declining trend, the rapid growth implying a large annual increase in school entrants. The country's vast and sparsely populated territory, coupled with an underdeveloped transport infrastructure, poses a challenge for the delivery of such public services.

The country has gone through a challenging political process, having had a series of military coups since its independence. However, it experienced relative political stability during most of the period of this case study (the first decade of the 2000s), following a successful multiparty democratic election in 1999. This generally favorable political situation was interrupted by another coup in early 2010, following President Tandja's disputed referendum to extend his

5. GNI at current U.S. dollars. World Bank (2012).

presidential term. About a year later, Mahamadou Issoufou became president (in April 2011) through a democratic election that was generally seen as free and fair.

In the late 1990s and the early 2000s, education in Niger was in an appalling state. In 2000, just before Niger unveiled its long-term education program, the gross enrollment rate of primary education was only 33 percent, while the average corresponding figure for sub-Saharan African countries was 81 percent.[6] There were also marked gender and geographical disparities.

While statistics indicate that other aspects of education in the country urgently needed attention, tackling the issue of access to primary education became the core strategy of the country's education development program throughout the early 2000s. One important reason for this was the international Education for All (EFA) initiative, which supported the strengthening of primary education.

Niger's education sector had several severe constraints to deal with. Among them was its lack of efficiency, which was lower than the subregional average in West Africa. Higher salaries for full-time teachers, compared with those of its neighbors, placed a heavy burden on the budget and were one of the major causes of inefficiency in the sector.[7] Another problem was the overly centralized educational structure and the general lack of capacity of the Ministry of Education.[8] These led to the poor management of financial and human resources, resulting in frequent arrears in salary payment, teacher absenteeism, and regular teacher strikes.

Ten-Year Program for Education Development

This difficult context provided the backdrop for the launch of the 2002 national education development program, Programme Décennal de Développement de l'Éducation au Niger (PDDE), or the Ten-Year Program for Education Development in Niger.[9] PDDE was part of a sectorwide approach that combined all donor support to the sector, coupled with a common-basket fund. PDDE was developed around three main pillars: access, quality, and institutional development. PDDE prioritized the primary education subsector along with preschool and literacy programs; the government committed to allocating about half of the sector's budget to primary education during PDDE's implementation period.

PDDE comprised several important initiatives that aimed to ensure school access while controlling the number of schools and teachers and their costs.

---

6. World Bank (2012).
7. Bourdon, Frölich, and Michaelowa (2010).
8. UNESCO (2005).
9. MEBA (2002a).

Actions taken include the introduction of a contract teacher scheme—which had already been started in the late 1990s with donor assistance—and a hiring freeze on full-time teachers.[10] Another key element of PDDE was decentralization, and the introduction of SBM formed an integral part of this policy. One measure taken in this connection was the restructuring of the entire ministry so that greater responsibilities were delegated to newly appointed school inspectors and pedagogical advisers who operated below the regional level. Another measure was the devolution of decisionmaking authority for the management of schools to school management committees.

PDDE was implemented through medium-term action plans, covering three-to four- year periods, along with annual action plans. Monitoring was done through an annual and midterm joint review, which informed the programming of activities in subsequent periods. The review, jointly undertaken by the government and external partners (including international NGOs), examined the progress in each of the three subcomponents of PDDE, including SBM policy.

School-Based Management

In a nutshell, SBM in Niger is based on local school councils, called COGES, and two layers of monitoring designed to ensure that COGES function effectively: the first layer consists of federations of COGES (Fédération Communale des COGES, or FCCs); the second layer consists of forums, in which multiple stakeholders, including FCC representatives, can come together to address problems of common interest.

COGES are the central local agents in Niger's SBM system. According to a ministerial decree in 2003, each COGES was to be composed of at least six core members: three representatives from parent-teacher associations, from which the COGES president would be selected; one representative either from a school mothers' association or another women's group, who could act as treasurer; a school principal, who would act as COGES secretary; and a schoolteacher (figure 11-1). In addition, COGES could invite any person, as needed, to help the committee fulfill its mission.

With the participation of the parents of pupils and community members, as well as schoolteachers, COGES play many roles in school management. These roles include managing local grants as well as influencing decisions on contract teachers, in accordance with relevant government decrees. Under the COGES system, parents and villagers are expected to create their school activity plans and to contribute to the execution of these plans, through either financial or in-kind contributions. Other tasks include managing school activities at

---

10. Bourdon, Frölich, and Michaelowa (2010).

Figure 11-1. *Structure of COGES*[a]

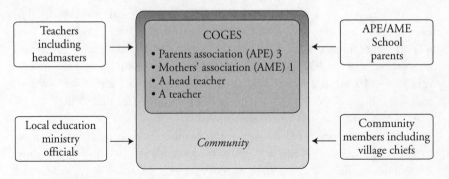

Source: Authors.
a. AME is Association de Mère d'École; APE is Association Parents des Écoles.

a community level; managing school infrastructure, equipment, and supplies; managing and monitoring the contracts of contract teachers; and managing school subsidies and community funds for local schools.[11]

When the COGES were put in place, it was understood that the local Nigerien government officials in charge would monitor the SBM system. As COGES were expanded to the entire country, it became evident, however, that monitoring by the limited number of COGES officers would no longer be viable. Around the time when the nationwide scaling up of COGES was decided on in 2005, there were only about fifty COGES officers in the entire country and close to 9,000 primary schools, making it necessary for one officer to cover more than 150 schools.

Given the budgetary limitations of the Nigerien government in hiring additional COGES officers, a new system had to be devised that would place as little burden as possible on these officers. The idea of an FCC with the principal task of monitoring COGES arose out of this necessity (figure 11-2).[12] The FCC system started in 2007 in two states and became functional nationwide by 2010. Its objective was to share experiences of school improvement activities through the COGES mechanism and to discuss concrete actions on important issues in the presence of major stakeholders. The activities of FCCs are financed through both the contributions from constituent COGES as well as locally mobilized resources including financial support from the local government.

11. MEBA (2003).
12. This idea was devised by Le projet École Pour Tous and supported by JICA.

Figure 11-2. *National COGES Monitoring Mechanism*

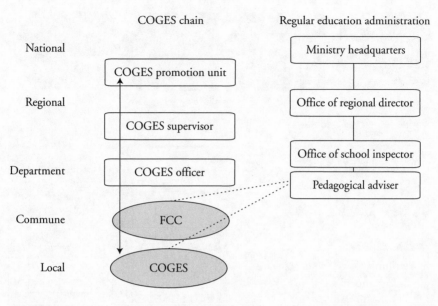

Source: Authors.

To further enhance the function of FCC, FCC forums were also introduced to address issues of common interest for many communities. This mechanism started in 2007 in two states and became functional nationwide by 2010. Its objective was to share experiences of school improvement activities through the COGES mechanism and to discuss concrete actions on important issues, such as the enrollment of girls in schools, in the presence of major stakeholders. The resulting overall institutional structure and main functions of the nationwide FCC system with FCC forums is shown in figure 11-3.

Scaling Up Pathways for Niger's School-Based Management

The approximately ten-year period of the development of Niger's SBM policy can be roughly subdivided into four phases:[13]

—First phase, 2002–05. During this period, SBM policy was officially adopted by the government, its legal and institutional frameworks were laid out, and pilot projects were started, covering 240 primary schools.

13. There were some overlaps between these phases, as some of the activities were conducted in parallel.

Figure 11-3. *The FCC System*

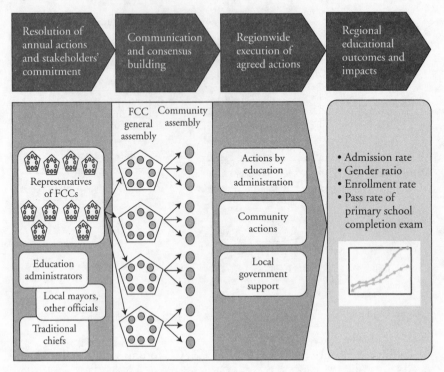

Source: Authors, adapted from Hara (2011, p. 152).

—Second phase, 2005–06. During this period, SBM policy was expanded by an April 2005 governmental decree to install COGES in all primary schools. As a result, the number of COGES increased from 240 to roughly 9,000 by 2005. At this stage, however, many of the COGES were yet to be fully functional.

—Third phase, 2004–08. During this phase, efforts were made to develop and test a standard model of COGES. This was to make sure that the COGES that were formally instituted nationwide in the 2005 decision would remain fully functional. The model was agreed on by stakeholders at a 2007 joint workshop and subsequently scaled up at a national level.

—Fourth phase, 2005 to present. During this phase, monitoring and evaluation systems were developed by implementing FCCs and introducing forums where stakeholders could come together to address educational issues.

In retrospect, SBM development in Niger could be said to have followed a rather ambitious and risky path, in that quantitative expansion and qualitative or systemic development progressed more or less simultaneously, since when the

Figure 11-4. *Overview of the Scaling-Up Pathway*

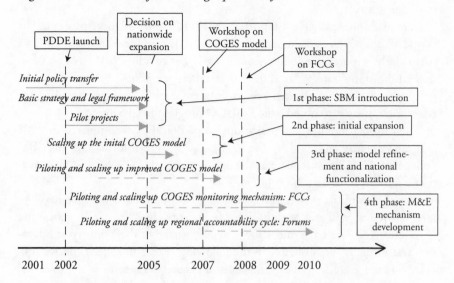

quantitative expansion was decided in 2005, systems to ensure the functionality of COGES were not fully in place (figure 11-4).

First Phase: SBM Introduction

In Niger the idea of establishing a democratic school committee in each school dates back to the second half of the 1990s. The Education Framework Act, enacted in 1998, was the country's first law clarifying the overall direction of national education policy. It called for contributions from all key stakeholders, including NGOs, private corporations, parents, and communities, with some clarification of roles and responsibilities in these efforts, along with a government commitment to provide universal access to quality primary education.[14]

The PDDE, introduced in 2002, formally mainstreamed SBM policy into its program. Its formulation was in part a follow-up action of the Dakar Conference on EFA in 2000 and was also triggered by the newly launched EFA Fast-Track Initiative (FTI) in 2002. Through the FTI, Niger was to get access to extra aid upon the endorsement of a coherent sector development plan by the EFA FTI board. The preparation process, which started in 2001, was undertaken through an extensive consultation with sector stakeholders, including donors and local actors such as ROSEN (a consortium of local NGOs active in education) and teacher unions. The government also undertook extensive

14. République du Niger (1998).

campaigns and outreach activities for EFA, including an annual EFA week and media program.[15]

Several donors actively supported the PDDE formulation process. The World Bank, which had the largest financial portfolio for education, played a particularly important role in encouraging Niger to adopt SBM as part of its decentralization strategy. In 2002, for instance, the World Bank facilitated a promotional tour that allowed key government decisionmakers, including the education minister, to observe the EDUCO program in El Salvador.

The formulation and national adoption of PDDE was completed in 2001 and subsequently endorsed by the EFA board.[16] PDDE formalized the SBM policy with COGES at its core as the national policy. The actual implementation of PDDE started in May 2003.

During this initial period, the government also proceeded with the development of a basic legal and organizational framework. In 2002 a joint committee to monitor COGES trials under the secretary general of the Ministry of Education was formally established.[17] In the following year, a ministerial decree provided a broad COGES policy rationale and general definitions of the roles and responsibilities of COGES stakeholders. The ministry also created a COGES Promotion Unit under the secretary general dedicated to coordinating and monitoring COGES policy. Other officers included COGES supervisors at the regional level and COGES advisers within the office of school inspectors, all of whom were to report directly to the COGES unit at headquarters.[18]

In parallel with the development of a basic strategy and legal framework for COGES implementation, the government, with the assistance of the World Bank, went ahead with the first COGES pilots in 240 schools in three regions—Diffa, Maradi, and Tillaberi—starting in February 2002. This preceded the formal adoption of PDDE. The government, through the engagement of contracted NGOs, undertook the training of pedagogical advisers, who served as education administrators at the lowest level, helping pilot schools and communities to organize COGES.

Second Phase: Initial Expansion

About one year after the beginning of the initial trials, an evaluation of the initial COGES pilots was undertaken with financial assistance from the World Bank. The results were shared at a workshop in September 2003 to confirm the feasibility and relevance of COGES as well as the lessons to be used toward standardization and scaling up.

15. Oumarou and Namata (2006).
16. UNESCO (2005).
17. MEBA (2002b).
18. MEBA (2004).

The overall assessment of the performance of the COGES trials was mixed.[19] The assessment certainly validates the relevance and feasibility of introducing SBM in the context of Niger. In the target areas, 88.9 percent of the population surveyed viewed COGES as their own organizations. In terms of their impact on school management, the assessment records a reduction in the loss of school materials in 74.4 percent of pilot schools. The interviews conducted in non-pilot areas show that all the key stakeholders—teachers, local government officials, local populations, and NGOs—welcomed the establishment of COGES to improve educational systems.

In spite of these positive results, the assessment also reveals that the approach and the model used during the initial trials were poorly designed and not ready for further expansion.[20] The report states that the initial trials did not pay sufficient attention to the functionality and capacity of COGES. Among its recommendations for further action, the report urges stakeholders to

—Further refine the approach to and instruments for organizing COGES

—Provide further capacity-building programs, especially for COGES members, to allow them to assume broader responsibilities

—Develop and strengthen the monitoring and coordination mechanism of COGES at various administrative levels

—Promote collaboration between the government and nongovernmental actors such as NGOs and international donors

—Provide clearer guidance on the roles and responsibilities of the multiple actors engaging in COGES

Following the evaluation, a debate began on when and how COGES should be scaled up. Two broad options were suggested. One was to continue an incremental approach, gradually expanding the coverage of COGES through the annual addition of a thousand new COGES. With this approach, it was expected that national scaling up would be completed in about six to seven years. Another option was establishing COGES in all primary schools as fast as possible.

The latter was eventually chosen as one of the agreed actions of the PDDE annual plan for 2004–05, which was linked to the World Bank's basic education project. Then at the joint COGES meeting in March 2005, the ministry presented a new COGES strategy, announcing its decision to complete scaling up the existing 9,000 schools within a matter of months.[21] Apart from fulfilling the PDDE action, the ministry explained that the rapid COGES expansion was necessary to enable it to distribute textbooks procured through World Bank financing to all schools with the help of COGES.[22]

19. Maïna (2003).
20. Maïna (2003).
21. This includes those schools under donor-assisted pilots.
22. EPT (2005).

The government proceeded by issuing a decree to institute COGES in all primary schools, providing basic training to officials involved in COGES matters using available materials, except those COGES that were already part of donor-assisted projects. Through this rapid exercise, COGES were officially installed in all primary schools by October 2005, when the annual joint PDDE review session was held.[23]

The same review, however, also raised concerns about the limited functionality of the newly installed COGES which the Ministry also acknowledged. To rectify the situation, the report strongly urged several actions including the clarification of the roles and responsibilities of stakeholders, further capacity building, and the development and introduction of sustainable monitoring mechanisms. This necessitated the qualitative development of the system, which was dealt with in the next phase.

Third Phase: Model Refinement and National COGES Functionalization

While the government (with the assistance of the World Bank) was proceeding with its own pilots and the initial scaling up, several donors simultaneously initiated their own education projects with COGES components. These projects started in the first few years of the 2000s in response to a government request for multiple donor trials for better COGES models. Donors included the European Union; the French NGO Aide et Action, which acts as an executive organization for L'Agence Française de Développement (AFD); UNICEF; the Irish NGO Concern Worldwide; and the Japan International Cooperation Agency (JICA).

All these projects had adopted a pilot approach in either targeting specific administrative units or targeting schools (numbering 70 to 1,000). These projects made efforts to adapt and test their own COGES approaches within the broad guidance established by the government. Key ministry officials, including the head of the COGES Promotion Unit, and donor representatives shared and discussed matters related to COGES at monthly PDDE partners' meetings as well as at specially organized COGES meetings.

Following the first round of national COGES scaling up in 2005, when most of the COGES were only partially functioning at best, the focus of these donor-assisted multiple pilots was on the development and field testing of a more refined COGES model, to help revitalize the existing COGES. The challenge, then, was to determine in what ways the different approaches of the pilots pursued by different donors could be mainstreamed into a common national strategy.

Through a dialogue, the government and the education partners agreed to undertake an external evaluation of the major donor-assisted COGES pilots

23. EPT (2005).

and to discuss the results of their evaluation at a workshop for a revised standard national COGES strategy. Over the following months, consultants started assessing the five major COGES pilots: the projects of the EU, the AFD, UNICEF, JICA, and Concern Worldwide. The three main themes of the assessment, with their underlying questions regarding replicability and sustainability, were the approach to establishing COGES, capacity building, and the mechanism of support, monitoring, and evaluation.

Due to the lack of field data and time limitations, the evaluation was done not by using rigorous impact-assessment methodologies but by relying on an ordinary project evaluation method, including document reviews, interviews with key actors both at headquarters and in the field, observations in the field, and interviews of local stakeholders.

At a three-day workshop in April 2007 organized by the Education Ministry, a broad range of stakeholders gathered and discussed the evaluation results with the objective of agreeing on a revised standard COGES strategy. Those who attended were key ministry officials including the secretary general, and staff of donor organizations and international NGOs. The main consensus that emerged at the workshop was that a model strategy for COGES should include the following components:[24]

—Democratic election of COGES members by secret ballot

—Full engagement of the community in making key decisions

—Reinforced capacity building

—Support of school activities mainly through the mobilization of local resources

—Support and monitoring mainly through government officers

—Formation of COGES federations at the community level to strengthen monitoring and support

Table 11-1 presents the two competing options discussed at the 2007 workshop. Plan B was eventually selected as the more suitable for Niger.

Following the validation of a revised COGES strategy at the workshop, the government embarked on a second round of scaling up in June 2007, with the objective of mainstreaming the revised COGES model to all primary schools where COGES was now established. The revised model was called the COGES minimum package. The term *minimum package* had a dual meaning: first, it had the minimum essential components to make COGES functional, and second, it was designed so that the costs to run COGES were kept to the minimum possible, including financial contributions from outside.

The scaling-up exercise was jointly supported by JICA and the World Bank, the former providing technical assistance in collaboration with Organisation

24. A major part of these components was drawn from the EPT initiative model.

Table 11-1. *Alternative Options Considered for COGES Institutional Setup*

	Plan A	Plan B
COGES member selection	Show of hands at the community assembly	Secret ballot at the community assembly
Community involvement	Frequent consultation through community assembly	Frequent consultation as well as key decisionmaking through community assembly
Donor-supported financial input for school activities	School activity plan financed by both local resources and donor-supported financial assistance	School activity plans financed within the limits of locally mobilized resources

Nigérienne des Educateurs Novateurs (ONEN), a Nigerien local NGO, and the latter providing financial assistance.[25]

One of the challenges in the scaling up of the functioning COGES model was holding democratic elections of COGES members. Before the second round of scaling up, there was a concern that incumbent COGES members, who had already been selected by consensus in the first round in 2005, would resist democratic elections in which they could be unseated. As it turned out, however, though there were some isolated incidents where unseated incumbents refused to step down, the election of COGES members generally progressed smoothly, partly thanks to carefully designed preparation with good training prior to the elections as well as the use of community assemblies for resolving such disputes.

In February 2008 the national scaling up of the COGES minimum model to all 10,000 primary schools in the eight regions was completed.[26]

Fourth Phase: The M&E Mechanism Development

After the national scaling up of the COGES minimum package, the next issue to emerge was the need to establish an adequate national mechanism to support and monitor COGES. Two mechanisms were put in place: the COGES federations, or FCCs, and the forums involving these FCCs.

The government made an effort to gradually develop and strengthen its capacity to monitor and support COGES. For example, COGES officers in most of the school inspector's offices were appointed. In addition, a senior education administrator was appointed as a COGES supervisor at the regional director's office. The role of the senior education administrator was as an adviser

25. World Bank (2009).
26. The roll-out of the "COGES minimum" was completed through the EPT in the two regions of Tahoua and Zinder ahead of the other six regions. Between 2005 and 2008, over a thousand new schools were added in an effort to improve school access.

to COGES officers and as a liaison between the regional office and the central COGES Promotion Unit at ministry headquarters. As already explained, by the time the government had established COGES in all 9,000 schools in 2005, it had become apparent that the government structure fell far short of being able to effectively monitor them. The idea of federating COGES came out of the need to devise a monitoring mechanism that imposed the least burden on COGES officers.

To develop a workable model for such a system, a few donor-assisted pilots went ahead to develop and test the FCC model. As a follow-up to the recommendations made at the COGES workshop in 2007, an external evaluation and another workshop for a common strategy on FCCs was added to the second mid-term PDDE action plan (2008 to 2010). A joint workshop for the validation of a standard FCC strategy was organized in July 2008, with major stakeholders attending. The pilots evaluated were those developed by EPT-JICA, Souteba-EU, and Concern Worldwide.[27] EPT and Concern Worldwide used a similar approach in most aspects, including financing and the formation of a federation.[28]

The final national model for FCC was decided based on a sustainable and replicable design that made maximum use of the locally available capacity of COGES as well as that of COGES officers.[29] To formalize what was agreed on at the workshop, in October 2008 the ministry issued a decree that formed the legal basis for the Fédération Communale des COGES.[30] In October 2009, with assistance from JICA and ONEN, the ministry started the national scaling up of FCCs to six regions (excluding only Tahoua and Zinder).[31] By around July 2009 the national scaling up of FCCs was completed in five regions (leaving Agadez, whose sparse population and underdeveloped transportation made it difficult to establish FCCs).

While the national scaling up of the COGES minimum package and FCCs was under way, a new initiative with the objective of consolidating COGES' functions began. The initiative's intent was to take advantage of the presence of FCCs to address issues of common interest to many communities through shared forums. These forums started in 2007, first in Tahoua and then in Zinder.

Forum participants, other than the FCC representatives, included key education officials such as regional directors, school inspectors, secretaries general, and national COGES coordinators, from both the region and headquarters. Also included were local actors: representatives of regional teacher unions and parent associations plus other social-political leaders, including governors, mayors,

27. Souteba is Programme de soutien a l'education de base.
28. MEN (2008a).
29. A major part of the accepted FCC model was drawn from the EPT initiative model.
30. MEN (2008b).
31. In these states the federations were already in place through the EPT project.

community council members, traditional chiefs, and local religious leaders. These regional forums typically followed an annual action cycle:
—Analysis and selection of a priority issue in the region
—Holding a regional forum
—Communicating through both COGES and the education administration structure
—Community activities
—Monitoring results and feedback

By 2010 all eight regions held such forums, which helped to broaden the stakeholder base for improving primary education below the regional level.

The forums also served to align the COGES structure with, and incorporate it into, the regular educational administration. Stakeholders, including inspectors, agreed that they would play a larger role in COGES-related activities by attending monthly regional inspectors' meetings starting in February 2008.[32] Monthly regional inspectors' meetings started to play a key role in a broader range of regional education issues beyond COGES matters, providing the space to share experience and information. For example, field data such as the enrollment rate and the level of local resource mobilization of COGES in school improvement activities, came to be shared with administrators. In recognition of their important role, the education minister issued a directive to formalize the monthly inspectors' meetings in January 2009.[33]

Achievements of Niger's School-Based Management

One achievement of Niger's school-based management policy is the continuing presence and functioning of COGES. In the 2010–11 fiscal year, regional education offices collected reports of school activities from 12,666 COGES, which is over 95 percent of the national total. An analysis of the collected reports suggests that, on average, a COGES conducts 5.6 activities. The local resources that were mobilized amounted, on average, to 135,301 CFA francs a year, which is equivalent to approximately $260 at current rates.[34]

Though the survey data on the level of community participation in COGES-related activities are limited, several interviews conducted during the project evaluation indicate that community members were well engaged in community general assemblies and activities. This general observation is supported by a recent comparative research project conducted in selected West and Central

---

32. Monthly meetings of COGES officers at the regional level had been taking place since the mid-2000s, well before the start of the inspectors' meeting. JICA (2007).

33. MEN (2010).

34. EPT (2011).

African countries.[35] Its Niger research team conducted surveys and interviews in six community councils, which were selected according to such criteria as climate, population structure, and geographical location. The team found that 146 out of 149 respondents answered that they knew of the existence of COGES in their local area. About 67 percent of respondents said that they were involved in the management of schools.

Another achievement of Niger's school-based management policy are the federations of COGES, or FCCs. Despite the difficult context of Niger, most FCCs remain active, operate reasonably effectively, and undertake such activities as sensitization training and the monitoring of COGES. Of the 266 FCCs in the country, 249, or 93.6 percent, have held three or more general assemblies and six or more secretariat meetings; 252 FCCs (94.7 percent) have conducted more than one activity related to school improvement.[36] In terms of financial mobilization, 11,210 COGES, or 84.3 percent of the total, have contributed to FCCs. The average amount of mobilized resources per FCC, including contributions from local COGES, was 398,465 CFA francs, or about $770.[37]

Educational outcomes have also been favorably affected by Niger's school-based management policy. For example, the primary admission rate improved in the years following the scaling up of the COGES minimum package (figure 11-5). However, there is no clear evidence for any significant changes in the quality of education at the national level, judging from the primary school completion rate and completion examinations.

Nevertheless, there are indications of the potential contribution of COGES and related activities to education quality. Take for instance the improvement of the pass rate of primary school completion exam (CFEPD) in the Zinder region. In 2008 Zinder recorded a considerably higher pass rate (67.2 percent) than the previous year (54.5 percent), and it was the top-rated region among the country's eight regions. This noticeable improvement coincided with the Zinder regional education forum of 2008, which adopted the improvement of the CFEPD pass rate as the annual priority action, along with the promotion of remedial classes and mock exams.[38] At the Zinder forum in 2009, participants cited the possible contribution of actions taken in 2008 to the improved education outcomes in the year.[39]

There have been several efforts to replicate the success of Niger's SBM policy. The first such move, beginning in 2007, was the extension of COGES

35. ROCARE/ERNWACA (2011).

36. Activities include use of the "sensitization caravan" and the use of community radio for information dissemination. Hara (2011).

37. EPT (2011).

38. Hara (2011).

39. EPT (2009).

Figure 11-5. *School Admission and Enrollment Rates, 2003–11*

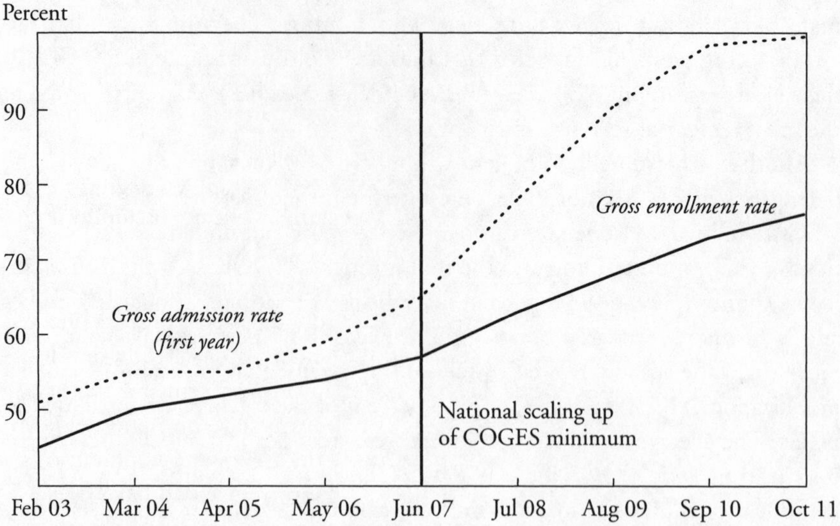

Percent

Source: Authors' calculations, based on MEBA/MEN (various years).

into pre-schools. This was supported by several donors including JICA (EPT) and UNICEF.[40] The Education Ministry has also embarked on an extension of COGES into junior secondary schools.[41]

As for the achievement of scaling up, several neighboring countries, including Burkina Faso, Senegal, and Mali, have started to apply the SBM model developed in Niger to their own pilot programs.[42] In Mali, where the decentralization of the local government has progressed more than in Niger, the model has been modified so that local governments take responsibility for monitoring school management committees in lieu of the decentralized branches of education ministries. So far, more than a thousand COGES have been established in these countries.

To identify the enabling—and, where applicable, impeding—factors that have affected the scaling-up process in the development of Niger's SBM policy, we revisit the pathways, using the analytical framework introduced at the beginning of this chapter.

40. EPT (2007).
41. JICA (2012).
42. JICA is supporting these projects, based on its experience in Niger. The equivalent of Niger's COGES is called Comité de Gestion de l'École (CGE) in Senegal and Comité de Gestion Scolaire (CGS) in Mali.

Dimensions of Scaling Up

There were two dimensions to the scaling up of Niger's SBM policy: horizontal (quantitative) scaling up and vertical (functional) scaling up. Horizontal scaling up expanded the initial pilot program of 240 schools to all 9,000 primary schools in the country.[43] However, the full operationalization of COGES policy had to await the completion of a vertical scaling-up process, which involved setting nationwide policy and establishing regulatory and institutional systems (including COGES) and monitoring and evaluation systems (including FCCs and forums).

One interesting observation about the scaling up of Niger's SBM policy is its sequence. As we observed above (figure 11-3), the decision to expand nationwide was made relatively early on, in 2005, when neither a fully developed functional COGES model nor appropriate monitoring systems for the project were in place. One could argue that the decision to scale up nationwide was premature and risky, for if it had not been for the timely development of the COGES model and the monitoring systems, the project could have faced the problem of suboptimal functionality. Fortunately, the efforts of all the stakeholders, including the government, villagers, teachers, and donors, helped to circumvent this mistake.

MONITORING AND EVALUATION. M&E was a key factor for learning and accountability in the process of scaling up SBM, and the successful introduction of FCCs and forums was critical in ensuring functional M&E for the project. The idea of the FCCs was to ensure proper monitoring, learning, and accountability, while imposing as little burden as possible on COGES officers. The FCCs addressed issues of mutual interest to many communities and helped align COGES activities with the normal educational administration. Both of these mechanisms have been functioning reasonably well.

Yet devising these mechanisms and putting them in place is one thing; making them operative and keeping them functional for a long time is quite another. Behind the successful operation of these mechanisms were carefully elaborated working procedures.[44]

IDEAS AND MODELS. A number of important ideas and models were developed by the project that supported the scaling up of the SBM policy in Niger. The most obvious one is the standardized institutional model of COGES. The model is based on the understanding that, in order for COGES to be functional,

---

43. Subsequently, the total number of primary schools equipped with COGES increased to about 13,000.
44. Hara (2011).

first, they had to be transparent and legitimate organizationally; second, full community engagement was needed in key decisions; and third, participation had to be authentic.

The functional COGES model, or the COGES minimum package, was devised to make sure that each COGES was armed with these abilities and characteristics. The model has three components:

—A democratic election system, which nominates organization leaders by secret ballot

—A school action plan, which incorporates all the actions to support the school agreed on and approved at the community assembly

—A monitoring system, which manages COGES

Masahiro Hara, who served as chief adviser for JICA's EPT project, recalls his experience on how this COGES minimum package model worked:

> As the project progressed, I found that the transparency of the organization was the key that allowed the will and latent potential of the residents to be brought out. Experience shows that, for example, it is generally easy to mobilize residents and their resources in villages where there is an encouraging atmosphere that allows residents to voice their opinions and share information during occasions such as resident assemblies and parent meetings.[45]

The most provocative part of the standard COGES model was the introduction of secret ballots in electing COGES leaders; the idea actually drew a lot of opposition, even when it was being piloted in the EPT project supported by JICA. As it turned out, however, it worked; the anonymous election system piloted in JICA's EPT project won the support of many residents, heightening residents' trust in COGES, leading to their improved performance. With this proven achievement, the component was accepted, after some debate, at the September 2007 workshop.

EXTERNAL CATALYSTS. At the policy level, the adoption of SBM policy in Niger itself was strongly influenced by the opinions of external donors. As noted at the outset, SBM was widely promoted through the global EFA initiative, mainly by UNESCO and the World Bank, with the latter serving as the secretariat of the FTI.[46] Not only was EFA a political statement, it was also linked to additional financial resources through the FTI mechanism.

---

45. Hara (2011, p. 82), translated by the authors.
46. EFA-FTI changed its name to Global Partnership for Education (GPE) with the movement toward a more autonomous management structure.

External donors seem to have strongly influenced the contents of the mid-term and annual actions plans as a quasi-conditionality in pressing specific policy actions, as in the case of the initial rapid scaling up of COGES in 2005, with the objective of distributing textbooks to schools. On the other hand, most of the COGES-related actions in the annual and midterm plans played the role of expediting policy implementations, such as the external evaluations, the joint workshop for national COGES-related strategies, and the development and revision of legal instruments. Overall, the policy cycles mentioned above, as well as the ownership of the policy by key education officials, helped maintain a space for dialogue and policy learning throughout the period.

Operationally, too, external actors played very important roles. As we noted earlier, the scaling-up process of Niger's SBM policy was only possible because of the knowledge and experience that was accumulated from the various projects supported by donors such as the World Bank, the EU, AFD, and JICA, along with international and local NGOs such as Aide et Action, Concern World-wide, and ONEN.

INCENTIVES AND ACCOUNTABILITY. Various studies have attested to the demand for better education among the Nigerien population.[47] A participatory survey undertaken as part of Niger's First Full Poverty Reduction Strategy Paper reported that education is a priority for the poor.[48] The fact that many communities had already taken action to improve school environments, such as the construction of straw classrooms without any external support, is another sign of people's strong demand for improved education.[49] In spite of this demand, the same assessments reported that people's trust in, and sense of ownership of, the schools and school education were generally low among Nigeriens.

Given these circumstances, strengthening weak accountability mechanisms and processes was considered to be key. At the community level, accountability mechanisms were generally unclear in the work of APE (Association Parents des Écoles) and their secretariats, which often resulted in distrust of APE secretariat members. As the education administration was highly centralized, there was no clear accountability framework linking local communities, schools, and the education administration. The situation was no better at the central level, given the absence of a clear results-oriented policy and institutional framework.

47. Oumarou and Namata (2006) report that awareness has been strengthened through the basic education awareness campaign, engaging broad stakeholders including trade unions and parents associations.

48. République du Niger (2002).

49. JICA (2002); Hara (2011). A field interview conducted by one of the authors in Niger also supports this point.

The Education Framework Act and the PDDE were intended to usher in a more results-oriented accountability framework, with a shorter accountability route through COGES. However, the accountability cycle, particularly at the community level, as well as its connection to the local education administration, continued to be weak in most parts of the country, except for some pockets that had donor-assisted pilots.

The introduction of the SBM policy helped ameliorate this problem. Talking about the advantages of the model developed in JICA's EPT project (which later developed into the standard COGES model), Hara observes the following:

> School action plans have been introduced in virtually all of the projects operating at the school level, but they have had numerous problems. Among these, I have always felt that the most detrimental was the fact that local resident participation in the planning process was partial, superficial, and inadequate.
>
> In many of the projects, action planning processes are determined by a small fraction of the central members of parents' associations and school management committees. The plans formulated by these groups are then approved, only formally or nominally, in general parents' associations or residents' assemblies. Local residents felt that these plans, which had been drafted without their knowledge, were being forced on them from above. Under these circumstances, the voluntary participation of residents could not grow.
>
> In our project, we designed the model so that local residents would be encouraged to participate directly in the planning process, and so that important topics would be discussed at residents' assemblies, such as assessing school conditions, identifying issues, finalizing actions, and various other evaluations.
>
> Thanks to this model, residents' assemblies began to be held more frequently, and information was consistently shared with the public; transparency, the most important functional component of the COGES, was maintained.[50]

POLITICAL SPACE. The transition to a multiparty democracy provided a generally favorable country context for the introduction of the SBM policy, which is itself participatory and democratic. Through democratic elections, people became more accustomed to the democratic process.

---

50. Hara (2011, pp. 85–86), translated by the authors.

The Tandja government was committed to poverty reduction and social development, with primary education as its top priority. Though criticism of its inefficacy and populist nature persisted, the launch of the special presidential program reinforced belief in the Tandja government's commitment.[51] The timing of the SBM policy coincided with the government's implementation of a general decentralization policy, including the establishment of local health and water committees. Thus successive sector ministers were generally supportive of the decentralization and COGES policies.

POLICY AND INSTITUTIONAL SPACE. Several instrumental developments during the late 1990s as well as the early years of the 2000s created a favorable policy and legal environment for SBM policy.

For instance, the Education Framework Act of 1998 articulated the policy of decentralization, with a larger role for the community and other nongovernmental actors in school management. PDDE was triggered by this act. The act also provided legitimacy for the politically challenging COGES policy, as evidenced by the continual reference to the act as the fundamental basis of COGES policy in almost all key government documents and donor reports.

The ownership of the approach by key civil servants was critical to the smooth implementation of the policy. Among these, administrators such as the secretary general, the director general of basic education, and the head of the Promotion Unit, who were directly responsible for its implementation, were supportive of the COGES policy from early on. Their participation in the promotional tour for the El Salvador EDUCO program early in 2003 might also have deepened their understanding of the policy.

With this generally favorable policy and legal framework in place at the beginning of the execution of the SBM policy, another challenge was how to localize the SBM framework, which was largely constructed from global best practices, initially without sufficient local adaptation. Over time, an incremental process of reformulating and revising implementation strategies and guidelines was followed in Niger, including enacting new and revised ministerial decrees that drew on the lessons and experiences gained through the pilots. The success of this institutional adaptation was made possible by close consultations via the various meetings, workshops, and conferences within the PDDE cycle.

FISCAL AND FINANCIAL SPACE. Partly affected by delays and volatility in the overall level of donor funding, the execution report of the first PDDE midterm plan notes that most of the allocated budget was absorbed by school

51. BBC (2010).

construction and teacher and administrator salaries, while the remainder of the very limited budget had to meet the two pillars of quality and institutional development.[52]

Under these circumstances, dealing with these harsh fiscal and financial constraints was a major concern for SBM planners and practitioners. A key factor for a reasonably successful scaling-up process was the adoption of a system that placed the utmost importance on cost savings at both the community level (COGES) and the district level (FCCs). Again, talking about the COGES model developed by the JICA project, Masahiro Hara notes that "a characteristic of our model for school action plans was that they did not rely on external funding; rather, we made sure that the plans were implementable with the available funds in the villages or schools, or were within reach of the local residents. Through this principle, our planned actions became more immediate, realistic, and reliable."[53]

Ibo Issa, national coordinator of ONEN and also an adviser for the EPT, commented: "For example, in planning, local residents' labor was given a monetary value, which was counted as the cost of the action, and this information was then shared publicly. It therefore became possible for even poor villagers with meager monetary endowments to participate in action plans. In this way a significant level of participation and contribution from local residents was achieved, leading to a variety of accomplishments."[54]

LEARNING SPACE. A notable aspect of Niger's SBM policy was that the learning process took place at multiple interlinked levels, thanks to the conscious efforts of various stakeholders.

As already noted, the PDDE policy process at the central level provided a critically important policy learning space, largely made possible through sustained partnerships between the government and the donor community including international NGOs. Activities that provided space for policy learning among actors included joint evaluations of alternative models, joint selection of the preferred model based on the results of the evaluations, and joint support for implementation certainly.

Such a supportive sector environment also facilitated the process of knowledge-sharing and knowledge-creation among stakeholders, especially through the organization of joint workshops. It should be remembered that the models and ideas presented in the 2007 workshop had been tried and tested by many actors in their respective pilot projects. It was this ample body of knowledge and

---

52. MEN (2007).
53. Hara (2011).
54. Ibo Issa, interview with one of the authors, Niamey, July 2011.

experience accumulated through small-scale piloting and feedback activities that solidified the decisionmaking process.

Multistakeholder learning also occurred at lower levels. This included regional forums, monthly meetings among inspectors and COGES officers, and general assemblies of FCCs and community assemblies with COGES. These mechanisms allowed the SBM policy to be effectively followed up at the national, regional, and local levels, and provided opportunities for experimentation and adaptation to suit the special and difficult conditions in Niger.

CULTURAL SPACE. The functioning of a COGES relies on people's acceptance of and participation in it. Therefore, a major challenge was the development of a participatory COGES model that would enhance collective practices in the community according to the local context. Past attempts such as APE and the initial attempt at a school committee in the late 1990s were not completely successful in this regard.

Among the several major bottlenecks that had led to ineffective practices in the past, the most crucial was insufficient transparency in the management of activities. Leaders were usually elected by consensus, and quite often a handful of influential people dominated these committees, regardless of their management capabilities. Even when leaders were committed to school reform, they often took action without broad community support.

One critical instrument to help ameliorate this problem is the election of COGES leaders by anonymous ballot. Hara and Issa testify that in their experience the system of electing leaders by secret ballot gained widespread local support and helped select motivated and capable leaders. Furthermore, it enhanced residents' trust in the COGES, and eventually led to their participation in various activities.[55]

Summary and Conclusions

Since its official commencement in 2002, school-based management in Niger has been steadily scaled up: COGES have been established in virtually all primary schools in the country; federations of COGES, or FCCs, which serve as monitoring and information-sharing systems, have been established; and forums, which serve to align SBM with the regular educational administration, have also been established. All in all, the scaling-up process can be judged as having been successful.

Among the factors that have contributed to this outcome, the following are the most noteworthy:

55. Hara (2011).

—Vertical scaling up (for example, the development of national policies and monitoring systems) generally went hand in hand with horizontal (quantitative) scaling up.

—The workable ideas and models of COGES and its monitoring system were devised through an active, participatory process among many concerned stakeholders (villagers, teachers, government, and donors).

—Although some of the model selection and scaling-up decisions were in part driven by donors, government ownership was preserved, key stakeholders were engaged, and critical partnerships were developed and sustained.

—Alternative models were tested with the support of various donors, who subsequently supported a single, sector-wide approach based on the results of interim joint evaluation.

—A continuous learning and adaptation process ensured that a model introduced from abroad was adapted to local conditions in Niger.

—The far-reaching accountability of the COGES organizational structure was ensured through the democratic election of COGES leaders by secret ballot and participatory decisionmaking.

—The system's cost was kept within the constraints faced by villagers and the government.

—Institution- and capacity-building efforts specifically focused on supporting the SBM institutional model.

One important caveat, however, is that the process of scaling up Niger's SBM did not progress according to a preplanned schedule; in fact, the process made its way step by step, each step driven by necessities as they arose and based on the preceding step. This in itself is not a shortcoming in a context where blueprints of long-term policy and institutional development are generally not much help. The fact that key actors, domestic and foreign, had a long-term vision and goal of achieving national scale and pursued this in a flexible, participatory approach, was critical.

Scaling up is often just a buzzword among development practitioners, and commitment to an adaptive process and planning for scaling up is given insufficient attention. However, actual scaling-up cases, such as that of Niger, can further our understanding of what constitutes an effective approach to scaling up development impact.

References

BBC. 2010. Profile: Mamadou Tandja (https://news.bbc.co.uk/2/hi/africa/8181537.stm).

Bourdon, Jean, Markus Frölich, and Katharina Michaelowa. 2010. "Teacher Shortages, Teacher Contracts and Their Effect on Education in Africa." *Journal of the Royal Statistical Society.* Series A (*Statistics in Society*) 173, no. 1: 93–116.

Bruns, Barbara, Deon Filmer, and Harry Anthony Patrinos. 2011. *Making Schools Work: New Evidence on Accountability Reforms.* World Bank.

Caldwell, Brian J. 2005. "School-Based Management." Education Policy Series 3. UNESCO.

EPT (Le projet École Pour Tous). 2005. "Monthly Report: May 2005." Niamey.

———. 2007. "Project Newsletter: November 2007."

———. 2009. "Monthly Report: March 2009."

———. 2011. "EPT Phase 2, 7th Progress Report."

———. 2012. *Newsletter of School for All Projects in West Africa,* vol. 5, October.

Hara, Masahiro. 2011. *Nishi Africa no Kyoiku wo Kaeta Nihonhatsu no Gijyutsu Kyoryoku* [A story of Japanese technical cooperation in a West African country]. Tokyo: Diamond.

Hartmann, Arntraud, and Johannes Linn. 2008. "Scaling Up: A Framework and Lessons for Development Effectiveness from Literature and Practice." Working Paper 5. Wolfensohn Center for International Development, Brookings.

JICA (Japan International Cooperation Agency). 2002. *Report of the Basic Study on the Basic Education in Francophone West African Countries* (in Japanese). Tokyo.

———. 2007. *Report of the Final Evaluation of the Project of Support to the Improvement of School Management through Community Participation ("School for All").*

———. 2012. "School for All: The Project on Support to Educational Development through Community Participation." JICA Knowledge Site.

Linn, Johannes. 2012. "Scaling-Up Development Interventions: A Review of UNDP's Country Program in Tajikistan." Working Paper 50. Global Economy and Development, Brookings.

Maïna, Ali Ramadan Sékou. 2003. *Etude pour l'Evaluation et la Généralisation des Comités de gestion des Etablissements Scolaires (COGES).* Niamey: Ministère de l'Education de Base et de l'Alphabétisation, République du Niger.

MEBA (Ministère de l'Education de Base et de l'Alphabétisation). 2002a. *Programme Decennal de Developpment de l' éducation de Base (PDDE).* Niamey.

———. 2002b. "Arrêté n°0045/MEB/DEB du 06 mai 2002, portant création, attributions et composition du comité national de suivi des comités de gestion des établissements du Cycle de Base I." Niamey.

———. 2003. "Arrêté 070/MEB1/A/SG/DECB/DAF du 16 mai 2003 portant création, composition et fonctionnement des Comités de Gestion des Etablissements Scolaires." Niamey.

———. 2004. "Arrêté n°00027/MEB1/SG du 17 Février 2004 Modifiant l'Arrêté n° 0098/MEB1/A du 4 juillet 2003 portant création. Attributions et composition d'une Cellule de Promotion des Comités de Gestion des Etablissements scolaires (CP/COGES)." Niamey.

MEBA (Ministère de l'Education de Base et de l'Alphabétisation)/MEBA (Ministère de l'Education de Base et de l'Alphabétisation) /MEN (Ministère de l'Education Nationale). Annuaire Statistique. Various Issues. 2006/07–2010/11. Niamey.

MEN (Ministère de l'Education Nationale). 2007. "Rapport d'Execution de la Premiere Phase du Programme Decennal de Developpment de l'Education. Niamey.

———. 2008a. "Evaluation des COGES Communaux dans les Regions de Tahoua, Zinder, Dosso et Tillaberi." Niamey: Cellule de Promotion des COGES.

———. 2008b. "Arrêté N°0168/MEN/SG/DGEB du 24 octobre 2008, portant création, composition et fonctionnement Fédérations Communales des Comités de Gestion des Etablissements Scolaires." Niamey.

———. 2010. "Document Cadre de Suivi dans la Mise en Oeuvre de la Gestion Décentralisée de l'école : Rôles et Responsabilités des Acteurs." Niamey: Cellule de Promotion des COGES.

Oumarou, Hamissou, and Issa Namata. 2006. "Basic Education Awareness Campaign Conducted in Niger with Trade Unions, Parents' Representatives and Political Authorities at Various Levels." *Prospects* 36, no. 1.

République du Niger. 1998. "LOI n° 98-12 du 1er juin 1998, portant orientation du système éducatif nigérien." Niamey.

———. 2002. "Full Poverty Reduction Strategy." Niamey.

ROCARE/ERNWACA (Educational Research Network for West and Central Africa). 2011. "Transnational Research Decentralization in West and Central Africa: Learning from Local and Intersectoral Lessons (Education, Water, Health)." Summary Report of Case Studies. Bamako.

UNESCO. 2005. "Capacité de mise en oeuvre des plans de développement de l'éducation: Cas du Niger." *Politiques et Stratégies d'éducation* 9.

World Bank. 2009. "Implementation Completion and Results Report on a Credit to the Republic of Niger for a Basic Education Project." Education Sector, Africa Region.

———. 2012. *World Bank Development Indicators 2012.*

12

Scaling Up Impact through Public-Private Partnerships

JANE NELSON

There is growing consensus among development practitioners, policymakers, and business leaders that public-private partnerships offer untapped potential for catalyzing and scaling effective development interventions. Such partnerships are not new. They have a long-standing and in some cases contested history both within developed countries and in the field of international development. Over the past fifty years they have been used, in particular, as a mechanism to share the costs and risks of financing, building, and operating public infrastructure projects, from transportation to energy and water utilities. In the past two decades, they have become more common in other sectors such as health, nutrition, education, agriculture, information and communications technology, and financial services. Today, they are widely promoted as a tool for leveraging diverse resources, skills, and capacities to overcome some of the governance gaps and market failures that limit the ability of either publicly subsidized models or for-profit models to scale up development impact on their own.

It is now rare for any communiqué from an intergovernmental conference or commission not to include an explicit call for more public-private partnerships. From milestone events and processes such as the Busan High Level Forum on Aid Effectiveness, the Rio+20 Conference, and the Post-2015 Development Agenda to annual World Bank meetings, UN general assemblies, and gatherings of the G-8 and G-20, such partnerships have become a fixture on the international development agenda. Yet there is no commonly agreed-on definition, taxonomy, or even mapping of the spectrum of public-private partnerships for development, which ranges from project-based contractual agreements, joint ventures, and memorandums of understanding to voluntary sector-specific or national alliances to global multistakeholder institutions and platforms.

Although numerous studies have been undertaken to evaluate individual partnerships, there has been relatively little comparative analysis on the efficacy of different partnership models in scaling up development interventions, with the exception of infrastructure and global health partnerships. Existing research and experience show that the impact of public-private partnerships has been mixed in terms of cost effectiveness, accountability, sustainability, and ability to achieve scale, but more analysis is needed. In particular, there is a need to better understand what types of governance and accountability structures, resourcing mechanisms, incentives, skills, and competencies underpin successful public-private partnerships as a key pathway to scaling.

This chapter offers a definition for the evolving spectrum of public-private partnerships, outlines key public and private sector motivations for engagement, and reviews some of the ways in which these partnerships can serve as pathways for scaling up development impact. It concludes with recommendations to governments, donors, and corporations on how to use such partnerships as a tool in more systematic and deliberate approaches to bringing development solutions to millions of poor people. The chapter focuses on the scaling potential of three broad levels and types of public-private partnership and the reinforcing relationships between them.[1]

Project-based partnerships between a single public sector entity and one or a small number of private enterprises usually bring two or more players together under a formal agreement to accomplish a certain objective or set of objectives within a set time frame. They typically include a project plan with well-defined roles and responsibilities and with monitoring and evaluation mechanisms that enable the partners to make course corrections as needed over the life of the project. Project-based partnerships relevant to serving the poor include partnerships to catalyze or scale up a specific for-profit inclusive-business model or new technology aimed at reaching large numbers of low-income producers or consumers through a market-based approach; joint ventures and contractual agreements aimed at sharing the costs and risks and improving the development impact of large-scale infrastructure projects to benefit the poor; and social investment or strategic philanthropy partnerships that have the potential

---

1. This framework draws on research being undertaken by the author and her colleagues at the Corporate Social Responsibility Initiative, Harvard Kennedy School, on different approaches that companies are taking to strengthen the broader ecosystem for inclusive business models. For an overview see Gradl and Jenkins (2011).

to enhance the delivery of a particular public good or service and to scale up through replication.

In *sector-specific or country-based alliances*, government engages in a formal but voluntary and precompetitive collaboration with a group of private enterprises or business associations to develop a shared vision and strategy for development and to mobilize domestic and foreign private resources to help finance and deliver this strategy, sometimes alongside donor resources. Such alliances can range from public-private partnerships to agree on and deliver a broad set of national development goals to more-targeted sector-focused efforts to achieve scale in tackling a specific but systemic development challenge. Systemic challenges that lend themselves to such precompetitive industry alliances with government include joint efforts to improve the country's investment climate, coordinate industry clusters and regional infrastructure priorities, increase agricultural productivity and food security along a particular commodity value chain or geographic corridor, strengthen health systems, fortify staple foods, improve education access and quality, develop a more inclusive banking system, or implement a national energy and climate resilience strategy.

Global multistakeholder partnership platforms are composed of a larger number of both public and private actors and usually aim either at scaling up the financing, development, and delivery of specific development goals, products, or services or at enhancing the level of public and private accountability and transparency or at spreading learning and innovation in a particular sector or value chain. These global public-private partnerships range from independently governed and financed institutions and vertical funds to formal multistakeholder partnerships hosted by an existing development organization to informal, online information and knowledge hubs and open innovation platforms and networks.

In most cases of successful scaling up, there are mutually reinforcing linkages between the different levels and types of public-private partnership outlined above and between these and other types of partnership and actors. Examples of these linkages are illustrated in the profiles in this chapter, which focus on public-private partnerships in four areas that offer high potential to reach many more poor people and to transform their opportunities and the quality of their lives: scaling up health interventions to tackle malaria; scaling up efforts to reduce micronutrient deficiencies; scaling up more-inclusive agricultural linkages between companies and smallholder farmers; and enhancing the pro-poor development impact of large-scale investment projects in mining and energy.

Evidence suggests that scaling up development impact in any sector or country almost always requires multiple layers of different actors, partnerships, and business models ranging from subsidy models to for-profit models, with a variety of hybrid or public-private partnership models in between. As Johannes Linn concludes in a series of briefs commissioned by the 2020 Vision for Food,

Agriculture and the Environment initiative, "Virtually all effective scaling-up experiences in agriculture, rural development, and nutrition, have involved a multiplicity of actors: national, state, and local governments; civil society organizations; private businesses; public and private external donors; and most importantly, farmers and rural communities."[2] The same argument can be made for scaling up impact in other sectors and circumstances. A diverse ecosystem of different interventions and relationships is needed, including, in many cases, new models of public-private partnership.

Despite the potential of new models of public-private partnership to help scale up development impact, it is clear that these cross-sector alliances are not a quick fix, nor are they easy to build and sustain. Most of them have high transaction costs. They usually require an extensive investment in time at the outset to build mutual trust and to design effective processes for governance and execution that set clear goals, roles, responsibilities, and levels of risk tolerance while allowing flexibility for adaptation and course correction over time. Most public-private partnerships also require persistence and long-term commitment over a decade or more. And they call for a specific set of managerial and mediation skills on the part of all the partners, in particular the individuals and institutions that play a leadership role in brokering and coordinating the partnership. This is especially the case in building nontraditional alliances between government, business, and civil society organizations, which often have different motivations, cultures, time horizons, and modes of operating and in some cases share a legacy of mutual mistrust or low-levels of understanding about one another.

Despite these strategic and operational challenges, in an era of constrained public sector resources, increasingly complex development challenges, new technologies and development actors, and growing awareness of the role of market-based solutions in helping to scale up development impact, the potential of new types of public-private partnerships cannot be ignored. As the examples in this chapter and others throughout the book illustrate, effective partnerships, whether they are public-private, public-public, private-private, or some other combination, are at the core of all successful scaling-up initiatives.

The Evolving Spectrum of Public-Private Partnerships

Over the past two decades, nonstate actors have become engaged to an unprecedented degree in many development interventions traditionally considered the preserve of government and public donors. Private capital from citizens, residents, and companies in many donor countries—in the form of foreign direct and portfolio investment, commercial bank loans, remittances, and financial

2. Linn (2012, p. 1).

and in-kind contributions from philanthropic and nonprofit sources—now far outstrips official development assistance from their governments. In the United States, for example, it accounts for more than 80 percent of resource flows to developing countries compared with less than 30 percent three decades ago.[3] Similar shifts are under way in other donor countries. At the same time, within developing countries themselves, domestic private capital and private resources are becoming increasingly important drivers of growth and development, including efforts to alleviate poverty.

In many cases the increased engagement of private sector enterprises and other nonstate actors in development interventions takes the form of a public-private partnership. This chapter focuses primarily on partnerships that include one or more public sector entities—governments and donors—and one or more for-profit firms, business associations, or market-oriented social enterprises. Private foundations and nongovernmental organizations (NGOs) are often important participants in these partnerships as well but are not the focus of this chapter. Over the past two decades, there has been a dramatic growth in the number, diversity, and reach of public-private partnerships. These range from thousands of single project–based initiatives between an individual public entity and private enterprise to an estimated several hundred global coalitions with multimillion dollar budgets and complex multistakeholder funding and governance structures.

Despite the growing practice of public-private partnerships, the achievement of a universally agreed-on definition and taxonomy remains elusive. The Donor Committee for Enterprise Development (DCED) states that "the term public-private partnership (PPP) covers a multitude of different formats and criteria of collaboration."[4] The World Bank concurs in its reference guide to PPPs: "There is no single, internationally accepted definition of 'Public-Private Partnership.'"[5] This guide defines such a partnership as "a long-term contract between a private party and a government agency, for providing a public asset or service, in which the private party bears significant risk and management responsibility."[6]

This definition captures most traditional examples of public-private partnership that have involved the financing and provision of public goods, public infrastructure, or public services. Their primary aim has been to improve public sector performance through the judicious use of private resources and expertise and through the transfer of some public sector risk to private sector actors. Such partnerships remain important today. They are the focus of renewed attention from governments, private sector operators, financial institutions,

---

3. Hudson Institute (2011).
4. "Partnership Mechanisms of DCED Member Agencies" (www.enterprise-development.org/page/partnershipmechanisms).
5. World Bank Institute and the Public-Private Infrastructure Advisory Facility (2012, p. 11).
6. World Bank Institute and the Public-Private Infrastructure Advisory Facility (2012, p. 11).

and the development community, especially in the form of contractual project-based partnerships or joint ventures established to finance, develop, and operate large-scale infrastructure and natural resource projects. However, they no longer cover the full spectrum of PPPs for development. In recent years there has been growing recognition of the value of public-private partnerships in at least three additional contexts.

The first is growth in public sector–led vertical funds, trust funds, and other innovative financing mechanisms that enable private enterprises and private foundations to voluntarily contribute financial (often philanthropic) and other resources directly to government or donor-sponsored development institutions and programs and to participate in the governance and decisionmaking structures of these initiatives. The aim in most cases is to pool private and public resources and expertise in order to improve and scale up public sector performance while at the same time creating a precompetitive platform to catalyze and scale up market-based solutions to meet public challenges. Examples include the involvement of companies and corporate or private foundations in the Global Fund to Fight AIDS, Tuberculosis, and Malaria, the Global Alliance for Improved Nutrition, the GAVI Alliance, the World Bank's Carbon Funds and Facilities, the Global Crop Diversity Trust, the Consultative Group to Assist the Poorest, and the United Nations' Sustainable Energy for All and Education First initiatives.

This type of public-private partnership is not entirely new. The Rockefeller Foundation and the Ford Foundation played vital roles contributing to public programs in the 1960s to fund and scale the Green Revolution, and they have helped to strengthen many other public institutions in developing countries for decades. There are also some long-standing and successful product-donation partnerships in the field of global health which are led and hosted by public sector institutions but substantially enhanced and in some cases dependent on voluntary private sector contributions. The private contribution by companies such as Merck and GlaxoSmithKline, in the case of the Mectizan Donation Program, and by business and professional services organizations such as Rotary International, in the case of the Global Polio Eradication Initiative, are philanthropic, but they are substantial and have been sustained for more than twenty years. Merck, for example, has donated more than 1.5 billion cumulative treatments for onchocerciasis and lymphatic filariasis, and GlaxoSmithKline 3 billion treatments of the antiparasitic treatment albendazole. Both companies have also provided technical and logistical assistance and financial contributions in addition to product donations.

Although the model itself is not new, what is new has been the dramatic growth in the level of private and corporate philanthropy over recent decades and growing expertise on development-related issues within the foundation and corporate sectors. This trend has led to an increase in the number of such public-private partnerships, in which voluntary private contributions of money, expertise, and, in some cases products are directly increasing the scale and impact of public-led initiatives.

The second major trend over the past decade has been the sharing of public sector resources or the transfer of risk to a public sector entity to improve private sector performance by overcoming market failures and barriers to scaling up market-based solutions to poverty reduction and sustainable development. This has been manifested through catalytic public financing, technical support, and public funding of research and development incentives.

The catalytic potential of public finance has been used to enable companies and entrepreneurs to build more-inclusive business models that explicitly aim at integrating or serving low-income producers, consumers, and employees while also being profitable (also described as base-of-the-pyramid or creating-shared-value business models).[7] The story of M-PESA in chapter 7 illustrates this approach. In 2003 a Financial Deepening Challenge Fund, created by the United Kingdom's Department for International Development, provided financial support, together with funding from Vodafone, to enable Kenya-based Safaricom (a Vodafone subsidiary) to carry out initial pilot testing on the business model that developed into M-PESA. By the end of 2011, M-PESA had signed up 15 million customers, equivalent to three in four Kenyan adults.

Public provision of technical support has also been employed to help companies develop pro-poor, inclusive business models, either directly through public grants or through contracting consultancy services. The UK Department for International Development's Business Innovation Facility is an example of this approach. Rather than providing finance, the facility supports companies and social enterprises to develop or scale up inclusive business models through the provision of advice, facilitation, and technical input, sourced from a wide

7. The term *inclusive business models* was coined in 2005 by the World Business Council for Sustainable Development and is also used by the International Finance Corporation and the United Nations Development Programme. It can be defined as "Sustainable business solutions that go beyond philanthropy and expand access to goods, services, and livelihood opportunities for low-income communities in commercially viable ways"; see www.inclusive-business.org/inclusive-business.html. The term *creating shared value* was coined in 2006 by Michael Porter and Mark Kramer. It can be defined as "policies and operating practices that enhance the competitiveness of a company while simultaneously advancing the economic and social conditions in the communities in which it operates"; Porter and Kramer (2006). The term *"serving the base of the pyramid"* or *bottom of the pyramid* was coined by the late C. K. Prahalad and Stu Hart in 2002. It can be defined as "serving individuals in the bottom of the four tiers of world population. Tier 1: 75–100M affluent consumers (middle and upper income people in developed countries and elites in developing countries); Tiers 2 and 3: 1.5–1.75B consumers (poor in developed nations and middle income in developing countries); Tier 4: 4B of the world's poorest, to rise to 6B in 40 years because of population growth patterns." Prahalad and Hart (2002, pp. 54–67).

network of public and private expertise.[8] The examples provided by the Shell Foundation, discussed in chapter 6, illustrate how the combination of funding and technical support from both the public and private sector has helped to scale up inclusive business models in the area of energy access.

The use of publicly funded research and development incentives has encouraged private-led science and technology innovations that have the potential to create breakthroughs in scaling up pro-poor solutions to health, agriculture, and financial inclusion. Examples of this approach include the Medicines for Malaria Venture, the GAVI Alliance, Advanced Market Commitments, the International Finance Facility for Immunization, and vaccine bonds. In 2012 the U.S. Agency for International Development launched two new initiatives— Development Innovation Ventures and Grand Challenges—that offer models for a new generation of public-private partnerships to spur scientific and technological innovation that has the potential to reach millions of poor people.[9]

A third major partnership trend in recent years has been the creation of public-private partnerships to improve the broader ecosystem or enabling environment for simultaneously achieving desired development outcomes and direct or indirect business benefits. Examples include collaboration aimed at creating a better private investment climate in a particular sector, region or country (for instance, the Africa Investment Climate Facility); cooperative efforts for institution strengthening and capacity building (for instance, South Africa's Business Trust and Educational Quality Improvement Program, where more than one hundred companies have worked with the government); the creation of norms and standards (for instance, the Voluntary Principles on Security and Human Rights, the Extractive Industries Transparency Initiative, the Equator Principles, and a variety of forestry and agricultural commodity roundtables); and alliances that promote knowledge sharing, policy dialogue, and joint advocacy efforts (such as the United Nations Global Compact, the Global Reporting Initiative, and the UN's Principles for Responsible Investment). These system-level multistakeholder partnerships usually aim to improve coordination among diverse stakeholders and strengthen overall systemic capacity and efficiency.

To encompass the growing variety of partnership models, this chapter proposes the following broader definition for public-private partnerships: "A voluntary collaborative agreement between one or more public sector entities and one or more private actors in which all participants agree to work together to

8. A detailed overview of the Business Innovation Facility, its goals, methodology, portfolio and progress updates is available on www.businessinnovationfacility.org.

9. Details of Development Innovation Ventures and Grand Challenges, along with other alliances to spur science and technology innovation for development, are available at www.usaid.gov/what-we-do/science-technology-and-innovation.

achieve a common purpose or to undertake a specific task and to share risks, responsibilities, resources, competencies and benefits."[10]

The partnerships and alliances that are evolving between public and private actors vary widely in how they are convened and by whom, their governance structures and degree of formality, their range of participants, their intended tenure, and their scope of activity. In many cases they are still led or catalyzed by governments and official donor agencies. In others they are driven by a combination of new technology platforms, inclusive business models, impact investing funds, corporate social responsibility initiatives, social entrepreneurship, and strategic philanthropy.

In terms of governance structures and degree of formality, most project-based partnerships are governed by either a contractual and legally binding agreement or a voluntary memorandum of understanding between the participating public and private partners, which is usually term limited and specific to that particular project. Most sector-specific and country-based alliances or multistakeholder partnership platforms are voluntary in nature, with a steering committee to govern them and consensus reached on funding, strategic direction, and programming activities. Many are hosted by a public institution, nongovernmental organization, or business association with secretariat support funded by participants. They range from those with formally defined membership structures and responsibilities to loose networks, technology hubs, and movements in which the participation of public, private, and civic actors is more fluid and flexible. Examples of the latter include the Scaling Up Nutrition movement, Every Woman Every Child, and Sustainable Energy for All, which have clearly defined secretariats, lead groups, and principles for engagement but encourage a vast array of public, private, and civil society organizations to make practical commitments to achieve the goals of the initiative.

Some public-private partnerships, especially global initiatives, have been more formally constituted as new legal entities with their own funding, governance, and operational structures. There are more than twenty global public-private health partnerships, for example, most of which are independently governed by a board of public and private participants and convene dozens of organizations to finance, research, develop, deliver, and advocate for improved global health outcomes focused on specific disease burdens. Well-known examples include the GAVI Alliance, the Global Fund to Fight AIDS, Tuberculosis, and Malaria, and the Global Alliance for Improved Nutrition.[11] Non-health-related multistakeholder partnerships that have been established over the

10. Nelson (2002, p. 46).
11. For a list of other global public-private health partnerships that fit this description, see Overseas Development Institute (2007).

past few decades as independent institutions include the Extractive Industries Transparency Initiative, the Africa Investment Climate Facility, the Marine Stewardship Council, and the Forest Stewardship Council. Some of these independently governed institutions that focus on mobilizing targeted financial support, providing a critical mass of expertise, and delivering measurable results are also termed vertical funds, several examples of which are explored in more depth in chapter 4.

There is also great variety in terms of duration. Some public-private partnerships are designed to be catalytic and term limited, for example, helping to finance and develop a scalable business model with the aim that over time it will become self-financing and sustainable. Others are structured to be ongoing joint ventures throughout the intended life of a project, as is the case in most major infrastructure and natural resource development projects and in some hybrid inclusive business models. Others do not have an explicit time horizon or exit strategy beyond a vision of achieving a broad development goal or set of targets.

In terms of scope of activities, most public-private partnerships are established to undertake one or more of the following set of interventions identified by McKinsey & Company: coordination; funding; product development; and delivery.[12] McKinsey points out that many of the public-private partnerships that have been most effective at achieving scale and impact combine several of these objectives and capabilities. Most of the examples profiled in this chapter illustrate the point.

In summary, the spectrum of public-private partnerships that have potential to help reach millions more poor people and to transform their lives is diverse and constantly evolving. Despite this diversity, most public-private partnerships meet the following three sets of conditions:

—First, they involve a formal but voluntary and collaborative agreement and sharing of authority, rather than simply a contract for services, between one or more public sector entities and one or more private sector entities, which may or may not be legally binding.

—Second, there is an explicit agreement to share or transfer resources, risks, and rewards between the participants, and there is shared discretion on and mutual accountability for the allocation of these resources, risks, and rewards.

—Third, there is a commitment to achieving mutual benefit; a desired public or development outcome (or set of outcomes); and a private or business benefit (or set of benefits, which may be direct or indirect).

12. McKinsey & Company (2009).

Government and Business Motivations for Engaging in Public-Private Partnerships

Partnerships are a means to an end, not an end in themselves. In the vast majority of cases, that end is the achievement of greater scale, greater systemic or transformational impact, or greater sustainability than the participants would be able to achieve on their own. Most public-private partnerships are established to address market failures, governance gaps, and other systemic obstacles that are beyond the capacity and resources of any one actor or sector to tackle on its own. They are driven by a shared recognition that many development problems are too complex and interdependent, and the financial, technical, and managerial resources for tackling them are too scarce or too widely dispersed among different actors, not to search for new approaches that draw on the resources, skills, and capacities of all sectors.

Government Motivations for Engagement

John Donahue and Richard Zeckhauser make the following case:

> No one believes, given the complexity and cost of the tasks we confront, that simply scaling up the standard governmental solutions is the answer. Government too often finds that it lacks the skill, the will, and the wallet to figure out a fix and get it done. Corporations—which some hope will be spurred by their sense of social responsibility to save us from the perils that beset us—are often struggling to save themselves, and resist devoting resources to any problem if a profit, direct or indirect, isn't part of the solution. And private charities have too few resources to take up every burden that government shrugs off.[13]

Donahue and Zeckhauser argue that "collaborative governance," which they define as "carefully structured arrangements that interweave public and private capabilities on terms of *shared discretion*," can serve as a force multiplier or a systemic way to ramp up the impact of government's efforts.[14] They outline two government motivations for collaboration with the private sector: the achievement of better outcomes through greater productivity and operational efficiency, better information, and greater legitimacy; and more resources. Their research focuses primarily on collaborative governance models within the United States, but the case made for public sector engagement in such models is relevant in most countries.

13. Donahue and Zeckhauser (2011, p. 3).
14. Donahue and Zeckhauser (2011, p. 4).

Over the past decade, a growing number of developing-country governments and donors have reengaged in public-private partnerships to provide public infrastructure assets and services. The World Bank, in particular, has committed to renewing its focus on infrastructure, following its withdrawal in the 1990s in part as a response to campaigns by nongovernmental organizations. Infrastructure projects in the areas of transportation, water, energy, and information and communications technology have grown from a low point in 2003 to account for more than 40 percent of the World Bank Group's portfolio by 2012. While cognizant of the fiscal, operational, and governance challenges of such partnerships and drawing on lessons from previous decades, the bank, along with other development finance institutions, the G-20, and many low- and middle-income country governments, now makes a strong pro-poor case for increasing the financing and delivery of infrastructure, and doing so in partnership with the private sector.

As stated in the foreword to the World Bank's Infrastructure Strategy Update FY2012–2015:

> Infrastructure can be a vector of change in addressing some of the most systemic development challenges of today's world: social stability, rapid urbanization, climate change adaptation and mitigation and natural disasters. Without an infrastructure that supports green and inclusive growth, countries will not only find it harder to meet unmet basic needs, they will struggle to improve competitiveness. Today, the infrastructure gap in low and middle-income countries is estimated at US$1 trillion. More and more, countries need to turn to the private sector as well as the public sector to build and operate their essential infrastructure.[15]

Figure 12-1 illustrates the public sector motivation for promoting public-private partnerships in the area of infrastructure development. Similar motivations are driving government and donor interest in the broader range of public-private partnerships to support more inclusive or pro-poor models of growth and sustainable development. From a public sector perspective, public-private partnerships, when implemented well, can play a crucial role in providing much needed financing, management skills and efficiencies, and, in some cases, the delivery systems or networks necessary to reach larger numbers of poor people with effective and affordable interventions that have the potential to transform their lives.

Business Motivations for Engagement

What is the motivation for private sector companies to engage in the often time-consuming, costly, and challenging process of building public-private partnerships? Four broad, and often interrelated, categories of business motivation can

15. World Bank Group (2012).

Figure 12-1. *What's Wrong with Infrastructure and How PPPs Can Help*

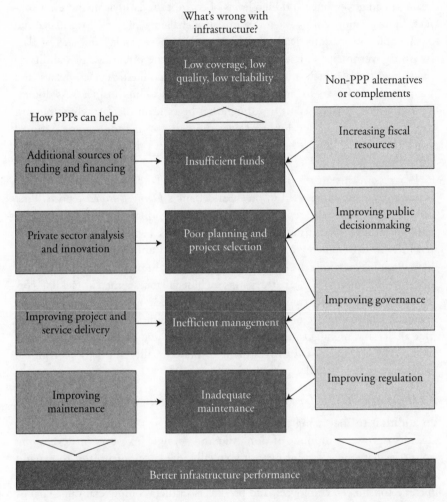

Source: World Bank Institute and the Public-Private Infrastructure Advisory Facility (2012, p. 16).

be summarized as improving the investment climate for business; creating and scaling inclusive products, services, and business models; managing and mitigating risks and negative externalities; and leveraging corporate social investment and philanthropy.

Improving the Investment Climate for Business

In many low- and middle-income countries the broader enabling environment—both public policies and institutions—remains an obstacle to private sector development and investment. In some cases, the challenge is severe as a result of bad governance and high levels of corruption, cronyism, and even conflict. In many more countries, it is primarily a challenge of weak governance and weak public institutions, leading to high levels of bureaucracy and lack of clarity over government policies and regulations and the public sector's ability to implement them, which in turn result in uncertainty, inefficiencies, delays, and higher risks and costs for making investments and doing business. As domestic and foreign private sector investment has become an increasingly important driver of growth and development over the past two decades, many national governments and donors have increased their focus on improving the investment climate.

Progress in this area is demonstrated by improvements in the performance of many countries, discussed in the World Bank's *Doing Business* reports. First published in 2003, the reports gather and analyze quantitative data to compare business regulations and policy reforms across 185 economies and, more recently, in different regions, cities, and sectors. Public-private partnerships have often played a role in supporting improvement in national and subnational investment climates. These partnerships include alliances aimed at tackling corruption and improving transparency on the collection and allocation of public finances; national or sector-specific investor roundtables where companies provide advice and highlight priorities to governments; and regional programs such as the public-private Africa Investment Climate Facility and various regional infrastructure and corridor partnerships.

Creating and Scaling Up Inclusive Products, Services, and Business Models

In addition to increasing private sector investment generally, over the past decade a growing number of domestic and foreign investors in developing countries have been exploring commercially viable opportunities to expand existing markets or to create new markets by more explicitly including low-income consumers, employees, and producers in their commercial value chains. Well-documented examples of making markets work for the poor include the growth in microfinance and mobile money services, market-based approaches to the development and delivery of health products and services, and the inclusion of small-scale farmers, producers, distributors, and retailers into large corporate value chains through models such as contract farming or out-growers' schemes, local content programs, franchising, and microdistribution centers and retail outlets. These approaches involve social enterprises or larger companies harnessing for-profit motives and capabilities in a manner that directly addresses one or more development challenges, with the explicit aim of creating shared value by achieving business benefit and economic value as well as development impact and social value. Michael Porter and Mark Kramer have identified three components of creating shared value:[16]

—Reconceiving products and markets: Companies can meet development needs while better serving existing markets, accessing or creating new markets, or lowering costs through innovation.

—Redefining productivity in the value chain: Companies can improve the quality, quantity, cost, and reliability of inputs and distribution and improve efficiency or reduce risk, while they simultaneously address a social or environmental challenge.

—Enabling local cluster development: Companies can enhance their broader operating environment while directly alleviating a social problem by developing more reliable local suppliers, a functioning infrastructure of roads and telecommunications, access to talent, and an effective and predictable legal system.

If the potential for building more inclusive business models or creating shared value is so great, why is it not being tapped by many more companies and entrepreneurs? Primarily because these new business models are often challenging to develop, and they are even more challenging to scale. This is the case for even the largest and best-resourced multinational corporations, let alone for the smaller companies and social enterprises that have led much of the innovation in this area.

A report by the Monitor Group and Acumen Fund concludes:

> Monitor's research in India and Africa [reviewing over 600 enterprises and inclusive business models], and Acumen Fund's decade of investing experience, provide an insight into the many challenges facing inclusive businesses. They sell to a hard-to-reach customer base with severely limited resources, and engage suppliers with limited capabilities. Their products are often in 'push' categories like preventative health care requiring high levels of awareness building and education, unlike 'pull' categories like mobile phones that consumers already desire. And these come on top of poor infrastructure and inefficient regulation. . . . A recent Monitor study of over 400 enterprises in Africa found that only 32 percent were commercially viable and had potential to scale, and only 13 percent were actually at scale.[17]

Partnerships with public donors, governments, and private foundations can help corporations and social enterprises to overcome some of these obstacles to creating and scaling up these new business models. Such partnerships can help

16. Porter and Kramer (2011).
17. Koh, Karamchandani, and Katz (2012, p. 4).

companies develop and deliver new products and services or extend their value chains beyond what the individual company or group of private enterprises could commercially justify doing on their own by

—providing catalytic financing or patient capital (which is important in that these models often take a long time to scale up and to become commercially viable);

—sharing the risk burden;

—investing in research and market information on low-income producers and consumers;

—supporting consumer education on the benefit of paying for market-based solutions;

—enhancing the physical, institutional, and information infrastructure needed to connect low-income producers and consumers to formal markets and services;

—helping low-income economic actors to aggregate in order to strengthen their own economic bargaining power, efficiency, or political voice; and

—improving the enabling regulatory and policy environment for inclusive business models and markets.

Partnerships appear to be essential to catalyzing and scaling up many inclusive business models—whether they are structured to provide time-limited catalytic support at the outset of piloting and scaling up a new business model or structured as an ongoing joint venture or hybrid model to sustain an inclusive business model that is unlikely to become fully commercially viable over time.

Managing and Mitigating Risks and Negative Externalities

In many cases, companies engage in public-private partnerships primarily to manage their risks, improve transparency and accountability, protect or enhance their brand and corporate reputation, increase their political influence, enhance their public legitimacy, minimize regulation and taxation, or create a more level playing field between leaders and laggards. All of these risk management and relationship management motives offer business benefits both direct and indirect.

One area where managing risks and relationships has been a key business driver in the emergence of new models of public-private partnership is the extractive sector and, to a lesser extent, forestry, agriculture, and manufacturing, where voluntary multistakeholder initiatives have been created to improve transparency and accountability of large-scale projects and to develop norms, principles, and standards to respect human rights and to minimize negative environmental and social externalities. Ideally, government regulations should ensure responsible corporate performance in relation to these issues.

In many developing countries where governance is weak, national regulations in areas such as human rights, labor, anticorruption, and the environment are often not effectively implemented and monitored, even though they usually exist on the books. This can create serious operational, reputational, and in some cases financial risks for companies that are increasingly under a global spotlight with respect to their performance on these issues. Public-private partnerships aimed at achieving mutual accountability and a level playing field within an industry are one approach to tackling these governance gaps and to improving the likelihood that the public revenues and other benefits generated by major investment projects will reach millions of citizens.

Leveraging Corporate Social Investment and Strategic Philanthropy

In some cases, especially when it comes to responding to humanitarian crises, meeting community needs, and seeding social entrepreneurship, the corporate motivation for participating in a partnership may be primarily philanthropic or driven by social investment and employee engagement. Even here, companies are becoming more rigorous and strategic in linking their philanthropic and employee volunteering activities to their core business interests and capabilities to achieve greater scale and sustainability. They are also recognizing that they can leverage the impact of their philanthropic resources—and often increase the legitimacy and effectiveness of their donations—by working in partnership with public and private humanitarian agencies and governments.

Although philanthropy—whether private or corporate—is unlikely on its own to reach the level of scale and sustainability that can be achieved through effective public policy or by making markets work for the poor, it can still play a valuable role. It can be especially important in catalyzing, coordinating, and testing new technologies and market-based approaches that have the potential to scale. Private foundations such as the Rockefeller Foundation, the Bill & Melinda Gates Foundation, the Aga Khan Development Network, the Skoll Foundation, and the Omidyar Network and innovative corporate foundations such as the Shell Foundation, the Syngenta Foundation, and the Google Foundation, for example, have played an important catalytic and convening role in supporting market-based development solutions and public policy innovations that have subsequently achieved scale or been replicated. The case of the Shell Foundation is profiled in chapter 6.

Monitor Group and the Acumen Fund point to lessons on the catalytic use of philanthropy and its value as patient capital in seeding the microfinance sector: "Now commercially attractive with billions of dollars of invested capital, microfinance was promising but unprofitable for many years. The sector received $20 billion in grants, soft loans and guarantees in its first two decades of development. This allowed early pioneers like Grameen to refine the model through many years of trial and error, providing the critical platform for later entrants to accelerate their progress towards break-even and investability."[18] Combining philanthropic or public donor funds and technical assistance with the execution capabilities, business models, technological innovation, and scaling potential of large corporations or effective social enterprises offers great potential for scaling up development impact.

In summary, governments, public donors, and development practitioners are growing more comfortable with the concept and the practice of commercially viable, market-based approaches to poverty reduction. They are starting to partner with companies in ways that directly support the profit motive where these companies can demonstrate their ability or their intention to directly support the achievement of development goals. As stated in a 2011 U.K. Department for International Development report:

> Our new approach to working with the private sector is about us doing more with and for private enterprise, extending our work in new areas, and doing it better. We want private sector thinking to become as much a part of [the Department for International Development's] DNA as our work with charities and governments. The new approach will deliver results for poor people: better job opportunities and incomes; more readily available and affordable finance for households and small businesses; and more accessible, better quality health care, schooling and basic services.[19]

At the same time, corporations and social enterprises are increasingly active as investors, operators, and donors in developing countries. Their growing interest in these countries is driven by a combination of new investment and business opportunities, risk management and stakeholder engagement imperatives, and social responsibility and strategic philanthropy goals. Given some of the challenges of operating in these countries, such as high political and social risk, market failures, and limited local capacity and resources, engagement in public-private partnerships has become an increasingly attractive and viable business strategy to help companies harness the benefits while managing the risks of doing business in frontier markets.

Pathways to Scaling Up through Public-Private Partnerships

Public-private partnerships can facilitate the scaling up of development impact by enabling governments and the public sector to deliver public goods and services more effectively, whether by strengthening rule making and implementation or improving public service delivery (for example, by enabling subsidy

18. Koh, Karamchandani, and Katz (2012, p. 8).
19. U.K. Department for International Development (2011, p. 2).

Figure 12-2. *Ecosystem of Public-Private Partnerships*

Large-scale but often difficult to implement or sustain without effective business models, financing, and delivery mechanisms on-the-ground

Global multi-stakeholder platforms

Country-based or regional alliances

Sector-based cooperation

Numerous, but often difficult to scale or replicate in the absence of an enabling ecosystem—markets, institutions, and policies

Project-based partnerships

Source: Author.

models to reach more poor people with better quality, reliability, and afford-ability of service); or by making markets work more effectively (for example, by improving the reach, scale, replicability, or sustainability of market-based solu-tions or for-profit inclusive business models that seek to benefit the poor); or through some combination of these.

As emphasized in chapter 1 and illustrated by the case studies in this book, the challenge of scaling up can be divided into two parts: financing scaled-up interventions, because poor people cannot afford to pay full cost for many ser-vices; and managing delivery to large numbers of beneficiaries.

In addition to these challenges is the challenge of coordinating different types of intervention and optimizing the use of subsidy models, for-profit models, and hybrid models to meet different levels of income, capability, and accessibility among low-income households. All of these scaling challenges require sustained commitment and usually new models of partnership. As outlined in the intro-duction to this chapter and illustrated in figure 12-2, three levels and types of public-private partnership—and the mutually reinforcing interactions between them—offer particular potential for helping to scale up development impact:

—project-based partnerships

—sector-specific or country-based alliances

—global multistakeholder partnership platforms

The following examples illustrate how these three levels and types of public-private partnership and the interactions between them can offer pathways to scaling up through a combination of market-based approaches and better public sector performance. The examples focus on interventions that have scaled up or demonstrate potential to scale up in improving access to health interventions, with a focus on tackling malaria; improving nutrition, with a focus on tackling micronutrient deficiencies; building more inclusive agricultural linkages between large companies and smallholder farmers; and managing the risks and enhancing the pro-poor development impact of large-scale investment projects in mining and energy.

Scaling Up Health Interventions to Tackle Malaria

Some of the most effective and long-standing public-private partnerships in terms of scaling up development impact have been in the area of health. Over the past two decades, health public-private partnerships have evolved from project-based and global multistakeholder partnerships focused on specific disease burdens, where the private sector contribution was primarily driven by corporate philanthropy and product donations, to a growing number of market-based product development and delivery partnerships also targeted at tackling specific diseases but using a range of tools from subsidized pricing to commercially viable business models and joint ventures. Today, public-private health partnerships are also looking increasingly at ways to strengthen health systems more broadly at a national or regional level, in addition to the financing, development, and delivery of particular products and technologies to tackle a specific disease burden.

Many individual health-care companies, and the partnerships in which they engage, employ a spectrum of different approaches to improving access to health care for low-income consumers, ranging from philanthropic donations to zero- or low-profit contributions to commercial solutions. They demonstrate that scaling up access to health care at all levels of the economic pyramid will require a systemic approach that combines both market-led and publicly subsidized or incentivized research and development (R&D), as well as both subsidized and for-profit delivery models, facilitated by effective partnerships to coordinate these different actors and approaches. Efforts to tackle malaria illustrate this ecosystem.

Malaria mortality rates have fallen by more than 25 percent globally since 2000, in large part owing to coordinated global efforts, effective national control programs, and a variety of public-private partnerships created to develop and deliver preventive, diagnostic, and therapeutic interventions. Despite this progress, an estimated 216 million cases of malaria still occur every year, resulting in some 655,000 deaths, mostly in Africa, and about $12 billion a year in direct economic losses.[20] Almost half the world's population, 3.3 billion people in more than 100 countries, remains at risk from this disease. To control and, over time, eradicate malaria, ongoing efforts are needed to scale

20. See www.rbm.who.int/keyfacts.html.

up the financing, discovery, development, and delivery of interventions and to strengthen health care systems. To achieve these goals, especially in the face of increasingly constrained public sector resources, the ecosystem of public-private partnerships that has emerged to fight malaria over the past decade will be more important than ever.

The following profiles illustrate some of the mutually reinforcing relationships between a few of these partnerships, from global multistakeholder platforms to regional and country-level alliances and project-based initiatives. They focus on the Medicines for Malaria Venture, the Global Fund to Fight AIDS, Tuberculosis, and Malaria, and the Roll Back Malaria Partnership at the global level, which have facilitated country-level coordinating mechanisms and also helped to initiate project-based partnerships between individual companies, donors, and governments.

GlaxoSmithKline, Novartis, Sanofi, and Pfizer are examples of global healthcare companies that have established public-private anti-malaria partnerships that span more than a decade. These partnerships run the full spectrum from large-scale product donations and low-cost or zero-profit provision of drugs and diagnostics for government-led programs to increasingly commercial R&D and inclusive or shared-value business models. New business models range from public-private partnerships to accelerate and scale up the development and delivery of vaccines, drugs, and diagnostics to partnerships aimed at training health-care workers and strengthening public health institutions.

In addition to pharmaceutical, biotechnology, and medical-device companies, firms with a large number of employees or consumers in malaria-endemic countries, such as those in energy, mining, agribusiness, chemicals, tourism, financial services, consumer goods, retail brand marketing, and information and communications technology have also become increasingly active partners in tackling malaria over the past decade. Examples include Anglo American, AngloGold Ashanti, Bayer, Chevron, Coca-Cola, ExxonMobil, Google, IBM, Marathon Oil, Shell, Standard Bank, Sumitomo, and Vodafone. All of these companies have been recognized in award programs for providing a combination of financial support, technical assistance, product development, distribution networks, facilities, public health education, health-worker training, advocacy, and governance input to successful public-private partnerships aimed at efforts to prevent and eradicate malaria. In addition to engaging in individual project-based partnerships, most of the companies named here have also participated in one or more of the following global and country-level alliances.

MEDICINES FOR MALARIA VENTURE. The Medicines for Malaria Venture (MMV) was established in 1999 as an independent foundation with initial public and private funding from the Swiss, British, and Dutch governments, the World Bank, and the Rockefeller Foundation. In addition to support from these donors, the core funders of the MMV today include the Gates Foundation, Crimalddi, ExxonMobil, Newcrest Mining, the MCJ Amerlior Foundation, the Wellcome Trust, the Irish, Spanish, and U.S. bilateral donor agencies, and the U.S. National Institutes of Health. Over the past decade, the MMV has become the leading product-development partnership in antimalarial drug research and development. It has achieved this by employing innovative and flexible approaches to intellectual property rights and the use of what it calls "socially responsible" contractual agreements with companies and by working through a virtual R&D network of more than 260 public, private, and non-profit partners in almost fifty countries as well as clinical centers in endemic countries. The Medicines for Malaria Venture states:

> We use public and philanthropic funds to engage the pharmaceutical industry and academic research institutions in undertaking R&D for diseases of the developing world that they would normally be unable or unwilling to pursue independently, without additional incentives. MMV itself does not often have the capacity or infrastructure to undertake early stage development projects in-house; instead, it relies on its partners for financing and other in-kind contributions (i.e. laboratories and expertise) and it itself allocates resources to the most promising projects, coordinates partner activities for various stages of the R&D process, manages the project portfolio and acts as a facilitator.[21]

An essential component of the MMV's successful model has been its ability to access not only public and private financial support but also in-kind contributions and the core capabilities of its private sector partners. The organization acknowledges that it "received 'in-kind' contributions such as the use of facilities, pharmaceutical technologies (i.e. high-throughput screening), staff resources, laboratories and unique resources such as general or tailored compound libraries. MMV estimates that its in-kind contributions by large pharmaceutical companies to be at least equivalent to the funds committed to projects by MMV."[22]

When the MMV was created in 1999, the pipeline for new antimalarials was virtually empty. Today, the organization can point to a number of achievements, ranging from the screening of millions of compounds to the discovery, regulatory approval, and affordable delivery of new treatments. For example, the MMV and its partners have been able to apply high-throughput screening technologies to screen more than 5 million compounds for their potential activity

---

21. See www.mmv.org/partnering/product-development-partnership-model.
22. See www.mmv.org/about-us/faqs/who-funds-mmv-and-how-much-has-it-raised-so-far.

against the malaria parasite and have identified more than 10,000 promising compounds. Three of these partners—GlaxoSmithKline, the Genomics Institute of the Novartis Research Foundation, and St. Jude Children's Research Hospital—have released their data into the public domain, making them available to thousands of scientists. In 2009 Novartis and the MMV launched Coartem Dispersible, the first high-quality artemisinin combination therapy (ACT) formulated especially for children (who account for more than 85 percent of deaths from malaria). By June 2012 more than 137 million treatments had been delivered to thirty-five malaria-endemic countries. In November 2010, with support from the MMV, Guilin Pharmaceutical became the first company to receive World Health Organization prequalification for its artesunate injection for the treatment of severe malaria, and by May 2012 more than 3.2 million vials had been delivered to malaria-endemic countries, sufficient to treat 1 million sick children and saving an estimated 24,000 lives during this eighteen-month period.[23]

In addition to ongoing work through the MMV and others to develop antimalarial drugs, there are also alliances focused on the difficult and long-term task of discovering and developing a malaria vaccine, such as the PATH Malaria Vaccine Initiative that is working with the Gates Foundation and GlaxoSmithKline. If successful, this joint work on a vaccine has the potential to protect millions of children and reduce the burden on health-care services. Commenting on its partnership with the Malaria Vaccine Initiative to develop the RTS,S malaria vaccine, GlaxoSmithKline states:

> We have invested $300 million in the vaccine so far and expect to invest another $50–100 million over the next few years. We do not expect to recoup these costs through sales of vaccine, as there is little or no market for vaccine in developed markets. Our ability to make significant investment returns on other innovative medicines in our portfolio enables us to support this important work. We will also donate at least 12.5 million doses of the vaccine to [the Malaria Vaccine Initiative], . . . which has [also] received more than $200 million in grants from the Bill & Melinda Gates Foundation to advance the clinical development of RTS,S, together with prominent African research centers.[24]

Phase 2 and phase 3 trials of the vaccine have shown promising results.

Partnerships to discover a malaria vaccine and to ensure the constant evolution of resistant antimalarial drugs and effective treatments are only part of the story. The control of malaria also relies on other interventions, such as the

23. See www.mmv.org/achievements-challenges/achievements.
24. GlaxoSmithKline (2012, p. 17).

use of insecticide-treated bed nets, personal and spatial mosquito repellants, and other vector-control methods, and on joint efforts to improve the access to and affordability of these interventions through innovative financing mechanisms and pricing models, widespread consumer awareness and education campaigns, and more effective and reliable delivery channels. Public-private partnerships have been crucial in scaling up impact in these areas as well.

THE GLOBAL FUND. The Global Fund to Fight AIDS, Tuberculosis, and Malaria has focused its own antimalaria efforts on scaling up access to affordable and reliable insecticide-treated nets, indoor residual spraying, and artemisinin combination therapy and more recently by hosting the Affordable Medicines Facility, malaria (AMFm). Although supported primarily by and working largely with governments, the Global Fund has partnered with the private sector in achieving its goals over the past decade. Established in 2001 as an independent vertical fund, the Global Fund's overall governance and scaling effectiveness is reviewed in more detail in chapter 4. Its partnerships with business to scale up malaria interventions, as well as those focused on HIV/AIDS and tuberculosis, include alliances at both the global and country level and with individual companies as well as collective initiatives such as the Global Business Coalition for Health. The Global Fund's partners include Novartis, Sanofi, Chevron, AngloGold Ashanti, Standard Bank, and Coca-Cola.

Novartis and Sanofi are working in a variety of partnerships with the Global Fund, the World Health Organization, the AMFm, the MMV, and others to develop and deliver new antimalarial treatments. During 2011, Novartis delivered 100 million treatments of its antimalarial drug, Coartem Dispersible. Novartis estimates that it has delivered more than 500 million antimalarial treatments since 2001 through its Malaria Initiative.[25] Sanofi established its own initiative in 2001, the Impact Malaria program. Among other activities, in 2007 it partnered with the Drugs for Neglected Diseases Initiative Foundation to develop an ACT drug. More than 100 million units were distributed in sub-Saharan Africa in the first three years after its launch.[26] The malaria programs of both companies combine research and development, tier pricing mechanisms, and information and education activities, most of which are undertaken in partnership with others. Tier pricing has become an important strategy throughout the industry. As Sanofi states:

> While donating medicines is indispensable in humanitarian emergencies, the tiered pricing policy is crucial to ensure the economic viability of

25. Novartis (2012).
26. Sanofi (2011).

our programs. Our antimalarial medication is sold according to a tiered-pricing policy that includes "no profit–no loss" prices to major international organizations, WHO, government purchasing agencies, and major sponsors such as UNITAID, the Global Fund and others. This price has become the standard reference price for new antimalarial drugs.[27]

Chevron made financial commitments to the Global Fund totaling US$55 million between 2008 and 2013 and engaged in governance processes at the global level while also investing time and resources to improve the outreach and performance of Global Fund grants at the country level in Indonesia, Thailand, Angola, South Africa, Nigeria, and the Philippines, where the company has operations and on-the-ground capacity. In these countries it has worked with national governments, nonprofit partners, and other companies to implement workplace programs, support capacity development, and undertake joint advocacy and awareness programs focused on both HIV/AIDS and malaria. The company reports that through the first three years of its investment in Global Fund grants, it "contributed to significant results, including: as many as 3.4 million people were directly reached through HIV/AIDS prevention programs; about 380,000 people completed voluntary HIV/AIDS counseling and testing; about 1 million malaria nets were distributed; and more than 1 million rapid diagnostic tests for malaria were distributed."[28]

In 2008, AngloGold Ashanti in Ghana was the first private company to be approved as a principal recipient of a Global Fund grant of up to US$150 million over five years to enable it to work with the Ministry of Health and other partners to scale up its successful integrated malaria-control program to an additional forty districts in Ghana. Initiated in 2006, the original Obuasi Malaria Program led to a decrease in the treatment of malaria cases by the Edwin Cade Hospital from an average of 6,800 a month to 700, and school attendance in the Obuasi District has increased by 70 percent since the inception of the program. The company set up a separate legal entity to administer the grant, and after initial delays in government approvals, the partnership was launched in mid-2011.[29] Other extractive sector companies such as Marathon Oil, Shell, BHP Billiton, and Anglo American have also been active in providing both financial support and technical assistance to coinvestment agreements with the Global Fund and to national and regional government-led malaria-control programs at the country level.

27. Sanofi (2011, p. 12).
28. Chevron (2011, p. 12).
29. Private Sector Case Study 1: Corporation as Principal Recipient.

Since 2008 Standard Bank, headquartered in South Africa, has provided financial and management expertise to Global Fund grant recipients and its Country Coordinating Mechanisms in six African countries on a demand basis.[30] Access Bank, headquartered in Nigeria, has launched a collective funding initiative with other Africa-based companies to benefit the Global Fund and to demonstrate the leadership role that African business leaders are willing to take in sharing responsibility with international donors.

Since 2010, through Project Last Mile, the Coca-Cola Company has partnered with the Global Fund, the Gates Foundation, Accenture Development Partnerships, Yale University's Global Health Leadership Institute, and the public sector Medical Stores Department in Tanzania to improve supply-chain management and develop a more effective distribution model for essential drugs and medical supplies. To date, the partnership has benefited an estimated 20 million people in the ten regions where the revised distribution model has been implemented, reduced lead time for medicine deliveries to the participating health facilities by as much as twenty-five days, improved availability of certain medicines by 20–30 percent in these facilities, and helped the Medical Stores Department to reorganize and expand its distribution system from 500 warehouse drop-off points to direct delivery to 5,000 health facilities.[31] Plans are under way to scale up the initiative to cover 75 percent of Tanzania and expand it to Ghana and Mozambique.

The Global Fund is also leveraging its impact by working with collective business initiatives such as the Global Business Coalition for Health and with regional and country-level business-led coalitions. Established as an independent organization in 2001 with fewer than twenty companies, the Global Business Coalition for Health (formerly the Global Business Coalition Against HIV/AIDS, TB, and Malaria) had more than 200 corporate members by 2012. Among other activities, it serves as the focal point for the Private Sector Delegation to the Global Fund and helps coordinate corporate contributions at the global level and facilitate private sector engagement at the country level. The Global Business Coalition for Health estimates that individual member companies are active in about ten Country Coordinating Mechanisms and that National Business Coalitions have been established in about twenty countries. In addition, it has worked with a group of about ten major corporate investors in Africa to establish the Corporate Alliance Against Malaria in Africa, which aims to cooperate with governments, the Global Fund, other donors, and nonprofit organizations to scale up the impact of malaria-control projects in mutually agreed-on countries.

30. See www.gbchealth.org/our-work/collective-actions/global-fund-private-sector-delegation/; Global Fund, "The Global Fund and Public-Private Partnerships."

31. Global Fund (2012). See also case study on the partnership at http://nexus.som.yale.edu/ph-tanzania/.

By mid-2012, malaria programs financed by the Global Fund had distributed a cumulative total of 270 million insecticide-treated nets, provided indoor residual spraying in dwellings 44 million times, and financed 260 million ACT drug treatments.[32] In 2008 the Global Fund board also agreed to host and pilot the newly created Affordable Medicines Facility, malaria, the development of which was facilitated by Roll Back Malaria and endorsed by the Medicines for Malaria Venture, among other organizations active in tackling malaria. An estimated 60 percent of malaria patients in sub-Saharan Africa buy their antimalarial treatments from the private sector. The AMFm is an innovative market-based financing mechanism that is structured to negotiate substantial price reductions with the private manufacturers of ACTs and then copay the ACTs ordered by approved public, private, and nonprofit first-line buyers. Based on early results, the AMFm is expected to support a tenfold fall in the costs of subsidized ACTs, making them more affordable to low-income patients and enabling them to compete with ineffective anti-malarials such as chloroquine.

ROLL BACK MALARIA. The Roll Back Malaria (RBM) Partnership offers a final example of a global public-private partnership that is working with other global platforms and a variety of public and private sector entities at the national and project level to scale up impact. It was established in 1998 by the World Health Organization, UNICEF, the United Nations Development Programme, and the World Bank to implement a coordinated response to the disease. Unlike the independent governance structures of the MMV and the Global Fund, Roll Back Malaria is essentially a public sector platform, managed by a secretariat in the World Health Organization. The private sector participates in the RBM's governance, funding, and working groups as one of eight constituencies.

Companies that agree to the RBM's conflict of interest policy and procedures are eligible to join the Private Sector Delegation, nominate two representatives to the RBM's board, and join regional networks and working groups to address key challenges such as advocacy, communication, harmonization, vector control, procurement and supply-chain management, monitoring, and evaluation. As of mid-2012 there were sixteen members of the Private Sector Delegation, across a range of industry sectors, coordinated by the International Business Leaders Forum.[33] In addition to their collective or representative input to the RBM's strategy, many of the private sector partners are also engaged in individual

---

32. See www.theglobalfund.org/en/about/diseases/malaria/.

33. Companies participating in RBM's Private Sector Delegation as of mid-2012 were Abt Associates; BASF; Bayer; Bestnet; Development Finance International; ExxonMobil; GlaxoSmithKline; Hill and Knowlton; Intelligent Insect Control; Novartis; Sanofi Aventis; sigma-tau SpA; Sumitomo Chemical Olyset Net; Syngenta; Trop Med Pharma Consulting; and Vetsergaard-Frandsen. See www.rbm.who.int/mechanisms/psConstituency.html.

project-based partnerships that address specific prevention, diagnostic, and treatment interventions or help to strengthen health-care systems more broadly.

The ExxonMobil Malaria Initiative, for example, is working with RBM, among other public, nonprofit, and academic partners, to support integrated malaria-control programs in a number of African countries. The company states that "since 2000, ExxonMobil and the ExxonMobil Foundation have contributed more than US$111 million toward the fight against malaria. Our funding has allowed our projects and operations to reach more than 66 million people by training nearly 180,000 health-care workers and providing 13.1 million bed nets, 1.6 million doses of anti-malarial drugs, and more than 875,000 rapid diagnostic tests. We also bring our expertise in business management."[34] The company also has a comprehensive and rigorous workplace-based antimalaria program, the adoption of which is required by its contractors, which helps to spread malaria-prevention behavior to thousands of African workers. In some countries, service stations are also used as part of a delivery system to distribute bed nets.

SMS for Life is another example of a project-based partnership in which RBM and the MMV are playing a role. Many public health facilities, especially in remote rural areas, run out of stocks of essential life-saving medicines on a regular basis. Novartis has partnered with the Tanzanian Ministry of Health, Vodafone, IBM, and the Roll Back Malaria Partnership to launch SMS for Life. This evolving business model uses a combination of mobile phones, SMS texting, mapping technology, statistical tools, and easy-to-use websites to monitor stock levels of ACT drugs and quinine injectables around the country. An initial six-month pilot conducted in three rural districts, covering 129 public health facilities and a population of 1.2 million people, showed impressive results, with stock-out rates reduced from 79 percent to less than 26 percent and the number of facilities with no doses of the Novartis ACT cut from 26 to 1 percent.[35] Scale-up to all 5,099 public health facilities in Tanzania is now being implemented through an extended partnership of the Swiss Agency for Development and Cooperation, the Medicines for Malaria Venture, Vodacom, and Novartis. At the same time, the scope of SMS for Life has been extended to also track stocks of rapid diagnostic tests, bed nets, and antibiotics and to explore ways to monitor patient surveillance data. As RBM states, "Overall, the SMS for Life system was built to be a generic and highly scalable solution that can be leveraged to support any medicine or product, and can be implemented in any country with minimal tailoring. Additionally the system could also be utilized for disease surveillance."[36]

34. ExxonMobil (2012, p. 42).
35. See www.malaria.novartis.com/innovation/sms-for-life/index.shtml.
36. Roll Back Malaria (2012).

These examples offer only an illustration of the multitiered ecosystem of individual project-based partnerships, country-level alliances, and global multistakeholder platforms that has evolved over the past decade to tackle malaria. Most successful inclusive business models that develop and deliver affordable health-care products for low-income consumers succeed in large part because of project-based partnerships between for-profit firms or market-oriented social enterprises and some combination of donors, governments, impact investors, or civil society partners. These partnerships provide project-level financing, technical assistance, market research, consumer education, and delivery networks beyond what the for-profit firm or social enterprise could achieve on its own. They may help to catalyze a self-sustaining market-based approach, or they may take the form of an ongoing joint venture or hybrid model that shares risks, costs, capabilities, and division of labor to reach low-income consumers over the long term. Yet though such project-based partnerships are necessary, they are usually not sufficient on their own to scale up impact. In addition, the success of such approaches often relies on the support of broader national or global public-private partnerships to mobilize industry-wide innovative financing mechanisms, to prioritize and stimulate research and development, to garner political attention and support, to share learning, to spread norms and operating standards, and to strengthen health-care systems.

There is no publicly available figure for the combined commercial, financial, philanthropic, and in-kind inputs that have been made by companies to scale up the impact of antimalaria partnerships during the past decade, let alone for the collective outputs and outcomes of these interventions. Even in the absence of reliable data, it is fair to say that the private sector has played an increasingly important role partnering with governments not only in mobilizing necessary resources but also in undertaking groundbreaking R&D and developing more affordable and reliable delivery mechanisms to control malaria. It is unlikely that most companies, even the research-based pharmaceutical and biotechnology companies, would have focused on tackling this disease beyond their own workplaces without the incentives and other support provided by public and philanthropic funding. Equally, governments alone could not have been as effective in providing financing, undertaking R&D, and strengthening delivery channels in the absence of their private sector partners. Such hybrid approaches warrant ongoing analysis to assess their impact relative to their costs and, where relevant, to attract additional private sector partners.

Scaling Up Nutrition Interventions to Tackle Micronutrient Deficiencies

Undernutrition, resulting from inadequate intake of nutritious food or the body's inability to make use of needed nutrients such as folate, iron, iodine, zinc, and vitamin A, severely undermines the quality of life and the learning and earning capacity of millions of people, especially in Asia and Africa, limiting economic growth and exacerbating cycles of poverty. The World Bank summarizes the challenge as follows:

> Under-nutrition imposes a staggering cost worldwide, both in human and economic terms. It is responsible for the deaths of more than 3.5 million children each year (more than one-third of all deaths among children under five) and the loss of billions of dollars in forgone productivity and avoidable health care spending. Individuals lose more than 10 percent of lifetime earnings, and many countries lose at least 2–3 percent of their gross domestic product to under-nutrition.[37]

The *Lancet* series on maternal and child malnutrition estimates that undernutrition accounts for 11 percent of the global burden of disease.[38]

The challenge of undernutrition, and specifically micronutrient deficiency, is complex and large scale. Yet there is evidence from both public health and economic research that fortifying staple foods—by adding essential vitamins and minerals during food processing—is one of the most cost-effective, high-impact, and direct interventions that can be made in addressing malnutrition and in achieving development goals more generally. The Copenhagen Consensus 2012 concluded:

> One of the most compelling investments is to get nutrients to the world's undernourished. The benefits from doing so—in terms of increased health, schooling, and productivity—are tremendous. New research by John Hoddinott et al. of the International Food Policy Research Institute shows that for just US$100 per child, interventions including micronutrient provision, complementary foods, treatments for worms and diarrheal diseases, and behavior change programs, could reduce chronic undernutrition by 36 percent in developing countries."[39]

Effective food fortification programs capable of reaching millions of people require an enabling public policy environment and effective national food fortification requirements and standards, the application of science and technology to food-processing value chains, appropriate incentives for both public and private food processing, marketing and distribution companies, consumer awareness and education, and affordable and reliable distribution channels—all of which require dedicated financing and management expertise to ensure that various parts of the food value chain are aligned and accountable. As with health more generally, a

37. Horton and others (2010, p. xix).
38. *Lancet* (2008).
39. Copenhagen Consensus (2012).

new generation of public-private partnerships has emerged over the past decade at the global, country, and project levels to meet these challenges. The following profile reviews the example of the Global Alliance for Improved Nutrition, looking at its role as a global multistakeholder partnership platform, its relationships with other global multistakeholder platforms focused on tackling micronutrient deficiencies, its support for country-led national food-fortification alliances, and two examples of the market-based partnerships to scale up food fortification that have been undertaken by its participating companies at a project level.

THE GLOBAL ALLIANCE FOR IMPROVED NUTRITION. GAIN was established in 2002 at a Special Session on Children convened by the UN General Assembly. It was constituted as an independent foundation in Switzerland with funding from both public and private sector donors. The alliance's board of directors and its advisory Partnership Council also consist of a combination of public health experts and representatives from governments, foundations, and private sector companies. From the outset, GAIN has been committed to working through national governments aligned with and in some cases supporting their national food fortification programs. At the same time, it has become increasingly focused on facilitating market-based solutions and engaging proactively with companies to cofinance and accelerate the development of new technologies and business models that can be more cost effective in fortifying staple foods and then delivering these through a combination of large-scale population-based programs and targeted programs aimed at vulnerable population groups such as infants and young children, pregnant women and nursing mothers, and people suffering from infectious diseases and humanitarian crises. To facilitate its work with the private sector and to enhance the effectiveness of learning, sharing best practices, and undertaking joint advocacy activities, GAIN established the GAIN Business Alliance in 2005, which has operated both at a global level and also in certain regions for the past eight years.[40]

The alliance's goal is to reach 1 billion people by 2015 with fortified foods that have sustainable nutritional impact. It also aims at ensuring that 500 million of these people are target individuals (such as women and children), keeping the cost per target individual reached less than 50 cents, and seeing a 20–30 percent reduction in the prevalence of micronutrient deficiencies in the locations where it operates. As of mid-2012 it could state: "In less than a decade, GAIN has been able to scale its operations by working in partnership with governments and international agencies, and through projects involving

40. Members of the GAIN Business Alliance in 2012 included Unilever (chair); Ajinomoto; AkzoNobel; Amway; BASF; bel; Britannia; Cargill; the Coca-Cola Company; Dal Group; Danone; DAM; Firmenich; Fortitech; GlaxoSmithKline; Indofood; Kemin; Kraft Foods; mana; Mars; Nutriset; PepsiCo; Pronutria; TetraPak.

more than 600 companies and civil society organizations in 30 countries, reaching over 667 million people with nutritionally enhanced food products. Half of the beneficiaries are women and children."[41]

The alliance's model takes a three-pronged approach. It focuses on building and supporting global nutrition and micronutrient networks; supporting national fortification alliances at the country level; and catalyzing market-based solutions through inclusive business models at the industry and project level.

Building and Supporting Multistakeholder Platforms at the Global Level. In addition to its own direct convening, catalyzing, and advocacy role as a global multistakeholder partnership, GAIN has helped to build and support a number of other global initiatives that aim at positioning nutrition as central to health and development, mobilizing resources, aligning policy, and sharing best practices to scale up proven nutrition interventions. These include initiatives such as the Scaling Up Nutrition movement, led by the United Nations, governed by a lead group consisting of selected heads of state, heads of UN agencies, donors, civil society, and business leaders, and implemented through five Scaling Up Nutrition networks (country, civil society, business, donor, and UN networks); the 1,000 Days partnership to promote investment in nutrition during the crucial days between conception and a child's second birthday; the Amsterdam Initiative Against Malnutrition, a Dutch-led public-private partnership focused on fighting malnutrition in Africa; Future Fortified, a global public awareness campaign; and the Access to Nutrition Index, which will encourage food and beverage companies to benchmark their performance on nutrition.[42]

GAIN is also engaged as a grant-making, technical assistance, and governance partner in other targeted multisector initiatives such as the Micronutrient Initiative and the Flour Fortification Initiative. Both of these are independent nonprofit organizations that apply a public-private partnership approach in their governance, financing, and operations.

—*Micronutrient Initiative.* The Micronutrient Initiative was established in 1992 and focuses its technical expertise on helping countries to strengthen and integrate delivery platforms for micronutrients. It achieves this by advising national governments on how to better use their resources to finance the marginal costs related to adding micronutrient supplementation to existing health programs and through its support of market-based solutions led by the food industry (ranging from multinational companies to small, locally based food

41. GAIN Investing in Partnerships.

42. Further details on each of these additional public-private partnerships and networks and their impacts to date can be found at the GAIN website or the partners' own websites; see www.gainhealth.org; www.scalingupnutrition.org; www.thousanddays.org; and www.futurefortified.org.

processors). In addition to long-standing support from the Canadian International Development Agency, the Micronutrient Initiative works with a variety of other bilateral donors, multilateral agencies, NGOs, private foundations, food industry associations, and corporations, including GAIN. As of 2011 the initiative was supporting programs that reached almost 500 million people in more than seventy countries. Since 1997 it has provided 75 percent of the vitamin A required for supplementation programs in developing countries (more than 5 billion capsules and oral doses of vitamin A). The Micronutrient Initiative is also leading efforts to reach the last 30 percent of households still not using iodized salt, by providing simple iodization techniques to small-scale, local salt producers.[43]

—*Flour Fortification Initiative.* The Flour Fortification Initiative was established in 2002 as a public-private network with the aim of scaling up flour fortification so that it becomes standard industrial milling practice in all countries. The initiative works with more than sixty partner organizations, supported by a staff team based at Emory University and governed by a multisector executive management team with representatives from the public, private, and civic sectors, including both GAIN and the Micronutrient Initiative.[44] It focuses on supporting both mandatory and voluntary flour fortification at the country level by facilitating national partnerships, providing training and communications expertise, mobilizing global leadership and advocacy, securing managerial and financial resources, and helping monitor fortification programs. The Flour Fortification Initiative and its partners can point to the following progress over the past decade: the number of countries with legislation requiring wheat flour fortification with at least iron and folic acid has more than doubled from thirty-three to seventy-five (covering a combined population of 2.09 billion); and the proportion of the world's industrially milled wheat flour that is fortified with at least iron or folic acid has risen from 18 percent to 30 percent.[45] This is still far from the initiative's goal for 80 percent of the world's wheat flour to be fortified by 2015, but its success demonstrates that progress can be made at scale through better coordination and partnership.

43. Micronutrient Initiative (2012).

44. As of 2012, the Flour Fortification Initiative's executive management team was cochaired by the CEO of the private sector company Interflour Group and the director of UNICEF's Programme Division. Other members included representatives from Buhler; Bunge Limited; Cargill; Emory University; Fleishman-Hillard; Global Alliance for Improved Nutrition; the International Association of Operative Millers; the International Federation for Spina Bifida and Hydrocephalus; the Micronutrient Initiative; Sydney West Area Health Service, Australia; the U.S. Centers for Disease Control and Prevention; the World Health Organization.

45. Flour Fortification Initiative, "About Us."

Supporting Country-Based Alliances. The Global Alliance for Improved Nutrition provides grants and technical assistance to support governments and help build national fortification alliances for large-scale impact in more than twenty countries. National fortification alliances bring together public and private partners to improve national nutrition policy, legislation, and regulation; to scale up the purchase of commercial premix and fortification equipment; to provide training in fortification techniques and quality assurance to government officials and employees in food plants, mills, and refineries; and to raise consumer awareness of the benefits of fortification. They aim thereby at catalyzing markets to work better for the poor by delivering affordable and sustainable nutrition products at scale. Some national fortification alliances are convened and led by government officials and departments and others by private sector leaders and industry associations, but GAIN requires all national alliances to have at least one representative from each of the following sectors: government, companies and industry associations; civil society; international agencies; and academia.

A key goal of each national fortification alliance is to advocate for and support the implementation and monitoring of legislation requiring mandatory fortification of staple foods such as maize flour, wheat flour, and vegetable oil. The alliances played a role, for example, in getting such legislation passed in 2011 in Tanzania and Uganda, with the prediction that by 2013 an estimated 45.6 million people in these two countries will purchase foods of improved nutritional quality.[46]

The National Food Fortification Program was established by GAIN in 2003, and over the past decade the program has supported large-scale projects in twenty-five countries selected on the basis of their high levels of vitamin and mineral deficiencies. A 2012 assessment of the national programs in Africa concludes that GAIN's investment in Africa in large-scale fortification programs has provided access to fortified foods for more than 270 million people to date.[47]

One of the barriers to scaling up food fortification programs faced by both government and industry partners at the country level is the ability to procure and monitor affordable and reliable premix. Premix is a commercially prepared blend of vitamins and minerals used to fortify staple foods, but it is often costly and of varying and unreliable quality. To help address this barrier to scaling up, GAIN launched a premix facility in 2009, working with Intertek, an international provider of quality health, environmental, safety, and social accountability standards and assurance, and with Crown Agents, an independent development organization with expertise in public finance, procurement, supply-chain

46. GAIN (2011a).
47. GAIN (2012c).

management, and institutional and systems strengthening. The facility can provide both public and private sector customers with a certification process, procurement support, financial assistance, and grant mechanisms as needed to reach more vulnerable groups and support humanitarian emergencies. As of mid-2012, the GAIN premix facility had reached an estimated 170 million consumers through premix orders worth US$18 million.[48]

Catalyzing Inclusive Business Models and Project-Based Partnerships. In addition to creating the GAIN Business Alliance to serve as a network for sharing best practices and building potential business partnerships, GAIN has also worked with individual companies and supported project-based partnerships to develop market-based approaches to food fortification. It has participated in a number of project-based partnerships between companies, donor agencies, foundations, and impact investors, such as the two following examples.

—*BASF, GIZ, and GAIN.* In 2008 the German development agency GIZ and the chemical company BASF joined forces to facilitate the establishment of functional markets for fortified food in developing countries. They created the Strategic Alliance for the Fortification of Oil and Other Staple Foods with the aim of strengthening inclusive ecosystems for food fortification in selected countries to reduce malnutrition. GAIN was one of their partners in providing technical assistance and supporting the creation of national food fortification alliances in some of the focus countries. The partners have taken a systemic approach, focusing on achieving scale. A country-level multistakeholder dialogue has been the foundation of this process. In addition, GIZ advises the public sector on malnutrition policies, and BASF works with local staple-food producers in developing technical capacities and business models. The goal of the fortification alliance has been to improve nutrition for 100 million people in eight target countries by the end of 2012. In May 2012 the alliance announced that it had already passed that threshold, having reached more than 140 million people with enriched staple foods. With a budget of only €2.8 million, the initiative has demonstrated the ability of a well-leveraged model combining both public policy support and market-based solutions.[49]

—*Britannia, the Naandi Foundation, and GAIN.* More than 47 percent of children under the age of five in India are malnourished, representing some 33 percent of the world's malnourished children. Britannia, founded in 1892, is one of India's largest and most widely recognized consumer-brand companies, selling biscuits, bread, cakes, and milk. Its products reach more than 300 million homes and are available in more than 3 million stores across the country;

48. GAIN (2012a).
49. Gradl (2012).

more than 40 percent of the consumption of Britannia brands occurs in rural areas; and it sells about 6 billion packets of biscuits every year.[50] In 2007, with brokering, technical assistance, and financial support from GAIN, Britannia partnered with the Indian-based Naandi Foundation (founded in 1998 by Dr. Reddy of Dr. Reddy's Laboratories, one of India's largest pharmaceutical companies) to develop fortified biscuits and deliver them to schoolchildren in Andhra Pradesh, working through the national government–mandated Midday Meal Program. The biscuits, called Iron Fortified Tiger Biscuits, benefit an estimated 150,000 children each day through the program. Building on this experience, the company developed a business model to sell the biscuits commercially, and by 2012 about 2 billion packets of the fortified Tiger Biscuits were being sold across the country.

More broadly—influenced in part by engagement with GAIN, the Naandi Foundation, and others such as the Navjyoti India Foundation, India's National Institute of Nutrition, the World Food Program, the World Bank Institute, and the Clinton Global Initiative—Britannia's CEO, Vinita Bali, made a public commitment to fortifying more of its leading brands to be sold in a commercially viable but affordable and accessible way, reaching millions more consumers. As of mid-2012, half of the total product volume sold by the company was enriched with essential vitamins and minerals, and the company estimated that it was reaching about 176 million children between the ages of three and twelve.[51] The Britannia Nutrition Foundation was created in 2009 with the goal of "secure[ing] every child's right to growth and development through the right to nutrition." Britannia aims at serving as a reliable authority on child nutrition matters, increasing resources for research, knowledge sharing and support for school feeding and humanitarian assistance programs, and educating at-risk populations about child nutrition.

These two examples illustrate different models of how multinational and national companies have worked with either public or private donors, with other local NGO or business partners, and with GAIN to develop and scale up specific business models or social investment programs that produce and deliver fortified foods. At the same time, the partners have worked together, and in some cases with national governments, to strengthen the broader ecosystem or market for fortified foods. This illustrates again the need for different levels and types of partnerships to build both inclusive business models and the broader markets and ecosystems that are often needed to scale up such models.

The Global Alliance for Improved Nutrition, and the other global multistakeholder networks that it works with, such as the Micronutrient Initiative

---

50. Britannia Industries Limited.
51. GAIN (2011b). See also GAIN (2008).

and the Flour Fortification Initiative, illustrate the potential for supporting both country-level public-private alliances and innovative new business models to scale up access to more nutritious fortified foods. Since its creation in 2012, GAIN has been one of the key conveners and advocates for what was previously a highly disparate, uncoordinated, and often mutually distrustful global nutrition community. It has played a role with other public and private actors in making a strong case for more effective and coordinated global investment in nutrition as a major driver of economic and social progress. It has also helped to make the case for country-led ownership of national nutrition programs. And it has become a key advocate for the vital role of market-based solutions and the private sector in tackling undernutrition. In so doing, GAIN has helped to overcome some, although not all, of the mistrust between the public health experts in the field of nutrition and commercial businesses, including food and beverage companies. Many public health leaders now publicly acknowledge that scaling up nutrition cannot be achieved without private sector investment and innovation alongside effective government leadership at the national level.

Scaling Up Agricultural Interventions to Empower Smallholder Farmers

There is growing recognition by governments, development experts, and a vanguard of private sector leaders of the crucial need to increase agricultural productivity over the next few decades in order to improve food security and nutrition, environmental sustainability and resilience, and rural livelihoods and incomes. The CEO of Unilever, Paul Polman, highlights what is at stake: "The challenges of food security—of providing a lot more, with a lot less—are complex, immense, frightening and urgent. They are urgent because our task is not only planning for 2050, when we will need to feed an extra 2 billion people. We also have to act for today, when 870 million people will go to sleep hungry." He argues:

> Governments and businesses need to direct investment towards strengthening whole value chains and improving support for smallholder farmers, particularly women. In the developing world, they make up 43 percent of farmers—rising to 50 percent in Eastern Asia and 80 percent in sub-Saharan Africa—but they have less access to the land, water rights, finance and education that could improve productivity. Aiding smallholder farmers is one of the most efficient ways of alleviating poverty, which makes it even more critical.[52]

Like attempts to expand access to affordable and reliable health and nutrition interventions, scaling up efforts to increase agricultural productivity and to build

52. Polman (2012).

more inclusive linkages between smallholder farmers and the inputs and markets that they need in order to thrive requires an ecosystem of different levels and types of partnership. Project-based partnerships that engage agribusiness companies to improve the productivity, income, and sustainability of large numbers of smallholder farmers, such as out-grower schemes and contract farming models, are usually more likely to scale up or replicate if the participating companies are also part of a broader ecosystem of precompetitive commodity or value-chain alliances, business-to-business partnerships with banks, information technology providers and retailers, industry-wide standards or certification programs, and country-based agriculture-corridor initiatives. Proactive engagement between farmers' groups, agribusiness companies, and policymakers is also necessary to ensure success. As a senior program manager at the International Fund for Agricultural Development notes in a brief on the institution's efforts to adopt a new systematic approach to scaling up agricultural and rural development:

> Impact at scale requires enabling government policy and an adequate public expenditure program. Policy that does not enable private investment in agriculture, for example, will inhibit scaling up, given that agricultural activities lie in the private sector and require private investment. Good pilot projects supported with donor money tend neither to gain traction nor to be replicated and scaled up when they reside in a poor policy environment that inhibits private investments.[53]

Sector-specific or national-level alliances to promote dialogue between government and the private sector on these issues, to agree on a joint vision, to set priorities, and to allocate roles and responsibilities can play a valuable part in promoting such an enabling policy environment while at the same time mobilizing investment dollars from the private sector.

Two recent examples of public-private partnerships that are taking this holistic ecosystem approach with a focus on building country-level alliances as well as facilitating individual project-based partnerships and investments are the New Vision for Agriculture and the New Alliance for Food Security and Nutrition. Both are at early stages of development, but they have gained strong support from both donor and partner governments and from a critical mass of the world's largest food and beverage companies. As such they offer interesting models and potential for scaling up impact.

NEW VISION FOR AGRICULTURE. The New Vision for Agriculture (NVA) was launched at the World Economic Forum's 2009 meeting in Davos, Switzerland, building on several years of research and dialogue and some pilot partnership projects. It is structured to develop a shared agenda for action between companies and governments and to foster country-level alliances and new investment to achieve more sustainable agricultural growth through market-based solutions. Led personally by the CEOs of major food and beverage companies and the heads of state and ministers of agriculture in participating countries, and supported by a variety of donor agencies, research partners, and nonprofit organizations, to date the NVA has mobilized country-level alliances in Tanzania, Vietnam, Mexico, Indonesia, and India, and Grow Africa, a regional public-private partnership underpinned by country-led initiatives in eight sub-Saharan African countries. It has also provided substantial policy input to food security initiatives being initiated by the G-20 and the G-8. As of mid-2012 the NVA was supported by twenty-eight global corporate champions, including a number of the world's largest food and beverage companies; fourteen government partners, including both donor and partner governments; and well over thirty other civil society and international organizations, as well as a growing number of domestic companies in the countries where it operates.[54]

The New Vision for Agriculture multistakeholder partnership platform is playing a catalytic leadership role at several levels. It has worked with McKinsey & Company, academic partners, and some of the participating companies to create a shared vision and to develop a six-part road map guiding companies and governments in practical action they can take to achieve sustained agriculture-sector transformation at the country level.[55] It has used practical examples and demonstration projects to raise awareness of the potential of market-based approaches to sustainable agriculture. It has made sure its goals are aligned with national and regional agricultural policies and has proactively engaged with and highlighted the vital leadership role of national governments. It has started to mobilize new investment dollars and develop innovative financing mechanisms. The companies that participate actively on the NVA's project board lead overall strategic development and are key drivers in building coalitions and initiating action and investment in the partner countries. In addition to focusing on specific value-chain interventions, the partners address cross-cutting themes at both global and country level, including environmentally sustainable production, finance, and risk management.

54. Companies that served on the NVA's project board in 2012 and provided strategic guidance, resources, and on-the-ground investment commitments were AgCo; BASF; Bayer AG; Bunge Limited; Cargill; the Coca-Cola Company; Diageo; DuPont; General Mills; Heineken NV; Kraft Foods; Louis Dreyfus; Maersk; Metro AG; Monsanto Company; Mosaic; Nestlé; PepsiCo; Rabobank; Royal DSM; SABMiller; Swiss Re; Syngenta; Teck Resources; Unilever; Vodafone; Walmart; and Yara International.

55. World Economic Forum with McKinsey & Company (2011). See also World Economic Forum with McKinsey & Company (2012).

The New Vision for Agriculture has demonstrated how companies can play a leadership role both individually, through their own value chains, and collectively, through transformational precompetitive partnerships focused on specific geographic corridors or agricultural commodities. In Tanzania, for example, the government, donors, and private sector partners established the Southern Agricultural Growth Corridor of Tanzania, focused on scaling up investments and impact in a clearly defined region of the country with backbone infrastructure and high agricultural potential. As of May 2012, twenty-one multinational and national companies had signed letters of intent for new investments ranging from smallholder out-grower schemes, access to finance, and training centers to investment in physical infrastructure such as irrigation, storage, and a fertilizer production facility. In Vietnam, Indonesia, India, and Mexico the alliances have chosen to focus on priority value chains, such as grains, oilseeds, fruits and vegetables, coffee and cocoa, tea, and fisheries. Different stakeholder groups have taken lead roles in different countries: in the Indian state of Maharashtra, the state government galvanized public-private partnership action by offering a cofinancing opportunity; whereas in Mexico, the local private sector has been a key driver of alliance activity.

The flexible partnership model facilitated by the New Vision for Agriculture has quickly replicated to engage a total of twelve countries in Asia, Africa, and Latin America. In the case of Grow Africa, government ministers from seven African countries (Burkina Faso, Ethiopia, Ghana, Kenya, Mozambique, Rwanda, and Tanzania) agreed to support a regional alliance convened jointly by the African Union, the New Partnership for Africa's Development (NEPAD), and the World Economic Forum in June 2011. Nigeria joined the initiative in late 2012. The alliance aims to attract new private sector investment, support new models of public-private partnership, and share knowledge and best practices. It provides an Africa-owned and country-led process to engage companies and donors in supporting market-based agriculture sector investment and partnerships.

NEW ALLIANCE FOR FOOD SECURITY AND NUTRITION. Grow Africa served as a platform for developing the private-sector investment commitments, which formed part of the G-8's New Alliance for Food Security and Nutrition launched by President Obama in May 2012. Like the NVA, the New Alliance aims at engaging public and private stakeholders to enable market-based approaches and private sector investment as a key part of achieving African food security and improving smallholder productivity and incomes. It is based on a model of country cooperation frameworks, initially focused on Tanzania, Ghana, and Ethiopia, that aims at identifying shared priorities and aligning government, donor, and company investments. At its launch, more than forty-five African and multinational companies committed in excess of $3 billion to increase their investments in different stages of the agriculture value chain. The G-8 governments have committed complementary financing, with a particular focus on smallholder farmers, and aim to bring agricultural innovations to scale, support more effective financing mechanisms and risk management, and improve nutrition.

Although these catalytic public-private platforms are still new, over the past decade some of world's largest food and beverage companies that are participating in these partnerships have already demonstrated a growing commitment to building more inclusive business models that include smallholder farmers. Their experience and the project-based partnerships and commitments that they have already developed offer potential for further scaling. Examples include:

—*Nestlé*. Nestlé sources milk, cocoa, and coffee from some 680,000 small-scale suppliers in developing and emerging economies through its Farmer Connect program, as part of the company's Sustainable Agriculture Initiative. A commitment to scaling up its investment in rural development is one of the three cornerstones of the company's creating shared-value model, the other two being water and nutrition.

—*Unilever*. Unilever estimates that it has around 1.3 million smallholder farmers linked into its supply chain. It has made a public commitment to improving the livelihoods of at least 500,000 of these farmers through its Sustainable Living Plan and to provide evidence that the company's interventions have had a positive impact.[56] The company is clear about its goals to improve the yields, sustainability, and security of its own sources of supply while also improving access to markets, training, other inputs, and higher productivity and incomes for smallholders.

—*SABMiller*. SABMiller has established Farming Better Futures programs in Africa, India, and Latin America. The programs aim at generating more inclusive growth by supporting local sourcing of agricultural raw materials from smallholder and commercial farmers and, in some cases, also providing technical assistance on water management and HIV/AIDS testing and treatment for farmers. Research by Ethan Kapstein of INSEAD shows that in 2012, SABMiller supported around 89,000 direct farming jobs in sub-Saharan Africa (excluding South Africa), which, in turn, support further indirect rural employment, leading to a total of more than 310,000 jobs. The company's plans to expand local sourcing through barley in Zambia, cassava in Southern Sudan, and sorghum in Ghana are likely to increase direct rural jobs to about 150,000.[57]

—*Other beverage companies*. Other beverage companies, such as Coca-Cola, Heineken, and Diageo, are investing in programs to include similar numbers of

56. Unilever (2012).
57. Wales (2012).

smallholder farmers as well as thousands of small-scale or micro distributors in their value chains.

Beyond agribusiness companies, a number of retailers, information technology companies, insurance companies, and banks are making public commitments to support thousands of smallholder farmers and rural enterprises through project-based partnerships with other companies, donors, and governments. Walmart, for example, has committed to selling US$1 billion in food sourced from 1 million smallholder and medium-sized farms by 2015, increasing farmers' income by 10–15 percent, and to providing training to 1 million farmers and farmworkers, half of whom will be women.[58] Rabobank is launching a lending facility in West Africa that will provide up to US$135 million in loans over five years to small and medium-sized companies participating in agricultural value chains, as part of the bank's long-standing and much broader efforts to improve access to finance for smallholder farmers and small enterprises active in agriculture. Similarly, Vodafone has made a public commitment to establishing the Connected Farmer Alliance in Tanzania, Mozambique, and Kenya, which will work in partnership with other companies and donors to increase the productivity, incomes, and resilience of more than 500,000 smallholder farmers by improving their access to mobile technology and their connections with larger agribusinesses.

A 2011 study undertaken by Vodafone, Accenture, and Oxfam identified twelve feasible opportunities for improving the lives and livelihoods of smallholder farmers in developing countries through the use of mobile technology by providing them with better access to markets, information, and finance. The researchers concluded that "in 26 countries across Vodafone's footprint, these 12 opportunities could together increase agricultural income by US$138 billion in 2020, an increase of 11 percent. Additional benefits could include avoidance of greenhouse gas emissions and reduced freshwater withdrawals. It is estimated that around 549 million mobile connections to services will be needed to realize these benefits."[59] Given the dramatic growth in mobile technology and applications, such a goal could feasibly improve agricultural productivity and incomes for at least some of the world's estimated 500 million smallholder farmers.

Most of the individual companies and inclusive business models profiled above are also engaged in different aspects of the New Vision for Agriculture and the New Alliance for Food Security and Nutrition at both the global and country levels. Again, this illustrates the ecosystem of different levels and types of partnership that are needed to achieve scale.

58. Walmart (2010).
59. Accenture and Vodafone, with Oxfam Great Britain (2011, p. 4).

Scaling Up Benefits from Extractive Projects to Improve Transparency and Risk Management

An estimated 3.5 billion people live in countries rich in oil, gas, and minerals.[60] They represent some 60 percent of the world's poorest people.[61] In many of these countries, national governments and state-owned enterprises partner with international energy and mining companies on projects to develop these natural resources. Such projects usually entail multibillion dollar foreign direct investment flows and the generation of millions of dollars in taxes, royalties, and other payments to national and subnational host governments as well as payments to local companies, the development of associated physical and institutional infrastructure, technology cooperation, local training, and the development of human capital. These activities have the potential to transform the quality of life for millions of people. Yet all too often the capital flows, income, and public revenues that they generate and the public assets and services that they make possible benefit only a small elite and fail to result in long-term benefits and progress for the majority of citizens in the nations, regions, and local communities where they operate. In some cases they lead to negative development outcomes, including permanent environmental damage, loss of local livelihoods, human rights abuses, and even conflict—the so-called resource curse.[62]

Over the past decade a number of public-private partnerships have been established to tackle the resource curse and to improve the pro-poor development impact of large-scale energy and mining projects in low-income countries. Most of these initiatives have been created in response to a combination of activist NGO campaigns, government-led consultations, regulations and standards, and voluntary action taken by industry leaders.[63] Together they form part

60. World Bank (2009).
61. Oxfam America (2010).
62. *Resource curse* refers to the paradox that many countries that are rich in nonrenewable mineral, oil, and gas resources and benefit from multibillion-dollar project finance agreements to develop these resources (usually funded by both public and private financial institutions) have often delivered worse development outcomes and less economic growth than countries that lack such natural resources, with the communities that live closest to the resources in question often the least likely to benefit from their development and most likely to be adversely affected by human rights, social, and environmental risks.
63. Influential NGO campaigns and global dialogues and consultation processes aimed at improving environmental, social, and governance performance in the extractive sector (and in some cases industry more broadly) over the past two decades have included the Publish What You Pay campaign (started in 2002 and ongoing); Oxfam's Ombudsman process and ongoing research and campaigns focused on oil, gas, and mining; the Mining Minerals and Sustainable Development initiative led by the Institute for Environment and Development between 2000 and 2002; the World Bank's Extractive Industries Review (from 2000 to 2004); multistakeholder consultations associated with the launch (in 2006) and revision (in 2011–12) of the International Finance Corporation's Policy and Performance Standards on Environmental and Social Sustainability; the official

of an evolving ecosystem of different types and levels of partnership aimed at addressing one or more of the following imperatives:

—The need for better governance, transparency, and accountability on the collection and allocation of revenues associated with large-scale energy and mining projects

—The need for comprehensive stakeholder consultation, risk management, and grievance mechanisms to identity and mitigate negative human rights, environmental, economic, and social impacts associated with such projects

—The need for integrated and systemic approaches to creating shared value and sustained prosperity for host communities, regions, and nations through a combination of tax revenues, regional development initiatives, local content programs, and social investment activities

—The need to build individual and institutional capacity in both governments and communities so that they are better equipped to engage with large-scale project developers and to understand and manage the risks and benefits of natural resource development

Experience suggests that to be effective such efforts require a combination of project-based partnerships, aimed at managing social and environmental risks and improving transparency, community engagement, grievance mechanisms, and local development benefits at the level of individual energy and mining projects; country-based or regional alliances to leverage resources and build the institutional and managerial capacity of communities and relevant government departments at all levels; and global multistakeholder partnership platforms to promote greater environmental, social, and governance accountability and revenue transparency standards on an industrywide basis.

The Extractive Industries Transparency Initiative and the Equator Principles for project finance are only two of many industry-led initiatives and multistakeholder platforms that have emerged over the past decade to improve the development impact of natural resource projects.[64] These two voluntary partnership

---

mandate of the UN secretary general's Special Representative on Business and Human Rights (from 2005 to 2011), which supported a comprehensive global multistakeholder consultation process and extensive research leading to endorsement by the UN Human Rights Council on the UN Guiding Principles on Business and Human Rights; and the development and updating since 2000 of various OECD Guidelines on Multinationals, Anti-Corruption, and Conflict Minerals.

64. Collective industry-led initiatives and public-private partnerships that have been created to improve the human rights, environmental, social, and governance performance and development impact of large-scale energy and mining projects over the past decade include the Voluntary Principles on Security and Human Rights (created in 2000 by the British and U.S. governments with a small number of global energy and mining companies and human rights NGOs); the International Council on Mining and Metals (created in 2001 by major mining companies that agree to adhere to a set of sustainable development principles); the Equator Principles (created in 2003 by the International Finance Corporation and leading project finance banks to improve environmental and social risk management in large-scale project finance in developing countries and undergoing a

models and others like them are by no means a panacea. Many of them face challenges in terms of the credibility and comparability of the data gathered, their ability to overcome entrenched interests and perverse incentives, and the capacity needed to drive large-scale transformation at a national level. This is the case even for governments and companies that participate in such voluntary initiatives, while some of the countries and state-owned enterprises that face the most serious problems chose not to participate and are therefore not held accountable to these evolving voluntary processes. Despite the challenges, these partnerships are helping to create practical frameworks, tools, and incentives to enable the public and private sector to better manage risk and to improve development benefits on an industry-wide basis.

EXTRACTIVE INDUSTRIES TRANSPARENCY INITIATIVE. The Extractive Industries Transparency Initiative (EITI) aims at strengthening governance and improving development outcomes in countries that are developing their oil, gas, and mineral resources by improving transparency and accountability in the extractives sector. It provides a global standard and methodology for monitoring and reconciling extractive company payments (in the form of taxes, royalties, and signature bonuses) and government revenues at the country level. This partnership approach has enabled effective scaling up of a voluntary assessment and disclosure process in a relatively short period of time for those countries and companies that have chosen to participate.

The EITI was officially launched by the former British prime minister Tony Blair at the World Summit for Sustainable Development in South Africa in 2002. Initially hosted by the U.K. government, an independent board was created in 2006 and a secretariat established in Oslo in 2007. The board is structured to be representative of the EITI's five core constituencies—implementing countries, supporting countries, civil society organizations, the extractive industry, and investment institutions. Together with the secretariat and a global conference every two years, the board is responsible for oversight of the initiative and ensuring the integrity of the EITI methodology and process. The EITI's funding also reflects its multistakeholder approach. Responsibility for funding, technical

---

consultative revision process in 2011–13); the Extractive Industries Transparency Initiative (created in 2002 by governments, energy and mining companies, NGOs, and financial institutions); the Partnering Against Corruption Initiative (created in 2003 by a group of CEOs in the extractive and construction sectors and led by the World Economic Forum); the Global Gas Flaring Reduction partnership (created in 2002 by the World Bank, governments, and energy companies); the Kimberley Process (created in 2000 by governments, companies, and NGOs, with a certification process initiated in 2002 to tackle the problem of conflict diamonds); and the creation of other industry-led action and public-private partnerships to tackle the challenge of other conflict minerals in 2011 and 2012. This list is not exhaustive, but is illustrative of the variety of public-private partnerships and industry-led initiatives that have emerged in this area over the past decade.

assistance, and in-kind support is shared by all public and private constituents. The World Bank administers a multidonor trust fund on behalf of the EITI; supporting countries, the private sector, NGOs, and the Norwegian government share responsibility for the international management costs of the initiative, and the governments of implementing countries cover the costs of validation.

Implementing countries apply to participate in the EITI and are accepted as candidate countries on the basis of meeting certain requirements, including the creation of a country-level multistakeholder group that oversees the implementation process at the country level. Candidate countries have one and a half years to publish a public EITI report that reconciles company payments with government receipts, and after undergoing an independent assessment (the EITI validation process) they are accepted as EITI-compliant countries. As compliant countries, they must maintain adherence to the twenty-one EITI process, disclosure, dissemination and review, and validation requirements. As of late 2012 there were fifteen EITI-compliant countries, twenty candidate countries, and one suspended country. More than sixty of the world's largest oil, gas, and mining companies have publicly committed to supporting the EITI, together with about eighty investment institutions that collectively manage an estimated US$16 trillion. Civil society organizations participate directly and through the Publish What You Pay campaign, which is supported by more than 300 NGOs worldwide. A number of intergovernmental organizations and international finance institutions at the global and regional levels have endorsed the EITI.

Critics of the process have raised concerns about the methodology and rigor of the EITI standard and validation process; the lack of links between the EITI process and other investment climate and governance reforms at the country level; challenges of weak institutional and implementation capacity in many implementing country governments at both the national and regional level; the quality of data, and their degree of aggregation, which makes it difficult to assess individual extractive projects; and the voluntary nature of the overall initiative, which allows resource-rich weakly governed countries to opt out. In response to these concerns and as part of its own oversight process, the EITI board commissioned an independent evaluation and initiated a comprehensive strategic review in 2012. Although gaps clearly exist, the EITI can point to the fact that within the seven-year period from 2005 to 2012, the number of national reports produced increased from zero to more than 100. The EITI's first overview of these reports states:

> Data from 109 fiscal periods has been disclosed by 30 countries under the oversight of the EITI. More than 900 companies have participated in EITI reporting processes around the globe. Some countries went back many years

to bring data into the public sphere. Nigeria has disclosed data starting from 1999. Other countries, notably Azerbaijan, have reported every year. Most reports cover the oil, gas and mining sectors although some countries have included other sectors as well. Liberia's 2009 Report includes mining, oil, forestry and agriculture. EITI Reports often go beyond revenue and payment information. Ghana, Mongolia and Peru include data on extractive sector flows to local governments. Central African Republic includes artisanal mining. Reports from Mali and Timor-Leste are disaggregated not only by company and revenue streams, but also by project.[65]

Collectively, the reconciliation reports published to date cover more than US$700 billion in payments and revenues, and discrepancies of more than US$20 billion have been explained and resolved. As reporting becomes more timely and regular, the EITI expects the average total revenues disclosed to reach US$300 billion a year.[66] A key focus for coming years is to make the data more accessible and to develop interactive tools to enable citizens, civil society organizations, and the media, as well as participating governments, companies, and financial institutions, to make more effective use of the information. The EITI secretariat is also exploring ways to support capacity building of governments at the national, regional, and local levels.

Monitoring company payments and government revenues is essential but not sufficient. Another key aspect of the challenge is ensuring that the revenues are budgeted and spent in a manner that furthers national development goals and reaches citizens at the regional and community levels. A number of innovative proposals have been made for ensuring that these goals are met, such as the Center for Global Development's Oil-to-Cash initiative, but the challenges remain high in terms of lack of political will and weak governance capacity in many countries.[67] Even as the EITI continues to strengthen its own processes and standards, it is only one component of an ecosystem of interventions and public-private partnerships that are needed to ensure both accountability for the revenues raised from extractive sector projects and the effective management and allocation of these revenues to achieve development goals.

65. Extractive Industries Transparency Initiative (2012b, p. 5).
66. Extractive Industries Transparency Initiative (2012b). See also Extractive Industries Transparency Initiative (2012a).
67. For a useful overview of proposals on the responsible allocation and governance of extractive resource revenues, see work done on this topic by the Center for Global Development (www.cgdev.org/section/initiatives/_active/revenues_distribution); Oxfam America (www.oxfamamerica.org/issues/oil-gas-mining); and the Responsible Mining Development Initiative, led by the World Economic Forum (www.weforum.org/reports/responsible-mineral-development-initiative).

EQUATOR PRINCIPLES. The Equator Principles offers another example of a voluntary accountability mechanism based on a partnership model that has scaled up in a relatively short period of time. The initiative was launched in June 2003 with ten banks cooperating as the founder signatories and with support from the International Finance Corporation. Based on the environmental and social standards of the International Finance Corporation, the Equator Principles require its signatories to voluntarily adhere to a set of environmental and social risk management criteria when financing projects in developing countries with capital costs above US$10 million. The principles were revised in June 2006 to include a public reporting requirement and again in 2012 to include requirements for managing climate impacts and greater consideration of human rights.

Today, less than ten years after their creation, the Equator Principles are supported by more than seventy-five financial institutions in almost thirty countries, including most of the world's major banks as well as some insurance companies, bilateral development agencies, and export credit agencies. The banks that support the Equator Principles are estimated to represent more than 75 percent of total project finance debt in emerging markets. This offers a good illustration of how a relatively small number of major corporations can achieve scale in a short period of time by engaging in a precompetitive coalition, convened in this case by the World Bank Group.

The Equator Principles are being applied to major projects such as the PNG LNG development in Papua New Guinea, a US$15.7 billion natural gas project financed by a public-private consortium of seventeen commercial banks, six export credit agencies, and ExxonMobil. As part of the lenders' requirements the project developer has implemented a comprehensive Environmental and Social Management Plan, which is independently audited. In addition, the company has committed to providing public reports on a quarterly basis and to implementing local stakeholder consultation and grievance mechanisms. PNG LNG has commissioned more than 100 independent scientific and social studies to help it better understand the risks and benefits associated with the project. The project operator is working in partnership with a variety of local and international environmental NGOs, economists, public health experts, and anthropologists, as well as the national, regional, and local governments to build the capacity of local institutions and professionals to more effectively manage these risks and benefits, and to create shared value.

Similar comprehensive risk management and benefit-sharing approaches are being undertaken as a result of public-private partnerships in other major extractive projects such as the Peru LNG project, the Tangguh LNG project in Indonesia, the Baku-Tbilisi-Ceyhan pipeline, the Oyu Tolgoi mining development in Mongolia, and the Juruti mining project in Brazil.

In some countries, such as Mozambique, Angola, Ghana, and Chile, extractive sector companies have joined together with the World Bank, bilateral donor agencies, and host governments to coordinate their efforts to identify, finance, and build the capacity of locally owned suppliers and to help build the local private sector. There are limited data available on the size and impact of these joint efforts to increase the local and national content or value-added of natural resource development projects. Relatively few energy and mining companies provide figures at a country level, but those that do suggest that their efforts are substantial. Shell, for example, reports that "wherever possible, we buy goods and services from local businesses. . . . In 2011, we estimate that almost $12 billion was spent in countries, that according to the UNDP Human Development Index 2010, have a gross domestic product of less than $15,000 a year per person. In these countries, Shell companies spend over 90% of this $12 billion with local companies."[68] Similarly, Statoil states, "We are making efforts to increase local purchase of goods and services in our operations in non-OECD countries. In 2011, we spent an estimated NOK 9.8 billion on goods and services from companies based in non-OECD countries, up from NOK 4 billion the previous year."[69]

This is an area that requires more research, especially given the high level of financial flows, the large economic, environmental, and social footprints involved, and the growing importance of the mining and energy sector to many low- and middle-income countries. The International Council on Mining and Metals notes, "There is no economic study group—including from within the World Bank or the International Monetary Fund—that systematically captures the important role of the extraction and production of mining, minerals and metals in the economies of each country in the world. Until now, this data limitation has prevented a country-by-country assessment of the varied macro-economic contributions of the mineral sector to national economies."[70] The same can be said for the energy sector and for the microeconomic and community contributions of both industries. Efforts to improve development outcomes for many of the world's poorest people cannot ignore the contributions and the challenges associated with developing oil, gas, and mineral resources or the potential for new models of partnership at global, national, regional, and project levels to scale up the responsible development of these resources.

68. Shell (2012, p. 4).
69. Statoil Annual Report (2012).
70. International Council on Mining and Metals (2012, p. 8).

Assessing the Impact of Public-Private Partnerships as Tools for Scaling Up

Public-private partnerships are still relatively new approaches to development. Other than long-standing infrastructure projects, most cross-sector initiatives did not exist a decade ago, especially large-scale multistakeholder platforms at the global, national, or industry sector level and market-oriented partnerships and hybrid business models at the project or value-chain level. Thus it is still relatively early to assess their impact. Beyond independent evaluations of individual public-private partnerships there has been relatively little comparative analysis of their effectiveness in scaling up development impact, let alone their ability to sustain promising results over a long period of time. There is now a growing need and opportunity to undertake this analysis and to explore opportunities for learning what works, what does not work, and how best to spread good practice.

In one of the most comprehensive impact assessments undertaken to date, the World Bank reviewed its portfolio of some seventy global programs, all of which involve a variety of public, private, or civil society participants in their funding, governance, or program delivery activities.[71] It carried out in-depth analysis of twenty-six of these programs, which represented 90 percent of all the bank's global program expenditures in 2004. Only six of these had been in existence for more than ten years. The World Bank's evaluation concluded that while most of these public-private partnerships had been innovative and responsive to addressing selected development challenges, and several had added measurable value, there were weaknesses that needed to be addressed in terms of their governance, management, and financing, particularly the level of participation in decisionmaking by developing country governments and intended beneficiaries.

In a 2007 study focused on twenty-three global public-private health partnerships, the Overseas Development Institute also concluded that while these partnerships had added significant value in tackling diseases of poverty, this contribution was undermined by some common and resolvable accountability challenges.[72] These included insufficient participation in decisionmaking by recipient countries and beneficiaries, inadequate use of critical governance procedures, failure to compare the costs and benefits of public versus private approaches, high transaction costs for managing the alliances, lack of partnership-building skills, and wastage of resources through inadequate use of existing country systems.

---

71. World Bank Group (2005).
72. Overseas Development Institute (2007).

Research conducted by McKinsey & Company in 2011 for the New Vision for Agriculture identified and analyzed multistakeholder partnerships that had achieved transformative change in the agricultural sector. The study concluded:

These experiences highlight six elements that are essential stepping stones toward success in a large-scale transformation effort. Effective direction from an early stage is critical to direct efforts at high-return opportunities, and includes leadership and alignment of stakeholders around shared goals, a clear strategy and priorities for implementing the transformation, and an investment and entrepreneurship pipeline. Delivery at scale requires specific means and methods, in particular—enabling hard and soft infrastructure, policies and investments, catalytic financing and risk management solutions, and robust mechanisms and institutions for delivery, implementation and durability.[73]

Similar conclusions were reached by an assessment of the U.S. Agency for International Development's Global Development Alliance in 2011; by research undertaken by the World Wildlife Fund in 2010 on multistakeholder sustainability initiatives aimed at driving more responsible production, sourcing, and manufacturing practices in global food chains; and in a review of large-scale United Nations–business partnerships undertaken in 2011 by the UN Global Compact in cooperation with Unilever, Dalberg consultants, and Harvard's Kennedy School of Government.[74]

Three sets of challenges—and success factors—in building effective public-private partnerships warrant further analysis to learn and share what works. First, there is a need for analysis on different models of governance, funding, and accountability that are being used by partnerships, and especially how they are ensuring transparency and accountability not only to the participants but also to beneficiaries. Second, more in-depth analysis is needed on the operating models and management and communication systems that partnerships are employing to manage the risks and harness the benefits of bringing together participants with different cultures, incentives, motivations, time frames, expectations, resource levels, and skills to ensure that the sum is greater than the parts and to manage and resolve conflict when it inevitably arises. Third, there is value in better understanding how partnerships integrate not only impact monitoring and evaluation into their planning and operations processes but also broader systemic learning and the sharing and adoption of good practice.

---

73. World Economic Forum, with McKinsey & Company (2012).
74. Mission Measurement and the U.S. Agency for International Development (2010); WWF Review (2010); UN Global Compact (2011).

The Organization for Economic Cooperation and Development and the Donor Committee for Enterprise Development are both supporting ongoing efforts to document and categorize new models of partnership between business and other development actors and to develop more-systematic approaches to learning and sharing what works in scaling up and sustaining impact. There is potential for greater research and coordination in this area.

Recommendations for Scaling Up through Public-Private Partnerships

When public-private partnerships are effective, they can help to achieve greater efficiency, increase legitimacy, and improve the leverage, scale, and impact of development efforts. To achieve these outcomes, concerted efforts are needed to make such partnerships better at leveraging diverse resources (public and private, commercial and nonprofit, financial and in kind), more operationally effective in improving outcomes, and more transparent and accountable to their relevant stakeholders. The following recommendations focus on the role that governments, donors (both public and private), and corporations can play in building partnerships that help scale up development impacts.

Governments and Donors

—*Convene partners.* At the country or industry sector level, government agencies and foundations can play a valuable role in convening companies on a precompetitive basis. This is often difficult for a company or even industry association to do on its own, whereas a government entity or foundation can provide a more neutral platform for companies that normally compete with one another to come together to address common development challenges and mobilize resources at scale. Given the growing focus on country ownership, government ministers and departments can play an especially important role in convening country-level alliances such as investor roundtables and a variety of corridor, cluster, and city initiatives or sector-based country-coordinating mechanisms to deliver health, education, food security, and other specific development goals at scale. Such government-led efforts can also ensure that multistakeholder alliances and private sector investments are better aligned to national development strategies and priorities, which often coordinate government and donor resources.

—*Provide catalytic and replication or scaling finance.* Donors and national governments can build on the early models and lessons learned from the use of competitive-bid catalytic financing mechanisms, such as innovation funds, challenge funds, advanced market commitments, and prizes. First, they can increase the amount of catalytic funding that is often needed to share the initial risks of testing new business models and the development of new products and technologies that aim at serving the poor or achieving improved environmental impact. Second, donors and governments should explore the creation of replication or scaling funds, based on a similar competitive-bid approach and supported by a combination of financial resources, technical advice, brokerage, and government policy dialogue and supporting reforms. The launch of the U.S. Agency for International Development's Development Innovation Ventures offers an interesting model of a three-stage and three-tiered funding approach that combines start-up catalytic financing for testing high-potential breakthrough solutions to development challenges; funds for scaling up proven successes; and larger amounts of funding to expand further on proven success. India's Public-Private Partnership for Integrated Agricultural Development scheme offers a national government-led example of a catalytic fund aimed at leveraging large-scale private sector investment and supporting smallholder farmers in a more integrated manner along agricultural value chains.

—Create joint networks and incentives for science and technology innovation. There is potential for donor and partner governments to cooperate more effectively with each other and with the corporate, foundation, academic, and research communities in financing and coordinating the identification, development, and delivery of new information technologies and life sciences and materials technologies that offer breakthrough approaches to improving development impacts in agriculture, health, climate-change mitigation and adaptation, energy, and water. Both long-standing and more recently established global multistakeholder platforms such as the Consultative Group on International Agricultural Research and the GAVI Alliance have demonstrated the potential to scale up the financing, research, development, and delivery of new science and technology. Much more can be achieved in this area through incentives such as prizes, competitions, and open-source innovation and design platforms. There is a particular need to explore the discovery and scaling up of new technologies and market-based solutions at the nexus of water, energy, and food security.

—Build the collective capacity and organizing capability of low-income producers, employees, and consumers. Governments, donors, and foundations can play a vital role in helping low-income producers, employees, and consumers to be better equipped and organized to either integrate into formal markets and value chains or to demand greater transparency and accountability from public service providers. This can involve training, extension and education services, public awareness campaigns, support in creating producer and consumer associations and cooperatives, strengthening of trade unions and worker councils, and efforts to improve the access of citizens and citizen groups to data and information and to social media platforms and networks.

—*Build capacity of government officials to engage more effectively in partner-ships.* Donors, foundations and other civil society organizations can play a greater role in helping to build the capacity of partner governments and specific ministries and government departments to engage in public-private partnerships. The German development agency GIZ, for example, has worked with the Part-nering Initiative in several African countries to help build government capacity for partnering with the private sector. Grow Africa works with governments to identify and develop investment opportunities that align with national plans and then to engage private sector investors and others to implement these oppor-tunities. Donors and foundations have supported governments in establishing multistakeholder, country, coordinating mechanisms in areas such as health, nutrition, and agriculture. There are untapped opportunities to bring together government officials, business leaders, and civil society leaders around specific development challenges to build trust, mutual understanding, common agendas, and the technical and managerial skills needed to work more effectively together.

Companies

—*Commercially develop inclusive business models, products, and services.* The number of large domestic and multinational companies that are dedicating senior executive support and resources to commercially develop and deliver more inclusive, pro-poor business models, products, and services is still small. Initiatives such as the International Finance Corporation's Inclusive Business unit, the Business Call to Action, Business Fights Poverty, and a growing num-ber of academic and consulting platforms are now studying examples of what works within companies to implement such approaches in terms of internal incentives, venture financing, dedicated business units, metrics, and manage-ment structures. These lessons and models need to be more widely shared, and more companies need to make public commitments to implement them within their core business operations and value chains. Governments and donors can provide incentives and catalytic financing support, but business executives need to take more of a leadership role to mobilize the necessary managerial, technical, and financial resources to take market-based solutions to scale.

—*Harness corporate philanthropy to support market-based solutions with the potential to scale.* A small number of companies and corporate foundations have demonstrated that corporate philanthropy can be used effectively to catalyze and scale up market-based approaches to poverty alleviation. In addition to finan-cial support, companies and their foundations can contribute valuable technical expertise and convening capability to help build the supporting ecosystem of institutions, value-chain linkages, human capital development, and public poli-cies that is often essential to scaling market-based solutions. The example of the Shell Foundation in chapter 6 illustrates this approach. Many more corporate foundations could be more innovative, catalytic, creative, and market oriented in their approaches to tackling development challenges.

—*Support open-source innovation and scaling approaches.* Lessons on the potential of open-source innovation are emerging from newly created corporate innovation platforms, such as IBM's Smarter Planet and Development Jams, Unilever's Sustainable Living Plan, Nestlé's Creating Shared Value initiative, and General Electric's EcoMagination. Companies, working alone or supported by private foundations and public donors, can do more to use social media technologies and competitions, combined with the technical expertise of their research and development departments and the financing capability of their business development departments, venture funds or philanthropic dollars, to identify, test, and scale up innovative approaches to tackling development challenges.

—*Continue to engage in precompetitive partnership platforms.* Even the largest and most committed companies can only achieve a certain level of scale working through their own business operations, value chains, and corporate foundations. The experience over the past two decades of precompetitive collective business action within a specific industry sector or value chain, or multistakeholder alliances focused on a specific challenge or geography, suggests high potential for strengthening market systems and public policies. Precompetitive models are likely to be especially important in industries and value chains that have a major impact on the quality of life of and opportunities for poor people, such as infrastructure, health, nutrition, energy, water, agriculture, natural resources, information technology, financial services, manufacturing, and tourism.

Conclusion

Over the past two decades, project-based partnerships, sector-specific and country-level alliances, and global multistakeholder partnership platforms have become increasingly important components of the development architecture. These diverse and often interrelated public-private partnerships offer the potential for overcoming some of the governance gaps and market failures that limit the ability of publicly subsidized and for-profit models to scale up development outcomes. Although they are often challenging to build and sustain, such partnerships can help leverage diverse financial and nonfinancial resources, improve operational efficiency and effectiveness, and increase the transparency and accountability of both public and private service delivery to low-income producers and consumers. They offer an important tool for governments, donor agencies, private sector enterprises, philanthropic foundations, and other civil society organizations in the ongoing effort to improve development effectiveness and to ensure that development interventions reach millions more poor people and improve their opportunities and the quality of their lives.

References

Accenture and Vodafone, with Oxfam Great Britain. 2011. *Connected Agriculture: The Role of Mobile in Driving Efficiency and Sustainability in the Food and Agriculture Value Chain.*

Britannia Industries Limited. 2008. *Health and Nutrition Initiatives* (www.britannia.co.in/bnf/media/britannia-in-health-nutrition.pdf).

Center for Global Development. 2013. "Oil-to-Cash: Fighting the Resource Curse through Cash Transfers" (www.cgdev.org/section/initiatives/_active/revenues_distribution).

Chevron. 2011. *2010 Corporate Responsibility Report.*

Conway, Gordon. 2012. *One Billion Hungry: Can We Feed the World?* Ithaca, N.Y.: Cornell University Press.

Copenhagen Consensus. 2012. "Outcome" (www.copenhagenconsensus.com/Projects/CC12/Outcome.aspx).

Department for International Development. 2011. *The Engine of Development: The Private Sector and Prosperity for Poor People.* London.

Donahue, John D., and Richard. J. Zeckhauser. 2011. *Collaborative Governance: Private Roles for Public Goals in Turbulent Times.* Princeton, N.J.: Princeton University Press.

Extractive Industries Transparency Initiative. 2012a. *Building on Achievements.* Board Paper 21-2-A. EITI International Secretariat. October 8.

———. 2012b. *Extracting Data: An Overview of EITI Reports Published 2005–2011.* Oslo.

ExxonMobil. 2012. *2011 Corporate Citizenship Report.*

GlaxoSmithKline. 2012. *Do More, Feel Better, Live Longer.* Corporate Responsibility Report 2011. London.

Global Alliance for Improved Nutrition (GAIN). 2008. Interview with Vinita Bali of Britannia Industries. Video. July 31 (www.gainhealth.org/country-stories/vinita-bali-top-business-woman-and-champion-malnutrition).

———. 2011a. *Changing Nutrition at the National Scale: The Collective Impact Approach to Achieving Mandatory Food Fortification Legislation across East Africa.*

———. 2011b. *Vinita Bali: Top Business Woman and Champion of Nutrition.* December 12.

———. 2012a. "Facts about Malnutrition" (www.gainhealth.org/about-gain/fastfacts).

———. 2012b. *An Innovative Approach to Improving the Nutritional Status of Children: The Grameen Danone Venture in Bangladesh.*

———. 2012c. *Lessons Learned from 10 years of Experience in Africa: Sharing Experiences in Food Fortification.* Food Fortification Workshop, Addis Ababa, Ethiopia, September 18–19.

Global Fund. 2012. "Coca-Cola and the Global Fund Announce Partnership to Help Bring Critical Medicines to Remote Regions." Press release. New York. September 25 (www.theglobalfund.org/en/mediacenter/newsreleases/2012-09-25_Coca-cola_and_the_Global_Fund_Announce_Partnership_to_Help_Bring_Critical_Medicines_to_Remote_Regions/).

Gradl, Christina. 2012. *Building a Strategic Alliance for the Fortification of Oil and Other Staple Foods (SAFO): A Case Study.* Harvard Kennedy School of Government, Corporate Social Responsibility Initiative.

Gradl, Christina, and Beth Jenkins. 2011. *Tackling Barriers to Scale: From Inclusive Business Models to Inclusive Business Ecosystems.* CSRI Report 47. Harvard Kennedy School of Government, Corporate Social Responsibility Initiative. September (www.hks.harvard.edu/m-rcbg/CSRI/pub_main.html).

Horton, Susan, and others. 2010. *Scaling Up Nutrition: What Will It Cost?* Directions in Development Series. World Bank.

Hudson Institute. 2011. *The Index of Global Philanthropy and Remittances 2011.*

International Council on Mining and Metals. 2012. *The Role of Mining in National Economies.* InBrief Series. London.

Koh, Harvey, Ashish Karamchandani, and Robert Katz. 2012. *From Blueprint to Scale: The Case for Philanthropy in Impact Investing.* Monitor Group in collaboration with Acumen Fund. April.

Lancet. 2008. "Maternal and Child Malnutrition." *Lancet* 371, no. 9608. (www.thelancet. com/series/maternal-and-child-undernutrition).

Linn, Johannes F. 2012. "Lessons on Scaling Up: Opportunities and Challenges for the Future." Brief 20 in *Scaling Up in Agriculture, Rural Development, and Nutrition.* International Food Policy Research Institute. June.

McKinsey & Company. 2009. *Public-Private Partnerships: Harnessing the Private Sector's Unique Ability to Enhance Social Impact.* Social Sector Office. Working document. December.

Micronutrient Initiative. 2012. *20 Years of Progress.* 2011–2012 Annual Report (www.micro nutrientinitiative.org).

Mission Measurement and the United States Agency for International Development. 2010. *(Re)Valuing Public-Private Alliances: An Outcomes-Based Solution.* Private Sector Alliances Division.

Nelson, Jane. 2002. *Building Partnerships: Cooperation between the United Nations System and the Private Sector.* United Nations.

Novartis. 2012. *Reaching More Patients: Expanding Access to Healthcare.* Novartis Corporate Responsibility. July.

Overseas Development Institute. 2007. *Global Health: Making Partnerships Work.* Briefing Paper 15.

Oxfam America. 2010. *Protect Community Rights and Resources.* Oxfam Fact Sheet.

Polman, Paul. 2012. *Now Is the Time for Action to Achieve Global Supply Security.* Opinion piece in *The Future of the Food Industry.* Special report. *Financial Times,* November 21.

Porter, Michael E., and Mark R. Kramer. 2006. "Strategy and Society: The Link between Competitive Advantage and Corporate Social Responsibility." *Harvard Business Review* 84 (12).

———. 2011. "Creating Shared Value: How to Reinvent Capitalism and Unleash a Wave of Economic Growth." *Harvard Business Review.* January–February 2011.

Prahalad, C. K., and Allen Hammond. 2002. "Serving the World's Poor, Profitably." *Harvard Business Review* 80(9): 48–57.

Prahalad, C. K., and Stuart. L. Hart. 2002. "The Fortune at the Base of the Pyramid." *Strategy+Business* 26: 54–67

Roll Back Malaria. 2012. "SMS for Life: An RBM Initiative" (www.rbm.who.int/psm/ smsWhatIsIt.html).

Sanofi. 2011. *Access to Medicines.* September. (http://en.sanofi.com/Images/29244_Sanofi_ Access_to_Medicine_2011.pdf)

Shell Global. 2012. "Our Performance." In *Shell Sustainability Report 2011.*

Sourang, Cheik M. 2012. "IFAD: Adopting a New Systemic Approach to Scaling Up Agricultural and Rural Development." Brief 17 in *Scaling Up in Agriculture, Rural Development, and Nutrition.* International Food Policy Research Institute. June.

Statoil. 2012. *Annual Report 2011.*

U.N. Global Compact. 2011. *Catalyzing Transformational Partnerships between the United Nations and Business.*

Unilever. 2012. *Unilever Sustainable Living Plan: Progress Report 2011.*

Wales, Andy. 2012. *Africa Economic Summit: Impact, Resources, and the Growing Middle Class.* Views and Debates blog (www.sabmiller.com/index.asp?pageid=1766&blogid=140).

Walmart. 2010. *Walmart Unveils Global Sustainable Agriculture Goals* (www.walmart.com).

World Bank. 2009. World Bank Oil, Gas and Mining Policy Division. August.

————. 2012. *Information and Communications for Development 2012: Maximizing Mobile.*

World Bank Group. 2005. *Addressing the Challenges of Globalization: An Independent Evaluation of the World Bank's Approach to Global Programs.* 2005. Operations Evaluation Studies Unit.

————. 2012. *Transformation through Infrastructure.* Infrastructure Strategy Update FY2012-2015.

World Bank Institute and the Public-Private Infrastructure Advisory Facility. 2012. *Public-Private Partnerships: Reference Guide.* Version 1.0. World Bank.

World Economic Forum with McKinsey & Company. 2011. *Realizing a New Vision for Agriculture: A Roadmap for Stakeholders.*

————. 2012. *Putting the New Vision for Agriculture in Practice: A Transformation Is Happening.*

World Wildlife Fund. 2010. *Certification and Roundtables: Do They Work?* Review of Multi-stakeholder Sustainability Initiatives. September.

Contributors

TESSA BOLD
Professor of Economics, Goethe University, Frankfurt

LAURENCE CHANDY
Fellow, Global Economy and Development, Brookings Institution

WOLFGANG FENGLER
Lead Economist, World Bank Office, Nairobi

DAVID GARTNER
Associate Professor of Law, Arizona State University, and Nonresident Fellow,
    Global Economy and Development, Brookings Institution

SHUNICHIRO HONDA
Research Associate, JICA Research Institute

AKIO HOSONO
Director, JICA Research Institute

MICHAEL JOSEPH
Director for Mobile Money, Vodafone, and Fellow, World Bank

HIROSHI KATO
Senior Special Adviser, JICA

HOMI KHARAS
Senior Fellow and Deputy Director, Global Economy and Development,
  Brookings Institution

MWANGI KIMENYI
Senior Fellow and Director, Africa Growth Initiative, Global Economy and
  Development, Brookings Institution

MICHAEL KUBZANSKY
Partner, Monitor Inclusive Markets

JOHANNES F. LINN
Senior Resident Scholar, Emerging Markets Forum, and Nonresident Senior
  Fellow, Global Economy and Development, Brookings Institution

GERMANO MWABU
Professor of Economics and Department Chair, University of Nairobi

JANE NELSON
Director, Harvard Kennedy School's Corporate Social Responsibility Initiative,
  and Nonresident Senior Fellow, Global Economy and Development,
  Brookings Institution

ALICE NG'ANG'A
Lecturer, Strathmore University, Nairobi

JUSTIN SANDEFUR
Research Fellow, Center for Global Development

PAULINE VAUGHAN
Consultant and former Head of M-PESA at Safaricom

CHRIS WEST
Director, Shell Foundation

Index